Great Men of the Bible

Volume II

OTHER ZONDERVAN BOOKS BY F. B. MEYER . . .

Great Verses Through the Bible
Our Daily Walk

CHRISTIAN
CLASSICS

Great
Men of the
Bible

Volume
II

F. B. Meyer

zondervan/marshall morgan & scott

GREAT MEN OF THE BIBLE, VOL. 2
Copyright © 1982, The Zondervan Corporation
Grand Rapids, Michigan and
Marshal Morgan & Scott
1 Bath Street, London ECIV 9LB

Library of Congress Cataloging in Publication Data

Meyer, F. B. (Frederick Brotherton), 1847–1929.
   Great men of the Bible.
    1. Bible—Biography. I. Cumbers, Frank Henry. II. Title.
BS571.M49   1981   220.9'2[B]   81-12940
ISBN 0-310-44281-8   AACR2

ISBN 0-551-00930-6

Printed in the United States of America

83 84 85 86 87 88 — 10 9 8 7 6 5 4 3 2

CONTENTS

Great Men of the Bible

Volume II

DAVID

1

Taken From the Sheep-cotes
1 Samuel 16:1

The story of David opens with a dramatic contrast between the fresh hope of his young life and the rejection of the self-willed king Saul, whose course was rapidly descending toward the fatal field of Gilboa.

Few have had a fairer chance than Saul. Choice in gifts, handsome in appearance, favored by nature and opportunity, he might have made one of the greatest names in history. His first exploit, the relief of Jabesh-gilead, justified the wildest anticipations of his friends. But the fair dawn was soon overcast.

The final announcement of his deposition was made at Gilgal. Saul, it is said, rejected the word of the Lord; and the Lord rejected him from being king.

From Gilgal Saul went up to his house at Gibeah, in the heights of Benjamin: while Samuel went to Ramah, a little to the south—his house was there; there he had judged Israel for twenty years.

In the selection of every man for high office in the service of God and man, there are two sides—the divine and the human. We must consider, therefore: (1) The Root of David in God; (2) The Stem of Jesse—that is, the local circumstances that might account for what the boy was; and (3) The White Bud of a Noble Life.

1. THE ROOT OF DAVID. Once in the prophecy of Isaiah, and twice in the Book of Revelation, our Lord is called the "Root of David." "The Lion of the Tribe of Juda, the Root of David, hath prevailed to open the book, and to loose the seven seals thereof" (Rev. 5:5).

The idea suggested is of an old root, hidden deep in the earth, which sends up its green scions and sturdy stems. David's character may be considered as an emanation from the life of the Son of God before He took on Himself the nature of man, and an anticipation of what He was to be and do in the fullness of time. Jesus was the Son of David, yet in another sense He was his progenitor. Thus we return to the ancient puzzle, that Jesus of Nazareth is at once David's Lord and Son (Mark 12:35–37).

There are four great words about the choice of David, the last of which strikes deeply into the heart of that great mystery.

a. *"The LORD hath sought him a man"* (1 Sam. 13:14). No one can know the day or hour when God will pass by, seeking for chosen vessels and goodly pearls. Let us be always on the alert, with our lamps burning and our nets mended and cleansed.

b. *"I have found David my servant"* (Ps. 89:20). There is ecstasy in the voice, like the thrice-repeated "found" of Luke 15. David was found long before Samuel sent for him. What was the moment of that blessed discovery? Was there not some secret glad response to the Master's call, like that which the disciples gave, when Jesus found them at their nets, and said, "Follow me"?

c. *He chose David to be his servant* (Ps. 78:70). The people chose Saul; but God chose David. This made him strong. The thought that he was divinely commissioned was his standby (2 Sam. 7:21). We are immovable when we touch the bedrock of God's choice, and hear Him say, "He is a chosen vessel unto me, to bear my name" (Acts 9:15).

d. *The LORD has appointed him to be Prince* (1 Sam. 13:14). Appointments are not due solely to human patronage, nor won by human industry; they are of God. Fit yourself for God's service; be faithful. He will presently appoint you; promotion comes neither from the east nor the west, but from above.

e. *"I have provided me a king"* (1 Sam. 16:1). That answers everything. The divine provision meets every need, silences every anxiety. God has provided against all contingencies, and has His prepared and appointed instrument. As yet the shaft is hidden in His quiver, in the shadow of His hand; but at the precise moment it is needed the most and can be most effective, it will be produced and launched on the air.

2. THE STEM OF JESSE. We turn for a moment to consider the formative influences of David's young life. The family dwelled on the ancestral property to which Boaz, that mighty man of wealth, had brought the Rose of Moab. His wealth may have been somewhat decayed through the exactions of the Philistine garrison, which seems to have been posted in the little town.

David says nothing of his father, but twice speaks of his mother as "the handmaid of the LORD." From her he derived his poetic gift, his sensitive nature, his deeply religious character. To the father he was the lad who kept the sheep, whom it was not worth while to summon to the religious feast; to his mother he was David the beloved. He honored both of his parents with dutiful care; and when it seemed possible that they might suffer serious hurt, amid the pelting storm of Saul's persecution, he moved them to the safe-keeping of the king of Moab, the land of his ancestress.

Young David may have owed something to the schools of the prophets, established by Samuel's wise prescience to maintain the knowledge of the law in Israel. They appear to have been richly endued with the gracious power of the Holy Ghost.

But nature was his nurse, his companion, his teacher. Bethlehem is situated six miles south of Jerusalem, by the main road leading to Hebron. Its site is two thousand feet above the level of the Mediterranean, on the northeast slope of the long gray ridge, with a deep valley on eaither side; these unite at some little distance to the east, and run down toward the Dead Sea. On the gentle slopes of the hills the fig, olive, and vine grow luxuriantly; and in the valleys are the rich cornfields, where Ruth once gleaned, and which gave the place its name, the House of Bread. The moorlands around Bethlehem, forming the greater part of the Judaean plateau, do not however present features of soft beauty; but are wild, gaunt, strong—character-breeding.

Such were the schools and schoolmasters of his youth. But preeminently his spirit lay open to the Spirit of God, which brooded over his young life, teaching, quickening, and ennobling him, opening to him the books of nature and revelation, and pervading his heart with such ingenuous trust as the dumb animals of his charge had in him.

3. THE WHITE BUD OF A NOBLE LIFE. He did not have the strong physique of his brother Eliab, who so impressed the aged prophet. But he was strong and athletic. His feet were nimble as a gazelle's; he could leap a wall or outstrip a troop; a bow of steel could be easily broken by his young arms; and a stone sent from his sling would hit the mark with unerring precision. He was too slight to wear a man's armor, and yet was able

to kill a lion or bear. His face glowed with health. The blue of his eyes and beauty of his fair complexion was in strong contrast to the darker visages of his companions. The sensitiveness of the poet's soul was combined with daring, resource, and power to command. His dress was a coarse and simple tunic; his accouterments were the wallet sling, the rod and staff.

Ah, guileless, blessed young man! You know little that you will die amid the blare of trumpets announcing the accession to the throne of your son, the splendid Solomon; still less you dream that your unsullied nature will one day be so sadly stained! Yet your God loves you, and you will teach us many lessons as we turn again the pages of your career and read them in the light that streams from the face of your greatest Son, who was born of the seed of David according to the flesh, but who was declared to be the Son of God by the resurrection of the dead!

2

"From That Day Forward"
1 Samuel 16:13

Few have had so varied a career as he: shepherd and monarch; poet and soldier; champion of his people, and outlaw in the caves of Judaea, beloved of Jonathan, and persecuted by Saul; vanquishing the Philistines one day, and accompanying them into battle the next. But in all he seemed possessed of a special power with God and man. The secret still eludes us, until we read the momentous words that sum up the result of a memorable day in the obscure years of opening youth. "The Spirit of the LORD came mightily upon David from that day forward."

1. IT BEGAN LIKE ANY ORDINARY DAY. No angel-trumpet heralded it; no faces looked out of heaven; with the first glimmer of light the boy was on his way to lead his flock to pasture lands heavy with dew. As the morning hours sped onward, many duties would engross his watchful soul.

A breathless messenger suddenly broke on this pastoral scene, with the tidings of Samuel's arrival at the little town, and that the prophet had refused to eat of the hastily-prepared banquet until the young shepherd had joined the invited guests. How the young eyes must have flashed with pleasure! Never before had he been wanted and sent for in this way. It was a genuine pleasure to feel that the family circle in great Samuel's eyes was not complete until he had come. He therefore left his sheep with the messenger, and started at full speed for home.

2. IT WAS THE CONSUMMATION OF PREVIOUS TRAINING. We must not suppose that now, for the first time, the Spirit of God worked in David's heart, and that he had probably never experienced, before the day of which we treat, that special unction of the Holy One symbolized in the anointing oil. This blessed anointing for service cannot be ours before we have experienced a previous gracious work on the heart. And it was because all these had been wrought in David by the previous work of the Holy Spirit, that he was prepared for this special unction. It may be, reader, that in the obscurity of your life you are being prepared for a similar experience.

3. IT WAS MINISTERED THROUGH SAMUEL. The old prophet had conferred many benefits on his native land, but none could compare in importance with his eager care for its youth. The creation of the schools of the prophets was due to him.

Driving a heifer before him, he entered the one long street of Bethlehem, and summoned the elders to a feast, so as not to arouse the suspicions of the jealous, moody king, who would ~~not~~ have tried to take his life if he had suspected the real object of his visit.

When David reached the village, a strange scene met his eye. There he saw his father Jesse, and his seven brothers, who were probably waiting for him in the ancestral home, preparatory to their all going together to the public banquet to which the leading men of the village had been invited. No sooner had he entered, flushed with exertion, health glowing on his face, genius flashing from his eye, royalty in his mien, than the Lord said to Samuel, "Arise, anoint him: for this is he!" Then Samuel took the horn of oil he had brought with him from Nob, and poured its contents on the head of the astonished lad.

It is likely that the bystanders did not realize the significance of that act; but David probably understood. Josephus indeed tells us that the prophet whispered in his ear the meaning of the sacred symbol. Did the aged lips approach the young head, and as the trembling hand pushed back the clustering locks, did they whisper in the young man's ear the thrilling words, "Thou shalt be king"? From that memorable day David returned to his sheep; and as the months went by slowly, he sometimes must have wondered when the hour of achievement would arrive. When would he have an opportunity to display and use his new-found force? He had to learn that we are sometimes strengthened with all might to patience and long-suffering as the prelude to heroic deeds; we have to wrestle with the lion and the bear on the hills of Bethlehen, that we may be prepared to meet Goliath in the valley of Elah.

4. IT WAS A DAY OF REJECTION. Seven of Jesse's sons were passed over. Seven is the perfect number: the seven sons of Jesse stand for the perfection of the flesh. This has to be cut down to the ground, lest it should glory in God's presence. The lesson is hard to learn, but its acquisition is imperative.

3

Summoned to the Palace
1 Samuel 16:18–19

After his anointing, David returned to his sheep. When Saul, advised by his courtiers, sent for him years later to charm away his melancholy, this was the specific indication he gave to Jesse, his father, "Send me David thy son, which is with the sheep." It says much for the simplicity and innocence of the boy's character that he should have returned to the fold, to lead and guard his helpless charge, faithfully fulfilling the routine of daily duty, and waiting for God to do what Samuel had spoken to him of.

A contemporary hand has given a brief picture of his character as it presented itself at this period to casual observers. One of Saul's young men said, "Behold, I have seen a son of Jesse the Bethlehemite, that is cunning in playing, and a mighty valiant man, and a man of war, and prudent in matters, and a comely person, and the LORD is with him."

1. THE MINSTREL. He had the poetic temperament, sensitive to nature, and he had the power of translating his impressions into speech and song. Thus we admire his marvelous power in depicting the sacred hush of dawn, where there is neither speech nor language, just before the sun leaps up as a bridegroom to run his race, and the solemn pomp of night, where worlds beyond worlds open to the wondering gaze. And to these we might add the marvelous description of the thunderstorms that broke over Palestine, rolling peal after peal, from the great waters of the Mediterranean, over the cedars of Lebanon to the far-distant wilderness of Kadesh, until the sevenfold thunders are followed by torrents of rain, and these by the clear shining in which Jehovah blesses His people with peace (Pss. 23, 19, 8, 29).

The Psalm began with David. The psalms that he composed in those early days were destined to be sung through the world, working on men effects like those worked on the king, of whom it is said that when David took the harp and played with his hand, Saul was refreshed.

2. THE YOUNG WARRIOR. There was abundant opportunity for the education of his prowess. The Philistines' frontier was not far away from his native town. Many skirmishes the men of Bethlehem had with the border warriors, who would sweep down on the produce of their vineyards and cornfields when the harvest was ripe. In these David acquired the character of being a man of valor and a mighty man of war.

But he would have been the last to attribute his exploits to his sinewy strength. By faith he had learned to avail himself of the might of God. Was he not His servant, designated for a great mission, summoned to wage uncompromising war with the uncircumcised?

> *For by Thee have I run through a troop;*
> *And by my God have I leaped over a wall. . . .*
> *It is God that girdeth me with strength. . . .*
> *He maketh my feet like hinds' feet. . . .*
> *He teacheth my hands to war. . . .*
> *Thou hast subdued under me those that rose up against me.*
>
> *Psalm 18*

3. PRUDENT IN SPEECH. The discernment of avid will appear as our story proceeds. He was as prudent to advise and scheme as he was swift to execute. Whatever emergency threatened, he seemed to know just how to meet it. And this was no doubt due to the fact that his spirit rested in God. The sad mistakes he made may be traced to his yielding to the sway of impulse and passion, to his forgetfulness of his habit of drawing near to God and inquiring of Him before taking any important step.

When men live like that, they cannot fail to be prudent in speech, discerning in counsel.

4. THE CHARM OF HIS PRESENCE. He was David the beloved. Wherever he moved, he cast the spell of his personal magnetism. So he passed through life, swaying the scepter of irresistible potency over men and women. Beloved of God and man, with a heart timid to the touch of love, the soil of his soul was capable of bearing crops to enrich the world; but it was also capable of the sharpest suffering possible to man.

5. GOD WAS WITH HIM. He thought of God as his Rock, Redeemer, Shepherd, and Host in the house of life, his Comforter in every darksome glen. In weariness he found green pastures; in thirst, still waters; in perplexity, righteous guidance; in danger, sure defense—in what the Lord was to his soul. God's Word, though he knew but a part of it, was perfect, right and pure. He set the Lord always before him; because He was at his right hand, he could not be moved; and therefore his heart was glad.

4

A Dark Background
1 Samuel 17:11

As we have said, a great contrast is evidently intended by the historian between Saul and David. The portrait of Saul is drawn in Rembrandt colors, to set forth the excelling beauty of God's designated king. We will notice some points in Saul's dark eclipse that will serve to illustrate salient features in the young shepherd's character.

1. FORSAKEN BY THE SPIRIT OF GOD. Browning conceives of him amid the silence of the dark tent, from which for days not a sound came to the anxious watchers; the blackness of darkness reigned, and within the figure of Saul was resting against the tent-prop without movement, speech, or appetite for food; shuddering for a moment under the first spell of music, and then resuming his insensibility to all.

Nothing in this world, or the next, can be compared for horror to the withdrawal of God from us. When God's presence is lost, every power in the soul rises in revolt. Ah! bitter wail, when a man cries with Saul, "I am sore distressed; for . . . God is departed from me, and answereth me no more!" (1 Sam. 28:15).

How different with David! The Lord was with him. To the clear, bright eye of his faith the living God was more real than the giant that stalked each morning before the hosts of Israel. Had He not delivered him from the paw of the lion and from the paw of the bear? And was He not as real amid the dignity of the court or the clash of the battlefield?

2. TROUBLED BY AN EVIL SPIRIT FROM THE LORD. Evidently the conception is of Jehovah surrounded by spirits, some good, and some evil. He has only to speak, and one powerful to exercise a malign and deadly influence hastens to do his bidding. This method of speech is unfamiliar. We prefer to say that God always means to do the best by every creature He has made: but that we have the power of extracting evil from his good; of transforming his sunshine and rain into hemlock and deadly nightshade and rank poison. But when we turn against God, it seems as though He has begun to be our enemy, and to fight against us; the reality being that, whereas we once went with the stream of the divine blessing, we are now wading against it with difficulty and peril. With the obstinate God shows Himself obstinate; and with the perverse, His angels, conscience, gratitude, the memory of the past, convictions of duty, which are intended to elevate and save, oppose their progress as mortal foes.

With David, on the other hand, the Spirit of God was constantly cooperating. He lived and walked in fellowship with the unseen.

3. SAUL'S DISCORD. The fact that music was the corrective of the king's malady seems to indicate that, being wrong with God, he was out of harmony with the universe, which is the circumference of which God is center. He was out with God, and consequently there was discord in his heart and life. Music falling on his ear recalled memories of his former better self, and laid a brief spell on the discordant elements of his soul; reducing them to a momentary order, destined, however, to be marred and spoiled as soon as the sweet sounds were withdrawn. Yes, it is always so. If you have not received the At-one-ment, if you are not at peace with God through Jesus Christ, you are at enmity, by wicked works and inward temper. Art, music, the engagements of daily business, the whirl of society, the exercises of religion may do what David's harp did for Saul, in producing a momentary stillness and sense of harmony with your environment; but it is only for a moment: when the spell is withdrawn, the old spirit of disorder asserts itself.

With David, on the other hand, the harp was the symbol of a soul at rest in God. And it was because his own spirit was in perfect harmony with the nature of God and with the universe, that he could cast the spell of calming and quieting influence over another. The servants of Saul were therefore justified in urging him, in one of his lucid moments, to permit them to seek out a man who was a cunning player on the harp. And the power that David exercised over him is an illustration of a similar charm that we may individually exert on the restless, storm-tossed spirits around us. Let us go forth to induce men to be reconciled to God, and to learn the mystery of that peace of which Jesus spoke.

4. SAUL'S UNBELIEF. If a man is wrong with God, faith is impossible; for it is the health-bloom of the soul. Therefore when Goliath stalked through the valley of Elah, and defied the armies of Israel, Saul became frightened. Under happier conditions he would have become the champion of his people; now he cowered in his tent.

To David, on the other hand, there was no such fear. His soul was full of God. He was his light and salvation, whom should he fear? He was life, of whom should he be afraid? There was no unsteadiness in the hand that slung the stone, no tremor in the heart. He was strong in faith, because his young heart was in living fellowship with Jehovah.

5

The Faith of God's Elect
1 Samuel 17

Having recovered from the chastisement inflicted on them by Saul and Jonathan at Michmash, the Philistines had marched up the valley of Elah, encamping on its western slope. Saul pitched his camp on the other side of the valley. Three figures stand out sharply defined on that memorable day.

1. THE PHILISTINE CHAMPION. Goliath was tall—nine feet six inches in height; he was heavily armed. His armor became a spoil for Israel; it was eagerly examined and minutely described. They even weighed it and found it to weigh five thousand shekels of brass, equivalent to two hundred pounds. He was protected by an immense shield,

carried by another in front of him, so as to leave his arms and hands free. He wielded a ponderous spear, while sword and javelin were carried at his side. He was quite a braggard, for he talked of the banquet he proposed to give to the fowls and beasts, and defied the armies of the living God.

2. SAUL. There was not among the children of Israel a better person than he; from his shoulders and upward he was taller than any of the people. He had also a good suit of armor, a helmet of brass, and a coat of mail; but he dared not adventure in conflict with what he considered were utterly overwhelming odds. He intimidated David with his materialism and unbelief: "Thou art not able to go against this Philistine to fight with him: for thou art but a youth, and he a man of war from his youth."

3. DAVID. He was only a boy, ruddy and handsome. He carried no sword in his hand; he carried a staff, probably his shepherd's crook; he wore no armor, no weapon except a sling in his hand and five smooth stones that he had chosen out of the torrent bed and put in his shepherd's bag. But he was in possession of a mystic spiritual power; the living God was a reality to him. He had no doubt that the Lord would vindicate His glorious name, and deliver into his hands this uncircumcised Philistine.

Let us study the origin and temper of this heroic faith.

a. *It had been born in secret, and nursed in solitude.* God was as real to him as Jesse, or his brothers, or Saul, or Goliath. His soul had so rooted itself in this conception of God's presence, that he took it with him, undisturbed by the shouts of the soldiers as they went forth to the battle, and the searching questions addressed to him by Saul.

This is the unfailing secret. Thus alone can the sense of God's presence become the fixed possession of the soul, enabling it to say repeatedly with the psalmist, "Thou art near, O God."

b. *It had been exercised in lonely conflict.* With a beautiful modesty David probably would have kept to himself the story of the lion and the bear, unless it had been extracted from him by a desire to magnify Jehovah. Possibly there had been many conflicts of a similar kind, so that his faith had become strengthened by use, as the sinews of his wiry young body by exertion.

c. *It stood the test of daily life.* There are some who appear to think that the loftiest attainments of the spiritual life are incompatible with the grind of daily toil and the friction of the home. It was not so with David. When Jesse, eager to know how it fared with his three elder sons, who had followed Saul to the battle, asked David to take them rations, and to take a present to the captain of their division, there was an immediate and ready acquiescence in his father's proposal; "he rose up early in the morning . . . and took, and went, as Jesse had commanded him." And before he left his flock he was careful to entrust it with a keeper. We must always be careful that we do not neglect one duty for another; if we are summoned to the camp, we must first see to the care of the flock. He who is faithful in the greater must first have been faithful in the least.

d. *It bore meekly misconstruction and rebuke.* Reaching the camp, he found the troops forming in battle array, and ran to the front. He had already found his brothers and greeted them, when he was arrested by the braggart voice of Goliath from across the valley and saw, to his chagrin, the men of Israel turn to flee, stricken with panic. When he expressed surprise, he learned from bystanders that even Saul shared the general panic, and had issued rewards for a champion. So he passed from one group of soldiers

18

to another, questioning, gathering further confirmation of his first impressions, and evincing everywhere the open-eyed wonder of his soul that "any man's heart should fail because of him."

Eliab had no patience with the words and bearing of his young brother. How dare he suggest that the behavior of the men of Israel was unworthy of them and their religion! What did he mean by inquiring so minutely after the particulars of the royal reward? Was he thinking of winning it? It was absurd to talk like that! "Why art thou come down? With whom," he said, with a sneer, "hast thou left those few sheep in the wilderness?" Ah, what venom lay in those few words! David, however, ruled his spirit, and answered softly "Surely," he said, "my father's wish to learn of your welfare was cause enough to bring me here." It was at this point that the victory over Goliath was really won. To have lost his temper in this unprovoked assault would have broken the alliance of his soul with God, and drawn a veil over his sense of His presence. But to meet evil with good, and maintain an unbroken composure, only cemented his alliance with the Lamb of God.

e. *It withstood the reasoning of the flesh.* Saul was eager for David to adopt his armor, though he dared not put it on himself. He was taken up with the boy's ingenuous earnestness, but advised him to adopt the means. "By all means trust God, and go; but be wise. We ought to adopt ordinary precautions."

But an unseen hand withdrew David from the meshes of temptation. He had already yielded so far to Saul's advice as to have put on his armor and girded on the sword: Then he turned to Saul and said, "I cannot go with these"; and he took them off. It was not now Saul's armor *and* the Lord, but the Lord alone; and he was able, without hesitation, to accost the giant with the words, "The LORD saveth not with sword and spear." Now let Goliath do his worst; he will know that there is a God in Israel.

6

"In the Name of the Lord of Hosts"
1 Samuel 17:45

While the two armies, on either side of the ravine, waited expectantly, every eye was suddenly attracted by the slight young figure which, staff in hand, emerged from the ranks of Israel, and descended the slope. For a little while David was hid from view, as he bent intent on the pebbles that lined the bottom, of which five smooth stones were presently selected and placed in his shepherd's bag. Then, to the amazement of the Philistines, and especially of their huge champion, he sprang up on the opposite bank, and rapidly moved toward him.

Goliath cursed David as he did so, and threatened him that his blood would color the mountain grass, while his unburied body would be a feast to the wild things of the earth and air. "Then said David to the Philistine, Thou comest to me with a sword, and with a spear, and with a shield: but I come to thee in the name of the LORD of hosts, the God of the armies of Israel whom thou hast defied."

1. THE TALISMAN OF VICTORY. "The name of the LORD of hosts." Throughout the Scriptures, a name is not simply, as with us, a label; it is a revelation of character. Thus the

name of God, as used so frequently by the heroes and saints of sacred history, stands for those divine attributes and qualities that combine to make Him what He is. The special quality that David had extracted from the bundle of qualities represented by the divine name of God is indicated in the words, *the Lord of hosts.*

To come in the name of the Lord of hosts implied his own identification by faith with all that was comprehended in this sacred name. A person in a foreign country speaks in a very different tone as an ordinary traveler, or if he acts as representative and ambassador of his country. In the former case he speaks in his own name, and receives what respect and obedience it can obtain; in the latter he is conscious of being identified with all that is associated with the name of his country. For a man to speak in the name of England means that England speaks through his lips; that the might of England is ready to enforce his demands; and that every sort of power that England wields is pledged to avenge any affront or indignity to which he may be exposed.

There is much for us to learn concerning this close identification with God before we will be able to say with Daivd, "I come to thee in the name of the LORD of hosts." It would be well worthwhile to become so absolutely identified with God that His name might be our strong tower, our refuge, our battlecry, our secret of victory.

2. THE CONDITIONS ON WHICH WE ARE WARRANTED IN USING THE NAME.

a. *When we are pure in our motives.* There was no doubt as to the motive that prompted David to this conflict. It is true that he had spoken to the men of Israel, saying, "What shall be done to the man that killeth the Philistine?" but no one supposed that he acted as he did because of the royal reward. His one ambition was to take away the reproach from Israel, and to let all the earth know that there was a God in Israel.

We must be wary here. It is so easy to confuse issues that are as wide apart as the poles, and to suppose that we are contending for the glory of God, when we are really combating for our church, our cause, our prejudices or opinions.

To fall into this sin, though unconsciously, is to forfeit the right to use His sacred name. How constantly we need to expose our hearts to the inspiration of the Holy Spirit, that He may wholly cleanse them, and fill them with an all-consuming devotion to the glory of God.

b. *When we are willing to allow God to occupy His right place.* David said repeatedly that the whole matter was God's. And David's attitude has been that of every man who has done great things in behalf of righteousness. We must recognize Jesus Christ as the essential warrior, worker, organizer, and administrator of His church, through the Holy Spirit. Whatever is rightly done, He must do. We are not called to work for Him, but to let Him work through us. His skill must direct us; His might empower us; His uplifted hands bring us victory.

c. *When we take no counsel with the flesh.* It must have been a hard thing for a young man to disagree with Saul, especially when the king was so solicitous for his welfare. It was well for him, indeed, that David withstood the siren song, and remained unaffected by the blandishments of royal favor. To have yielded to Saul would have put him beyond the circle of the divine environment.

3. THE BEARING OF THOSE WHO USE THE NAME.

a. *They are willing to stand alone.* The young man asked no comradeship in the fight. He was perfectly prepared to bear the whole brunt of the fray without sympathy or succor; so sure was he that the Lord of hosts was with him, and that the God of Jacob was his refuge.

b. *They are deliberate.* David was free from the nervous trepidation that so often unfits us to play our part in some great scene. Calmly and quietly he went down the slope and selected the pebbles that best suited his purpose. In this quietness and confidence he found his strength. He did not flee because the Lord went before him, and the Holy One of Israel was his protection.

c. *They are fearless.* When the moment came for the conflict, David did not hesitate, but ran toward the Philistine army to meet their champion. There was no fear of the result in that young heart; no tremor in the voice that answered the rough taunt; no falter in the arm that wielded the sling; no lack of precision in the aim that drove the stone to the one part of the Philistine's body that was unprotected and vulnerable.

d. *They are more than conquerors.* The stone sank into the giant's forehead; in another moment he fell stunned to the earth. There was no time to lose; before Goliath could recover himself, or his startled comrades overcome their stupefied amazement, his head had been separated from his body by one thrust of his own sword. And when the Philistines saw that their champion was dead, they fled. The spoils of victory lay with the victor. David took the head of the Philistine as a trophy, and put his armor in his tent.

Let us live alone with God. The weakest man who knows God is strong to do exploits. This is the victory that overcomes the world, the flesh, and the devil—even our faith.

7

Jonathan
1 Samuel 18:1

In heaven's vault there are what are known as binary stars, each probably a sun, but blending their rays so that they reach the watcher's eye as one clear beam of light. So do twin souls find the center of their orbit in each other, and there is nothing in the annals of human affection nobler than the bond of such a love between two pure, high-minded and noble men. Nowhere is it more fragrant than on the pages that contain the memorials of the love of Jonathan and David.

David was in all probability profoundly influenced by the character of Jonathan, who must have been considerably older. It seems to have been love at first sight. "When [David] had made an end of speaking unto Saul, the soul of Jonathan was knit with the soul of David, and Jonathan loved him as his own soul." That night a royal messenger may have summoned David to Jonathan's pavilion, on entering which he was amazed to be greeted with the warm embrace of a brotherly affection, which was never to wane. The young soldier must have shrunk back as unworthy; he must have ruefully looked down at his poor apparel as unbefitting a royal alliance. But all such considerations were swept away before the impetuous rush of Jonathan's affection, as he stripped himself of robe and apparel, of sword and bow and girdle, and gave them all to David. "Then Jonathan and David made a covenant, because he loved him as his own soul."

1. CONSIDER THE QUALITIES OF THIS FRIEND whom Jehovah chose for the molding of the character of his beloved.

a. *He was every inch a man.* The prime condition of two men walking together is that they should agree. And the bond of a common manliness knit these twin souls from the first. Jonathan was every inch a man; as dexterous with the bow as his friend with his sling. He was able to flash with indignation, strong to bear without quailing the brunt of his father's wrath, fearless to espouse the cause of his friends at whatever cost. He was also capable of inspiring a single armor-bearer with his own ardent spirit of attacking an army, of turning the tide of invasion, and of securing the admiration and affection of the entire people who, standing between him and his father, refused to let him die.

b. *He was very sensitive and tender.* It is the fashion in some quarters to emphasize the qualities supposed to be especially characteristic of men—those of strength, courage, endurance—to the undervaluing of the more tender graces often associated with women. But in every true man there must be a touch of woman, as there was in the ideal Man, the Lord Jesus. In Him there is neither male nor female, because there is the symmetrical blending of both: and in us, too, there should be strength and sweetness, courage and sympathy.

c. *Jonathan had a marvelous power of affection.* He loved David as himself; he was prepared to surrender without a pang his succession to his father's throne, if only he might be next to his friend. We judge a man by his friends and the admiration he excites in them. Any man whom David loved must have been possessed of many of those traits so conspicuous in David himself.

d. *He was distinctly religious.* When first introduced to us he is accompanied by his armor-bearer. He climbs single-handed to attack the Philistine garrison strongly entrenched behind rocky crags, he speaks as one familiar with the ways of God, to whom there is no restraint "to save by many or by few"; and when the appointed sign is given, it is accepted as a sigh of the victory that the Lord is about to give (1 Sam. 14).

When the two friends are about to be torn from each other, with little hope of renewing their blessed intercourse, Jonathan finds solace in the fact of the divine appointment, and the Lord being between them. Between them, not in the sense of division, but of connection; as the ocean unites us with distant lands. However far we are parted from those we love, we are intimately near in God.

And when, in the last interview the friends ever had, they met by some secret arrangement in a wood, "Jonathan came to David there, and strengthened his hand in God." All that those words imply it is not easy to write: our hearts interpret the words, and imagine the stream of holy encouragement that poured from that noble spirit into the heart of his friend.

2. CONSIDER THE CONFLICT OF JONATHAN'S LIFE. He was devoted to his father. He was always found associated with that strange dark character.

When his father first ascended the throne of Israel, the Lord was with him, and Jonathan knew it (1 Sam. 20:13). It must have been a delight to him to feel that the claims of the father were identical with the claims of God, and the heart of the young man must have leaped up in a blended loyalty to both. But the fair prospect was soon overcast. The Lord departed from Saul, and his power to hold the kingdom immediately waned. The Philistines invaded his land, his weapons of defense failed him, his people followed trembling, and Samuel told him that his kingdom could not continue. Then followed that dark day when Saul intruded on the priestly office in offering sacrifice. The ominous sentence was spoken, "The LORD hath sought him a man after his own heart, and the LORD hath commanded him to be captain over his people."

From that moment Saul's course was always downward; but Jonathan clung to him as if he hoped that by his own allegiance to God he might reverse the effects of his father's failure, and still hold the kingdom for their race.

At first this was not so difficult. There was no one to divide his heart with his father. But when he woke up to find how truly he loved David, a new difficulty entered his life. Not outwardly, because though Saul eyed David with jealousy, there was no open rupture. David went in and out of the palace, was in a position of trust, and was constanly at hand for the intercourse for which each yearned. But when the flames of hostility, long smoldering in Saul's heart, broke forth, the true anguish of his life began. On the one hand, his duty as son and subject held him to his father, though he knew his father was doomed, and that union with him meant disaster to himself; on the other hand, all his heart cried out for David.

His love for David made him eager to promote reconciliation between his father and his friend. It was only when repeated failure had proved the fruitlessness of his dream that he abandoned it; and then the thought must have suggested itself to him: Why not join your fortunes with his whom God has chosen? The new fair kingdom of the future is growing up around him—identify yourself with it, though it be against your father.

The temptation was pleasing and masterful, but it fell blunt and ineffectual at his feet. In some supreme moment he turned his back on the appeal of his heart and elected to stand beside his father. From that choice he never flinched. When David departed where he would, Jonathan went back to the city. His father might sneer at his league with the son of Jesse, but he held his peace; and when finally Saul started for his last battle with the Philistines, Jonathan fought beside him, though he knew that David was somehow involved in alliance with them.

Jonathan died as a hero; not only because of his prowess in battle with his country's foes, but also because of his victory over the strangest passion of the human heart, the love of a strong man, in which were blended the strands of a common religion, a common enthusiasm for all that was good and right.

8

Outside the House, and In
Psalm 59:9, 17

In the Hebrew the difference between the words "wait" and "sing," as appearing in this passage, is slight. They are spelled alike, with the exception of a single letter. The parallelism, therefore, between these two verses is very marked.

> Upon Thee, O my strength, I will wait,
> For God is my high tower.
> Unto Thee, O my strength, I will sing,
> For God is my high tower.

The inscription indicates the occasion on which this Psalm, one of the oldest, was written. "A Psalm of David: when Saul sent, and they watched the house to kill him."

1. THE EVENTS THAT LED UP TO THIS ASSAULT ON DAVID'S HOUSE. As the victorious army returned home from the valley of Elah, the whole land went forth in greeting. To the song of victory there came this refrain, which was strikingly discordant to the soul of the king:

> Saul hath slain his thousands,
> And David his ten thousands.

In that hour the first jealous thought awoke in Saul's heart. "Saul was very wroth, and the saying displeased him . . . and Saul eyed David from that day and forward."

But Saul was more than jealous. He deliberately set himself to thwart God's purpose. Samuel had distinctly told him that the Lord had torn the kingdom of Israel from him, and had given it to a neighbor of his who was better than he was. And, without doubt, as he saw the stripling return with Goliath's head in his hand, the dread certainty suggested itself to him that this was the divinely designated king. Saul said to himself, "I am king, and will see to it that this prediction at least will not come true. A dead man cannot reign; and there are many ways short of direct murder by which a man's life can be taken. But this is what it must come to." He supposed that if only he could take David's life, God's purpose would miscarry, and Samuel's predictions be falsified.

Saul's murderous passion sought to fulfill itself in many ways. On the following day, as David attempted to soothe him with his harp, he twice hurled his javelin at the minstrel, in the hope that if it pinned him to the wall the act might be imputed to insanity; but on each occasion the weapon sped harmlessly past, to quiver in the wall behind, instead of in that young heart.

Next, Saul gave him an important military commission, and made him his captain over a thousand, in the hope that this sudden elevation into the slippery place of worldly prominence and power might turn his head, and lead him to some traitorous deed, for which death would be the obvious penalty. But David behaved wisely in all his ways, so that the king, who watched closely for his falling, became more than ever convinced that he was God's ward, and stood in awe of him.

Then he offered the young soldier the hand of his eldest daughter in marriage, and treacherously withdrew the offer as the time of the wedding approached—the intention being to arouse his ardent spirit to retaliate, and so become liable to the charge of treason; but all his efforts failed to arouse even a transient impulse for revenge.

Again, when he offered his second daughter, Michal, as prize to be won by the evidence of one hundred Philistines having been slain, David returned unscathed with double the number required; and the love of the people grew.

Thwarted thus far, the God-forsaken monarch, driven by the awful fury of his jealousy, told Jonathan and all his servants that they had to rid him of David's tormenting presence; but of course that plot failed, for Jonathan delighted much in David, while all Israel and Judah loved him. Jonathan indeed elicited from him the promise that his friend should not be put to death. But shortly after, as the young minstrel endeavored to charm away the spirit of melancholy, the javelin again quivered past him from Saul's hand, and would have transfixed David to the wall, if he wasn't so agile. It was evening, and David fled to his young wife and home. And Saul, intent on murder, "sent messengers unto David's house, to watch him, and to slay him in the morning."

Michal's quick thinking saved her husband's life. She let him down through the window and he escaped, while an image, covered with a quilt and placed in the bed, led Saul's emissaries to suppose that he was sick. When, shortly after, the king proposed to snatch his prey from the midst of the sacred college, and from the very presence of Samuel, three sets of messengers were rendered powerless. Saul was arrested by God's Spirit and he prostrated himself before that Spirit, and lay helpless on the earth (1 Sam. 19:24).

That must have been a marvelous experience for David. To the eye of sense there was absolutely nothing to prevent the king's messengers, or the king himself, from taking him. But by faith he knew that he was being kept within the curtains of an impalpable pavilion, and that he was hidden beneath an invisible wing. The Presence of God encircled and protected both Samuel and David. And thus our God will still do for each of His persecuted ones.

2. DAVID'S COMPOSURE AMID THE ASSAULTS OF HIS FOES. This hunted man is a lesson for men and angels. Saul is his inveterate foe; traps and snares are laid for him on all sides. Yet all the while his heart is tranquil and reposing—yea, it actually breaks forth into praise, as the closing verses of this psalm prove. What was the secret of his serenity?

It lay first in the conviction of what God was. God was *his strength*—that was God within him; God was *his high tower*—that was God without and around him. There was no demand for which God was not sufficient, no peril which He could not keep at bay. O weakest of the weak, remember Jesus Christ, and take Him to be the strength of your life; be strong, yes be strong in the grace that is in Christ Jesus.

Or see those fugitive soldiers, hotly pursued by their enemies. In the distance is a cliff on which is perched a fortress, whose mighty walls and towers, if only they can be reached, will ensure protection. Breathlessly they scale the ascent, rush across the drawbridge, let down the portcullis, and fling themselves on the ground, and know that they are safe. God is all that to the soul that has learned to put Him between itself and everything.

David's composure lay, next, in his attitude toward God. "O my strength, I will *wait* on thee." The word so translated is used in the Hebrew of the shepherd watching his flock, of the watchman on the tower, of the sentry passing to and fro upon his beat. Is this our habitual attitude? Too many direct their prayer, but do not look up the ladder for the descending angels, laden with the heavenly answer. We pray, but we do not wait; we ask, but we do not expect to receive; we knock, but we are gone before the door is opened.

This lesson is for us to learn—to depend on God; to wait for the vision; to believe that He who taught us to trust cannot deceive our trust; to be sure that none who wait on Him can be ashamed. This is waiting on God: this will keep us calm and still; this will change our waiting into song.

9

The Message of the Arrows
1 Samuel 20:21–37

Jonathan had considerable influence with his father. Saul did nothing, either great or small, which he did not "uncover to his ear." For his love's sake, as well as for his father's, Jonathan was extremely eager to affect a reconciliation between him to whom he owed the allegiance of son and subject, and this fair shepherd-minstrel-warrior, who had so recently cast a sunny gleam on his life.

It was the eve of the feast of the new moon, when Saul invited the chief men of his kingdom to a banquet; and the friends agreed that this was an opportune moment for testing the real sentiments of Saul. David suggested that he should absent himself from the royal banquet so he could visit his father's home at Bethlehem instead. It would be quite easy for him to do this, and yet be back by the third day. In the meantime, Jonathan was to carefully watch his father's behavior, and mark his tone, noting whether it was cruel or kind.

The general outline of this scheme was arranged within the palace, but it seemed wiser to continue the conversation in some secluded spot. Jonathan proposed the ingenious plan in which his directions to a young boy would express by a swift telegraphy the secret that would either lift David to peace and safety, or thrust him into the depths of despair.

1. THE ARROWS TAUGHT THAT A STRONG AND NOBLE FRIEND WAS STANDING IN THE BREACH. It was no child's play that Jonathan undertook in the sacred name of friendship; and probably he was quite prepared for the outburst that followed his protest for his absent friend. On the first feast day, Saul noticed David's absence, but said nothing; on the second, however, when David's seat was still vacant, he turned sharply on his son Jonathan and asked the reason, "Wherefore cometh not the son of Jesse to meat, neither yesterday, nor to-day?" Jonathan instantly gave the preconcerted answer about David's desire to see his family, and made out that he himself had given permission for his absence. Saul's fury knew no bounds: with stinging allusion to Jonathan's mother, his own wife, as the source of his son's perversity; with demands that David should be instantly brought to him and put to death—the monarch clearly showed his inveterate hatred for David. Jonathan made one vain attempt to reason with the furious monarch, but the king cast his spear at him to smite him. Then Jonathan knew that they had to prepare for the worst; and he left the table in fierce anger, being grieved for his friend because his father had done him shame.

Never be ashamed to own a friend. When you have entered into an alliance with another soul, whom you love as Jonathan loved David, dare to stand up for him at all cost. But there is something still nobler, and that is when anyone dares in any company to avow his loyalty to the Lord Jesus. Like David, He is now in obscurity and disrepute; His name is not popular; His gospel is misrepresented; His followers are subjected to rebuke and scorn. Jonathan's arrows showed that he did not hesitate to stand alone for David; therefore let our words assure Him, that we will bear scorn, reproach, and death for His dear name.

2. THE ARROWS SPOKE OF IMMINENT DANGER. "Jonathan knew that it was determined of his father to slay David. As the lad ran, Jonathan shot an arrow beyond him: "And as soon as the lad was gone, David arose out of a place toward the south, and fell on his face to the ground, and bowed himself three times: and they kissed one another, and wept one with another, until David exceeded." There was no need for Jonathan to enter into explanations, for David knew that the Lord had sent him away.

"The arrows are beyond thee." You have hoped against hope; you have tried to keep your position; you have done your duty, pleaded your cause, sought the intercession of your friends, prayed, wept, agonized: but it is all in vain. The message of those arrows cannot be resisted. There is no alternative but to leave and go, though you know not where. But take these thoughts for your comfort.

a. *There are things we never leave behind.* David had an inalienable possession in the love of his friend, in the devotion of the people, in the memory of God's goodness, in his experience of His delivering care, in the sense of the divine presence that was ever beside him. There are threads woven into the fabric of our life that can never be extracted or obliterated.

b. *There is a divine purpose determining our course.* To the lad there was but royal caprice in the flight of the arrow. "What are you doing, my little fellow?" "I am picking up the prince's arrows; we generally go for game, but he is playing at it today." That was all he knew; how little did he understand the purpose of his master, and still less realize that each flitting arrow was, so to speak, taken from God's quiver and directed by His hand. There is no chance in a good man's life.

c. *The going forth is necessary to secure greater happiness than we leave.* Had David lingered in the palace, his life would have been forfeited, and he would have missed all the glory and bliss with which his cup ran over years later. This was the way to the throne. Only thus could the sentence whispered in his ear by Samuel years before be realized.

Follow the arrow's flight then—beyond the warm circle in which you have so long been sheltered; beyond the known to the unknown. Like another Abraham, go into the land that God will show you.

3. The arrows taught that human love must suffer separation. This was the last meeting of these two noble hearts for a long time. Indeed, the friends met only once more, shortly before Jonathan's death. They had realized that this must be so. "Go in peace," Jonathan said finally, as though he could no longer bear the awful anguish of that parting. "Then David arose and departed to become a fugitive and an outlaw, liable at any moment to capture and violent death; while Jonathan returned thoughtfully and sadly to the palace, where he would have to spend the rest of his life in contact with one who had no sympathy for his noble sentiments, who had outraged his tenderest sensibilities.

These are the house that leave scars on hearts, and whiten the hair. But Christ comes to us in these dark moments, as He did to the disciples, on whom had broken the full import of their Master's approaching departure. To believe that He is ordering each detail, to trust Him utterly—there is nothing like this to bridge the yawning gulf of separation.

10

Almost Gone
1 Samuel 21; Psalm 56

It is not easy to walk with God. The air that beats around the Himalayan heights of divine fellowship is rare and hard to breathe; human feet tire after a little, and faith, put to it, is inclined to give up the effort of keeping step with the divine pace. David found it so, and he fell into a terrible lapse, the steps and consequences of which, together with his recovery, must engages us for a little.

1. THE STEPS OF DAVID'S DECLENSION. The *first* sign of what was impending was his remark to Jonathan, that there was but a step between himself and death (1 Sam. 20:3). Evidently his faith was beginning to falter, for nothing could have been more definite than the divine assurances that he was to be king. He looked at God through the mist of circumstances, which certainly to the eye of sense were sufficiently threatening, instead of looking at circumstances through the golden haze of God's very present help. But David possibly relied too absolutely on what he had received, and neglected the daily renewal of the heavenly unction (John 1:33–34; 1 John 3:24).

Next, he adopted a subterfuge, which was not worthy of him, nor of his great and mighty Friend. Late in the afternoon of the day preceding the weekly Sabbath, the king's son-in-law arrived, with a mere handful of followers at the little town of Nob, situated among the hills about five miles to the south of Gibeah. It was a peaceful secluded spot, as became the character and calling of its inhabitants, who were engaged in the service of the sanctuary. Eighty-six men who wore the linen ephod lived there with their wives, their children, their oxen, asses, and sheep. Into the tranquil course of existence in that holy and retired spot hardly a ripple came from the storms that swept the outer world; the path to the simple sanctuary was trodden only by occasional visitors, such as Doeg, who came to pay their vows, or be cleansed from ceremonial pollution.

It was necessary to answer the questions, and allay the suspicions of the priest, so David led Ahimelech to believe that his young attendants and himself had been on this expedition for at least three days; that the king had especially insisted on privacy and secrecy; and that a large escort awaited him at a distance. But a chill struck his heart while he was making these excuses to the simple-minded priest, and enlisting his willing cooperation in the matter of provisions and arms, as he saw the dark visage of Doeg, the Edomite, "the chiefest of the herdmen that belonged to Saul." He knew that the whole story would be mercilessly retold to the vindictive and vengeful monarch. Uneasiness for his unsuspecting host and fear for himself filled his heart; and as soon as the Sabbath was over he left the spot, and hurriedly struck out across the hills in a southwesterly direction until he cut the deep depression of the valley of Elah, where he had achieved the great victory of his life. Ten miles beyond lay the proud Philistine city of Gath, which at that time had sent its champion forth in all the pride of his stature and strength. Behind, David had left an implacable foe. What worse fate could await him at Gath than that which threatened him each hour he lingered within the limits of Judah! He therefore resolved to make the plunge, probably hoping that the shepherd boy of years ago would not be recognized in the mature warrior, or that the Philistines would be glad to have his aid in their wars against his countrymen.

Perhaps because of Goliath's sword hanging at his belt, he was instantly recognized. His hands had been drenched in Philistine blood; his fortunes reared from the dust at the expense of bereaved hearts and homes throughout the Philistine territory. David saw the immense peril in which he stood of imprisonment of execution. He saved himself by descending to the unworthy scheme of counterfeiting the behavior of a madman, drumming on the leaves of the city gate, and allowing his spittle to fall down on his beard. His device succeeded; and Achish dismissed him with the humorous remark to his servants that he had enough madmen around him, and had no need of another. This certainly was one of the least dignified episodes in David's varied life, very unworthy of God's anointed; and the shame was that there would have been no need for it if he had not departed through unbelief from the living God.

2. THE PSALM OF THE SILENT DOVE. At first sight we are startled with the apparently irreconcilable discrepancy between the scenes we have just described and Psalm 56, the inscription of which associates it with them. Closer inspection will reveal many resemblances between the singer's circumstances and his touching words: and we are reminded that beneath much that is unworthy and contemptible there may burn a true devotion, an eager yearning after God, a soul of good amid things evil.

The major part of this exquisite psalm consists of two stanzas, which culminate in the same refrain; the remainder is full of hope and praise, and expression of the joy with which the psalmist anticipates walking before God in the light of life.

a. *First Stanza* (1–4). He turns to God from man; to the divine mercy from the serried ranks of his foes, who, surging around him, threaten to engulf and swallow him up; he counts himself as a lonely dove far from its native woods; his heart trembles and misgives, amid the many that fight proudly against him. Yet he contrasts fear with faith, arguing with himself as to the baselessness of his dread, and contrasting man's fleshy might with God's supreme power. A new song is in his mouth, the burden of which is, "I will not be afraid." Oh, happy soul who has learned to take your stand on God as your Rock and Fortress!

b. *Second Stanza* (5–9). Again he is in the depths. Never a moment of intermission from the wrestling of his words; not a glint of respite from the hostility of their thoughts; not a step that is not watched by the scrutiny of those who lie in wait for his soul. He wanders fitfully from shelter to shelter; his tears fall thick and fast; his enemies are as numerous as the hairs of his head. Yet we hear the voice of faith again ringing out the positive assurance, "I know that God is for me."

c. *Third Stanza* (10–13). There is no further relapse. His heart is fixed, trusting the Lord; the vows of God are on his head. He looks back on the dark abyss into which his soul had almost gone, and knows that he is delivered from it forever. As the morning breaks he sees the mark of his footprints to the edge of the precipice, and recognizes the divine power and grace that has delivered his feet from falling. And now he is sure that from this day on he will walk before God in the light of life. In the extreme anguish of those hours at Gath, the backslider had returned to God, and once again sat, as a child at home, anointed with oil, with a table spread before him in the presence of his enemies.

3. THE CONSEQUENCES TO AHIMELECH. A child of God may be forgiven and restored, yet the consequences of his sin may involve sufferings to many innocent lives. So it was in this instance. It happened shortly after, when Saul was endeavoring to excite his servants sympathy by enumerating the wrongs he had suffered at the hand of David, and Doeg took the opportunity of ingratiating himself in the royal favor by narrating what he had seen at Nob. He told the tale as to make it appear that the priest and his house were accomplices with David's action, and perhaps were bent on helping David to gain supreme power. It was in vain that Ahimelech protested his innocence, enumerated David's services, and referred to the many occasions on which David had sought

his help. He persisted in the avowal of his unconsciousness of the quarrel between Saul and his son-in-law, but before night fell the white vesture of the priests was soaked with their blood, and every living thing in the little mountain town was smitten with the edge of the sword. By one ruthless act, the entire priestly community was exterminated.

But there was one survivor, for Abiathar escaped, carrying the ephod in his hands; and one day, to his horror, David beheld the dishevelled, blood-smeared form of the priest as he sped breathless and panic-stricken up the valley of Elah, to find shelter with the outlaw band in the Cave of Adullam. We shall hear of him again.

Meanwhile, let children of God beware! Sin is bitter to the conscience of the sinner, and in its consequences on others. Seeds may be scattered beyond recovery, to bear bitter harvests in the lives of those who, through their mysterious union with ourselves, are inextricably involved in the consequences of our deeds.

11

The Cave of Adullam
1 Samuel 22; Psalm 34

Leaving Gath, with a thankful heart for God's delivering mercy, David hastily recrossed the frontier, and found himself again in the kingdom of Saul. His life, however, was in great jeopardy, and he did not dare to expose himself to the royal jealousy. There was apparently no alternative but to adopt the life of a fugitive and wanderer amid the hills of Judah, with which his shepherd life had made him so familiar.

Two miles up the valley of Elah from Gath there is a labyrinth of hills and valleys, deeply honey-combed with caves. One of these, near the ancient Canaanite city of Adullam, and called after it, afforded David for a considerable period the shelter for which he was searching. Its position made it possible for him to cross from one country to another, as occasion required. His whole family fled to David, dreading, no doubt, the violence of Saul's hatred; and there also came every one who was in distress, and every one who was in debt, and every one who was discontented, and he became captain over them.

We need not now enlarge on David's filial love, which traversed the entire distance from Adullam to Moab to secure an asylum for his father and mother. But the double journey, first to secure the shelter, and then to escort the aged couple there, shows us a pleasing trait in David's character. There was no lack of obedience to the first commandment with promise. It is, however, the cave and the more motley group of his adherents that we now want to consider.

1. THE CAVE AND ITS LESSONS. There can be no doubt that the Holy Ghost desires us to trace an analogy between David's history and that of the Lord Jesus, in His present rejection and banishment from the throne of the world.

a. *A rejected king was on the throne.* Though anointed by Samuel, Saul by disobedience had forfeited his right to reign. The sentence of deposition had been pronounced, and was awaiting execution at the appropriate moment. Similarly, the dark fallen spirit, Satan, was once an angel set on the holy mountain of God, and perfect in his ways from the day he was created, until unrighteousness was found in him. Satan still holds the throne of the world. He has cast his javelin at the king after God's own heart. In the Temptation and in Gethsemane he would rather have pinned Him to the wall. But all his attempts must fail. As Saul fell on the field of Gilboa, so the prince of darkness will be finally cast into the bottomless pit.

b. *David's kingdom was hidden.* It was a true kingdom, though in mystery, veiled in the darkness of Adullam's Cave, and concealed in the labyrinth of valleys and hills. Such was also the experience of the divine King, who fell into the mystery of forsaken-ness on the Cross, and the mystery of rejection in the grave; and whose person and kingdom are now altogether hidden from the world of men. For the present, his king-dom is "in mystery."

c. *David and his followers were separated.* Driven outside the camp of Israel, they had no alternative. With the feasts and pageants, the counsels and decisions, the home-politics and foreign wars of Saul, they had no immediate connection. The lot of an exile, the path of the wanderer and stranger, were meted out to David and those who were willing to share his lot. There must have been a perpetual sadness and loneliness in his soul.

The true King of men is still outside human politics and society. We cannot have Him and them. Those who desire to be His subjects must go out to Him outside the camp, willing to forsake all that they have, and be counted the refuse of all things.

d. *David was content to await God's time.* Whatever provocation Saul gave, David never retaliated. However easy the opportunity of gaining an advantage over his vindic-tive pursuer, he never availed himself of it. He was prepared to wait God's time, and to receive supreme power in God's way. So it is through these passing centuries that our Savior is waiting. Now is the time of the kingdom and *patience* of Jesus Christ; here is the patience of the saints; while the eager expectation and yearning of the whole creation is waiting for the manifestation of the sons of God.

2. THE CAVE AND ITS INMATES. The tidings of David's return to Judah and of his retreat in the shelter of the cave, spread swiftly throughout the whole land; and those who were afflicted by misery, poverty, and bitterness of soul began to flock around him. The young leader soon found himself at the head of four hundred men, a very motley crew! The sacred historian says that their faces were like the faces of lions, and that they were as swift as deer on the mountains; but their tempers were probably turbulent and fierce, requiring all the grace and tact and statesmanship of which the young ruler was capable, to reduce them to discipline and order. It was surely no small feat to so organize such materials that they became the nucleus of the greatest army of their time, and carried the standard of Israel to the fullest limits it ever reached.

It is impossible not to turn from David to Him who, though cast out from the scheme of this world and its prince, is ever gathering around his standard the poor and outcast, the leper and sinner, the blind and bruised and broken-hearted, those who are in distress, in debt, and discontented, and making them into soldiers who will win the world for Himself.

Did these wild, rough soldiers find a new center for their life in David? We have found a new object in the Lord Jesus, for whom to live is life indeed, and for whom to die is gain.

Did they put off the manners and customs of their old life, and allow the shuttle of love and devotion to weave the fabric of a new character? We have to put off the old man with his doings, and put on the new man.

Did they love David for removing their discontent, alleviating their distress, and relieving them from the disorder and anxiety of their existence? Much more should we love Him, who has done more for us than even David did for his poor followers. He has paid our debts with His precious blood; relieved us from our creditors by meeting them Himself; clothed us in His perfect beauty; allayed our sorrows; calmed and stilled our souls.

3. THE CAVE AND ITS SONG. Many allusions connect the thirty-fourth Psalm with the Cave of Adullam. It was there that the little host needed the encamping angel; there that the young lions roared as they ranged the wilds in search of food; there also that God's care was perpetually laid under requisition to keep the bones of the fugitives lest they should be broken by falling down the crags (vv. 7, 10, 20).

The soul that is living a separated life, with sin judged, forsaken, and forgiven, behind it, may count on these four blessings:

a. *Deliverance*—even in the midst of difficulties and perplexities that have been caused by its own misdeeds (vv. 4, 7, 17, 19).

b. *Enlightenment*—for what the dawn is to the weary watcher, that God will be to the soul that has long groped in the dark, if only the face is turned toward His (v. 5).

c. *Perfect provision*—so that it will lack nothing it really needs (v. 10).

d. *The sense of God's nearness*—nearer than the nearest, more real than the presence of absence of any (v. 18).

12

The White Stone
1 Samuel 23:6; Psalm 27

It is not perfectly clear where David was when he was joined by Abiathar. If we consider the time, we are required to fix the massacre of the priests shortly after his flight to Gath; and in that case, Abiathar must have come to him while David was in his first prolonged hiding place in the Cave of Adullam. It is on this supposition that we have already sketched the fugitive coming there, breathless and dishevelled.

1. DAVID'S HABITUAL PRACTICE. The special reason that made David glad to welcome Abiathar was that he brought with him, rescued from the sack of the little town, the sacred ephod, within which were the sacred Urim and Thummim. The words signify "Light and Perfection"; it is by no means certain what they refer to. The most probable explanation, however, is the following:

The high priest's inner garment was a white linen tunic, over which he wore a blue robe, and above this the ephod, made of white interwoven linen, with blue and purple and scarlet and gold threads. To this was affixed the breastplate, in which were twelve precious stones, corresponding to the twelve tribes of Israel. In this breastplate were probably either one or two very beautiful and resplendent diamonds, through which God manifested His will. If to any question reverently put to Him by the priest the answer was no, the light in these precious stones dimmed; if on the contrary, it was yes, they flashed with splendor.

It was obviously a great gain to David to have at hand this priceless method of communication between Jehovah and himself. Already Gad was with him, as the representative of the prophetic office; now Abiathar and the ephod represented the most precious prerogative of the priesthood. By one or other of these, and probably in these earlier days especially by the latter, he was able at any moment to know the will of God.

If tidings come that the Philistines are plundering Keilah, he dare not pursue until he has asked the Lord. If the cowardly townspeople propose to betray their deliverer, he dares not leave the little city until he has received divine directions to go. In one of the most awful experiences of his life, when his men spoke of stoning him instead of taking up his cause, he said to Abiathar the priest, "I pray thee, bring me hither the ephod." Then Abiathar brought the ephod to him, and David inquired of the Lord. Long after he had become acknowledged king of the land, in his conflicts with the Philistines he was careful to inquire of the Lord as to the very method of attack (1 Sam. 30:7, 2 Sam. 5:17–25).

Evidently this was the holy practice of his life: to wait on God until time had been given for the clear disclosure of the divine purpose and plan.

2. THE LESSON FOR OURSELVES. When Israel came up out of Egypt, they were led across the desert by the pillar of cloud and fire. After they were settled in their own land, the Urim and Thummim took its place. After awhile, this method of ascertaining God's will fell into disuse, and the prophets spoke as they were moved by the Holy Spirit. These, even in the early church played a very important part in the ordering of God's people in His way.

But the voices of the prophets were silenced as the apostolic age came to a close. What is our oracle of appeal? In one of the last messages given by the ascended Lord to His church, through the apostle John, it was foretold that he who overcame would receive a *white stone,* and the word *white* means resplendent, or lustrous. It may therefore denote a diamond, and probably refers to those ancient stones in the high priest's breastplate, that dimmed or flashed with the divine oracles.

In other words, each child of God has his own Urim and Thummim stone, which is a conscience void of offense, a heart cleansed in the blood of Christ, a spiritual nature that is pervaded and filled by the Holy Spirit of God.

When we are in doubt or difficulty, when many voices urge this course or the other, then let us be still in God's presence; let us study His Word in the attitude of devout attention; let us lift up our nature into the pure light of His face, eager to know only what God the Lord shall determine—and before long a very distinct impression will be made, the unmistakeable forthtelling of His secret counsel. It is not wise, in the earlier stages of Christian life, to depend on this alone, but to wait for the corroboration of circumstances. But those who have had many dealings with God know well the value of secret fellowship with Him, to ascertain His will. The journals of George Fox are full of references to this secret of the Lord, which is with those who fear Him.

Are you in difficulty about your way? Go to God with your question, get direction from the light of His smile or the cloud of His refusal. If you will dare to wait silently and expectantly, though all around you insist on immediate decision or action, the will of God will be made clear.

13

Songs Born of Sorrow
1 Samuel 23

It is remarkable how many of David's psalms date from those dark and sad days when he was hunted as a partridge on the mountains. His path may be tracked through the Psalter, as well as in the sacred narratives of his wanderings. Keilah, Ziph, Maon, Engedi, yielded themes for strains that will live forever. We will now trace the parallel lines of David's history and song.

1. A CLUSTER OF PSALMS.

a. *Keilah.* While hiding in the forest of Hareth, tidings came to David of a foray of the Philistines on one of the hapless border towns. "Behold, the Philistines fight against Keilah, and they rob the threshingfloors." The year's harvest was at that time spread out for threshing; it was an opportune moment therefore for the plunderer. The labors of the year were being carried off, and the cattle "lifted by Israel's bitter and relentless foe." David arose and went down from the hill country of Judah into the plains, met the marauders on their return journey, heavily laden with booty and impeded with cattle. He slaughtered many of them and brought back all the spoil to the rejoicing townsfolk who, in return for his services, gladly lodged and entertained him and his men.

It must have been very welcome to the weary little band. To again be in a town that had "gates and bars" was a welcome exchange to life in the dens and caves of the earth. And this gleam of comfort probably elicited from the minstrel-chieftain Psalm 31, "Blessed be the LORD: for he hath shewed me his marvellous kindness in a strong city."

b. *Ziph.* His stay in Keilah was brought to a close by the tidings, given perhaps by Jonathan, that Saul was preparing an expedition to take him. These tidings were confirmed through the ephod, by which David appealed to the God of Israel; and other information was communicated that the cowardly and ungrateful townspeople, when forced to choose between the king and himself, did not hesitate to save themselves by surrendering their deliverer. Then David and his men, in number about six hundred, arose and departed out of Keilah, and went wherever they could go. They perhaps broke up into small parties, while the leader, with the more intrepid and devoted of his followers, made his way to the neighborhood of Ziph, about three miles south of Hebron.

This was about the lowest ebb in David's life. The king was searching for him every day with a malice that made it evident that he had come out to seek his life. In addition to this relentless hate, there was the meditated treachery of the Ziphites, who sought to obtain favor with the king by betraying David's hiding place. Tidings of their intended treachery came to David and he moved further south to the wilderness of Maon, where a conical hill gives an extended view of the surrounding country. But the men of Ziph conducted the king to the spot with such deadly accuracy, that before David and his band could escape, the little beleaguered group found the hill on which they gathered surrounded by the royal troops, and their escape rendered impossible. It was fortunate for them that at this juncture a breathless messenger burst in on Saul with the words, "Haste thee, and come; for the Philistines have invaded the land."

Then David drew a long sigh of relief, and sang Psalm 54; "Save me, O God, by thy name, and judge me by thy strength."

c. *Engedi.* From Maon, when the heat of the pursuit was over, David moved his quarters eastward to the strongholds of the wild goat on the shores of the Dead Sea. It is said that gray weather-beaten stones mark the site of an ancient city, and traces of palms have been discovered encrusted in the limestone. This was David's next resort— Engedi, the haunt of the wild goat. Here, again the psalmist sets his experiences to music in two priceless songs. Psalm 57, "Be merciful unto me, O God, for my soul trusteth in thee"; and Psalm 142, "I cried unto the LORD with my voice; with my voice unto the LORD, did make my supplication."

Wilderness experiences also gave rise to other psalms, all of them marked by a recurrence of the same metaphors borrowed from the wilderness and rocky scenery; of the same protestations of innocence; of the same appeals for the overshadowing wing of the most high; of the same delicately-worded references to Saul. Among these are Psalms 11, 13, 17, 22, 25, 64.

2. SOME CHARACTERISTICS OF THESE PSALMS. We cannot deal with these psalms in detail, but one or two features arrest the most superficial glance.

a. *There is a conscious rectitude.* His conscience was void of offense toward God and man. If challenged as to his absolute sinlessness, he would have acknowledged that he was constantly in need of the propitiating sacrifices that would plead for him with God. But, in respect to Saul, or to any treachery against him or his house, he protested his absolute innocence, and turned confidently to God with clean hands and a pure heart, as one who had not lifted up his soul unto vanity, or sworn deceitfully (Ps. 7:3–5; 24).

b. *There is great evidence of suffering.* Of all sources of pain, there is none so hard to bear as the malice of our fellows. This is what David suffered from most of all: that though he was absolutely innocent, though he was willing to give himself to prayer and ministry on their behalf, yet his slanderers pursued him with unrelenting malice— "Their teeth are spears and arrows, and their tongue a sharp sword" (Ps. 57:4).

c. *But his appeal was to God.*

> Save me, O God, by thy name,
> And judge me by thy might! (Ps. 54:1)
>
> Behold, God is mine helper. (Ps. 54:4)
>
> I will cry unto God most high;
> Unto God that performeth all things for me.
> He shall send from heaven, and save me. . . .
> God shall send forth his mercy and his truth. (Ps. 57:3)
>
> Refuge failed me; no man cared for my soul.
> I cried unto thee, O LORD.
> I said, "Thou art my refuge." (Ps. 142:4–5)

What depths of pathos lie in these stanzas of petition! He commits himself to Him who judges righteously. If any should read these lines who are unjustly maligned and persecuted, let them rest in the Lord and wait patiently for Him. Some little time may elapse before the hour of deliverance may strike, but soon God will arise and lift the poor out of the dust, "to make them sit with princes and inherit the throne of glory."

14

David's Self-restraint
1 Samuel 24 and 26; Psalm 40:1–3

As David reviewed his life, and recorded his experiences, he was well aware of the innumerable evils that had encompassed him, and of the many who had sought in vain to destroy his soul; but from all he had been delivered. Mark his record of God's dealings with him, as he stands on the eminence of the years and looks down and back—

"He *inclined unto me, and heard my cry.*
He *brought me up also out of an horrible pit, out of the miry clay,*
And *set my feet upon a rock, and established my goings.*
And *hath put a new song in my mouth, even praise unto our God.*" (Ps. 40:1–3)

And if we further inquire what his attitude was, during all these long and sad experiences, he answers:

"*I waited patiently for the* LORD."

We wait *for* the Lord by patience and submission. It is very needful to learn this lesson of silence, patience, and resignation; and it is interesting to see in the two incidents before us how perfectly David had acquired it.

1. THE BASIS OF WAITING FOR GOD. There must be a promise to justify us, or some definite commitment of God on which we can rest. When Jonathan and David met for the last time in the wood of Ziph, Jonathan had given this to his friend. He had spoken like a messenger from God. "Fear not," he had said, "for the hand of Saul my father shall not find thee; and thou shalt be king over Israel, and I shall be next unto thee." He had even said that this, too, was Saul's conviction: "That also Saul my father knoweth."

Besides this, he was conscious of faculty and God-given power; of the ability to grasp the helm of the distracted kingdom, and guide the sorely-tossed bark into calmer waters. He became convinced that God had a great purpose in his life, and settled it in his own mind that he would wait patiently for the Lord to do as He had said, and that he would not lift his finger to secure the kingdom for himself. Whenever the moment came for him to sit on the throne as the acknowledged king of his people, it should be from first to last the divine gift, and the divine performance.

2. TWO NOTABLE INCIDENTS.

a. *Engedi.* One afternoon when Saul, with three thousand men, was in hot pursuit of David, amid the wild and tangled rocks of Engedi, a strange incident put him completely in David's power. David and his men were in the inmost recesses of an immense cavern when Saul entered that same cave. His men had gone forward but the intense solitude and silence within and without threw him off his guard, so he lingered a little in the entrance.

How little did the king realize the intense interest with which he was being watched by six hundred pairs of eyes, and the peril to which he was exposed! The whole band was thrilled with excitement.

Now was the opportunity for David to end their wanderings and hardships by one thrust of the spear. They whispered "Seize your opportunity!" David restrained them, and curbed his own passion that tore like fire through every vein, and contented himself with creeping near and cutting off the skirt of the king's robe to prove to him afterward how completely he had been in his power. But even then, after Saul had left and David's men crowded around, full of sullen remonstrance at his weakness, he was struck with remorse, and he said to them, "The LORD forbid that I should do this thing unto my master, the LORD's anointed, to stretch forth mine hand against him, seeing he is the anointed of the LORD."

b. *Hachilah.* Earlier at this spot David had been nearly trapped. This time the tables were turned. Once more Saul, probably instigated by a malign influence that we shall consider in our next chapter, was in pursuit of his rival, "having three thousand chosen men of Israel with him." Having ascertained by means of scouts the exact situation of the royal camp, David went to inspect it in person from an overhanging cliff. On the outskirts the wagons made a rude barricade; within these were the soldiers' quarters, and in the innermost circle Saul and Abner were posted. But the watches were badly kept, and no precaution was taken against sudden attack.

A sudden inspiration seized David, and he proposed to Abishai and Ahimelech the Hittite that they should visit the camp by night. Abishai gladly volunteered to accompany him, and guided by the clear moonlight they crept down the hill, crossed the ravine, picked their way through the wagons and the sleeping ranks of the soldiers, stood for a moment whispering over the prostrate form of the king. They took his spear and the waterbottle that was hanging around Saul's neck, and then "gat them away, and no man saw it, nor knew it, neither awaked; because a deep sleep from the LORD was fallen upon them." Once again Saul had been in his power, but he had restrained himself.

On each of these occasions David acted with the magnanimity that became a hero and a saint. He would take no mean advantage of his adversary. He elected to await the slow unfolding of the divine purpose.

3. THE BEHAVIOR THAT WAITING FOR GOD INDUCES.

a. *It restrains from crime.* Bitter indeed would David's remorse have been if he had listened to his comrades and had taken Saul's life. It would have robbed his harp of all its music. There would then have been some justification for Shimei's cursing words on that dark day later in his life; but as it was, though they cut him to the quick, he knew that Absalom's rebellion and seizure of his throne could not be, as Shimei suggested, a requital in kind for his dealings with Saul. True, months of anxiety and suspense were still to pass before the coronation shouts rang through the streets of Hebron; but there was nothing to regret, no death's head at the bottom of his cup of joy. Be still, O heart! wait for God; this will keep you from acts and words which, if allowed, would shadow the rest of your life.

b. *It inspires courage.* What an intrepid spirit this was that dared to cry after the king and hold up the skirt of his robe; that challenged the two bravest men of his little army to a feat, from which one of them shrank! Ah! the man who is living the divine purpose has the secret of quenchless courage. He fears nothing, except to do wrong, and to grieve God.

c. *It gives great rest.* Surely it was out of such experiences as these that David wrote Psalm 37 which, though it belongs to a later period, forever preserves the conclusions of this.

Fret not thyself because of evildoers,
Neither be thou envious against the workers of iniquity.
For they shall soon be cut down like grass,
And wither as the green herb.

Live on the divine purpose. Rest; sit still and trust—God is working out the plan of your life; you cannot hurry Him; it will only expend the energy of your soul to no purpose. In his own time, the best time, He shall give you the desires of your heart.

d. *It induces penitence in others.* When David gave such unmistakable evidences of his self-restraint, continued loyalty, and surviving affection, in spite of all that had been done to quench it, Saul lifted up his voice and wept, and confessed that he had "played the fool, and have erred exceedingly." Saul recognized David's nobility; and he went so far as to admit that he would be king. Nothing but such forbearance on David's part could have brought him so near repentance.

It is in this way that we may still win men. We win most when we appear to have yielded most; and gain advantages by refusing to take them wrongfully. The man who can wait for God is a man of power.

15

Cush: a Benjamite
Psalm 7

It is somewhat surprising to find Saul in search of David, after the first of the incidents described in the previous chapter. At Engedi it seemed as though the reconciliation between them was complete. And yet, after so short a time, Saul is again on the warpath.

These capricious changes may, of course, have been due to the malady from which he was suffering, but another explanation has been suggested, and one which casts fresh light on the seventh Psalm. Dr. Maclaren, whose work on the Psalter has brought the whole church into his debt, is especially emphatic in connecting the psalm with this part of David's history, and indicates its value in helping us to understand the rapid vacillations in Saul's behavior. The title has, "concerning the words of Cush, the Benjamite." Who was this Cush? If the psalm is examined carefully, it will be found to bear a close resemblance to the words spoken by David, when Saul and he held the brief discussion outside the cave at Engedi, and afterward at the hill Hachilah.

Indeed, the correspondences are so many and minute that they establish, almost beyond question, the date of the psalm as synchronous with the incidents described in the last chapter; and if so, we can infer the cause of Saul's renewed passion. It seems more than likely that Cush was one of Saul's intimate friends and constant companions, and that he was incessantly at work poisoning the king's mind with malignant and deliberate falsehoods about David. When Saul was away from this man, and under the spell of David's noble and generous nature, he laid aside his vindictiveness, and responded to the appeals of old friendship and chivalry; but when he returned to his palace, and Cush had fresh opportunities of influencing him, he yielded to the poorer side of his character and resumed his desperate attempt to thwart the divine purpose. Thus, like a shuttlecock he was tossed to and fro between the two men. Now inclined to mercy by David, and then to vengeance by Cush.

Such slanderers are to be found in the salons of modern society, as in the palace of the first king of Israel; and they cause as much torture to sensitive and tender natures today as they did to David in the wilds of Engedi. Let us learn how to deal with them.

1. SEARCH YOUR HEART TO SEE IF THESE SLANDERS HAVE FOUNDATION IN FACT. It may be that there is more truth in these hurtful words than you are inclined, at first sight, to admit. Perhaps those quick, envious eyes have discerned weaknesses in your character, of which your closest friends are aware, but they have shrunk from telling you. It is a good rule before you destroy the anonymous letter, or dismiss the unkind statement that has been making the rounds of your society, to sit down before the judgment seat of Christ, and in its white light ask yourself whether you can say with David:

> My shield is with God,
> Who saveth the upright in heart.

2. IF THERE IS NO BASIS FOR THEM REJOICE! How thankful we should be that God has kept us from being actually guilty of the things of which we are accused! We might have done them, and worse. It was only by His grace that we have not been guilty of committing them. That we have the witness of good conscience, and of His Spirit in our hearts should be a perennial source of gladness.

3. TAKE SHELTER IN THE RIGHTEOUS JUDGMENT OF GOD. We are His servants, and if He is satisfied with us, why should we break our hearts over what our fellow servants say? He put us into the positions we occupy, and if He please to keep us there, all that men may say or do will not be able to dislodge us.

4. DESPISE MORE COMPLETELY THE CARNAL LIFE. Why do we smart under these unkind and slanderous words, which are as baseless as they are uncharitable?

If we were really nothing, and God were all in all; if we were dead to the flesh and alive only to God—surely it would be a matter of indifference what became of our good name on the lips of foolish and sinful men.

5. LET GOD VINDICATE YOUR GOOD NAME. Any unjust imputation or stigma that rests on us is part of the evil of the world, and is a manifestation of its sinfulness. It is impossible for us to cope with or remove it; so we must wait patiently until God arises to avenge our wrong and vindicate our characters. David acted in this way. He appealed to the righteous God who tries the hearts.

Such is the true and wisest policy. Be still; give no place to wrath; concern yourself rather with the misery of that soul from which these wild words proceed; try to overcome the evil of his heart by your generous good; and leave vindication and vengeance alike to God.

16

A Cool Hand on a Hot Head
1 Samuel 25

The news passed throughout the land, like fire in prairie grass, that Samuel was dead; and Israel gathered to lament the prophet and saint, and perform the last honoring rites. David came to take part in the funeral rites of his master and friend. He did not, however, trust himself in such near proximity to Saul a moment longer than was absolutely essential; and as soon as all was over, he started again for the sparsely-populated region of Paran, at the extreme south of Judah. To those borderlands, so long desolated by border warfare his coming brought tranquility and safety. The sheepmasters had every reason to be grateful for his protection; and, as one well put it, "The men were very good unto us, and we were not hurt, neither missed we anything, as long as we were conversant with them; they were a wall unto us both by night and by day, all the while we were with them keeping the sheep."

Where such services were accepted and counted on, it was obviously fair, and indeed according to the custom of the time, that some recompense in kind should be made. So David was perfectly justified in sending ten young men to greet the opulent sheep master, Nabal, in the day of prosperity, to which the efforts of himself and his men had so largely contributed, to remind him of his obligations, and ask for whatever he might feel free to give. Nabal's miserly treatment of this request touched David to the quick.

The story centers in Nabal, David, and Abigail.

1. NABAL, THE MISER. His character is drawn, after the manner of Scripture, in three or four bold outline strokes, and need not detain us. What an apt thumbnail sketch is given of the whole race of Nabals in the confidential remark passed between his servant and his wife, "He is such a son of Belial, that a man cannot speak to him"!

a. *He was very great,* the historian says. But it was the meanest kind of greatness. There are four kinds of greatness; young men, choose the best for your life's goal! It is little to be great in possessing; better to be great in doing; better still to conceive and promulgate great thoughts; but best to be great in character.

b. *He was a fool,* his wife said. "As his name is, so is he; Nabal is his name, and folly is with him." He surely must have sat for the full-length portrait of the fool in our Lord's parable, who thought his soul could take its ease and be merry because a few big barns were full.

c. *He was a man of Belial,* his servant said; and indeed his treatment of David's modest request well bore out the character. He as good as said that David was raising a revolt against his master Saul. He also asserted his preference to give his bread and flesh to those who, like his shearers, had worked for them, rather than to some vain men who were hanging idly about to live on the ripe fruit that might fall into their mouths.

2. DAVID, PRECIPITATE AND PASSIONATE. One of the most characteristic features in David's temper and behavior through all these weary years was his self-control. Year

after year he rested on God's promise, and let Him fulfill the word on which He had caused him to hope. On two occasions he had controlled himself, when Saul lay in his power. But the rampart of self-restraint built by long habit went down, like a neglected sea wall, before the sudden paroxysm of passion that Nabal's words aroused. In hot fury he said to his men, "Gird ye on every man his sword." And about four hundred men did as David commanded.

At this hour David was on the brink of committing a crime that would have cast a dark shadow on all his remaining years. From this shame and disgrace he was saved by Abigail.

3. ABIGAIL, THE BEAUTIFUL INTERCESSOR. She was a woman of good understanding and of a beautiful countenance—a fit combination. Her character had written its legend on her face. The two things do not always go together.

It is remarkable how many Abigails get married to Nabals. God-fearing women, tender and gentle in their sensibilities, high-minded and noble in their ideals, become tied in an indissoluble union with men for whom they can have no true affinity. In Abigail's case this relationship was in all probability not of her choosing; but the product of the Oriental custom that compelled a girl to take her father's choice in the matter of marriage.

But if any young girl of good sense and earnest aspirations who reads these lines, secretly knows that, if she had the chance, she could marry into money or position, irrespective of character, let her remember that to enter the marriage bond with a man, deliberately and advisedly, for such a purpose, is a profanation of the divine idea, and can end in only one way. She will not raise her husband to her level, but will sink to his.

Nabal's servants knew the quality of their mistress, so they told her all. She immediately grasped the situation, sent a small procession of provision-bearers along the way that David would come, and followed them immediately on her ass. She met the avenging warriors in the shelter of the mountain, and the interview was as creditable to her woman's wit as to her grace of heart. Frank and noble as David always was, he did not hesitate to acknowledge his deep indebtedness to this lovely woman, and to see in her intercession the gracious intervention of God. "And David said to Abigail, Blessed be the LORD God of Israel, which sent thee this day to meet me; and blessed be thy advice, and blessed be thou, which hast kept me this day from coming to shed blood, and from avenging myself with mine own hand."

What a revelation this is of the ministries with which God seeks to avert us from our evil ways! They are sometimes very subtle and slender, very small and still. Ah! how often we could have saved ourselves actions that later caused lasting regret, had we only heeded. And above all these voices and influences, there has been the gracious arresting influences of the Holy Spirit, striving with passion and selfishness, calling us to a better life. Blessed Spirit, come down more often and stop us in our mad career.

The idyll ended happily. Nabal died in an apoplectic fit, caused by his debauchery, or his anger at his wife's treatment of David and his men. David proposed marriage to Abigail, to whom he owed so much, which she gracefully and humbly accepted, not thinking herself worthy of such high honor.

41

David

17

A Fit of Mistrust
1 Samuel 27

The Psalms which, with more or less probability may be assigned to this period of David's life, are marked with growing sadness and depression. Among them may be considered 10, 13, 17, 22, 25, 64, and perhaps 40 and 69. Those of the first group have many features in common. The scenery of the wilderness, the psalmist like a hunted wild thing, the perpetual insistence on his innocence and invocation of Jehovah's interference, the bitter description of his sorrows—such are the characteristic features of these Psalms. But there is a tone of despair:

Why standest thou afar off, O Lord?
Why hidest thou thyself in times of trouble (10:1).

How long wilt thou forget me, O Lord for ever?
How long wilt thou hide thy face from me? (13:1).

My God, my God, why hast thou forsaken me?
Why art Thou so far from helping me, and from the words of my roaring? (22:1).

Save me, O God;
For the waters are come in unto my soul.
I sink in deep mire, where there is no standing:
I am come into deep waters, where the floods overflow me (69:1).

It is as though the sufferer was near the limits of his endurance. It seemed hopeless to effect any permanent alteration in Saul's feelings toward him, as long as Cush, and Doeg, and Abner, and others who had proved themselves his inveterate foes, were able so readily to instill their poison into the royal ear. It had become so increasingly difficult to elude the hot pursuit of the royal troops, whom long practice had familiarized with his hiding places and haunts. And it became more and more perplexing to find sustenance for the large body of followers now attached to him. Every day he had to provide for six hundred men, besides women and children; and the presence of these more tender souls made it perilously difficult to maintain a perpetual condition of migration or flight. He now had two wives; and from what is said of the sack of Ziklag, shortly afterward, we should judge that the larger number of the outlawed band consisted of those who had wives, and sons, and daughters, and property (1 Sam. 3:3, 6, 19, 22).

In days of healthier faith these considerations would not have been able to do much to shake the constancy of his much-tried soul. He would have trusted in his God. But of late his faith had become impaired, so that he said in his heart, "I shall now perish one day by the hand of Saul: there is nothing better for me than that I should speedily escape into the land of the Philistines; and Saul shall despair of me, to seek me any more in any coast of Israel: so shall I escape out of his hand."

1. LET US EXAMINE THIS SUDDEN RESOLUTION.

a. *It was the suggestion of worldly policy.* "David said in his heart." On other occasions, as we have observed more than once, it had been his custom to summon the priest with the sacred ephod, or to inquire of God through Gad; but in this resolution he had recourse to neither the one nor the other. Do not say in your heart what you will or will not do; but wait on God until He makes known His way. As long as that way is hidden, it is clear that there is no need of action, and that He considers Himself responsible for all the results of keeping you where you are.

b. *It was very dishonoring to God.* Had He not sworn to make David king, to cast forth his enemies as out of a sling, and to give him a sure house? Had not these promises been confirmed by Samuel, Jonathan, Abigail, and Saul himself? Had not the golden oil designated him as God's anointed? How impossible it was that God should lie or forget His covenant!

Then it was unworthy of David to say, in effect: "I am beginning to fear that God has undertaken more than He can carry through. True, He has kept me up to this point, but I question if He can make me surmount the growing difficulties of my situation. Saul will, sooner or later, accomplish his designs against me; it is a mistake to attempt the impossible. I have waited until I am tired; it is time to use my own wits, and to extricate myself while I can from the nets that are being drawn over my path."

c. *It was highly injurious.* Philistia was full of idol temples and idolatrous priests (2 Sam. 5:21). It lay outside the inheritance of the Lord, the sacred land of Palestine, deemed by the pious Israelites of those days to be the special location and abiding place of the Most High, and to be banished from those sacred borders seemed like going into a wild and desolate land of estrangement and God-abandonment. What fellowship could David look for with the divine Spirit who had chosen Israel for His people and Jacob for the lot of His inheritance? How could he sing the Lord's songs in a strange land?

d. *It was the entrance on a course that demanded the perpetual practice of deceit.* He was received at Gath with open arms. Before, when he had sought the shelter of the court of Achish, he had but a handful of companions; now he was the leader of a formidable band of warriors, who might easily turn the scale of strength in the long struggle between Israel and Philistia. "And David dwelt with Achish at Gath, he and his men, every man with his household."

This proximity to the royal palace and the court became extremely irksome to the Hebrews, however. Their movements were always under inspection, and it was difficult to preserve their autonomy and independence. Therefore, finally David asked that one of the smaller towns might be assigned to him; and to his great comfort he received permission to settle at Ziklag, a town in the south country, originally allotted to Judah, then transferred to Simeon, and later captured by the Philistines, but not occupied by them (Josh. 15:31; 19:5; 1 Chron. 4:30).

The sense of security and relief to these hunted men must have been very great as they found themselves within the slender fortifications of the little town. For sixteen months they had a measure of repose and safety. "It was told Saul that David was fled to Gath: and he sought no more again for him."

But David's mind was constantly at work, weaving a tissue of duplicity and cruelty. Maintenance for himself and his followers must, of course, be provided; so he turned his sword on the petty tribes of the south country, who were in alliance with Philistines, but who were the hereditary foes of his own people. Among these were the Geshurites, and Girzites, and the Amalekites, all nomad tribes living by plunder. To obviate any report of his proceedings reaching the ears of Achish, David was compelled to adopt the policy of saving neither man nor woman alive: and when Achish, by virtue of his feudal lordship, required of him an account of his expedition, he said evasively that he had been raiding against the south of Judah, or against tribes that were known to be under the direct protection of Israel. "And Achish believed David, saying, He hath made his people Israel utterly to abhor him; therefore he shall be my servant for ever."

David's behavior at this time was utterly unworthy of his high character as God's anointed servant. *It was also a barren time in his religious experience.* No Psalms are credited to this period. The sweet singer was mute.

How precisely do these symptoms of old-time declension and relapse correspond with those which we have observed in ourselves and others! When we descend to the lowlands of expediency and worldly policy, a blight comes on the landscape of the soul, a silence on the song of the heart. We realize that we have purchased our deliverance from the pressure of adverse circumstances at too great a cost.

18

The Mercy of God That Led to Repentance
1 Samuel 29–30

Throughout that season of declension and relapse we have been considering, the loving mercy of God hovered tenderly over David's life. This is illustrated by the present period of David's history. There was a special focusing of divine gentleness and goodness to withdraw him from his purpose, to keep back his soul from the pit. We now trace the successive stages in this loving process of divine restoration.

1. IN INCLINING STRONG AND NOBLE MEN TO IDENTIFY THEMSELVES WITH DAVID'S CAUSE. "Now these are they," says the chronicler, "that came to David to Ziklag, while he yet kept himself close because of Saul the son of Kish: and they were among the mighty men, helpers of the war" (1 Chron. 12:1). And he proceeds to enumerate them. Some came from Saul's own tribe, experienced marksmen, who could use with equal dexterity the right hand and the left in slinging stones and handling the bow and arrow. Some came from the eastern bank of the Jordan, swimming it at the flood, mighty men of valor, men trained for war. Some came from Benjamin and Judah, assuring David that there was no ground for his suspicions of their loyalty.

Evidently the spirit of discontent was abroad in the land. The people, weary of Saul's oppression and misgovernment, were beginning to realize that the true hope of Israel lay in the son of Jesse. Thus from day to day "there came to David to help him, until it was a great host, like the host of God" (1 Chron. 12:22).

2. IN EXTRICATING HIS SERVANT FROM THE FALSE POSITION INTO WHICH HE HAD DRIFTED. The Philistines suddenly resolved on a forward policy. They were aware of the disintegration that was slowly dividing Saul's kingdom; and had noticed with secret satisfaction the growing numbers of mighty men who were leaving it to seek identification with David, and therefore, presumably, with themselves. Not content with the border hostilities that had engaged them so long, they resolved to strike a blow in the very heart of the land, the fertile plain of Esdraelon, destined to be one of the greatest battlefields of the world. It became drenched with the blood of great leaders such as Sisera, Saul, and Joash, and of vast hosts such as Philistine and Hebrew, Egyptian and Assyrian, Roman and Maccabaean, Saracen and Anglo-Saxon. "The Philistines gathered together all their

armies to Aphek; and the Israelites pitched by a fountain which is in Jezreel."

When this campaign was being meditated, the guileless king assured David that he would accompany him. This was perhaps said as a mark of special confidence. He had seen no fault in his *protegé* from the first hour of his coming into his court; he had no hesitation, therefore, in summoning him to march beside him, and even to be captain of his bodyguard. "Therefore will I make thee keeper of mine head for ever." It was a relief to the gentle nature of the king to turn from his imperious lords to this generous, open-hearted soul, and entrust himself to his strong care.

However, it was a very critical juncture for David. He had no alternative but to follow his lord into the battle, but it must have been with a sinking heart. It looked as though he would be forced to fight Saul, from whom for so many years he had fled; and Jonathan, his beloved friend; and the chosen people, over whom he hoped one day to rule. He could not but reply evasively, and with forced composure and gaiety: "Thou shalt know what thy servant can do"; but every mile of those fifty or sixty that had to be traversed must have been trodden with sad face and troubled heart. There was no hope for him in man. It may be that his heart already was turning in eager prayer to God, asking Him to extricate him from the net that his sins had woven for his feet.

If by your mistakes and sins you have reduced yourself to a false position like this, do not despair; hope still in God. Confess and put away your sin, and humble yourself before Him, and He will arise to deliver you.

An unexpected door of hope was suddenly opened in this valley of Achor. When Achish reviewed his troops in Aphek, David and his men passed on in the rear with the king. This aroused the jealousy and suspicion of the imperious Philistine princes, and they came to Achish with fierce words and threats. "What do these Hebrews here? Make this fellow return, that he may go again to his place which thou hast appointed him, and let him not go down with us to battle." In vain Achish pleaded on behalf of his favorite; the Philistines would have none of it. They pointed out how virulent a foe he had been, and how tempting the opportunity for him to purchase reconciliation with Saul by turning traitor in the fight. In the end, therefore, the king had to yield. It cost him much to inform David of the inevitable decision to which he was driven; but he little realized with what a burst of relief his announcement was received. It was with unfeigned satisfaction that he received the stringent command to depart from the camp with the morning light.

3. BY THE DIVINE DEALINGS WITH HIM IN RESPECT TO THE BURNING OF ZIKLAG. It was by God's great mercy that the Philistine lords were so set against the continuance of David in their camp. They thought that they were executing a piece of ordinary policy, dictated by prudence and foresight; little realizing that they were the shears by which God was cutting the meshes of David's net. Their protest was lodged at exactly the right moment; had it been postponed but for a few hours, David would have been involved in the battle, or have not been back in time to overtake the Amalekites, redhanded in the sack of Ziklag.

As David was leaving the battlefield, a number of the men of Manasseh, who appear to have deserted to Achish, were assigned to him by the Philistines, lest they also should turn traitors on the field. Thus he left the camp with a greatly increased following. Here, too, was a proof of God's tender thoughtfulness, because at no time of David's life was he in greater need of reinforcements than now.

Contrary to custom, David had left no men to defend Ziklag during his absence. It is difficult to understand the laxity of his arrangements for its safeguard in those wild and perilous times; but apparently not a single soldier was left to protect the women and children. Yet it turned out well, for when a band of Amalekites fell suddenly on the little town, there was none to irritate them by offering resistance.

In the first outburst of grief and horror, nothing but the gracious interposition of God could have saved David's life. On reaching the spot they considered home, after three days' exhausting march, the soldiers found it a heap of smoldering ruins; and instead of the welcome of wives and children, silence and desolation reigned supreme. Those who sometime earlier had cried, "Peace, peace to thee, thou son of Jesse, thy God helpeth thee," now spoke of stoning him. The loyalty and devotion that he had never failed to receive from his followers were suddenly changed to vinegar and gall.

But this was the moment of his return to God. In that dread hour, with the charred embers smoking at his feet, with the cold hand of anxiety for the fate of his wives feeling at his heart, he suddenly sprang back into his old resting place in the bosom of God.

From this moment David is himself again, his old strong, glad, noble self. For the first time, after months of disuse, he asks Abiathar to bring him the ephod, and he inquires of the Lord. With marvelous vigor he arises to pursue the marauding troop, and he overtakes it, leading them to the work of rescue and vengeance with such irresistible impetuosity that not a man of them escaped, except four hundred young men who rode on camels and fled. And when the greed of his followers proposed to withhold the rich plunder from those whose fear had caused them to stay back by the brook Besor, he dared to stand alone against all of them, and insisted that it should not be so, but that he who went down to the battle, and he who stayed back with the supplies should share alike. Thus he who had power with God had power also with man.

And when, shortly after, the breathless messenger burst into his presence with the tidings of Gilboa's fatal rout, though it meant the fulfillment of long-delayed hopes, he was able to bear himself humbly and with unaffected sorrow, to express his lament in the most exquisite funeral ode in existence, and to award the Amalekite his deserts.

He was sweet as well as strong, as courteous as well as brave. For when he returned to Ziklag, his first act was to send of the spoil taken from the Amalekites to the elders of all the towns on the southern frontier where he and his men were accustomed to staying, acknowledging his indebtedness to them, and so far as possible repaying it.

Thus the sunshine of God's favor rested afresh on his soul. God had brought him up from the horrible pit and the miry clay; had set his feet on a rock, and established his going; and had put a new song of praise in his mouth. Let all backsliders give heed and take comfort.

19

Thrice Crowned
2 Samuel 1–4

Two whole days had passed since that triumphant march back from the slaughter of Amalek to the charred and blackened ruins of Ziklag. What should he do next? Should he begin to build again the ruined city? Or was there something else in the divine program of his life?

On the third day a young man rushed breathless into the camp, his clothes torn and earth on his head. He headed straight for David, and fell to the ground at his feet. In a moment more his tidings were told, each word stabbing David to the quick. Israel had fled before their enemy; large numbers had fallen on the battlefield; Saul and Jonathan were dead also. That moment David knew the expectations of years were on the point of being realized; but he had no thought for himself or for the marvelous change in his fortunes. His generous soul, oblivious to itself, poured out a flood of the noblest tears man ever shed, for Saul and for Jonathan his son, and for the people of the Lord, because they had fallen by the sword.

1. Davidʼs treatment of Saulʼs memory. There could be no doubt that Saul was dead. His crown and the bracelet worn on his arm were already in David's possession. The Amalekite had made it appear that the king's life had been taken, at his own request, by himself. "He said to me," so the man's tale ran, "Stand, I pray thee, upon me, and slay me: for anguish is come upon me, because my life is yet whole in me. So I stood upon him, and slew him, because I was sure that he could not live after that he was fallen." David seems to have been as one stunned until evening, and then he aroused himself to show respect to Saul's memory.

a. *He gave little attention to the Amalekite.* The bearer of the sad news had been held under arrest, because he admitted he had slain the Lord's anointed; and as the evening fell the wretched man was again brought into the chieftain's presence. David asked, an expression of horror in his tone, "How wast thou not afraid to stretch forth thine hand to destroy the Lord's anointed!" Then calling one of the young men, he told him to slay the Amalekite.

b. *He next poured out his grief in the Song of the Bow,* which has passed into the literature of the world as an unrivaled model of a funeral dirge. The Dead March in *Saul* is a familiar strain in every national mourning.

The psalmist bursts into pathetic reminiscences of the ancient friendship that had bound him to the departed. He forgets all he had suffered at the hands of Saul; he thinks only of the ideal of his early manhood. His chivalrous love refuses to consider anything but what had been brave and fair and noble in his king. "Lovely and pleasant," such is the epitaph he inscribes on the memorial stone.

But for Jonathan there must be a special stanza. Might had also been given to him. Had he not, singlehanded, attacked an army, and brought about a great deliverance? But with all his strength, he had been gentle. A brother-soul; every memory of whom was very pleasant. A knightly nature; dreaded by foe, dearly loved by friend; terrible as a whirlwind in battle, but capable of exerting a woman's love, and more.

> *Thy love to me was wonderful,*
> *Passing the love of women.*

c. *Moreover, he sent a message of thanks and congratulation to the men of Jabesh-gilead.* The indignity with which the Philistines had treated the royal bodies had been amply expiated by the devotion of the men of Jabesh-gilead. They had not forgotten that Saul's first act as king had been to deliver them from a horrible fate. They had organized an expedition that had taken the bodies of Saul and his three sons from the walls of Bethshan, to which, after being beheaded, they were affixed; they had carried them through the night to their own city, where they had burned them to save them from

47

further dishonor—the ashes being reverently buried under the tamarisk tree in Gilead.

As soon as David heard of this act, he sent messengers to the men of Jabesh-gilead, thanking them for their chivalrous devotion to the memory of the fallen king, and promising to reward the kindness as one done to the entire nation, and to himself.

2. DAVID'S ATTITUDE WITH RESPECT TO THE KINGDOM. There is something very beautiful in his movements at this juncture, evidencing how completely his soul had come back to its trust in God.

This was the more remarkable when so many reasons might have been given for immediate action. The kingdom was overrun by Philistines; indeed it is probably that for the next five years there was no settled government among the northern tribes. It must have been difficult for David's patriot heart to restrain itself from gathering the scattered forces of Israel and flinging himself on the foe. He knew, too, that he was God's designated king, and it would have been only natural for him to step up to the empty throne, assuming the scepter as his right. Possibly none would have disputed a vigorous decisive policy of this sort. Abner might have been outmaneuvered, and have shrunk from setting up Ishbosheth at Nahanaim. So mere human judgment might have reasoned. But David was better advised. He inquired of the Lord, Shall I go up into any of the cities of Judah? And when the divine oracle directed him to proceed to Hebron, he does not appear to have gone there in any sense as king or leader, but settled quietly with his followers among the towns and villages in its vicinity, waiting until the men of Judah came, and claimed him king. Then for a second time he was anointed.

3. THE CHARACTERISTICS OF DAVID'S REIGN IN HEBRON. For seven years and six months David was king in Hebron over the house of Judah. He was in the prime of life, thirty years of age, and seems to have given himself to the full enjoyment of the quiet sanctities of home. Sandwiched between two references to the long war that lasted between his house and that of Saul is the record of his wives and the names of his children (3:2–5).

Throughout those years he preserved that same spirit of waiting expectancy that was the habit and temper of his soul, and which was so rarely broken in on. He sat on the throne of Judah, in the city of Hebron—which means *fellowship*—waiting until God had smoothed the pathway to the supreme dignity He had promsied. The only exception to this policy was his request that Michal should be returned to him; it would perhaps have been wiser for them both if she had been left to the husband who seemed really to love her. But David may have felt it right to insist on his legal status as the son-in-law of the late king, and as identified by marriage with the royal house.

The overtures for the transference of the kingdom of Israel were finally made by Abner himself, in entire independence of David; it was he who had communications with the elders of Israel, and spoke in the ears of Benjamin, and went finally to speak in the ears of David in Hebron all that seemed good to Israel and to the whole house of Benjamin.

Throughout these transactions David quietly receives what is offered; and only asserts himself with intensity and passion on two occasions, when it was necessary to clear himself of complicity in dastardly crimes, and to show his abhorrence of those who had perpetrated them.

It was a noble spectacle when the king followed the bier of Abner, and wept at his grave. He forgot that this man had been his persistent foe, and remembered him only as a prince and a great man. Then followed the dastradly assassination of the puppet king, Ishbosheth. His had been a feeble reign throughout. Located at Mahanaim, on the eastern side of Jordan, he had never exercised more than a nominal sovereignty. All his power was due to Abner, and when he was taken away the entire house of cards crumbled to pieces, and the hapless monarch fell under the daggers of traitors. David solemnly swore that he would require at their hands the blood of the murdered man.

Then came all the tribes of Israel to that "long stone town on the western slope of the bare terraced hill," and offered him the crown of the entire kingdom. They remembered his kinship with them as their bone and flesh; they recalled his former services when, even in Saul's days, he led out and brought in their armies. Then David made a covenant with them, and became their constitutional king and was solemnly anointed, for the third time; king over the entire people.

It is to this period that we must attribute Psalm 18, which undoubtedly touches the highwater mark of thankfulness and adoration. Every precious name for God is laid under contribution; the figure of his coming to rescue his servant in a thunderstorm is unparalleled in sublimity, but there is throughout an appreciation of the tenderness and love of God's dealings with His children.

> Thou hast given me the shield of thy salvation;
> Thy right hand hath holden me up,
> And thy gentleness hath made me great. (Ps. 18:35)

20

O for the Water of the Well of Bethlehem!
2 Samuel 5:17–25; 21:15; 23:8

It must have been a rare and imposing assembly that came to crown David king of all Israel. For three days they remained with him, keeping high festival; all Israel participated in the joy of the occasion.

The Philistines, however, were watching the scene with profound dissatisfaction. As long as David was content to rule as a petty king in Hebron, they were not disposed to interfere; but when they heard that they had anointed David king over all Israel, all the Philistines went down to seek him. They poured over into Judah in such vast numbers that he was forced to retire with his mighty men and faithful six hundred to the hold which, by comparison of passages, must have been the celebrated fortress-cave of Adullam (2 Sam. 5:17 and 23:13–14).

1. A SUDDEN REVERSAL OF FORTUNE. It was but yesterday that David was the center of the greatest assembly of warriors that his land had seen for many generations; but today he is driven from Hebron, back to that desolate mountain fastness in which years before he had taken refuge from the hatred of Saul. It was a startling reversal of fortune. It is probable, however, that he took refuge in God. These were days when he walked very closely with his almighty Friend, and he did not for a moment waver in his confidence that God would establish him firmly in his kingdom.

It was salutary that David should be reminded at this crisis of his history that he was as dependent on God as ever.

2. Gleams of light. The misty gloom of these dark hours was lit by some notable incidents. Prodigies of valor were performed around the person of their Prince, whom his followers delighted to call the Light of Israel, albeit for the hour obscured by clinging mists (21:17).

What marvels may be produced by the inspiration of a single life! We cannot but go back in thought to that hour when, near that very spot, an unknown youth stepped forth from the frightened hosts of Israel to face the dreaded Goliath. Alone, as far as human strength went, he had encountered and defeated that terrible antagonist; but now, after some fourteen or fifteen years had run their course, he no longer stood by himself; there were scores of men, animated by his spirit, inspired by his faith, who pushed him gently back, and told him that they must be permitted to bear the brunt of the conflict, since his life, which was the fountain source of all their energy, must be carefully withheld from needless peril.

Thus the lives of great men light up and inspire other lives. They mold their contemporaries.

3. A touching incident. Adullam was not far from Bethlehem. Often, in his earliest years, David had led his father's flocks to pasture amid the valleys where he was now sheltering; and the familiar scenes recalled memories.

One sultry afternoon an irresistible longing suddenly swept across him to taste the water of the well of Bethlehem, which was by the gate. Almost involuntarily he gave expression to the wish. He did not suspect that any of his stalwarts were within earshot, or if they were, that they would be foolhardy enough to attempt to gratify his whim.

Three of his mightiest warriors overheard their chieftain's wish, stole secretly out of the cave and down the valley, burst through the host of the Philistines, drew water from the well, and, before they had been missed, placed the brimming vessel in David's hands. It was the priceless expression of a love that was stronger than death. He could not drink it. To him the vessel seemed gleaming crimson with the blood it might have cost. With that instinctive chivalry of soul that made him in all the changes of his fortune so absolutely kingly as to compel the devotion of his adherents, he arose and poured it out as a libation to God, as though the gift were fit only to be made to Him; saying, as he did so, "My God forbid it me that I should do this thing: shall I drink of the blood of these men that have put their lives in jeopardy?"

How often we sigh for the waters of the well of Bethlehem! Oh, to see again that face; to feel the touch of that gentle hand; to hear that voice! Oh, to be again as in those guileless happy years, when the forbidden fruit had never been tasted, and the flaming sword had never been passed! Oh, for that fresh vision of life, that devotion to the Savior's service, that new glad outburst of love! Oh, that one would give us to drink of the water of the well of Bethlehem, which is beside the gate! They are vain regrets; there is nothing strong enough to break through the ranks of the years, and bring back the past. But the quest of the soul may yet be satisfied; not in Bethlehem's well, but in Him who was born there, shall the soul's thirst be quenched forever.

4. The overthrow of the Philistines. Prosperity had not altered the attitude of

David's soul in its persistent waiting on God. As he was when he first came to Hebron, so he was still; and in this hour of perplexity, he inquired of the Lord, saying, "Shall I go up to the Philistines? wilt thou deliver them into mine hand?" In reply, he received the divine assurance of certain victory; and when the battle began, it seemed to him as if the Lord Himself was sweeping them before Him, like a winter flood. The routed foe had no time even to gather up their gods, which fell into the conqueror's hands.

Again the Philistines came up to assert their old supremacy, and again David waited on the Lord for direction. It was well that he did so, because the plan of action was not as before. In the first battle the position of the Philistines was carried by assault; in the second it was turned by ambush.

This movement in the mulberry trees, which indicated that the ambush had to begin an advance on the foe, suggests the footfalls of invisible angelic squadrons passing onward to the battle. "The LORD is gone out before thee, to smite the host of the Philistines." Then David broke on their ranks and pursued them from Gibeon down into the heart of the maritime plain.

21

Jerusalem, the Holy City
2 Samuel 5

One of the first acts of the new king was to secure a suitable capital for his kingdom. And his choice of Jerusalem was a masterpiece of policy and statesmanship. Surely it was more; it was the result of the direct guidance of the Spirit of God.

It was highly desirable that the capital should be accessible to the whole country; it must be capable of being strongly fortified; it must combine strength and beauty so as to arouse the national pride and devotion. It must be hallowed by sacred associations so as to become the religious center of the people's holiest life. All these features blended in Jerusalem, and commended it to David's divinely-guided judgment.

1. ITS PREVIOUS HISTORY. To the Jew there was no city like Jerusalem. It was the city of his God, situated in his holy mountain: "Beautiful in elevation, the joy of the whole earth." The mountains that stood around her seemed to symbolize the environing presence of Jehovah. The exile opened his windows toward Jerusalem as he knelt in prayer. The noblest bosom that ever throbbed with true human emotion heaved with convulsive sobs at the thought of the desolation impending over her. Jesus wept when He beheld the city and said: "O Jerusalem, Jerusalem . . . how often would I have gathered thy children together, even as a hen gathers her chickens under her wings; and ye would not" (Matt. 23:37).

But it had not always been so. Her birth and nativity were of the land of the Canaanite. For years after the rest of the country was in occupation of Israel, Jerusalem was still held by the Jebusites.

2. THE CAPTURE. Making a levy of all Israel, David went up to Jerusalem. For the first time in seven years, he took the lead of his army in person. The Jebusites ridiculed the attempt to dislodge them. They had held the fortress for so long, and were so

confident of its impregnable walls, that in derision they placed along the walls a number of cripples, and boasted that these would be strong enough to keep David and his whole army at bay. But it appears, from the narrative given by Josephus, that Joab, incited by David's proclamation of making the captor of the city his commander-in-chief, broke in by a subterranean passage, excavated in the soft limestone rock, made his way into the very heart of the citadel, and opened the gates to the entire army.

Whether this story is true or not, it is certain that through Joab's prowess the city soon fell into David's hands; and he dwelled in the stronghold, afterward known as Zion, or the City of David. This was only part of what was afterward known as Jerusalem. Moriah, where later the temple was erected, was probably an unoccupied site. Araunah, the Jebusite, had a threshing floor there.

David's first act was to extend the fortifications: he "built round about from Millo and inward"; while Joab seems to have repaired and beautified the buildings in the city itself. This first success laid the foundation of David's greatness.

3. A FAIR DAWN. It has been suggested that we owe Psalm 101 to this hour in David's life. He finds himself suddenly called to conduct the internal administration of a great nation. It was highly desirable that the country should be reassured as to the character of the men whom the king was prepared to entrust with its concerns. For these purposes this psalm may have been prepared. In any case, it suits exactly such an occasion and purpose.

The royal psalmist declares that he will behave himself wisely in a perfect way. He will set no base thing before his eyes. His earliest and best energies would be devoted to the destruction of all the wicked of the land; while his eyes would be on all the faithful of the land; he would choose as his most favored attendants those who walked in a perfect way.

22

The Conveyance of the Ark to Mount Zion
2 Samuel 6

As soon as David had acquired a capital, he was eager to make it the religious, as well as the political, center of the national life. With this object in view, he resolved to place in a temporary structure near his palace the almost forgotten ark; which, since its return from the land of the Philistines, had found a temporary resting place in the "city of the woods," some eleven miles southwest of Jerusalem, in the house, and under the care of Abinadab.

He would not, however, take any step on his own initiative, but consulted with the captains of thousands and of hundreds, even with every leader. With their acquiescence he went everywhere throughout all the land of Israel gathering priests, Levites, and people to bring back the sacred emblem.

1. THE MISTAKE OF THE CART. It was a great procession that wended its way that day to the little town. In addition to a vast host of priests and Levites, and a great concourse of people, there were thirty thousand chosen soldiers, whose presence would be sufficient to protect the assembly from any hostile raid or surprise.

We probably owe Psalm 132 to this occasion, in which the royal singer records the determination to establish a place of the Lord, a tabernacle for the mighty one of Jacob.

But one fatal mistake marred the events of the day, and postponed the fulfillment of the nation's high hope and resolve. It was strictly ordained in the law of Moses that Levites alone, who were especially consecrated to the task, should bear the ark on their shoulders, not touching it with their hands, lest they should die (Num. 4:15; 7:9). Nothing could be clearer than this specific injunction, or more obvious than the reason for it, in enforcing the sanctity of all that pertained to the service of the Most High. This command had, however, fallen into disuse along with much else; and it was arranged that the ark should be carried on a new cart driven by the two sons of Abinadab.

The oxen started amidst a blast of song and trumpet, and for the first two miles all went well. But then they came upon a piece of rough road on which the oxen stumbled, and the ark shook so violently as to be in danger of being cast to the ground. Then Uzzah, the younger son of Abinadab, put out his hand to steady it, and instantly fell dead. The effect on the procession was terrific. Horror silenced the song, and panic spread through the awed crowd, as the tidings of the catastrophe spread backward through its ranks. David was greatly dismayed. He was afraid of God that day, and said, How shall I bring the ark of God home to me? So he directed that the ark should be deposited in the house of Obed-edom, a Levite, who lived in the vicinity, and there it remained for three months. The terrified crowds returned to Jerusalem in consternation and dismay.

2. THE SHOULDERS OF LIVING MEN. "The LORD blessed Obed-edom and all his household." Josephus states that from the moment the ark rested beneath his roof, a tide of golden prosperity set in, so that he passed from poverty to wealth; an evident sign that Jehovah had no controversy with those who obeyed the regulations and conditions laid down in the ancient law.

Again a large assembly was gathered. This time, however, the prescribed ritual was minutely observed; and the children of the Levites bore the ark of God on their shoulders, with the staves attached, as Moses commanded according to the word of the Lord. As the ark entered the city, David, clad in a linen ephod, leaped and danced before the Lord.

So they brought in the ark of the Lord, and set it in its place, in the midst of the tent that David had pitched for it; and he offered burnt offerings and peace offerings before the Lord. Then he turned to bless the people in the name of the Lord of hosts; and distributed to them bread, and wine, and raisins. The one cloud that marred the gladness of the day was the biting speech of Michal, who had no sympathy with her husband's religion. Poor woman! perhaps she was still smarting over the loss of Phalti. Or she was possibly jealous at David's independence of her and her father's house— hence the venom in her speech to the man whom she had loved, and whose life she had once saved.

3. THREE MAJESTIC PSALMS. On this occasion three of the greatest psalms were composed: 15, 68, and 24. Psalm 15 was evidently composed with direct reference to the death of Uzzah, and in answer to the question:

> Lord who shall abide in thy tabernacle?
> Who shall dwell in thy holy hill?

Psalm 68 was chanted as a processional hymn. It begins with the ancient formula, uttered in the desert march each time the camp was struck:

> Let God arise, let his enemies be scattered:
> Let them also that hate him flee before him.

As the ark was borne forward in its majestic progress, the symphony was softly played which told of the ancient days in which He went before His people and marched through the wilderness, while the earth trembled, and the heavens dropped at His presence.

As the Levite bearers drew near the ascent of the road up to the citadel of Zion, the choristers broke into a strophe of unrivaled grandeur, the full meaning of which could be fulfilled only in the ascension of the Christ Himself, far above all principality and power into the presence of His Father:

> Thou hast ascended on high, Thou hast led captivity captive:
> Thou has received gifts for men;
> Yea, for the rebellious also, that the LORD God might dwell among them.

An enumeration of the constituent parts of that mighty host follows. Finally, the psalmist anticipates the gathering of distant nations to that sacred spot:

> Princes shall come out of Egypt;
> Ethiopia shall soon stretch out her hands unto God.

But Psalm 24 is perhaps the master ode of the three. It begins with a marvelous conception, when we consider the narrowness of ordinary Jewish exclusiveness:

> The earth is the LORD's, and the fulness thereof;
> The world, and they that dwell therein.

The first half of the psalm answers the question as to the kind of men who may stand before God (vv. 3–6). They must be clean in hands, and pure in heart, not lifting their soul to vanity nor swearing deceitfully. The requirement of the holy God is the righteousness that He alone can give to those who seek His face.

The second half declares God's willingness to abide with man on the earth. The low-browed gates were commanded to lift up themselves, and open to the entering king. In thunders of voice and instrument, the white-robed choirs, halting before the closed portals, cried:

> Lift up your heads, O ye gates;
> And be ye lift up, ye everlasting doors,
> And the King of glory shall come in.

Then from within, a single voice, as though of some startled and suspicious warder, demands:

> Who is this King of glory?

A question, which met with the immediate, emphatic, and mighty response:

> The LORD strong and mighty,
> The LORD mighty in battle.

Again the challenge to open. Again the inquiry.

Again the magnificent reply, that the King of glory—for whom admittance was demanded to this ancient city, is the Lord of Hosts. So the ark at last reached its resting place.

23

"Thou Didst Well That It Was in Thine Heart"
2 Samuel 7; 2 Chronicles 6–8

With the assistance of Hiram, king of Tyre, a palace of cedar had been erected for David on Mount Zion. It was a great contrast also to the temporary structure that served as a house for the ark. One day, calling Nathan the prophet, David announced to him his intention of building a house for God. For the moment, the prophet cordially assented to the proposal, but in the quiet of the night, when he was more able to comprehend the thought of God, the word of the Lord came to him, and told him to stop the king from taking further steps in that direction.

The next day he broke the news to David with the utmost delicacy and gentleness. The offer was refused, but the refusal was wrapped up in so many assurances of blessing that the king was hardly sensible of disappointment amid the rush of overwhelming gladness that Nathan's words aroused. "Wilt thou build a house for God?—He will build thee an house."

1. A CONCEPTION OF A NOBLE PURPOSE. It was a great thought that came to David. It was in part suggested by the urgency of the situation. After the ark had come to its new home, Asaph and others had been appointed to celebrate, and thank, and praise the Lord, and minister before Him (1 Chron. 16:4–37); and it is supposed that at this period the twenty-four courses of priests were appointed, an arrangement that lasted to the time of our Lord. It is also supposed that the Levites were now organized—twenty-four thousand to help the priests, four thousand as musicians and singers, four thousand as guards and watchmen; while the remainder were scattered throughout the land to teach the law, execute justice, and perform other public offices. An immense body of men was thus gathering around the ark and palace, for whom it was necessary to find suitable headquarters. But surely there was a deeper reason; to show his love for God, his reverence, devotion, and lasting gratitude.

It is thus, especially in young life, that great conceptions visit the soul; ideals of surpassing beauty cast a light on the future; resolves of service for God. Young people, never surrender your ideal, nor disobey the heavenly vision.

2. THE IDEAL IS NOT ALWAYS REALIZED. There is no definite No spoken by God's gentle lips. He presses His promises and blessings on us, and leads us forward in a golden haze of love, which conceals His negative. Like David, we cannot point out the word or moment of refusal. We are lovingly carried forward from sentence to sentence in life's long speech of divine care and bounty, and it is only in moments of review that we find that our purpose is not destined to work itself out just as we thought.

3. GOD EXPLAINS HIS REASONS LATER. What we do not know now, we will know later. Years later David said to Solomon his son, not born at this time, "The word of the LORD

came to me, saying, Thou hast shed blood abundantly, and hast made great wars: thou shalt not build a house unto my name" (1 Chron. 22:8). The blood-stained hand might not raise the temple of peace. It would have wounded David needlessly to have been told this at this time. It was enough to wrap up the divine No in a promise of infinite blessing, but as the years passed the reason for God's refusal grew clear and distinct before him. Meanwhile, David remained patient, and said to himself: God has a reason, I cannot understand it; but it is well.

Some day we will understand that God has a reason in every No that He speaks through the slow movement of life. The time will come, probably in this life—certainly in the next—when we will understand why He led us as He did.

4. AN UNREALIZED CONCEPTION MAY YET BE FILLED WITH IMMENSE BLESSING. God will credit us with what we would have been if we could. He who has the missionary's heart, though he be tied to an office chair, is considered as one of that noble band; the woman at Zarephath, who did nothing more than share her last meal with the prophet, will have a prophet's reward; the soul that thrills with the loftiest impulses, but that cares for the widowed mother or dependent relative, will be surprised one day to find itself credited with the harvest that would have been reaped had those seed germs been cast on more propitious soil. In the glory David will find himself credited with the building of the temple of Mount Zion.

5. DO THE NEXT THING. The energy that David would have expended in building the temple wrought itself out in gathering the materials for its construction. "I have prepared with all my might for the house of my God . . ." (1 Chron. 29:2, etc.). If you cannot have what you hoped for, do not sit down in despair and allow the energies of your life to run to waste; but arise, and gird yourself to help others to achieve. If you may not build, you may gather materials for him who will. If you may not go down into the mine, you can hold the ropes.

Then David the king went in and sat before the Lord, and he said, "Who am I, O Lord GOD . . ." (2 Sam. 7:18). We have no words to characterize the exuberant outflow of his soul in that transcendent hour. There was no complaint that the purpose of his heart was thwarted, amid the successive billows of glory that swept over his soul.

24

"Yet Have I Set My King"
2 Samuel 8; 1 Chronicles 18, 19, 20

The time of rest that succeeded the removal of the ark was broken in on by a succession of fierce wars. One after another the surrounding nations gathered together, either singly or in confederacies, against David. "The nations raged; the kingdoms were moved."

The Philistines. For the last time they arose; but David subdued them.

The Moabites. The hereditary alliance, dating from the time of Ruth, between the Hebrew monarch and his restless neighbors was insufficient to restrain them; and Benaiah was commissioned to lead an expedition against them. This was so successful that their entire army fell into his hands and was dealt with according to the terrible custom of the time, only one-third being spared.

The Syrians. The king of Zobah and the Syrians of Damascus were utterly defeated; vast spoils of gold and brass fell into David's hand, and the border of Israel was carried to the line of the Euphrates, so that the ancient promise made by God to Abraham was fulfilled.

Edom. While David was engaged in the north, the Edomites invaded Judah, and Abishai was sent against them. On the west shore of the Dead Sea he encountered them, and slew eighteen thousand in the valley of Salt. The whole land, even to Petra, its rock-bound capital, was slowly reduced to submission; and, with the exception of Hadad, who made his way to Egypt, the royal family was exterminated.

Ammon. A friendly overture on the part of David was met with gross insult; and Hanun, apprehending the infliction of fitting revenge, formed a vast coalition. The combined forces amounted to thirty-two thousand, with a strong contingent of cavalry and chariots, against which David could only send the Hebrew infantry, the use of horses being forbidden by the Mosaic legislation. By God's good hand, however, victory was won; the tide of Israelite invastion swept over the hostile country. Rabbah, the capital city, fell into David's hand; the people were put to work with saws, arrows, and axes, probably preparing the materials for the erection of public works, and perhaps the temple itself.

These years of war gave birth to some of the grandest of the psalms, among which may be numbered 2, 20, 21, 60, 110.

1. THE FOE. The nations rage; the people imagine a vain thing; the kings of the earth set themselves and the rulers take counsel together against the Lord, and against his anointed. They trust in chariots and in horses; their kings think that they will be saved by the size of their armies. So tremendous is their assault, that all help of man seems vain.

2. THE ATTITUDE OF FAITH. While the tight ranks of the foe are in sight, the hero-king is permitted a vision into the unseen and eternal. There is no fear on the face of God, no change in His determination to set His king on His holy hill. In fact, it seems that the day of his foe's attack is that in which he received a new assurance of sonship, and is invited to claim the nations for his inheritance, and the farthest parts of the earth for his possession. As he anticipates the battle, he hears the chime of the divine promise above the tumult of his fear:

> Thou shalt break them with a rod of iron;
> Thou shalt dash them in pieces like a potter's vessel.

In perfect peace he anticipates the result; the Lord will send the rod of His strength out of Zion, and will make His enemies His footstool, so that in years to come he may combine the office of priest and king, as Melchizedek did on the same site centuries before.

3. THE WARRIORS OF THE PRIEST-KING. Catching the contagion of his faith, they triumph in God's salvation, and in His name set up their banners. They believe that God, as a Man of war, is going forth with their hosts, and will tread down their

adversaries. *They are dressed not in armor, but in the fine linen of the priests;* "the beauties of holiness," a phrase that suggests that the warfare was conducted by religious men, as an act of worship to God (Ps. 110).

What an exquisite concept of David's ideal for his soldiers, and of the knightly chivalry, of the purity, truth, and righteousness, in which all the soldiers of the Messiah should be arrayed!

4. THE COMPLETENESS OF THE VICTORY. The armies of the alien cannot stand the onset of those heaven-dressed soldiers. As the triumphant army returns, leaving desolation where their foes had swarmed, they express in song their gratitude to their almighty Deliverer.

> God is unto us a God of deliverances.

All this has a further reference. In David we have a type of the Messiah. For it is true that against the Holy Servant Jesus, whom God has anointed, both Gentiles and the peoples of Israel have gathered together. Men have refused His rule, and continue to refuse it; but God has sworn, and will not repent, that to Him every knee shall bow, and every tongue confess, saying, "The kingdoms of this world are become the kingdoms of our Lord, and of his Christ: and he shall reign for ever and ever" (Rev. 11:15).

25

The Sin of His Life
2 Samuel 11–19

The chronicler omits all reference to this terrible blot on David's life. The older record sets down each item without extenuation or excuse. The gain for all penitents would so much outweigh the loss to the credit of the man after God's own heart.

1. THE CIRCUMSTANCES THAT LED TO DAVID'S SIN. The warm poetic temperament of the king especially exposed him to a temptation of this sort; but the self-restrained habit of his life would have prevailed, had there not been some failure to trim the lamp.

For seventeen years he had enjoyed an unbroken spell of prosperity; in every war he was successful, and on every great occasion he increased the adulation of his subjects. But such prosperity is always filled with peril.

In direct violation of the law of Moses, he took more concubines and wives; fostering in him a habit of sensual indulgence, which predisposed him to the evil invitation of that evening hour.

He had also yielded to a fit of sluggishness, unlike the martial spirit of the Lion of Judah; he allowed Joab and his brave soldiers to do the fighting around the walls of Rabbah, while he waited at Jerusalem.

One sultry afternoon the king had risen from his afternoon siesta, and was lounging on his palace roof. In that hour of enervated ease, to adopt Nathan's phrase, a traveler came to him, an evil thought. To satisfy this hunger he entered into the home of a poor man and took his one ewe lamb, although his own folds were filled with flocks. We will not extenuate his sin by dwelling on Bathsheba's willing complicity, or on her strict ceremonial purification; it is enough to say she despised her married vows to her absent husband. The Scripture record lays the burden of the sin on the king alone, before whose absolute power Bathsheba may have felt herself obliged to yield.

One brief spell of passionate indulgence, and then!—his character blasted irretrievably; his peace vanished; the foundations of his kingdom imperilled; the Lord displeased; and great occasion given to his enemies to blaspheme! Moments of leisure are more to be dreaded than those of strenuous toil.

A message came one day to David from his companion in sin that the results could not be hidden. It made his blood run with hot fever. The law of Moses punished adultery with the death of each of the guilty pair. Instant steps must be taken to veil the sin! Uriah must come home! He came, but his coming did not help the matter. He refused to go to his home, though on the first night the king sent him there a meal of meat straight from his table, and on the second made him drunk. The chivalrous soul of the soldier shrank even from sleeping with his wife while the great war was still in process.

There was no alternative but that he should die; for dead men tell no tales. If a child was to be born, Uriah's lips, at least, should not be able to disown it. He bore to Joab, all unwitting, the letter that was his own death warrant. Joab must have laughed to himself when he got it. Uriah was set in the forefront of the hottest battle and left to die; the significant item of his death being inserted in the bulletin sent to the king from the camp. It was supposed by David that only he and Joab knew of this thing; Bathsheba probably did not guess the costly method by which her character was being protected. She lamented for her dead husband, as was customary of a Hebrew matron, congratulating herself meanwhile on the fortunate coincidence; and within seven days was taken into David's house. What a relief! The child would be born under the cover of lawful wedlock! There was one fatal flaw, however, in the whole arrangement: "The thing that David had done displeased the LORD." David and the world were to hear more of it. But oh, the bitter sorrow that he should have fallen in this way! The psalmist, the king, the man, the lover of God, all trampled in the mire by one dark, wild, passionate outburst. My God, grant that I may wear the white flower of a blameless life to the end!

2. DELAYED REPENTANCE. The better the man, the dearer the price he pays for a short season of sinful pleasure. For twelve whole months the royal sinner wrapped his sin in his bosom, closed his lips, and refused to confess. But in Psalm 32 he tells us how he felt. His bones wasted away through groaning all day long. Day and night God's hand lay heavily on him.

Nathan's appearance on the scene must have been a positive relief. The prophet, by right of old acquaintance, sought a private audience. He told what seemed to be a real and pathetic story of high-handed wrong; and David's anger was greatly worked up against the man who had perpetrated it. The spirit that always characterizes the sullen, uneasy conscience, flamed out in his sentence. The Levitical law in such a case only demanded fourfold restoration (Exod. 22:1). The king pronounced sentence of death. Then, as a flash of lightning on a dark night suddenly reveals to the traveler the precipice over which he is about to step, the brief, awful, stunning sentence, "Thou art the man!" revealed David to himself and brought him to his knees. Nathan reminded him of the unstinted goodness of God. "Thou hast despised his word; thou hast slain

Uriah; thou hast taken his wife. The child shall die; thy wives shall be treated as thou hast dealt with his; out of thine own house evil shall rise against thee." "I have sinned against the LORD," was David's only answer.

When Nathan had gone, David beat out that brief confession into Psalm 51, that all the world might use it. But long before his pathetic prayer was uttered, as soon as he acknowledged his sin, without the interposition of a moment's interval between his confession and the assurance, Nathan had said, "The LORD also hath put away thy sin."

Penitent soul! Dare to believe in the instantaneous forgiveness of sins. You have only to utter the confession, to find it interrupted with the outbreak of the Father's love. As soon as the words of penitence leave your lips, they are met by the hurrying assurances of a love which, while it hates sin, has never ceased to yearn over the prodigal.

25

The Stripes of the Children of Men
2 Samuel 12–19

Sin may be forgiven, as David's was, and yet a long trail of sad consequences can follow. The law of cause and effect will follow on, with its linked chain of disaster: these facts stand out upon the pages that tell the story of God's chastisements, alleviations, and deliverances.

1. GOD'S CHASTISEMENTS. Bathsheba's little child was very sick; it was the child of sin and shame, but the parents hung over it. For seven days the mother watched it, and the father fasted and lay on the earth. He suffered more in seeing the anguish of his young son than if ten times its pain had been inflicted on himself. It cuts to the quick when the innocent suffer for our crimes. On the seventh day the child died.

Two years later, one of his sons treated his sister as David had treated Uriah's wife. In Ammon's sin David beheld the features of his own unbridled passions; and in his murder by Absalom two years after, David encountered again his own blood-guiltiness. Absalom's fratricide would never have taken place if David had taken instant measures to punish Ammon. But how could he inflict that penalty for his son's impurity when he had not for himself (Lev. 18:9–29)? Nor could he punish Absalom for murder, when he remembered that he, a murderer, had eluded the murderer's fate.

Soon Absalom's rebellion broke out. What swept Ahithophel, David's most trusty counselor, into the ranks of that great conspiracy? The answer is given in the genealogical tables, which show that he was the grandfather of Bathsheba, and that his son Eliam was the comrade and friend of Uriah.

The most disastrous and terrible blow of all was the rebellion of Absalom. His beautiful figure; ready wit; apparent sympathy with the anxieties and disappointments of the people, fretting under the slow administration of the law; his extravagent expenditure and splendor—all these had for four years been undermining David's throne, and stealing away the hearts of the people. So when Absalom erected his standard at Hebron and was proclaimed king throughout the land, it was evident that the people had lost their former reverence and love for David, and they hurried to pay their homage at the shrine of the new prince.

We need not recount the successive steps of those stormy days. The panic-stricken flight of the king, "Arise, and let us flee . . . make speed to depart"; the barefoot ascent of Olivet; the anguish that wept with loud voice; the shameful cursing of Shimei; the apparent treachery of Mephibosheth; the humiliation of David's wives in the sight of that sun that had witnessed his own sin; the gathering of all Israel together to Absalom in apparent oblivion of the ties that for so many years had bound them to himself.

Such were the strokes of the Father's rod that fell thick and fast on His child. They appeared to emanate from the slander and hate of man; but David looked into their hearts and knew that the cup that they held to his lips had been mixed by heaven, and was not the punishment of a Judge, but the chastisement of a Father.

Apart from the story of Christ, there is nothing in the Bible more beautiful than David's behavior as he passed through this tangled growth of thorns. "Carry back the ark of God," he said to Zadok; "He will bring me and show me again, both it, and his habitation." but if not, "behold, here am I, let him do to me as seemeth good unto him." And when Shimei, called him a man of blood because of his dealings with Saul's house, David said to Abishai, "The LORD hath permitted him to curse, and who shall say, Wherefore hast thou done so?" Let us never forget the lesson. Pain and sorrow may be devised against us by the slander of an Ahithophel, a Shimei, or a Judas: but if God permits such things to reach us by the time they have passed through the thin wire of His sieve they have become His will for us; and we may look up into His face and know that we are being trained as children.

2. GOD'S ALLEVIATIONS. They came in many ways. The bitter hour of trial revealed a love on the part of his adherents of which the old king may have become a little oblivious.

Ahithophel's defection cut him deeply, but Hushai the Archite came to meet him with every sign of grief, and was willing, as his friend, to plead in the council chamber of Absalom.

Shimei might curse him; but Ittai the stranger, a man of Gath, with all his men, swore allegiance for life or death.

Zadok and Abiathar were there with the ark, their old animosity forgotten in their common sorrow for their master; Ziba met him with summer fruits, clusters of raisins, and loaves of bread; Shobi, and Machir, and Barzillai made abundant provision for his hungry, weary, and thirsty followers; his people told him that he must not enter the battle because his life was priceless, and worth ten thousand of theirs.

Thus he came to sing some of his sweetest songs, and among them Psalms 3, 4, 61, 62, 143.

The two former are his morning and evening hymns, when his cedar palace was exchanged for the blue canopy of the sky. He knows that he has many adversaries, who say, "There is no help for him in God," but he figures that he is well guarded.

> Thou, O LORD, art a shield for me;
> My glory, and the lifter up of mine head.

He is not afraid of ten thousands of the people; he lies down in peace to sleep, and awakes in safety, because the Lord sustains him.

3. GOD'S DELIVERANCE. The raw troops that Absalom had so hasitly mustered were

unable to stand the shock of David's veterans, and fled. Absalom himself was killed by the ruthless Joab, as he swayed from the arms of a huge terebinth. The pendulum of the people's loyalty swung back to its old allegiance, and they eagerly contended for the honor of bringing the king back. Even the men of Judah, conscious of having forfeited his confidence by so readily following Absalom, repented, and urged him to return. Shimei cringed at his feet. Mephibosheth established his unfaltering loyalty. Barzillai was bound to the royal house forever by his profuse acknowledgments and the royal offers to Chimham.

Many were the afflictions of God's servant, but out of them all he was delivered. When he had learned the lesson the rod was stayed. He had been chastened with the rod of men, and with the stripes of the children of men; but God did not take His mercy from him as He did from Saul: his house, his throne, and kingdom, in spite of many conflicting forces, was made sure. There are always the rod, the stripes, the chastisements; but in them all there is the love of God, carrying out His redemptive purpose. Then follows the afterglow of blessing, the calm ending of the life in a serene sundown.

27

Sunset and Evening Star
1 Chronicles 20–29

A period of ten years of comparative rest was granted David, between the final quelling of the revolts of Absalom and Sheba and his death. The recorded incidents of those years are few. It is probable that David walked softly and humbly with God, concentrating his attention on the erection of the temple. If he might not build it himself, he would strive with all his might to help him who would.

1. ITS SITE. This was indicated in the following manner. David conceived the plan of numbering Israel and Judah. The chronicler says that Satan moved him to it, while the older record attributes the suggestion to the anger of the Lord. The sin of numbering the people probably lay in its motive. David was animated by a spirit of pride and prestige.

In spite of the remonstrances of Joab and others, the king persisted; and the officers went throughout the land, numbering the people. Excluding the tribes of Levi and Benjamin, and the city of Jerusalem, the fighting men of Israel numbered about a million, and those of Judah five hundred thousand.

When the enumeration was nearly complete, and the officers had reached Jerusalem, David's heart struck him, and he said to the Lord: "I have sinned greatly in that I have done." A night of anguish could not, however, wipe out the wrong and folly of nine months. David might be forgiven, but he had to submit to one of three modes of chastisement. It was wise on his part to choose to fall into the hands of God; but the plague that devastated his people with unparalleled severity hurt him deeply.

Sweeping through the country, it came at last to the holy city, and it seemed as if the angel of the Lord were hovering over it, sword in hand, to begin his terrible commission. Then it was that David cried to the Lord, pleading that His judgments might be stopped: "Better let thy sword be plunged into my heart, than that one more of my people should perish. I have done perversely; but these sheep, what have they done?" And the angel of the Lord stayed by the threshingfloor of Araunah, or Ornan, a Jebusite, who is thought by some to have been the deposed king of the old Jebusite city. There on Mount Moriah, where centuries before the angel had stopped the uplifted knife of Abraham, God said, "It is enough; stay thine hand." That spot became the site of the temple. At the direction of the prophet Gad, David purchased the threshingfloor, the threshing instruments, and the oxen that trod out the grain. He insisted on paying the full price that he might not give God that which cost him nothing; and from that day forward Mount Moriah became the center of national worship, the site of successive temples, and the scene of the manifestation of the Son of Man.

2. Its BUILDER. The last year of David's life, and the fortieth of his reign, was embittered by a final revolt of the discordant elements that had so often given him trouble. Joab at last turned traitor to his old master; and Abiathar, instigated probably by jealousy of Zadok, joined him in embracing the cause of Adonijah, the eldest surviving son.

When the account of the revolt was brought to David, it stirred the old lion heart, and though he had reached the extreme point of physical exhaustion, he aroused himself with a flash of his former energy to take measures for the execution of the divine will communicated to him years before. Not many hours passed before tidings broke in on Adonijah's feast at Enrogel, that Solomon had been anointed king in Gihon, by the hand of Zadok the priest and Nathan the prophet, and that he had ridden through the city on the royal mule, escorted by Benaiah and his men-at-arms. Within an hour all of Adonijah's supporters had melted away, and he was clinging, as a fugitive, to the horns of the altar.

It was probably about this time that David gave Solomon the charge to build the house for God. He enumerated the treasures he had accumulated, and the preparatory works that had been set on foot. It is almost impossible for us to realize the immense weight of precious metal, the unlimited provision of brass, iron, and timber, or the armies of workmen. The surrounding countries had been drained of their wealth and stores to make that house magnificent.

At the close of this solemn charge, he added instructions to direct Solomon in his behavior toward Joab and Shimei. These charges have the appearance of vindictiveness, but we must give the dying monarch credit for being animated with a single purpose for the peace of his realm. Had vengeance been in his heart, he might have taken it then.

3. Its PATTERN. The Jewish polity required that the king should not only be anointed by the priest but also recognized by the entire people. It was therefore necessary that David's choice should be ratified in a popular assembly, which gathered at the roayl command (1 Chron. 28:1). For the last time monarch and people stood together before God. Again he recited the circumstances of his choice, of his desire to build the temple, and the substitution of Solomon for himself. Then turning to the young man that stood beside him, he urged him to be strong and carry out the divine purpose.

Next followed the gift of the pattern of the house that had been communicated to David by the Spirit of God, and an inventory of the treasures from which each article was to be constructed. To David's imagination the splendid temple stood before him complete in every part. The contribution from his private fortune had been most generous, and with this as his plea he turned to the vast concourse, asking princes and people to fill their hands with gifts. The response was beautiful. It is probable that never before or since has such a contribution been made at one time for religious purposes; but, better than all, the gifts were made willingly and gladly.

With a full heart David blessed the Lord before the congregation. His lips were touched with the old fire. Standing on the threshold of the other world, his days seemed as a shadow in which there was no abiding; and then the king and father pleaded for Solomon that he might keep the divine statutes and build the house. Last, he turned to the people, and urged them to join in ascriptions of praise, and there was such a shout of jubilation, of blessing and praise, that the sky rang again; while a great religious festival crowned the proceedings.

It was a worthy conclusion to a great life! How much longer David lived we cannot tell. One record says simply that "David slept with his fathers, and was buried in the city of David"; another, that "he died in a good old age, full of days, riches, and honour."

ELIJAH

1

The Source of Elijah's Strength
1 Kings 17

This chapter begins with the conjunction "And": it is therefore an addition to what has gone before, and it is *God's* addition. When we have read to the end of the previous chapter, we might suppose that was that, and that the worship of Jehovah would never again acquire its lost prestige and power. And, no doubt, the principal actors in the story thought so to. Ahab thought so; Jezebel thought so; the false prophets thought so; the scattered remnant of hidden disciples thought so.

But they had made an omission in their calculations—they had left out Jehovah Himself. When men have done their worst, and finished, it is time for God to begin. And when God begins, He is likely, with one blow, to reverse all that has been done without Him.

Things were dark enough. After the death of Solomon, his kingdom split into two parts—the southern under Rehoboam his son; the northern under Jeroboam. Jeroboam was desperately eager to keep his hold on his people, but he feared he would lose it if they continued to go, two or three times a year, to the annual feasts at Jerusalem. He resolved therefore, to set up the worship of Jehovah in his own territories. So he erected two temples, one at Dan, in the extreme north, the other at Bethel, in the extreme south. And in each of these he placed a golden calf, that the God of Israel might be worshiped "under the form of a calf that eateth hay." This sin broke the second commandment, which forbade the children of Israel making any graven image; or bowing down before the likeness of anything in heaven above, or in the earth beneath. Jeroboam's wickedness was never forgotten in Holy Scripture. Like a funeral knell, the words ring out again and again: "Jeroboam, the son of Nebat, who made Israel to sin."

After many revolutions, and much bloodshed, the kingdom passed into the hands of a military adventurer, Omri. The son of this man was Ahab, of whom it is said, "he did more to provoke the LORD God of Israel to anger than all the kings of Israel that were before him." This came to pass because he was a weak man, the tool of a crafty, unscrupulous, and cruel woman.

When the young and beautiful Jezebel left Tyre to become the consort of the newly-crowned king of Israel, it was no doubt regarded as a splendid match. Tyre at that time sat as queen on the seas, in the zenith of her glory: her colonies dotted the shores of the Mediterranean as far as Spain; her ships whitened every sea with their sails; her daughter, Carthage, nursed the lion-cub Hannibal, and was strong enough to make Rome tremble. But, like many a splendid match, it was filled with misery and disaster.

As she left her palace home, Jezebel would be vehemently urged by the priests—beneath whose influence she had been trained—to do her utmost to introduce into Israel the rites of her hereditary religion. Nor was she slow to obey. First, she seems to have erected a temple to Astarte in the neighborhood of Jezreel, and to have supported its four hundred and fifty priests from the revenues of her private purse. Then Ahab and she built a temple for Baal in Samaria, the capital of the kingdom, large enough to contain immense crowds of worshipers (2 Kings 10:21). Shrines and temples then began to rise in all parts of the land in honor of these false deities, while the altars of Jehovah, like that at Carmel, were ruthlessly broken down. The land swarmed with the priests of Baal and of the groves. The schools of the prophets were shut up; grass grew in their courts. The prophets themselves were hunted down and slain by the sword. "They wandered about in sheepskins and goatskins, being destitute, afflicted, tormented" (Heb. 11:37); so much so, that the pious Obadiah had great difficulty in saving a few of them, by hiding them in the limestone caves of Carmel, and feeding them at the risk of his own life. But God is never at a loss. The land may be overrun with sin; the lamps of witness may seem all but extinguished; but He will be preparing a weak man in some obscure highland village; and in the moment of greatest need will send him forth as His all-sufficient answer to the worst plottings of His foes. So it has been; and so it shall continue to be.

1. ELIJAH WAS OF THE INHABITANTS OF GILEAD. Gilead lay east of the Jordan; it was wild and rugged. The inhabitants partook of the character of their country—wild, lawless, and unkempt. They dwelt in rude stone villages, and subsisted by keeping flocks of sheep.

Elijah's childhood was like the other young men of his time. In his early years he probably did the work of a shepherd on those wild hills. As he grew to manhood, his erect figure, his shaggy locks, his cloak of camel's hair, his muscular, sinewy strength—which could outstrip the fiery horses of the royal chariot, and endure excessive physical fatigue—distinguished him from the dwellers in lowland valleys.

As he grew in years, he became characterized by an intense religious earnestness. He was "very jealous for the LORD God of hosts." As messenger after messenger told how Jezebel had thrown down God's altars, and slain His prophets, and replaced them by the impious rites of her Tyrian deities, his indignation burst all bounds; he was "very jealous for the LORD God of hosts."

But what could he do—a wild, untutored child of the desert? There was only one thing he could do—the resource of all much-tried souls—he could pray; and he did: "he prayed earnestly" (James 5:17). And in his prayer he seems to have been led back to a denunciation made, years before, by Moses to the people, that if they turned aside and served other gods and worshiped them, the Lord's wrath would be sent against them; and He would shut up the heaven so that there should be no rain (Deut. 11:17). And so he set himself to pray that the terrible threat might be literally fulfilled. "He prayed earnestly that it might not rain" (James 5:17).

And as Elijah prayed, the conviction entered his mind that it should be even as he prayed; and that he should go to acquaint Ahab with the fact. Whatever might be the hazard to himself, both king and people must be made to connect their calamities with the reason for them. That the drought was due to his prayer is also to be inferred from the words with which Elijah announced the fact to the king: "There shall not be dew nor rain these years, *but according to my word.*"

This interview needed no ordinary moral strength. What chance was there of his escaping with his life? Yet he went and came back unhurt, in the panoply of a might that seemed invulnerable.

What was the secret of that strength? If it can be shown that it was due to something inherent in Elijah, and peculiar to him, then we may as well turn away from the inaccessible heights that mock us. But if it can be shown, as I think it can, that this splendid life was lived, not by its inherent qualities, but by sources of strength that are within the reach of the humblest child of God who reads these lines, then every line of it is an inspiration.

Elijah's strength did not lie in himself or his surroundings. He was of humble extraction. When, through failure of faith he was cut off from the source of his strength, he showed more cowardice than most men would have done; he lay down on the desert sands and asked to die.

2. ELIJAH GIVES US THREE INDICATIONS OF THE SOURCE OF HIS STRENGTH.

"As the LORD God of Israel liveth." To everyone else Jehovah might seem dead; but to him, He was the one supreme reality of life. And if we would be strong, we too must be able to say: "I know that my Redeemer liveth." The person who has heard Jesus say, "I am he that liveth," will also hear Him say, "Fear not! be strong, yea, be strong."

"Before whom I stand." Elijah was standing in the presence of Ahab, but he was conscious of the presence of a greater than any earthly monarch, the presence of Jehovah. Gabriel himself could not employ a loftier designation (Luke 1:19). Let us cultivate this habitual recognition of the presence of God, for it will lift us above all other fear. Besides this, a conviction had been impressed on his mind that he was chosen by God as His servant and messenger, and in this capacity he stood before Him.

The word "Elijah" may be rendered—Jehovah is my God; but there is another possible translation—Jehovah is my strength. This gives the key to his life. What a revelation is given us in this name! Oh, that it were true of each of us! Yet, why should it not be? Let us from this day forth cease from our own strength which, at best, is weakness; and let us appropriate God's by daily, hourly faith.

2

Beside the Drying Brook
1 Kings 17

We are studying the life of a man of like passions with ourselves—weak where we are weak, failing where we would fail; but who stood singlehanded against his people, stemmed the tide of idolatry and sin, and turned a nation back to God. And he did it by the use of resources that are within reach of us all. This is the fascination of the story.

Faith made him all he became, and faith will do as much for us if only we can exercise it as he did. Oh, for Elijah's receptiveness, that we might be as full of divine power as he was, and as able therefore to do exploits for God and truth!

But, before this can happen, we must pass through the same education as he. We must go to Cherith and Zarephath before we can stand on Carmel.

Notice, then, the successive steps in God's education of His servants.

1. GOD'S SERVANTS MUST LEARN TO TAKE ONE STEP AT A TIME. This is an elementary lesson, but it is hard to learn. No doubt Elijah found it so. Before he left Tishbe for Samaria, to deliver the message that burdened his soul, he would naturally inquire what

he should do after he had delivered it. How would he be received? What would be the outcome? If he had asked those questions of God, and waited for a reply before he left his highland home, he would never have gone at all. Our Father shows us only one step at a time—and that, the next; and He bids us take it in faith.

But as soon as God's servant took the step to which he was led, and delivered the message, then "the word of the LORD came unto him, saying, Get thee hence . . . and hide thyself by the brook Cherith." And it was only when the brook had dried up that the word of the Lord came to him, saying, "Arise, get thee to Zarephath."

I like that phrase, "the word of the LORD came unto him." He did not need to go to search for it; it *came* to him. And so it will come to you. It will find you out, and tell you what you are to do.

It may be that for long you have had on your mind some strong impression of duty; but you have held back, because you could not see what the next step would be. Hesitate no longer! Step out on what seems to be the impalpable mist: you will find a slab of concrete beneath your feet, and every time you put your foot forward you will find that God has prepared a stepping stone, and the next, and the next; each as you come to it. God does not give all the directions at once, lest we should get confused; He tells us just as much as we can remember and do. Then we must look to Him for more; and so we learn the sublime habits of obedience and trust.

2. GOD'S SERVANTS MUST BE TAUGHT THE VALUE OF THE HIDDEN LIFE. "Get thee hence, and turn thee eastward, and hide thyself by the brook Cherith." The man who is to take a high place before his fellowmen must first take a low place before his God. And there is no better way of bringing a man down than by dropping him suddenly out of an area in which he was beginning to think himself essential, teaching him that he is not at all necessary to God's plan, and compelling him to consider in the sequestered vale of some Cherith how mixed are his motives, and how insignificant his strength.

Every saintly soul that would wield great power with people must win it in some hidden Cherith. We cannot give out unless we have previously taken in. Our Lord found His Cherith at Nazareth and in the wilderness of Judaea, amid the olives of Bethany and the solitudes of Gadara. Not one of us can dispense with a Cherith where we may taste the sweets and imbibe the power of a life hidden with Christ, and in Christ by the power of the Holy Ghost.

3. GOD'S SERVANTS MUST LEARN TO TRUST HIM ABSOLUTELY. We give at first a timid obedience to a command that seems to involve many impossibilities; but when we find that God is even better than His word, our faith grows exceedingly, and we advance to further feats of faith and service. At last nothing is impossible. This is the key to Elijah's experience.

How strange to be sent to a brook, which would of course be as subject to the drought as any other! How contrary to nature to suppose that ravens, which feed on carrion, would find such food as man could eat; or, having found it, would bring it regularly morning and evening! How unlikely, too, that he could remain hidden from the search of the bloodhounds of Jezebel anywhere within the limits of Israel! But God's command was clear and unmistakable. It left Elijah no alternative but to obey.

There is strong emphasis on the word *there*. "I have commanded the ravens to feed thee *there*." Elijah might have preferred many hiding places to Cherith, but that was the only place to which the ravens would bring his supplies; and, as long as he was there, God was pledged to provide for him. Our supreme thought should be: "Am I where God wants me to be?" If so, God will work a direct miracle rather than allow us to perish for lack. God sends no soldier to war on his own strength.

We will not stay to argue the probability of this story being true. The presence of the supernatural presents no difficulties to those who can say "Our Father," and who believe in the resurrection of our Lord Jesus. But if corroboration were needed, it could be multiplied many times from the experience of living people who have had their needs supplied in ways as marvelous as the coming of ravens to the lonely prophet. God has infinite resource; and if you are doing His work, where He would have you, He will supply your need, though the heavens fall. Only trust Him!

4. GOD'S SERVANTS ARE OFTEN CALLED TO SIT BY DRYING BROOKS. "It came to pass after a while, that the brook dried up." What did Elijah think? Did he think that God had forgotten him? Did he begin to make plans for himself? We will hope that he waited quietly for God. Many of us have had to sit by drying brooks; perhaps some are sitting by them now—the drying brook of popularity, ebbing away as it did from John the Baptist. The drying brook of health, sinking under a creeping paralysis, or a slow decline. The drying brook of money, slowly dwindling before the demands of sickness, bad debts, or other people's extravagance. The drying brook of friendship, which for long has been diminishing, and threatens soon to cease. Ah, it is hard to sit beside a drying brook—much harder than to face the prophets of Baal on Carmel.

Why does God let them dry? He wants to teach us not to trust in His gifts but in Himself. Let us learn these lessons, and turn from our failing Cheriths to our unfailing Savior. All sufficiency resides in Him.

3

Ordered to Zarephath
1 Kings 17

A friend of mine, spending a few days in the neighborhood of our English lakes, came upon the most beautiful shrubs he had ever seen. Arrested by their extraordinary luxuriance, he learned that it was due to a judicious system of transplanting, constantly pursued. Our heavenly Father is constantly transplanting us. And these changes, if they are rightly accepted, result in the most exquisite manifestations of Christian character and experience.

Jeremiah says, "Moab hath been at ease from his youth, and he hath settled on his lees, and hath not been emptied from vessel to vessel, neither hath he gone into captivity: therefore his taste remained in him, and his scent is not changed" (Jer. 48:11). Grape juice, when first pressed from its deep red chalice, is impure and thick; it is left in vessels for a time until fermentation has done its work, and a thick sediment, called lees, has settled to the bottom. When this is done, the liquid is carefully drawn off into another vessel, so that all the sediment is left behind. This emptying process is repeated again and again, until the liquid has become clear and beautiful.

Will this not cast light on God's dealings with Elijah? Once he stood in the vessel

"Home"; then he was emptied into the vessel "Jezreel"; then into the vessel "Cherith"; and now into the fourth vessel, "Zarephath": and all so that he might not settle on his lees, but might be urged toward a goal of moral greatness which otherwise he would never have reached; but which qualified him to take his stand years later on the Transfiguration Mount, the associate of Moses, the companion of Christ.

And yet, when a human spirit is entirely taken up with God, as Elijah was, these changes become comparatively harmless and trifling—as a gnat sting to a soldier in the heat of battle. To fulfill His plans, to obey the least intimation of His will, to wait on His hand; is the one passion of the happy spirit to whom, as to Elijah, this grace is given.

There are several lessons here.

1. FAITH AWAITS GOD'S PLANS. "It came to pass after a while, that the brook dried up, because there had been no rain in the land." Week after week, with unfaltering and steadfast spirit, Elijah watched that dwindling brook. The dwindling brook became a silver thread, and the silver thread stood presently in pools at the foot of the largest boulders; the pools shrank, and then the brook was dry. Only then, to his patient and unwavering spirit "the word of the LORD came unto him, saying, Arise, get thee to Zarephath."

Most of us would have become anxious and worn with planning long before that. And probably, long before the brook was dry, we would have devised some plan, and asking God's blessing on it, would have started off elsewhere. He often extricates us because His mercy endures forever; but if we had only waited first to see the unfolding of His plans, we would never have found ourselves landed in such an inextricable labyrinth. Would that we were content to wait for God to unveil His plan, so that our life might be simply the working out of His thought, the exemplification of His ideal!

2. GOD'S PLANS DEMAND IMPLICIT OBEDIENCE. "So he arose and went to Zarephath," as before he had gone to Cherith, and as soon he would go to show himself to Ahab.

In many Christian lives there comes a command clear and unmistakable. We must leave some beloved Cherith, and go to some unwelcome Zarephath; we must speak some word, take some step, cut off some habit: and we shrink from it—the cost is too great. But as soon as we refuse obedience, dark clouds fling their shadows far and near.

We do not win salvation by our obedience, that is altogether the gift of God. But being saved, we must obey.

3. IMPLICIT OBEDIENCE SOMETIMES BRING US INTO A SMELTING FURNACE. "Zarephath" means a smelting furnace, and lay outside the land of Canaan. Many things might have made it distasteful to the prophet. It belonged to the land from which Jezebel had brought her impious tribe. It was as much cursed by the terrible drought as Canaan. It was impossible to reach it except by a weary journey of 100 miles through the heart of the land, where his name was detested and his person denounced. And then to be sustained by a widow belonging to a heathen people! Surely it was a smelting furnace for cleaning out any alloy of pride, or self-reliance, or independence that might be lurking in the recesses of his heart.

And there was much of the refining fire in the character of his reception. When he reached the straggling town it was probably toward nightfall, and at the city gate a widow was gathering a few sticks to prepare the evening meal. This was evidently the widow of whom God had spoken. Faint with thirst, and weary with long travel, but never doubting that his needs would be amply met, he asked her to give him a little water in a vessel that he might drink. The widow may have had some premonition of his coming. There would seem to be some suggestion of this having been so, in the words, *"I have commanded* a widow woman there to sustain thee."

She was therefore not surprised at the prophet's request, and silently went to get a cup of cold water (Matt. 10:42). Encouraged by her willingness, Elijah asked her to bring with her a piece of bread. It was a modest request, but it unlocked the silent agony of her soul. She did not have a cake, but a handful of meal in a barrel and a little oil in a cruse; and she was about to make one last meal for herself and her son, who was probably too weak through long privation to be with her; and, having eaten it, they had no alternative but to lie down together and die. It was very depressing for the man of God, after his long and weary march.

4. WHEN GOD PUTS HIS PEOPLE INTO THE FURNACE, HE WILL SUPPLY ALL THEIR NEED. Circumstances were certainly very depressing, but what are they to a man whose inner self is occupied with the presence and power of God? God had said that Elijah should be fed, and by that widow; and so it would be, though the earth and heaven would pass away. And so with heroic faith Elijah said: "Fear not; go and do as thou hast said. . . . For thus saith the LORD God of Israel, The barrel of meal shall not waste, neither shall the cruse of oil fail, until the day that the LORD sendeth rain upon the earth.

Our only need is to inquire if we are at that point in God's pattern where He would have us be. If we are, though it may seem impossible for us to be maintained, the thing impossible will be done. We will be sustained by a miracle, if no ordinary means will suffice. "Seek ye first the kingdom of God, and his righteousness; and all these things shall be added unto you" (Matt. 6:33).

4

"The Spirit and Power of Elias"
1 Kings 17

In Elijah's time, only those of elevated character knew what His eternal fullness meant. "Holy men of God spake as they were moved by the Holy Ghost" (2 Peter 1:21). Elijah was one of these men filled with the Holy Ghost. Elisha's one desire was that he should be heir to the Spirit that was so manifestly on his master (2 Kings 2:9). "The spirit of Elijah" was a familiar phrase on the lips of the sons of the prophets (2 Kings 2:15). And when the angel of God spoke to Zacharias in the temple, he could find no better illustration of the presence of the Holy Ghost in his promised child than by saying, "He shall go before him in the spirit and power of Elias" (Luke 1:17).

The glorious ministry of Elijah was therefore due, not to any inherent qualities in himself, but to the extraordinary indwelling of the Holy Ghost—given to him as to other holy men of God—through faith. The question for us all is whether the Holy Ghost is working with and through us in power; if He is, then though our nature be paltry and weak, He will effect through us the same mighty deeds as He did through men who were our superiors in mental and moral force. No, we may even glory in our infirmities that this divine power may rest on us more conspicuously, and that the glory may be more evidently God's.

Now the question arises: May we, ordinary Christian people, hope to receive the Holy Spirit in that extraordinary and special measure in which He rested on Elijah?

Our blessed Lord, as the perfect servant, had it when, being full of the Holy Ghost, He returned in the power of the Spirit to Galilee, and traced His marvelous power to the fact of the Holy Spirit being on Him (Luke 4:1, 14, 18). The apostles had it from the Day of Pentecost, when they received the fullness of the Spirit for witness-bearing.

This is surely what we want. And this is what we may have. This special anointing for service is not only for men like Elijah, or Paul, or Peter, who soar far beyond us into the azure skies; but for us all.

But there are three conditions with which we must comply, if we would receive and keep this blessed gift.

1. WE MUST BE EMPTIED. God cannot fill us if we are already filled. It took apparently three years and six months for Elijah; it was a long and weary time of waiting, but it was well spent. In proportion as he became emptied of self, he became filled with the Spirit of Power; so that Carmel itself, with all its heroic deeds, was gloriously possible to him.

Are we willing to pay this price? Are we prepared to have God empty us of all that is in any way contrary to His will? If not, let us ask Him to work in us to will His own good pleasure—plunging the cold stubborn iron into the glowing furnace of His grace until it can be bent into perfect conformity to His own glorious will. But if we are willing, let us believe that He does fill us, as soon as we yield ourselves to Him. Grace, like nature, abhors a vacuum; and just as the cold fresh air will rush in to fill an exhausted receiver, as soon as it has a chance to enter, so does the grace of the Holy Spirit enter the heart that can boast of nothing but an aching void.

Many Christians, seeking this blessed fullness, look within for evidences of the reception and indwelling of the Spirit, and refuse to beleive in His presence unless they detect certain symptoms and signs that they consider befitting. This is entirely wrong. The evidence is not of feeling, but of faith.

If we have complied with God's directions, we must believe, whether we feel any difference or not, that God has done His part and has kept His promise given us through Jesus Christ our Lord. When we leave the place where we have solemnly dedicated ourselves to God, and sought to be filled with the Spirit, we must not examine our feelings to discover whether there is such a difference in us as we might expect; but we must cry, in the assurance of faith: "I praise You, blessed One, that You have not failed to perform Your chosen work; You have taken up Your abode in me: henceforth You shall have Your way with me, to will and do Your own good pleasure."

We should not seek to know the presence of the Holy Ghost by any signs pointing to Himself. The surest symptoms that He is within are: sensitiveness as to sin, tenderness of conscience, the growing preciousness of Jesus, the fragrance of His name, and sympathy with His purposes. Have you these in growing measure? Then you know something of His gracious filling.

2. WE MUST BE OBEDIENT. Christ reiterated His appeals for the keeping of His commands, in almost every sentence of His closing discourses with His disciples (John 14:15, 21, 23–24). Instant and implicit obedience to the teaching of the Word, and to

the inner promptings of the Holy Spirit, is an absolute condition of keeping, or increasing, the store of sacred influence. Nor is such obedience hard; for all God's commands are able to be kept, and His grace is sufficient. It is from the heights of unwavering obedience that we catch sight of the wide and open sea of blessedness. The exact obedience of Elijah is the inviolable condition of receiving and keeping "the spirit and power of Elias."

3. WE MUST LIVE ON THE WORD OF GOD. Elijah , the widow, and her son, lived on their daily replenished stores; but the prophet had other meat to eat that they knew nothing of: "Man shall not live by bread alone, but by every word that proceedeth out of the mouth of God" (Matt. 4:4). It was on that word that Elijah fed during those long and slow-moving days.

This is the further absolute condition of becoming and remaining filled with the Holy Ghost. The Spirit works with and through the Word. If we then neglect the reverent study of Scripture, we cut ourselves off from the very vehicle through which God's Spirit enters human spirits. And this is the great fault of our times. Christian people will attend conventions, plunge into all kinds of Christian work, read many good books about the Bible and Christian living; but they give the Bible itself the most cursory and superficial heed. And it is for this reason that the Bible does not speak to them. There is no book that will so repay time spent over its pages as the Word of God. A neglected Bible means a starved and strengthless spirit; a comfortless heart; a barren life; and a grieved Holy Ghost. If the people who are now perpetually running about to meetings for crumbs of help and comfort would only stay at home and search their Bibles, there would be more happiness in the church, and more blessing on the world. It is very prosaic counsel, but it is true.

We must reserve for our next chapter some account of the life that this Spirit-filled man lived in his little household. But we may note the remarkable admission of the widow: "I know that thou art a man of God" (1 Kings 17:24).

We talk of the man of letters, the man of honor, the man of mark, but how infinitely better to be known as a man of God—one of God's men, a man after God's own heart!

5

The Test of the Home Life
1 Kings 17

Many men might look like heroes and saints in the solitudes of Cherith, or on the heights of Carmel, and yet wretchedly fail in the home life of Zarephath. It is one thing to commune with God in the solitudes of nature, and to perform acts of devotion and zeal for Him in the presence of thousands; but it is quite another to walk with Him day by day in the midst of a home, with its many calls for the constant forgetfulness of self. There is a constant need for the exercise of gentleness, patience, self-sacrifice, self-restraint.

In our last chapter, we saw something of the power and Spirit with which Elijah was filled and endued. But we are now to follow him into a home, and see how he bears the test of home life; and we shall learn to admire and love him more. He lived a truly human life; he was the same man in the widow's house as on Carmel's heights. He shows that when a man is full of the Holy Ghost, it will be evidenced by the entire tenor of his daily walk and life style. In this he reminds us of Luther, whose family life was a model of beauty—an oasis in the desert. Let those who know him only as the Reformer read his letters to his little daughter, and they will be captivated by the winsomeness and tenderness of that great and gentle soul.

1. ELIJAH TEACHES US CONTENTMENT. The fare in the widow's home was frugal enough, and there was only just enough for their daily needs. Human nature, which was as strong in the prophet as in the rest of us, would have preferred to be able to count sacks of meal and barrels of oil. But this is usually not God's way; nor is it the healthiest discipline for our better life.

God's rule is—day by day. The manna fell on the desert sands day by day. Our bread is promised to us for the day. And they who live like this are constantly reminded of their blessed dependence on their Father's love.

If God were to give us the choice between seeing our provision and keeping it ourselves, or not seeing it and leaving Him to deal it out, day by day, most of us would be almost sure to choose the former alternative. But we would be far wiser to say, "I am content to trust You, Father. You keep the stores under Your own hand; they will give me less anxiety; they will not lead me into temptation; they will not expose me to jealousy of others more favored than myself."

And those who live this way are not worse off than others. No, in the truest sense they are better off. Better off, because the responsibility of maintaining them rests wholly on God; and they are delivered from the fret of anxiety, the strain of daily care, and the temptations that make it almost impossible for a rich man to enter the kingdom of God. The main thing is to understand the precious promise, "Seek ye first the kingdom of God and his righteousness, and all these things shall be added unto you." Then let us go on doing our duty, filling our time, working out the plan of our life. Our Father has ample resources: His are the cattle on a thousand hills; and His the waving cornfields, and the myriad fish of the ocean depths. He has prepared a supply for our need, and He will deliver it in time, if only we will trust Him.

If these words are read by those who are dependent on daily supplies—with little hope of ever owning more than the daily handful of meal, and the little oil at the bottom of the cruse—let them be comforted by the example of Elijah. The bottom of the barrel may have been scraped today, but on going to it tomorrow there will be just enough for tomorrow's needs. The last drop of oil may have been drained today, but there will be more tomorrow, and enough. Anxiety will not do you good; but the prayer of faith will. "Your Father knoweth what things ye have need of."

2. ELIJAH ALSO TEACHES US GENTLENESS UNDER PROVOCATION. We do not know how long the mother watched over her dying child, but she spoke unadvisedly and cruelly to the man who had brought deliverance to her home: "Art thou come unto me to call my sin to remembrance, and to slay my son?"

A remark, so uncalled-for and unjust, might well have stung the prophet to the quick, or prompted a bitter reply. And it would have doubtless done so had his goodness been anything less than inspired by the Holy Ghost. But without further remark Elijah simply said, "Give me thy son."

If the Holy Spirit is really filling the heart, a marvelous change will come over the rudest, the least refined, the most selfish person. There will be a gentleness in speech, in the very tones of the voice; a tender thoughtfulness in the smallest actions; a peace passing understanding on the face; and these will be the evident seal of the Holy Ghost. Are they evident in you?

> Gentle Spirit, dwell with me,
> I myself would gentle be;
> And with words that help and heal,
> Would Thy life in mine reveal.

3. ELIJAH TEACHES ALSO THE POWER OF A HOLY LIFE. Somewhere in the background of this woman's life there was a dark deed that dwarfed all other memories of wrongdoing, and stood out before her mind as her sin—"my sin" (1 Kings 17:18). What it was we do not know; it may have been connected with the birth of that son. It had probably been committed long years before, and had filled her with agony of mind, but in later years the sharp sense of remorse had become dulled; sometimes she even lost all recollection of her sin for weeks and months together.

It is remarkable how different the mental stimulus is that is required by different casts of mind, to awaken dormant memories. In the case of the woman of Zarephath it was Elijah's holy life, combined with her own terrible sorrow. Beneath the spell of these two voices her memory gave up its dead, and her conscience was quickened into vigorous life. "Art thou come unto me to call my sin to remembrance?"

4. ELIJAH TEACHES, LASTLY, THE SECRET OF GIVING LIFE. It is a characteristic of those who are filled with the Holy Ghost that they carry with them everywhere the spirit of life, even resurrection life. Thus was it with the prophet. But mark the conditions under which alone we will be able to fulfill this glorious function.

a. *Lonely wrestlings.* "He took him out of her bosom, and carried him up into a loft, where he abode, and laid him upon his own bed. And he cried unto the LORD." We are not specific enough in prayer, and we do not spend enough time dwelling with holy fervor on each beloved name. What wonder that we achieve so little!

b. *Humility.* "He stretched himself upon the child." How wonderful that so great a man should spend so much time and thought on that slender frame, and be content to bring himself into direct contact with that which might be thought to defile! We must seek the conversion of children, winning them before Satan or the world get them. But, to do so, we must stoop to them; becoming as little children to win little children for Jesus.

c. *Perseverence.* "He stretched himself . . . three times, and cried unto the LORD." He was not soon daunted. It is in this way that God tests the genuineness of our desire. These deferred answers led us to lengths of holy boldness and persistence of which we should not otherwise have dreamed, but from which we shall never go back.

And his supplications met with the favor of God. "The LORD heard the voice of Elijah; and the soul of the child came into him again, and he revived." And as the prophet presented him to the grateful and rejoicing mother, he must have been beyond all things gratified with her simple testimony to the reality and power of the life that the Holy Ghost had established in him: "Now by this I know that thou art a man of God, and that the word of the LORD in thy mouth is truth."

6

Obadiah—A Contrast
1 Kings 18

After many days the word of the Lord again summoned Elijah to be on the move. Months, and even years, had passed in the retirement of Zarephath; the widow and her son had become bound to him by the most sacred ties; the humble home, with its loft and barrel of meal and cruse of oil was hallowed with memories of the unfailing care of God.

It must have been a great trial for him to go; and how great was the contrast that awaited him! He had probably heard of Ahab's search for him. There was not a nation or kingdom where the incensed monarch had not sought to find him. It was not likely therefore that he would be received with much courtesy. No, the probability was that he would be instantly arrested, and perhaps put to torture to compel an annulment of the words that had placed the realm under the terrible interdict of drought. But he had no alternative but to go. He who had said, "Go hide thyself," now said, "Go show thyself." And so, with implicit obedience "Elijah went to shew himself unto Ahab."

It must have been very bitter to him to see the devastation that had been wrought in the land. We have no idea, in these temperate regions, of the horrors of an Eastern drought. All this had been brought about instrumentally by the prophet's prayer; and it would have been intolerable, had he now eagerly hoped that his people would learn the exceeding sinfulness and evil of sin.

Though the famine was bad everywhere, it seems to have been more severe in Samaria. And it was this famine that brought out the true character of Ahab. We might have supposed that he would set himself to alleviate the miseries of his people; but no, his one thought was about his horses and mules; and his only care was to keep some of them alive. And so he starts on a mission to find grass. What selfishness! Mules and asses before his people! Seeking for grass, instead of seeking for God!

It is startling to find such a man as OBADIAH occupying so influential a position at Ahab's court. "Obadiah, which was the governor [or steward] of his house." Now, according to his testimony, Obadiah had feared the Lord from his youth (1 Kings 18:12). This is also the testimony of the sacred historian concerning him: "Obadiah feared the LORD greatly" (v. 3). And he had given conspicuous proof of his piety, for when Jezebel had swept the land with the wave of persecution, hunting down the prophets of the Lord, and consigning them to indiscriminate slaughter, he had rescued a hundred of the proscribed men, hiding them by fifty in a cave, and feeding them with bread and water. But though a good man, there was evidently a great lack of moral strength, of backbone, of vigorous life, in his character; otherwise he could never have held the position he did in the court of Ahab and Jezebel.

There is no possible harm in a Christian man holding a position of influence in a court or society where he can do so at no cost of principle. On the contrary, it may enable him to render priceless service to the cause of God. But very few can occupy such a position without dropping something of their uncompromising speech, or dipping their colors to the flag of expediency. And there is every indication that this was the weak point with Obadiah.

Obadiah did not believe in carrying matters too far. Of course, he could not fall in with this new order of things, but then there was no need for him to force his religious notions on everyone. He was often shocked at what he saw at court, but then it was no business of his. He was often sad at heart to witness the sufferings of the prophets of the Lord, and was half inclined to take up their cause; but then a single man could not do much, and he could perhaps help them better in a quiet way by staying where he was, though it might sometimes be a strain on his principles. The poor man must often have been in a great conflict between reconciling his duty to Jehovah with his duty to his other master, Ahab. And Elijah shrewdly hinted at it when he said, "Go, tell *thy* lord, Behold, Elijah is here!"

There are many Obadiahs everywhere around us, and even in the professing church. They know the right, and are secretly trying to do it; but they say as little about religion as they can. They never confess their true colors. They are as nervous of being identified by declared Christians as Obadiah was when Elijah sent him to Ahab. They are sorry for those who suffer persecution for righteousness' sake; but it never occurs to them to stand by their side. They content themselves with administering some help to them, as Obadiah did to the harried prophets; and while they conceal that help from the world, they put it in as a claim to the people of God for recognition and protection, as Obadiah did. "Was it not told my lord what I did?" (1 Kings 18:13). What a contrast between Obadiah and Elijah!

1. THERE IS A CONTRAST BETWEEN THE INSIDE AND THE OUTSIDE OF THE CAMP FOR WITNESS-ING. Much is said on both sides of the case. Many among us feel that the children of God should stay in the camp of the world—joining in its festivities, going to its places of amusement, and taking the lead in its fashion and its course. In this way they hope to temper and steady it; to make it Christian. It is a fair dream, and if it were only true, it would save a world of trouble. The poor prophets of the Lord might come back from their caves; Elijah might become Ahab's vizier; and Obadiah's conscience might be at rest. Indeed, Elijah's policy would be a supreme mistake, and we had better all become Obadiahs at once.

But there are two insurmountable difficulties in the way of our accepting this theory of leveling up from within.

a. *It is in direct opposition to the teaching of Scripture.* "Come out from her, my people," is the one summons that rings like a clarion note from shore to shore. "Come out from among them, and be ye separate, saith the Lord; and touch not the unclean thing." (2 Cor. 6:17). There is not a single hero or saint who moved the people of his time from within: all, without exception, have raised the cry, "Let us go forth without the camp." They have joined the constant stream of martyrs, confessors, prophets, and saints, of whom the world was not worthy, but who can trace their kinship to Him of whom it is written, "He suffered without the gate." The only scriptural course for God's witnesses is to go to Him outside the camp. In the world, but not of it—wearing the pilgrim garb, manifesting the pilgrim spirit, uttering the pilgrim confession.

b. *This theory will not work.* The man who goes into the world to level it up will soon find himself on the level with it. Was this not the case with Obadiah? Compare the influence exerted on behalf of Sodom by Abraham on the heights of Mamre, with that of Lot who, not content with pitching his tent toward the city gate, went to live inside, and even became one of the aldermen of the place (Gen. 19:1). But why do we need to multiply instances? The Christian woman who marries an ungodly man is in imminent danger of soon being dragged down to his level. The church that admits the world into its circle will find that it will get worldly quicker than the world will become Christian.

The safest and strongest position is outside the camp. Archimedes said that he could move the world if he only had a point of rest given him outside it. Thus, a handful of God's servants can also influence their times, if only they resemble Elijah, whose life was spent altogether outside the court and the world of his time.

2. THERE IS A CONTRAST BETWEEN PREVENTIVE AND AGGRESSIVE GOODNESS. Obadiah sought simply to prevent a great harm being done. He shielded the prophets from the sword of Jezebel, and from the touch of famine. And this was good. Preventive goodness like this serves a very useful purpose. It rears homes and refuges and bulwarks of defense, behind which persecuted and threatened lives may thrive. But the world needs something more. There is an urgent demand for men like Elijah and John the Baptist, who dare oppose the perpetrators of evil deeds, and who arraign them before the bar of God and compel them to bow before the offended majesty of a broken law.

For this there is needed a positive enduement of power that cannot be had by the half-hearted, but is the glad prerogative of those who are servants of God. Obadiah had no power of this kind. How could he have? On the other hand, Elijah was full of it, and, because he was he succeeded in arresting the tides of sin when they were in full flood.

It is not enough to shelter the prophets; we must go and show ourselves to Ahab. May God send to His church a handful of lion-like men, like Elijah, of whom this is the majestic record: "Elijah went to show himself unto Ahab"; to confront the royal culprit, to arrest the king.

3. THERE IS A CONTRAST BETWEEN THE CAUTION OF EXPEDIENCY AND THE FEARLESSNESS OF FAITH. When Elijah told Obadiah to tell his master that he was awaiting him, the astonished courtier was incredulous. Indeed, he thought either that the prophet did not know the way in which the king had sought for him, or that the Spirit of the Lord would carry him off before they could meet. It never occurred to him that Elijah dare meet the king if he really knew how matters stood. And even supposing that *he* were foolhardy enough to do this himself, surely God would prevent him from slipping into the lion's lair. In any case, he wished to have nothing to do with it. Twice over he repeated the words, "he shall slay me." And it was only when Elijah assured him that he would surely show himself to Ahab before the sun went down, that he reluctantly went to meet Ahab and told him. How unable he was to form a true conception of the fearlessness of Elijah!

And what was the source of that fearlessness? God was more real to Elijah than Ahab. How could he be afraid of a man who would die? The fear of God had made him impervious to all other fear. Faith sees the mountain full of horses and chariots of fire. And so, with unblanched face and undismayed heart, God's Elijahs go on to do His commands, though their way is blocked by as many devils as there are shingles on the roof. The Obadiahs assert that they will never dare to carry their proposals through; but they live to see their predicitons falsified.

4. THERE IS A CONTRAST BETWEEN THE RECEPTION GIVEN BY THE UNGODLY TO THESE TWO TYPES OF CHARACTER. Ahab could tolerate Obadiah because he never rebuked him. But as soon as Ahab saw Elijah, he accosted him. "It came to pass, when Ahab saw Elijah, that

Ahab said unto him, Art thou he that troubleth Israel?" (v. 17). Years later, speaking of another devoted servant of God whose advice was demanded by Jehoshaphat, this same Ahab said, "I hate him; for he doth not prophesy good concerning me, but evil" (1 Kings 22:8).

There is no higher testimony to the consistency of our life than the hatred of the Ahabs around us. If all men speak well of you, you may begin to question whether you are not becoming mere Obadiahs. But if Ahab accuses you of troubling him, rejoice.

There, face to face, we leave Ahab and Elijah. We need not ask who is the more royal of the two; nor need we spend our time in looking for Obadiah. We cannot but admire the noble bearing of the prophet of God. But let us remember it was due, not to his inherent character, but to his faith. And if we will acquire a similar faith, we may anticipate similar results in our own lives.

7

The Plan of Campaign
1 Kings 18

When Elijah left Zarephath, it is more than probable that his mind was utterly destitute of any fixed plan of action. He knew that he must show himself to Ahab, and that rain was not far away, for these were his definite marching orders—"Go, shew thyself unto Ahab; and I will send rain upon the earth." But more than that he knew nothing.

The plan of this great campaign for God against Baal, for truth against error, may have been revealed to Elijah on his journey from Zarephath all at once. But it is quite as likely that it was revealed bit by bit. This is so often God's way.

If we seek to think ourselves into Elijah's attitude of heart and mind as he left the shelter of Zarephath and began to pass through the incidents that culminated in Carmel, it seems to have been threefold.

1. HE WAS FILLED WITH A CONSUMING PASSION FOR THE GLORY OF GOD. "Let it be known this day that thou art God in Israel." This prayer is the key to his heart. He neither knew nor cared to know what would become of himself, but his soul was on fire with a holy jealousy for the glory of God. He could not bear to think of those wrecked altars or martyred prophets. And when he was compelled to face these things, his spirit was stirred to its depths with indignation and sorrow.

Well would it be if each one of us were similarly inspired! Only trust Him to do it; ask and expect Him to fill you with the fire of that zeal that burned in the heart of Elijah, consuming all that was base, corrupt, and selfish, and making the whole man a fit agent for God.

2. HE WAS PROFOUNDLY CONVINCED THAT HE WAS ONLY A SERVANT. "Let it be known this day that thou art God in Isarel, *and that I am thy servant.*" This was the attitude of Elijah's spirit—surrendered, yielded, emptied; plastic to the hands that reach down out of heaven molding men.

Are we not too fond of doing things for God, instead of letting God do what He chooses through us? We do not recognize His absolute ownership. We often miss doing what He sorely wants to do, because we insist on carrying out some little whim of our own.

3. ELIJAH WAS EAGERLY DESIROUS TO KNOW AND WORK OUT GOD'S PLAN. "Let it be known this day that thou art God in Israel, and that I am thy servant, and *that I have done all these things at thy word.*" When once a man feels that he is working out God's plan, and that God is working out His plan through him, he is invincible. And this was one element in Elijah's splendid strength.

This question as to our relation to God's plan is most important, because the power and blessing of God are only to be enjoyed in all their fullness by those who are where He would have them be. Would we have divine supplies? We must keep step with the divine plan. The fire burns only when we erect the altar according to God's Word. We must be incessant in uttering the cry, "What wilt thou have me to do?"

There are many ways of learning God's plan. Sometimes it is revealed *in circumstances*—not always pleasant, but ever acceptable, because they reveal our Father's will. No circumstance happens outside His permission, and therefore each is a King's messenger, bearing His message, though we are sometimes puzzled as to how to understand it. Sometimes God's plan is revealed *by strong impressions of duty*, which increase in proportion as they are prayed over, and are tested by the Word of God.

There are many voices by which God can speak His will to the truly surrendered spirit, and we must be content to wait quietly. As a rule we do nothing as long as we are in any uncertainty, but we are to examine ourselves, and to be ready to act as soon as we know.

The plan, as Elijah unfolded it to Ahab, was eminently adapted to the circumstances of the case. All Israel was to be gathered to Carmel, which reared itself above the plain of Esdraelon, a noble site for a national meeting ground. Special care was to be taken to secure the presence of the representatives of the systems that had dared to rival the worship of Jehovah; "the prophets of Baal four hundred and fifty, and the prophets of the groves four hundred, which eat at Jezebel's table." A test was then to be imposed on these rival systems, which the adherents of Baal could not possibly refuse; for he was the Sun-god, and this was a trial by fire.

Elijah knew that the altar of Baal would remain smokeless. He was equally sure that Jehovah would answer his faith by fire. He felt convinced also that the people, unable to escape the evidence of what they had seen, would forever disavow the accursed systems of Phoenicia, and would return once more to the worship of the God of their fathers.

"So Ahab sent unto all the children of Israel, and gathered the prophets together unto Mount Carmel." This summoning of the people must have taken a few days. Where and how did Elijah spend that interval?

In my opinion, Elijah spent those memorable days of waiting on Carmel itself, sheltering himself and the lad in some wild cave at night, and by day going carefully over the scene of the approaching conflict. How constantly he would trust in his God, and pour out litanies of supplication for the people, and gird himself for the coming conflict by effectual fervent prayer. The answer by fire would never have come that day if the previous days had not been spent in the presence of God.

It is a sublime spectacle—this yielded, surrendered man, waiting on Carmel, in steadfast faith, the gathering of the people, and the unfolding of the purpose of God. He had no fear about the issue; he expected soon to see a nation at the feet of God.

And he was all this, not because he was different from ourselves, but because he had gotten into the blessed habit of dealing with God at first hand, as a living reality, in whose presence it was his privilege and glory always to stand.

8

The Conflict on the Heights of Carmel
1 Kings 18

It is early morning on Mount Carmel. From all sides the crowds are making their way toward this spot which, from the earliest times, has been associated with worship. No work is being done anywhere; every thought of young and old is concentrated on that mighty convocation to which Ahab has summoned them. See how the many thousands of Israel are slowly gathering and taking up every vantage spot from which a view can be had of the proceedings.

The people are nearly gathered, and there is the regular tread of marshaled men; four hundred prophets of Baal, conspicuous with the sun symbols flashing on their brows; but the prophets of Astarte are absent: the queen, at whose table they ate, has overruled the summons of the king. And now, through the crowd, the litter of the king, borne by stalwart carriers, threads its way, surrounded by the great officers of state.

We fix our thought on that one man, of sinewy build and flowing hair who, with flashing eye and compressed lip, awaits the quiet hush that will presently fall on that mighty concourse. One man against a nation! See, with what spiteful glances his every movement is watched by the priests.

The king alternates between fear and hate; but he restrains himself because he feels that somehow the coming of the rain depends on this one man. And if there are sympathizers in the crowd they are hushed and still. Even Obadiah discreetly keeps out of the way. But do not fear for Elijah! He is only a man of life passions with ourselves, but he is full of faith and spiritual power; he can avail himself of the very resources of Deity, as a slender rod may draw lightning from the cloud. This very day, by faith—not by any inherent power, but by faith—you will see him subdue a kingdom; nothing shall be impossible to him. He spoke seven times during the course of that memorable day, and his words are the true index of what was passing in his heart.

1. Elijah remonstrated. "Elijah came unto all the people, and said, How long halt ye between two opinions! If the Lord be God, follow him; but if Baal, then follow him."

At present their position was illogical and absurd. Their course was like the limp of a man whose legs are uneven; or like the device of a servant employed to serve two masters—doing his best for both, and failing to please either. His sincere and simple soul had no patience with such glaring folly. The time had come for the nation to be stopped in its attempt to combine the worship of Jehovah and of Baal; and to be compelled to choose between the two issues that presented themselves.

The people seemed to have been stunned and ashamed that such alternatives should be presented to their choice, for they "answered him not a word."

2. Elijah threw out a challenge. "The God that answereth by fire, let him be

God." It was a fair proposal, because Baal was the lord of the sun and the god of those productive natural forces of which heat is the element and sign. The priests of Baal could not therefore refuse.

And every Israelite could recall many occasions in the glorious past when Jehovah had answered by fire. It was the emblem of Jehovah, and the sign of His acceptance of His people's service.

When Elijah therefore proposed that each side should offer a bullock, and await an answer by fire, he secured the immediate agreement of the people. "All the people answered and said, It is well spoken."

That proposal was made in the perfect assurance that God would not fail him. God will never fail the man who trusts Him completely. Be sure that you are in God's plan; then forward in God's name!—the very elements will obey you and fire will leap from heaven at your command.

3. ELIJAH DEALT OUT WITHERING SARCASM. The false priests were unable to insert the secret spark of fire among the wood that lay on their altar. They were compelled therefore to rely on a direct appeal to their patron deity. And this they did with might and strength. Round and round the altar they went in the mystic choric dance, breaking their rank sometimes by an excited leap up and down at the altar; and all the while repeating the monotonous chant, "Baal, hear us! Hear us, Baal!" But there was no voice, nor any that answered.

Three hours passed in this way. Their Sun-god deity slowly drove his golden car up the steep of heaven, and ascended his throne in the zenith. It was surely the time of his greatest power, and he must help them then, if ever. But all he did was to bronze to a deeper tinge the eager, upturned faces of his priests.

Elijah could hardly conceal his delight in their defeat. He knew it would be so. He could afford to mock them by suggesting a cause for the indifference of their god: "Cry aloud: for he is a god; either he is talking, or he is pursuing, or he is in a journey, or peradventure he sleepeth, and must be awaked."

"And they cried aloud, and cut themselves after their manner with knives and lancets, till the blood gushed out upon them." Surely their sincere efforts were enough to touch the compassion of any deity, however hard to move! And, since the heavens still continued silent, did it not prove to the people that their religion was a delusion and a sham?

Thus three more hours passed by until the hour had come when, in the temple of Jerusalem, the priests of God were accustomed to offer the evening lamb. But "there was neither voice, nor any to answer, nor any that regarded." The altar stood cold and smokeless, the bullock unconsumed.

4. ELIJAH ISSUED AN INVITATION. His time had come at last; and his first act was to invite the people nearer. He wanted the answer of fire to be beyond dispute; he therefore invited the close scrutiny of the people as he raised up the broken altar of the Lord. As he sought, with reverent care, those scattered stones, and built them together so that the twelve stood as one—meet symbol of the unity of the ideal Israel in the sight of God—the sharp glances of the people, in his close proximity, could see that there was no inserted torch or secret spark.

5. ELIJAH GAVE A COMMAND. His faith was exuberant. He was so sure of God that he dared to heap difficulties in his way, knowing that there is no real difficulty for infinite power. The more unlikely the answer was, the more glory there would be to God. Oh, matchless faith! which can laugh at impossibilities and can even heap them one upon another, to have the pleasure of seeing God vanquish them.

The altar was raised; the wood laid in order; the bullock cut in pieces: but to prevent any possibility of fraud and to make the coming miracle still more wonderful, Elijah said, "Fill four barrels with water, and pour it on the burnt sacrifice, and on the wood." This they did three times, until the wood was drenched and the water filled the trench, making it impossible for a spark to travel across.

How sad that few of us have faith like this! We are not so sure of God that we dare to pile difficulties in His way. Yet what this man had, we too may have, by prayer and fasting.

6. ELIJAH OFFERED A PRAYER. Such a prayer! It was quiet and assured, confident of an answer. Its chief burden was that God would vindicate Himself that day in showing Himself to be God indeed, and in turning the people's heart back to Himself.

Is it not wonderful that "the fire of the LORD fell, and consumed the burnt sacrifice, and the wood, and the stones, and the dust, and licked up the water that was in the trench"? It could not have been otherwise! And let us not think that this is an old story, never to be repeated. Our God is a consuming fire; and when once the unity of His people is recognized and His presence is sought, He will descend, overcoming all obstacles.

7. ELIJAH ISSUED AN ORDER FOR EXECUTION. The order went forth from those stern lips: "Take the prophets of Baal; let not one of them escape." The people were in the mood to obey. Only a moment before they had rent the air with the shout, "The LORD, he is the God, the LORD, he is the God!" They saw how hideously they had been deceived. And now they closed around the cowed and vanquished priests, who saw that resistance was in vain, and that their hour had come.

"Elijah brought them down to the brook Kishon, and slew them there." One after another they fell beneath his sword while the king stood by, a helpless spectator of their doom, and Baal did nothing to save them.

And when the last was dead, the prophet knew that rain was not far off. He could almost hear the footfall of the clouds hurrying up toward the land. He knew what we all need to know, that God Himself can only bless the land or heart that no longer shelters within its borders rivals to Himself. May God impart to us Elijah's faith, that we also may be strong and do great things!

9

Rain At Last!
1 Kings 18

We can in a very inadequate degree realize the horrors of an Eastern drought. The anguish of the land was directly attributable to the apostasy of its people. The iniquities of Israel had separated from them their God, and Elijah knew this right well. This prompted him to act the part of executioner to the priests of Baal, who had been the ringleaders in the national revolt from God, but whose bodies now lay in ghastly death on the banks of the Kishon, or were being carried out to sea.

Ahab must have stood by Elijah in the Kishon gorge and been an unwilling spectator of that fearful deed of vengeance, not daring to resist the outburst of popular indignation or to attempt to shield the men whom he had himself encouraged and introduced. When the last priest had died, Elijah turned to the king and said, "Get thee up, eat and drink; for there is a sound of abundance of rain." It was as if he said, "Get up to where your tents are pitched on the broad upland sweep; the feast is spread in your gilded pavilion; feast on its dainties; but be quick! for now that the land is rid of these traitor priests and God is once more enthroned in His rightful place, the showers of rain cannot be delayed any longer. Be quick! or the rain may interrupt your feast."

What a contrast between these two men! "Ahab went up to eat and to drink. And Elijah went up to the top of Carmel; and he cast himself down upon the earth, and put his face between his knees." It is no more than we might have expected of the king. When his people were suffering the extremities of drought, he cared only to find grass enough to save his horses; and now, though his faithful priests had died by hundreds, he thought only of the banquet that awaited him in his pavilion. I think I can see Ahab and Elijah ascending those heights together: no sympathy, no common joy; the king turns off to his tents while the servant of God climbs steadily up to the highest part of the mountain, and finds an oratory at the base of a yet higher promontory.

Such contrasts still show themselves. The children of this world will spend their days in feasting and their nights in revelry, though a world is rushing to ruin. Woe to the land when such men rule! May our beloved country be preserved from having such leaders as these! And may our youth be found, not garlanded and scented for the Ahab feasts, but with Elijah on the bleak mountains, where there may be no fancy feasts but where the air is fresh, and life is free, and the spirit is braced to noble deeds.

1. THERE ARE CERTAIN CHARACTERISTICS IN ELIJAH'S PRAYER THAT WE MUST NOTICE AS WE PASS, BECAUSE THEY SHOULD FORM PART OF ALL TRUE PRAYER.

a. *It was based on the promise of God.* When Elijah was summoned from Zarephath to resume his public work, his marching orders were capped by the specific promise of rain: "Go, shew thyself unto Ahab; and I will send rain upon the earth." God's promises are given, not to restrain, but to incite to prayer. They are the mold into which we may pour our fervid spirits without fear. Though the Bible is crowded with golden promises from cover to cover, yet they will be inoperative until we turn them into prayer.

When we are asked therefore *why* men should pray, and *how* prayer avails, we should answer no more than this: "Prayer is the instinct of the religious life; it is one of the first principles of the spiritual world." It is clearly taught in the Word of God to be accepted by the Almighty. It has been practiced by the noblest and saintliest of men, who have testified to its certain efficacy. We are content therefore to pray, though we are as ignorant of the philosophy of the *modus operandi* of prayer as we are of any natural law.

When your child was a toddling, lisping babe, it asked many things wholly incompatible with your nature and its own welfare; but as the years passed, increasing experience has molded its requests into shapes suggested by yourself. So, as we know more of God through His promises, we are led to set our hearts on things that lie on His open palm waiting to be taken by the hand of an appropriating faith. This is why all prayer, like Elijah's, should be based on promise.

b. *It was definite.* This is where so many prayers fail. We do not pray with any expectation of attaining definite and practical results. Let us correct this. Let us keep a list of petitions that we will plead before God. Let us direct our prayer, as David did (Ps. 5:3), and look up for the answer; and we will find ourselves obtaining new and unwonted blessings. Be definite!

c. *It was earnest.* "Elijah prayed earnestly." The prayers of Scripture all glow with the white heat of intensity. Prayer is not answered unless it is accompanied with such earnestness as will prove that the blessing sought is really needed.

Such earnestness is, of course, to be dreaded when we seek some lower benefit for ourselves. But when, like Elijah, we seek the fulfillment of the divine promise—not for ourselves, but for the glory of God—then it is impossible to be too much in earnest, or too full of the energy of prayer.

d. *Elijah's prayer was humble.* "He cast himself down upon the earth, and put his face between his knees." It is not always so—that the men who stand straightest in the presence of sin bow lowest in the presence of God? True, you are a child; but you are also a subject. True, you are a redeemed man; but you cannot forget your original name, *sinner*. True, you may come with boldness; but remember the majesty, might, and power of God, and take your shoes from off your feet. Our only plea with God is the merit and blood of our great High Priest. It becomes us to be humble.

e. *It was full of expectant faith.* It beat strongly in Elijah's heart. He knew that God would keep His word, and so he sent the lad—possibly the widow's son—up to the highest point of Carmel, and urged him to look toward the sea, because he was sure that before long his prayer would be answered, and God's promise would be kept. We have often prayed, and failed to look out for the blessings we have sought.

There is a faith that God cannot refuse, a faith to which all things are possible. It laughs at impossibility, and can move mountains and plant them in the sea. May such faith be ours! such faith was Elijah's.

f. *It was very persevering.* He said to his servant, "Go up now, look toward the sea." And he went up, and looked, and said, "There is nothing." How often have we sent the lad of eager desire to scan the horizon! And how often has he returned with the answer, *There is nothing!* And because there is nothing when we have just begun to pray, we stop praying. We leave the mountain brow. We do not know that God's answer is even then on the way.

Not so with Elijah. "And he said, Go again seven times." He came back the first time, saying, "There is nothing—no sign of rain, no cloud in the clear sky": and Elijah said, "Go again." And that was repeated seven times. It was no small test of the prophet's endurance, but with the ordeal there came sufficient grace so that he was able to bear it.

Our Father frequently grants our prayer and labels the answer for us, but keeps it back that we may be led on to a point of intensity. He from which we shall never recede. Then when we have outdone ourselves, He lovingly turns to us, and says, "Great is thy faith: be it unto thee even as thou wilt!" (Matt. 15:28).

g. *And the prayer was abundantly answered.* For weeks and months before, the sun had been gathering up from lake and river, from sea and ocean, the drops of mist, and now the gale was bearing them rapidly toward the thirsty land of Israel. "Before they call, I will answer; and while they are yet speaking, I will hear" (Isa. 65:24). The answer to your prayers may be nearer than you think. On the wings of every moment it is hastening toward you. God will answer you, and soon!

Soon the boy, from his tower of observation, beheld on the horizon a tiny cloud, no bigger than a man's hand, moving quickly across the sky. No more was needed to convince an Oriental that rain was near. It was, and is, the certain precursor of a sudden hurricane of wind and rain. The boy was sent with an urgent message to Ahab, to come down from Carmel to his chariot in the plain beneath, lest Kishon, swollen by the rains, should stop him on his way home. The boy barely had time to reach the royal pavilion before the heavens were black with clouds and wind, and there was a great rain.

The monarch started amid the pelting storm, but faster than his swift horses were the feet of the prophet, energized by the hand of God. He snatched up his streaming mantle and twisted it around his loins; and amid the fury of the elements, with which the night closed in, he outran the chariot, and ran like a common courier before it to the entrance of Jezreel, some eighteen miles away.

Thus by his faith and prayer this one man brought back the rain to Israel. Why should we not learn and practice his secret? Then we too might bring from heaven spiritual blessings that would make the parched places of the church and the world rejoice and blossom as the rose.

10

How the Mighty Fell!
1 Kings 19

Amid the drenching storm with which the memorable day of the convocation closed in, the king and the prophet reached Jezreel. They were probably the first to bring tidings of what had occurred. Elijah went to some humble lodging for shelter and food; while Ahab retired to the palace where Jezebel awaited him. All day long the queen had been wondering how matters were going on Mount Carmel. She cherished the feverish hope that her priests had won the day, and when she saw the rain clouds steal over the sky she attributed the welcome change to some great interposition of Baal, in answer to their pleadings. We can imagine some scene such as this taking place between the royal pair when they met.

"How have things gone today? No doubt, well; the rain has anticipated your favorable reply."

"I have nothing to tell you that will give you pleasure."

"Why?"

"The worst has happened."

"What do you mean? Where are my priests?"

"You will never see them again. They are all dead; by this time their bodies are floating out to sea."

"Who has dared to do this thing? Did they not defend themselves? Did you not raise your hand? How did they die?"

"And Ahab told Jezebel all that Elijah had done, and withal how he had slain all the prophets with the sword."

Jezebel's indignation knew no bounds. Ahab was sensual and materialistic; if only he had enough to eat and drink, and the horses and mules were cared for, he was content. In his judgment there was not much to choose between God and Baal. Not so Jezebel. She was as resolute as he was indifferent. Crafty, unscrupulous, and intriguing, she molded Ahab to her mind.

To Jezebel the crisis was a grave one. Policy as well as indignation prompted her to act at once. If this national reformation were permitted to spread, it would sweep away before it all that she had been laboring at for years. She must strike, and strike at once; so that very night, amid the violence of the storm, she sent a messenger to Elijah, saying, "So let the gods do to me, and more also, if I make not thy life as the life of one of them by to-morrow about this time." That message betrays the woman. She did not dare kill him, though he was easily within her power; so she contented herself with threats. Her mind was set on driving him from the country, so that she might be left free to repair the havoc he had caused. And, sad to say, in this she was only too successful.

Elijah's presence had never been so necessary as now. The work of destruction had begun, and the people were in a mood to carry it through to the bitter end. The tide had turned, and was setting toward God; and Elijah was needed to complete the work of reformation by a work of construction. From what we have seen of him, we should have expected that he would receive the message with unruffled composure; but, "he arose, and went for his life."

Accompanied by his servant, and under cover of night, he hurried through the driving storm, across the hills of Samaria; nor did he slacken his speed until he had reached Beersheba. He was safe there; but even there he could not stay, so he plunged into that wild desert waste that stretches southward to Sinai.

Through the weary hours he plodded on beneath the burning sun, his feet blistered by the scorching sands; no ravens, no Cherith, no Zarephath were there. At last the fatigue and anguish overpowered even his sinewy strength, and he cast himself beneath the slight shadow of a small shrub of juniper, and asked to die. "It is enough: now, O LORD, take away my life; for I am not better than my fathers."

What might have been! If only Elijah had held his ground he might have saved his country; and there would have been no necessity for the captivity and dispersion of his people. The seven thousand secret disciples would have dared to come forth from their hiding places, and show themselves; and would have constituted a nucleus of loyal hearts, by whom Baal had been replaced by Jehovah; his own character would have escaped a stain that still remains.

The Bible saints often fail just where we would have expected them to stand. Abraham was the father of those who believe, but his faith failed him when he went down to Egypt and lied to Pharaoh about his wife. Moses was the meekest of men, but he missed Canaan because he spoke unadvisedly with his lips. So Elijah shows himself to be indeed "a man of like passions with ourselves."

What proof there is here of the veracity of the Bible! Had it been merely a human composition, its authors would have shrunk from delineating the failure of one of its chief heroes. Is there not even a gleam of comfort to be had out of the woeful spectacle of Elijah's fall? If it had not been for this, we would always have thought of him as being too far removed from us to be in any sense a model. But now as we see him stretched under the shade of the juniper tree asking for death, we feel that he was what he was, only by the grace of God, received through faith. And by a similar faith we may appropriate a similar grace to ennoble our unimposing lives.

SEVERAL CAUSES ACCOUNT FOR THIS TERRIBLE FAILURE.

1. *His physical strength and nervous energy were completely overtaxed.* Consider the tremendous strain he had undergone since leaving the shelter of the quiet home at Zarephath. The long excitement of the convocation, the slaughter of the priest, the intensity of his prayer, the eighteen miles swift run in front of Ahab's chariot, followed by the rapid flight that had hardly been relaxed for a single moment until he cast himself upon the desert sand—all had resulted in sheer exhaustion. He was suffering deeply from reaction.

2. *He was deeply sensitive to his lonely position.* "I only, am left." Some men are born to loneliness. It is the penalty of true greatness. At such a time the human spirit is apt to falter unless it is sustained by a heroic purpose, and by an unfaltering faith. You remind me that Elijah might have had the company of the young boy. But remember that there is company which is not companionship. We need something more than human beings; we need human hearts, and sympathy, and love.

3. *He looked away from God to circumstances.* Up to that moment Elijah had been animated by a great faith, because he had never lost sight of God. "He endured, as seeing him who is invisible" (Heb. 11:27). Faith always thrives when God occupies the whole field of vision. But when Jezebel's threats reached him, we are told most significantly, *"when he saw that,* he arose, and went for his life." While Elijah set the Lord always before his face, he did not fear, though a host was camped against him. But when he looked at his peril, he thought more of his life than of God's cause. *"When he saw that,* he arose, and went for his life."

Let us refuse to look at circumstances even though they roll before us as a Red Sea and howl around us like a storm. Circumstances, natural impossibilities, difficulties, are nothing in the estimation of the soul that is occupied with God.

It is a great mistake to dictate to God. Elijah did not know what he said when he told God that he had had enough of life, and asked to die. If God would have taken him at his word, he would have died under a cloud; he would never have heard the still small voice; he would never have founded the schools of the prophets, or commissioned Elisha for his work; he would never have swept up to heaven in a fiery chariot.

What a mercy it is that God does not answer all our prayers! How gracious He is in reading their inner meaning and answering them! This, as we shall see, is what He did for His tired and complaining servant.

How many have uttered those words, "It is enough!" The Christian worker, whose efforts seem in vain: "It is enough. Let me come home. The burden is more than I can bear. The lessons are tiresome. School life is tedious; holidays will be so welcome. I cannot see that anything will be gained by longer delay. It is enough!"

Little do we know how much we would miss if God were to do as we request. To die now would be to forego immeasurable blessings that await us within forty days' journey from this; and to die like a dog, instead of sweeping, honored and beloved, through the open gates of heaven. It is better to leave it all in the wise and tender thought of God, and we will yet live to thank Him that He refused to gratify our wish when, in a moment of despondency, we cast ourselves on the ground and said, "Let us die, It is enough!"

11

Lovingkindness Better Than Life
1 Kings 19

Many of us have learned some of our deepest lessons of the love of God, in having experienced its gentle kindness amid shortcoming and failure, like that which marred Elijah's course.

That failure, as we have seen, was most disastrous. It inflicted lasting disgrace on Elijah's reputation. It arrested one of the most hopeful movements that ever visited the land of Israel. It struck panic and discouragement into thousands of hearts that were beginning to gather courage from his great zeal. It snapped the only brake by which the headlong descent of Israel downward to destruction could have been prevented.

But God's eye followed with tender pity every step of His servant's flight across the hills of Samaria. He did not love him less than when he stood, elated with victory, near the burning sacrifice. And His love assumed, if possible, a more tender, gentler aspect, as He stooped over him while he slept. The love of God came on Elijah as, worn in body by long fatigue, and in spirit by the fierce war of passion, he lay and slept under the juniper tree.

And God did more than love him. He sought, by tender helpfulness, to heal and restore His servant's soul to its former health and joy. At His command an angel twice prepared a meal on the desert sand and touched him and urged him to eat. No upbraiding speeches; no word of reproach; no threats of dismissal; but only sleep and food and kind thoughts of the great journey he was intent on making to Horeb, the mount of God.

It may be that these words will be read by those who have failed. You once avowed yourselves to be the Lord's but all that is over now. You have fallen, as Milton's archangel, from heaven to hell. You have failed; and perhaps failed, as Elijah did, where everyone expected you to stand. And you are ashamed; you want to hide yourself from all who knew you in happier days; you have given up heart and hope. But remember: though forsaken by man, you are not forgotten of God. He loves you still, and waits beside you in order to restore your soul, and give you back the years that may have seemed wasted.

1. GOD'S LOVE IN ITS CONSTANCY. It is not difficult to believe that God loves us when we go with the multitude to the house of God, with the voice of joy and praise, and stand in the inner sunlit circle; but it is hard to believe that He feels as much love for us when, exiled by our sin, our soul is cast down within us. It is not difficult to believe that God loves us when, like Elijah at Cherith and on Carmel, we do His commandments, hearkening to the voice of His word; but it is not so easy when, like Elijah in the desert, we lie stranded or as dismasted and rudderless vessels roll in the trough of the waves.

Yet we must learn to know and believe the constancy of the love of God. We may not feel it. We may imagine that we have forfeited all claim to it.

O child of God, lying amid the wrecks of what might have been, take heart! hope still in the love of God; trust in it; yield to it; and you will yet praise Him, who is the health of your countenance and your God.

2. GOD'S LOVE MANIFESTED IN SPECIAL TENDERNESS BECAUSE OF SPECIAL SIN. We do not read that an angel ever appeared to Elijah at Cherith or Zarephath, or awakened him with a touch that must have been as thrilling as it was tender. Ravens, and brooklets, and a widow had ministered to him before; but never an angel. He had drunk of the water of Cherith; but never of water drawn by angel hands from the river of God. He had eaten of bread and flesh foraged for him by ravens, and of meal multiplied by miracle; but never of cakes molded by angel fingers. Why these special proofs of tenderness? A special manifestation of love was needed to convince the prophet that he was still dearly loved; and to lead him to repentance.

It may be that you are sleeping the sleep of insensibility or despair, but all the while the love of God is inventing some unique manifestation of its yearning tenderness. He hates your sin, as only infinite love can. All the time that you are grieving Him and wandering from Him, He is encompassing you with blessings. Yield to Him! Turn again to the Lord. He will receive you graciously.

3. GOD'S LOVE IN ITS UNWEARIED CARE. It is most likely that it was evening when the angel came the first time and touched him, and urged him to arise and eat; for we are told that he went *a day's journey* into the wilderness before he sat down under the juniper bush. And when the angel of the Lord came *the second time*, it would probably be as morning was breaking over the world. And thus, through the intervening night, the angels of God kept watch and ward about the sleeping prophet.

None of us can measure the powers of endurance in the love of God. It never tires.

4. GOD'S LOVE ANTICIPATING COMING NEED. This always stands out as one of the most wonderful passages in the prophet's history. We can understand God giving him a good meal and sleep, as the best means of recruiting his spent powers. This is what we should have expected of One who knows our frame and remembers that we are dust, and who pities us as a father pities his children. But it is wonderful that God should provide for His servant all he would need for the long journey that lay before him: "Arise and eat; because the journey is too great for thee."

That journey was undertaken at his own whim; it was one long flight from his post of duty; it was destined to meet with a grave rebuke at its close: "What doest thou here, Elijah?" And yet the Lord graciously gave him food, in the strength of which he could endure the long fatigue. The explanation must again be sought in the tender love of God. Elijah's nature was clearly overwrought. Without doubt he had steadfastly made up his mind for that tedious journey to the Mount of God. Nothing would turn him from his fixed purpose. And therefore, as he would go, God anticipated his needs, though they were the needs of a truant servant and a rebellious child. In wrath He remembered mercy, and presented him with the blessings of His goodness, and imparted, through a single meal, sufficient strength for a march of forty days and forty nights.

Surely these thoughts of the love of God will arrest some from pursuing any longer the path of the backslider. You have failed; but do not be afraid of God, or think that He will never look on you again. Rather cast yourself on His love; tell Him how deeply you mourn the past; ask Him to restore you; give yourself to Him again; and believe that God will again use you as a chosen vessel.

12

The "Still, Small Voice"
1 Kings 19

Refreshed by sleep and food, Elijah resumed his journey across the desert to Horeb. Perhaps no spot on earth is more associated with the manifested presence of God than that sacred mount. There the bush burned with fire; there the law was given; there Moses spent forty days and nights alone with God. It was a natural instinct that led the prophet there, and all the world could not have furnished a more appropriate school.

Forty times the prophet saw the sun rise and set over the desert waste. Thus, at last, the prophet came to Horeb, the mount of God. We have to consider how God dealt with His dispirited and truant child.

1. GOD SPOKE TO HIM. In some dark cave, among those jagged precipices, Elijah lodged; and as he waited in lonely reflection, the fire burned in his soul. But he didn't have to wait long. "Behold, the word of the LORD came to him."

That word had often come to him before. It had come to him at Tishbe. It had come to him in Samaria, after he had given his first message to Ahab. It had come to him when Cherith was dry. It had come to summon him from the solitudes of Zarephath to the stir of active life. And now it found him out, and came to him again. There is no spot on earth so lonely, no cave so deep and dark, that the word of the Lord cannot discover us and come to us.

But though God had often spoken to him before, He had never spoken in quite the same tone—"What doest thou here, Elijah?" The accent was stern and reproachful.

If the prophet had answered that searching question of God with shame and sorrow; if he had confessed that he had failed, and asked for forgiveness; if he had cast himself on the pity and tenderness of his almighty Friend—there is not the least doubt that he would have been forgiven and restored. But instead of this, he evaded the divine question. He did not try to explain how he came there, or what he was doing. He chose rather to dwell on his own loyalty for the cause of God; and to bring it out into striking relief by contrasting it with the sinful backslidings of his people. "I have been very jealous for the LORD God of hosts: for the children of Israel have forsaken thy covenant; thrown down thine altars, and slain thy prophets with the sword; and I, even I only, am left; and they seek my life, to take it away."

There was no doubt truth in what he said. He was full of zeal and holy devotion to the cause of God. He had often mourned over the national degeneracy. He keenly felt his own isolation and loneliness. But these were not the reasons why at that moment he was hiding in the cave; nor were they the real answer to that searching question, "What doest thou here, Elijah?"

How often is that question still put! When a person endowed with great faculties

93

digs a hole in the earth, and buries the God-entrusted talent, and then stands idle all day, again the question must be asked, "What doest thou here?"

Life is the time for doing. There is plenty to do. Evil to put down; good to build up; doubters to be directed; prodigals to be won back; sinners to be sought. "What doest thou here?" Up, Christians, leave your caves, and do! Do not do in order to be saved; but being saved, *do!*

2. GOD TAUGHT HIM BY A BEAUTIFUL NATURAL PARABLE. He was commanded to stand at the entrance to the cave. Presently there was the sound of the rushing of a mighty wind; and in another moment a violent tornado swept past. Nothing could withstand its fury. It tore the mountains, and broke in pieces the rocks before the Lord; the valleys were littered with splintered fragments; *but the Lord was not in the wind.* And when the wind had died away, there was an earthquake. The mountain swayed to and fro, yawning and cracking; the ground heaved as if an almighty hand were passing beneath it; *but the Lord was not in the earthquake.* And when the earthquake was over, there was a fire. The heavens were one blaze of light, each pinnacle and peak glowed in the kindling flame; the valley beneath looked like a huge smelting furnace; *but the Lord was not in the fire.*

How strange! Surely these were the appropriate natural symbols of the divine presence. But listen! a still small whisper is in the air—very still, and very small; it touched the listening heart of the prophet. It seemed to be the tender cadence of the love and pity of God that had come in search of him. Its music drew him from the cave, into the innermost recesses of which he had been driven by the terrible convulsions of nature. "And it was so, when Elijah heard it that he wrapped his face in his mantle, and went out, and stood in the entering in of the cave."

What was the meaning of all this? It is not difficult to understand. Elijah was most eager that his people should be restored to their allegiance to God; and he may have spoken often this way with himself: "Those idols will never be swept from our land unless God sends a movement swift and irresistible as the *wind*, which hurries the clouds before it. The land can never be awakened except by a moral *earthquake*. There must be a baptism of *fire*." And when he stood on Carmel, and beheld the panic among the priests and the eagerness among the people, he thought that the time—the set time—had come. But all that died away. That was not God's chosen way of saving Israel.

But in this natural parable God seemed to say: "My child, you have been looking for Me to answer your prayers with striking signs and wonders; and because these have not been given in a marked and permanent form, you have thought Me heedless and inactive. But I am not always to be found in these great visible movements; I love to work gently, softly, and unperceived; I have been working so; I am working so still; and there are in Israel, as the results of My quiet gentle ministry, 'seven thousand, all the knees that have not bowed to Baal, and every mouth that has not kissed him'." Yes, and was not the gentle ministry of Elisha, succeeding the stormy career of his predecessor, like the still small voice after the wind, the earthquake, and the fire? And is it not probable that more real good was effected by his unobtrusive life and miracles than was ever wrought by the splendid deeds of Elijah?

We often fall into similar mistakes. When we wish to promote a revival, we think we need large crowds, much evident impression, powerful preachers; influences com-

BRUISED REED SMOULDERING WICK

parable to the wind, the earthquake, and the fire. But surely Nature herself rebukes us. Who hears the roll of the planets? Who can detect the falling of the dew? Whose eye has ever been injured by the breaking of the wavelets of daylight on the shores of our planet? "There is no speech, nor language; their voice is not heard." At this moment the mightiest forces are in operation around us, but there is nothing to betray their presence. And thus it was with the ministry of the Lord Jesus. He did not strive, nor cry, nor lift up, nor cause His voice to be heard in the streets. He comes down as showers on the mown grass. His Spirit descends as the dove, whose wings make no tremor in the still air. Let us take heart! God may not be working as we expect; but He is working. If not in the wind, then in the breeze. If not in the earthquake, then in the heartbreak. If not in the fire, then in the still, small voice. If not in crowds, then in lonely hearts; in silent tears; in the broken sobs of penitents; and in multitudes who, like the seven thousand of Israel, are unknown as disciples.

But Elijah refused to be comforted. It seemed as if he could not shake off the mood in which he was ensnared. And so when God asked him the second time: "What doest thou here, Elijah?" he answered in the same words with which he had tried to justify himself before. "And he said, I have been very jealous. . . ."

It is pleasant to think of those seven thousand disciples, known only to God. We are sometimes sad as we compare the scanty number of professing Christians with the masses of ungodly. But we may take heart: there are still other Christians. That harsh-seeming governor is a Joseph in disguise. That wealthy owner of the garden in Arimathea is a lowly follower of Jesus. That member of the Sanhedrin is a disciple; but secretly, for fear of the Jews. But if you are one of that number, I urge you, do not remain so: it robs the cause of God of your help and influence; it is an act of treachery to Christ Himself. Beware lest, if you are ashamed of Him, the time may come when He will be ashamed of you.

It is quite true that confession means martyrdom in one form or another; and sometimes our heart and flesh shrink back as we contemplate the possible results of refusing the act of obeisance to Baal. But at such times, let us encourage ourselves by anticipating the august moment when the dear Master will speak our names before assembled worlds, and own us as His. And let us also ask Him in us and through us to speak out and witness a good confession.

13

"Go, Return!"
1 Kings 19

It is a very solemn thought that one sin may forever, so far as this world is concerned, destroy our usefulness. It is not always so. Sometimes—as in the case of the apostle Peter—the Lord graciously restores and recommissions for His work, the one who might have been counted unfit ever again to engage in it. But against this one case we may put three others.

The first case is that of Moses. No other man has ever been honored as was he, "with whom God spake face to face." Yet, because he spoke unadvisedly with his lips, and smote the rock twice, in unbelief and passion, he was compelled to bear the awful sentence: "Because ye believed me not, to sanctify me in the eyes of the children of Israel, therefore ye shall not bring this congregation into the land which I have given them." (Num. 20:12).

The second case is that of Saul, the first, ill-fated king of Israel, whose reign opened so auspiciously, but who soon brought on himself the sentence of deposition. Yet it was only for one single act. Alarmed at Samuel's long delay, and at the scattering of the people, he intruded rashly into a province from which he was expressly excluded, and offered the sacrifice with which the Israelites were ready to prepare for battle. Thus early in his reign Saul was rejected.

The third case is that of Elijah. He was never reinstated in quite the position he had occupied before his fatal flight. True, he was asked to return on his way, and work was indicated for him to do. But that work was the anointing of three men who were to share among them the ministry that he might have fulfilled if only he had been true to his opportunities, and faithful to his God. "Go, return on thy way to the wilderness of Damascus: and when thou comest, anoint Hazael to be king over Syria: and Jehu the son of Nimshi shalt thou anoint to be king over Israel: and Elisha the son of Shaphat of Abelmeholah shalt thou anoint to be prophet in thy room." Those words rang out the death knell of Elijah's fondest dreams. Evidently, he was not to be the deliverer of his people from the thraldom of Baal. Others were to do his work; another was to be prophet in his place.

All those who hold prominent positions among us, as public teachers and leaders, may well take warning by these solemn examples. We may not all be tempted, as Elijah was, to unbelief and discouragement. But there are many other snares prepared for us by our great enemy. Any one of these may compel God to cast us away from His glorious service; employing us only in such humbler ministry or to anoint our successors.

As children, He will never cast us away; but as His servants He may. Let us beware! One false step; one hurried desertion of our post; one act of disobedience; one outburst of passion: any one of these may lead our heavenly Father to throw us aside. But we will never again ride on the crest of the flowing tide. Others will finish our uncompleted task.

But with the danger there are sufficient safeguards. Let God prune you with the golden pruning knife of His holy Word. Offer your spirit constantly to the Holy Spirit, that He may detect and reveal to you the beginnings of idolatries and heart sins. Be jealous of anything that divides your heart with your Lord. Have perpetual recourse for cleansing, to the blood shed for the remission of sin.

But now, turning to the further study of the words with which God dismissed His servant from Horeb, let us notice three distinct thoughts.

1. THE VARIETY OF GOD'S INSTRUMENTS. Hazael, king of Syria; Jehu, the rude captain; and Elisha, the young farmer. Each was as different as possible from the others, and yet each was needed for some special work in connection with that idolatrous people. Hazael was destined to be the rod of divine vengeance to Israel at large. Ah! Cruel indeed was his treatment of them! (2 Kings 8:12; 10:32; 12:3, 17). Jehu was to be the scourge of the house of Ahab, removing its root and branch. Elisha's ministry was to be genial and gentle, as summer rain and evening dew; like the ministry of our Lord Himself, whom he prefigured, and of whom his name significantly spoke.

It is remarkable how God accomplishes His purposes through men who only think of working their own wild way. Their sin is not diminished or condoned because they are executing the designs of heaven; it still stands out in all its malignant deformity. And yet, though they are held accountable for the evil, it is nonetheless evident that they do whatever God's hand and God's counsel determine before to be done.

Men may do evil things against us, for which they will be condemned; and yet those very things, being permitted by the wisdom and love of God, are His messages to us. Before they can reach us, they must pass through His environing, encompassing presence; and if they do, then they are God's will for us: and we must meekly accept our Father's discipline, saying, "Not my will, but thine be done."

2. NO ONE CAN ENTIRELY ESCAPE FROM GOD'S PERSONAL DEALINGS. God's nets are not all constructed with the same meshes. Men may escape through some of them; but they cannot escape through all. "Him that escapeth the sword of Hazael shall Jehu slay: and him that escapeth from the sword of Jehu shall Elisha slay."

We do not read that Elisha ever wielded the sword; and yet the ministry of gentle love is sometimes more potent in slaying souls than the more vigorous ministry of a Hazael or Jehu: and out of such slaying comes life.

And as we look around us on the entire range of ministry by which the world is filled, we may be sure that every one has at least one chance; and that God so orders the lives of men that once at least during their course they are encountered by the kind of argument that is most appropriate to their character and temperament, if only they will give ear and yield.

3. GOD NEVER OVERLOOKS ONE OF HIS OWN. Elijah thought that he alone was left as a lover and worshiper of God. It was a great mistake. God had many hidden followers. We know nothing of their names or history. They were probably unknown in camp or court; obscure, simple-hearted, and humble. Their only testimony was one long refusal to become involved in the foul rites of idolatry. But they were all known to God; He cared for them with an infinite solicitude; and it was for their sake that He raised up the good and gentle Elisha to carry on the nurture and discipline of their souls.

It has often been a subject of wonder to me how these seven thousand secret disciples could keep so close as to be unknown by their great leader. It is to be feared that the godliness of these hidden followers was very vague and colorless, needing the eye of omniscience to detect it. But for all that, God did detect it.

You may be very weak and insignificant and yet, if you have but a spark of faith and love, if you strive to keep yourself untainted by the world, you will be owned by Him. But remember: if your inner life is genuine, it will not remain forever secret—it will break out as a long-hidden fire; it will force its way into the light as the buried seed in which there is the spark of life.

It may be that God, by these lines, will speak to some backslider, saying: Go, return! Return to Me, from whom you have wandered. Return to My work, which you have deserted. Return to the posture of faith from which you have fallen. "Return, ye backsliding children; and I will heal your backslidings." Oh, that the response may be, "Behold, we come to Thee; for Thou art the Lord our God!"

14

Naboth's Vineyard
1 Kings 21

In a room of the palace, Ahab, king of Israel, lies upon his couch, his face toward the wall, refusing to eat. What has taken place? Has disaster befallen the royal arms? Is his royal consort dead? No; the soldiers are still flushed with their recent victories over Syria. The worship of Baal has quite recovered the terrible disaster of Carmel; Jezebel—resolute, crafty, cruel, and beautiful—is now standing by his side, anxiously seeking the cause of this sadness.

The story is soon told. Jezreel was the Windsor of Israel; and there stood the favorite residence of the royal house. On a certain occasion, while Ahab was engaged there, his eye lighted on a neighboring vineyard, belonging to Naboth the Jezreelite; which promised to be so valuable an addition to his property that he resolved to procure it at all cost. He therefore sent for Naboth and offered either a better vineyard in exchange or the worth of it in money. To his surprise and indignation, Naboth refused both. And Naboth said to Ahab, "The LORD forbid it me, that I should give the inheritance of my fathers unto thee."

At first sight this refusal seems churlish and uncourteous. But by the law of Moses, Canaan was considered as being, in a peculiar sense, God's land. The Israelites were His tenants; and one of the conditions of their tenure was, that they should not alienate that which fell to their lot, except in cases of extreme necessity; and then only until the year of Jubilee. Naboth anticipated that if it once passed out of his hands, his patrimony would become merged in the royal possession, never to be released. Taking his stand then on religious grounds, he might well say: "The Lord forbids me to do it." His refusal was in part, therefore, a religious act.

But there was, without doubt, something more. In his mention of "the inheritance of his fathers," we have the suggestion of another, and most natural reason, for his reluctance; his fathers had for generations sat beneath those vines and trees; there he had spent the sunny years of childhood. He felt that all the juice ever pressed from all the vineyards of the neighborhood would never compensate him for the heartache from those clustered memories.

Naboth's refusal made Ahab leap into his chariot and drive back to Samaria; and turn his face to the wall in a sulk, "heavy and displeased." At the close of the previous chapter (1 Kings 20:43) we learned that he was displeased with God; now he is agitated by the same strong passions toward man. In a few more days the horrid deed of murder was perpetrated; which at one stroke removed Naboth, his sons, and his heirs, and left the unclaimed property to fall naturally into the royal hands. There are many lessons here that would claim our notice if we were dealing with the whole story, but we must pass them by, to center our attention exclusively on the part played by Elijah amid these terrible translations.

1. HE WAS CALLED BACK TO SERVICE. How many years had elapsed since the word of the Lord had last come to Elijah, we do not know. Perhaps five or six. All this while he must have waited wistfully for the well-known accents of that voice, longing to hear it once again. And as the weary days, passing slowly by, prolonged his deferred hope into

deep and yet deeper regret, he must have been driven to continued soul-questionings and searchings of heart; to bitter repentance for the past, and to renewed consecration for whatever service might be imposed on him.

It may be that these words will be read by some, once prominent in Christian service, who have lately been cast aside. The Great Master has a perfect right to do as He will with His own, and takes up one and lays down another; but we should inquire whether the reason may not lie within our own hearts; in some inconsistency or sin that needs confession and forgiveness at the hands of our faithful and merciful High Priest, before ever again the world of the Lord can come to us.

It is also possible that we are left unused for our own deeper teaching in the ways of God. Hours, and even years, of silence are full of golden opportunities for the servants of God. In such cases, our conscience does not condemn us or accost us with any sufficient reason arising from ourselves. Our simple duty then is to keep clean, and filled, and ready; standing on the shelf, meet for the Master's use; sure that we serve if we only stand and wait; and knowing that He will accept, and reward, the willingness for the deed.

2. ELIJAH WAS NOT DISOBEDIENT. Once before, when his presence was urgently required, he had arisen to flee for his life. But there was no vacillation, no cowardice now. He arose and went down to the vineyard of Naboth, and entered it to find the royal criminal. It was nothing to him that there rode behind Ahab's chariot two ruthless captains, Jehu and Bidkar (2 Kings 9:25). He did not for a moment consider that the woman who had threatened his life before might now take it, maddened as she was with her recent spilling of human blood. Who does not rejoice that Elijah had such an opportunity of wiping out the dark stain of disgrace. His time of waiting had not been lost on him!

3. HE WAS ACTING AS AN INCARNATE CONSCIENCE. Naboth was out of the way; and Ahab may have comforted himself, as weak people do still, with the idea that he was not his murderer. How could he be? He had been perfectly quiet. He had simply put his face to the wall and done nothing. He did remember that Jezebel had asked him for his royal seal, to give validity to some letters that she had written in his name, but then how was he to know what she had written? Of course if she had given instruction for Naboth's death it was a great pity, but it could not now be helped; and he might as well take possession of the inheritance! With such excuses he succeeded in stilling the fragment of conscience that alone survived in his heart. And it was then that he was startled by a voice he had not heard for years, saying, "Thus saith the LORD, Hast thou killed, and also taken possession?" "Hast thou killed?" The prophet, guided by the Spirit of God, put the burden on the right shoulders.

If an employer, by paying an inadequate and unjust wage, tempts his employees to supplement their scanty pittance by dishonest methods, he is held responsible, in the sight of heaven, for the evil he might have prevented if he had not been wilfully and criminally indifferent.

Acts of high-handed sin often seem at first to prosper. Naboth meekly dies; the earth sucks in his blood; the vineyard passes into the oppressor's hands; but there is One who sees and will most certainly avenge the cause of His servants. "Surely I have seen yesterday the blood of Naboth, and the blood of his sons, saith the LORD; and I will requite thee in this plat" (2 Kings 9:26). That vengeance may tarry, for the mills of God grind slowly; but it will come as certainly as God is God. And in the meanwhile in Naboth's vineyard stands Elijah the prophet. This lesson is enforced again and again by our great dramatist, who teaches men who will not read their Bibles that sin does not pay in the end; that however successful it may seem at first, in the end it has to reckon with an Elijah as conscience and with God as an avenger—and He never misses His mark.

4. HE WAS HATED FOR THE TRUTH'S SAKE. "And Ahab said to Elijah, Hast thou found me, O mine enemy?" Though the king did not know it, Elijah was his best friend; Jezebel his direst foe. But sin distorts everything.

When Christian friends remonstrate with evildoers, and rebuke their sins, and warn them of their doom, they are hated and denounced as enemies. The Bible is detested, because it so clearly exposes sin and its consequences. It cannot be otherwise.

Let us not be surprised if we are hated. Let us even be thankful when men detest us—not for ourselves, but for the truths we speak. Let us "rejoice, and be exceeding glad." When bad men think thus of us, it is an indication that our influence is opposite their lives.

5. HE WAS A TRUE PROPHET. Each of the woes that Elijah foretold came true. Ahab postponed their fulfillment, by a partial repentance, for some three years; but at the end of that time he went back to his evil ways, and every item was literally fulfilled. He was wounded by a "chance" arrow at Ramoth-gilead, "and the blood ran out of the wound into the midst of the chariot"; and as they washed his chariot in the fountain of Samaria, the dogs licked his blood. Twenty years later there was nothing of Jezebel left for burial; only her skull, and feet, and palms escaped the voracious dogs as she lay exposed on that very spot. The corpse of Joram, their son, was cast forth unburied on that same plot, at the command of Jehu, who never forgot those memorable words. God is true, not only to His promises, but also to His threats.

Every word spoken by Elijah was literally fulfilled. The passing years amply vindicated him. And as we close this tragic episode in his career, we rejoice to learn that he was stamped again with the divine imprimatur of trustworthiness and truth.

15

The Old Courage Again
2 Kings 1

In order to understand the striking episode before us, we must not judge by our own high standards of forgiveness and love, learned in the life and death of Jesus Christ, the last and supreme revelation of God.

The Old Testament brims with striking teaching of the holiness and righteousness of God. God, our Father, was as merciful and long-suffering then as now; and there were given many sweet glimpses of His loving heart. But men cannot take in too many thoughts at once. Line must be on line, precept on precept. And so each preliminary age had some one special truth to teach. The age of the Mosaic Law, which shed its empire over the times of Elijah, was preeminently the era in which those awful and splendid attributes of the divine character—God's holiness, justice, righteousness, and severity against sin—stood out in massive prominence. It was only when those lessons had been completely learned that mankind was able to appreciate the love of God that is in Jesus Christ our Lord.

Critics—who insensibly have caught their conceptions of infinite love from the gospels that they say they despise—find fault with the Old Testament because of it austere tones and its severe enactments. They point out many things inconsistent with the gentler spirit of our times. There is nothing surprising here! It could not have been otherwise, in a gradual unfolding of the nature and character of God. The holy men who lived in those days had never heard the gentle voice of the Son of Man speaking the Sermon on the Mount. They had, however, very definite conceptions of the righteousness and holiness of God, and His swift indignation on sin. This stimulated them to do deeds from which our nature shrinks. But for this, Levi had never slain his brethren, or Joshua the Canaanites; Samuel had never hewed Agag in pieces before the Lord; and Elijah had never presumed to slay the priests of Baal or call down fire from heaven to destroy the captians and their men.

And, as we read these deeds, we may well sink into quiet self-questioning. We do well to ask whether, granting that we forego the outward manifestation, there is the same hatred of sin, the same zeal for the glory of God, the same inveterate enthusiasm for righteousness—as there was in those days of force, and decision, and unswerving righteousness.

These considerations will help us to understand the narrative that awaits us, and will relieve the character of Elijah from the charge of vindictiveness and passion, so that we can consider, without compunction, the rising up again in his breast of something of his old undaunted courage and heroic bearing.

Ahaziah, the son of Ahab, had succeeded to his father's throne and his father's sins. He shrank in cowardly fear from the hardihood of the camp and the dangers of the field, leaving Moab to rebel, without attempting its resubjugation, and leading a self-indulgent life in his palace. But the shafts of death can find us in apparent security as well as amid threatening dangers. He was leaning on the railing that fenced the flat roof of the palace, when suddenly it gave way, and he was flung to the ground. When the first panic was over, the king sent messengers to one of the ancient shrines of Canaan, dedicated to Baalzebub, the god of flies, the patron saint of medicine, who had some affinity with the Baal of his parents. This was a deliberate rejection of Jehovah; it could not pass unnoticed; and Elijah was sent to meet his messengers as they were speeding across the plain of Esdraelon, with the announcement of certain death: "Thus saith the LORD, thou shalt not come down off that bed on which thou art gone up, but shalt surely die."

The servants did not know the stranger. However, they were so impressed by that commanding figure and authoritative tone, and so awed by that terrible reply, that they determined to return at once to the king. And they told him the reason of their speedy return. Ahaziah must have guessed who he was who had dared to cross their path, and send him such a message. But, to make assurance surer, he asked them to describe the mysterious stranger. They replied that he was "a man of hair." Long and heavy tresses of unshorn hair hung heavily down on his shoulders; his beard covered his breast, and mingled with the rough skins that formed his only dress. It was enough; the king recognized him at once, and said, "It is Elijah the Tishbite."

Two emotions now filled his heart. He wanted, in exasperation, to get Elijah in his power, to vent on him his wrath, and he perhaps cherished a secret hope that the lips that had announced his death might be induced to revoke it. He therefore resolved to capture him, and for that purpose sent a captain and a troop of fifty soldiers; and when they were struck down in death, another captain and his band. "Thou man of God, the king hath said, Come down!"

There was no personal vindictiveness in the terrible reply of the old prophet. I believe he was filled with consuming zeal for the glory of God, which had been trodden so rudely under foot. "If I be a man of God, let fire come down from heaven, and consume thee and thy fifty." And in a moment the fire came down and laid the impious blasphemers low. That there was no malice in Elijah is clear from his willingness to go with the third captain, who spoke with reverence and humility. "And the angel of the Lord said, Go down with him; be not afraid of him. And Elijah went down with him unto the king."

1. A THOUGHT IS SUGGESTED HERE OF THE MEEKNESS AND GENTLENESS OF CHRIST. How wonderful it is to think that He who, by a single word, could have brought fire from heaven to destroy the soldiers who came to take Him in Gethsemane, but left that word unspoken. He threw them on the ground for a moment, to show them how absolutely they were in His power; but He held back from touching one hair of their heads. He was under the compulsion of a higher law—the law of His Father's will; the law of self-sacrificing love; the law of a covenant sealed before the foundation of the world.

The only fire He sought was the fire of the Holy Ghost. Oh, matchless meekness! Oh, wondrous self-control! May grace be given to each of us, His unworthy followers, to walk in His steps, and to emulate His spirit; not calling for the fire of vengeance, but seeking the salvation of those who would do us hurt; dealing out not the fire of heaven, but those coals of fire, heaped on the head of our adversaries, which shall melt them into sweetness, and gentleness, and love.

2. THERE IS ALSO SUGGESTED HERE THE IMPOSSIBILITY OF GOD EVER CONDONING DEFIANT AND BLASPHEMOUS SIN. It is true that God yearns over men with unutterable pleading tenderness. "He is not willing that any should perish; but that all should come to repentance" (2 Peter 3:9). In every outbreak of human sin, in the lot of every lost man and woman, over every street fight, at every tavern doorstep, amid the blasphemous orgies of every den of impurity and shame—that love lingers, full of tears, and longings, and entreaties. "God so loved the world."

And yet, side by side with this love to the sinner, there is God's hatred of his sin. This longsuffering lasts only so long as there is a possible hope of the transgressor turning from his evil ways. The wrath of God against sinful men, who have definitely elected their sin, slumbers only; it is not dead. It broods over them, held back by His desire to give every one the chance of salvation. Yet the time of forbearance will end at last, as the waiting did in the days of Noah. Then fire will fall, of which the material flame that fell on these soldiers is a slight and imperfect symbol. And it will be discovered how bitter a thing it is to encounter the wrath of the Lamb, "when the Lord Jesus shall be revealed from heaven with his mighty angels, in flaming fire taking vengeance on them that know not God, and obey not the gospel of our Lord Jesus Christ" (2 Thess. 1:1–8).

We need more proclamation of this side of the gospel. There is an alarming lack among us of the sense of sin. Our vast populations are indifferent to the message of mercy, because they have not been aroused with the message of the holy wrath of God against sin. We need again to have one come in the power of Elijah to do the work of John the Baptist, and to prepare men by the throes of conviction for the gentle ministry of Jesus Christ. The crying need of our times is a deeper conviction of sin. Then when Elijah's fire of conviction has smitten human confidences low in the dust, there will be room for an Elisha to bind up broken hearts with the message of mercy.

3. WE ARE ALSO ASSURED OF ELIJAH'S FULL RESTORATION TO THE EXERCISE OF A GLORIOUS FAITH. Some time earlier the message of Jezebel was enough to make him flee. But in this case he stood his ground, though an armed band came to capture him. And when he was told to go down with the third captain to the king he did not hesitate, though it was to go through the streets of the crowded capital and into the very palace of his foes. Do you ask the secret, and why he was able to stand so calmly beside the bed of the dying monarch, delivering his message, and leaving unharmed? Ah, the answer is not far away. He was again dwelling in the secret of the Most High and standing in the presence of Jehovah. His faith was in lively and victorious exercise. He was able to gird himself with the panoply of God's armor, invulnerable to the darts of men and devils.

Is it not beautiful to behold this glorious outburst of the faith of Cherith, Zarephath, and Carmel? The old man, nearing his reward, was as vigorous in this as in his first challenge to Ahab. Glory be to Him who restores the soul of His faltering saints, and desires to use them once more in His glorious service!

16

Evensong
2 Kings 2

In God's gracious providence it fell to Elijah that after a life full of storm and tempest, at eventide there was light and peace and rest. It was as if the spirit of the world he was about to enter were already shedding its spell over his path.

There is always something beautiful in the declining years of one who in earlier life has dared nobly and been successful. The old force still gleams in the eye, but its rays are tempered by that tenderness for human frailty, and that deep self-knowledge that years alone can yield. Such an evening to life seems to have been Elijah's, and it must have been comforting to him that there was granted a time of comparative calm at the close of his tempestuous career.

Those years of retirement were valuable in the highest degree, both in their immediate results on hundreds of young lives, and in their far-off results on the future.

1. THE WORK OF THE CLOSING YEARS OF ELIJAH'S LIFE. His life has been called a "One-man Ministry"; and this one man was, as Elisha exclaimed, "The chariot of Israel, and the horsemen thereof." He made his age. Towering above all the men of his time by heroic exploits and by deeds of superhuman might he battled singlehanded against the tides of idolatry and sin that were sweeping over the land.

Though largely successful in keeping the cause of true religion from dying out, Elijah must often have realized the desirability of carrying on the work more systematically, and of leavening the country more thoroughly with the influence of devoted men. So, under divine direction, he carefully fostered, if he did not altogether inaugurate, the "schools of the prophets." When we use the word "prophet," we think of it as indicating a person who can foretell the future; and thus much confusion is introduced into our reading of Scripture. It includes this idea as a fragment of a larger meaning. The original word means "boiling or bubbling over"; and so a prophet was one whose heart was bubbling over with good matter, and with those divine communications that struggled within him for utterance. He was the mouthpiece and spokesman of God. So these schools of the prophets were colleges in which a number of young men gathered, their hearts open to receive and their tongues to utter the messages of God.

In his declining years Elijah gathered around him the flower of the seven thousand, and educated them to receive and transmit something of his own spiritual force and fire. These were the missionary seminaries of the age.

These young men were formed into separate companies of fifty, in different towns. They were called "sons"; the chief among them, like the *abbot* of a monastery, was called "father." Clad in a simple dress, they had their food in common, and dwelled in huts slightly made of the branches of trees. They were well-versed in the sacred books which they probably transcribed for circulation and read in the hearing of the people. They were frequently sent forth on the errands of God's Spirit—to anoint a king, to upbraid a high-handed sinner, or to take the part of oppressed and injured innocence. It was therefore no small work for Elijah to put these schools on so secure a basis that, when he was gone, they might perpetuate his influence and guard the flames he had kindled.

2. THE ATTITUDE OF HIS SPIRIT IN ANTICIPATING HIS TRANSLATION TO GLORY. We are deeply impressed by the calmness of spirit of the prophet's closing days. He knew that before many suns had set he would be standing in the light of eternity, mingling with his peers, understanding all the mysteries that had puzzled his eager spirit, and beholding the face of God. But he spent the days, as he had often spent them before, visiting the schools of the prophets, and quietly conversing with his friend until the chariot swept him from his side. And as we consider that scene we learn that a good man should so live that he need make no extra preparation when death suddenly summons him; and that our best method of awaiting the great exchange of worlds is to go on doing the duties of daily life.

Wesley gave a wise and true reply to the question, "What would you do if you knew that you would have to die within three days?" "I should just do the work which I have already planned to do: ministering in one place; meeting my preachers in another; lodging in yet another, till the moment came that I was called to yield my spirit back to Him who gave it." When our summons comes, we should wish to be found just doing the work we have been appointed to do, and in the place where duty would demand our presence at that hour. The workshop and the factory are as near heaven as the sanctuary; the God-given task as fair a height for ascension as Olivet or Pisgah.

3. THE AFFECTIONATE LOVE WITH WHICH ELIJAH WAS REGARDED. It strongly showed itself in Elisha. In spite of many persuasions to the contrary, he went with him down the steep descent to Bethel and Jericho. The sacred historian accentuates the strength of

their affection as he says three times, *they two* went on; *they two* stood by Jordan; *they two* went over. And again the strength of that love approved itself in the repeated acclamation: "As the LORD liveth, and as thy soul liveth, I will not leave thee." It is sweet to think that there were in the rugged strong nature of Elijah such winsome qualities as could elicit so deep and tenacious an affection. We catch a glimpse of a more tender side for which we had hardly given him credit.

Unusual emotion also welled up in the hearts of the young men whose reverence shared the empire with their love, as they beheld their master for the last time. With delicate reticence they would not speak on a subject that he did not mention, but drawing Elisha aside, they asked him whether the moment of separation had not come. "Yes," he said in effect, "but do not speak of it. Let there be no parting scene. Give and receive the parting farewells in expressive silence." And thus the old man tore himself away from them.

But in all their intercourse, how real and near the Lord seemed! To Elijah it was the Lord who was sending him from place to place. To Elisha it was the living Lord to whom he constantly appealed; living on the other side of the great change through which his master was to pass to Him. To the prophets, it was the Lord who was taking their head and leader to Himself. Surely those who speak thus have reached a position in which they can meet death without a tremor. And what is death but, as we shall see in our next chapter, a translation!

What is the Lord to you? Is He a dear and familiar friend, of whom you can speak with unwavering confidence? Then you need not fear to walk Jordan's shore. Otherwise, it becomes you to get to His precious blood, and to wash your garments white, that you may have right to the tree of life, and may enter in through the gates into the city.

17

The Translation
2 Kings 2

We have reached at length one of the most sublime scenes of Old Testament story. We would have been glad to learn the most minute particulars concerning it, but the historian contents himself with the simplest statements. Just one or two broad, strong outlines, and all is told that we may know. The veil of distance, or the elevation of the hills, was enough to hide the receding figures of the prophets from the eager gaze of the group that watched them from the neighborhood of Jericho. And the dazzling glory of the celestial cortege made the only spectator unable to scrutinize it too narrowly. What wonder, then, if the narrative is given in three brief sentences! "They still went on, and talked, that, behold, there appeared a chariot of fire, and horses of fire, and parted them both asunder; and Elijah went up by a whirlwind into heaven."

The two friends halted for a moment before the broad waters of the Jordan, which threatened to bar their onward steps; and Elijah took off his well-worn mantle, and wrapped it together and struck the waters, and they parted here and there, leaving a clear passage through which they went.

Elijah

1. THE FITNESS OF THIS TRANSLATION.

a. *There was fitness in the place.* Not Esdraelon, not Sinai, not the schools of Gilgal, Bethel, or Jericho; but amid the scenery familiar to his early life; in view of localities forever associated with the most memorable events of his nation's history; surrounded by the lonely grandeur of some rocky gorge—*there God chose to send His chariot to bring Elijah home.*

b. *There was fitness in the method.* He had himself been as the whirlwind that sweeps all before it in its impetuous course, leaving devastation and ruin in its track. It was fitting that a whirlwind-man should sweep to heaven in the very element of his life. Nothing could be more appropriate than that the stormy energy of his career should be set forth in the rush of the whirlwind, and the intensity of his spirit by the fire that flashed in the harnessed seraphim. What a contrast to the gentle upward motion of the ascending Savior!

c. *There was fitness in the exclamation* with which Elisha bade him farewell. He cried, "My father, my father! the chariot of Israel, and the horsemen thereof!" That man, whom he had come to love as a father, had indeed been as an armed chariot of defense to Israel. Alas, that such men are rare! But in our time we have known them, and when they have been suddenly swept from our side we have felt as if the church had been deprived of one main source of security and help.

2. THE REASONS FOR THIS TRANSLATION.

a. *One of the chief reasons was, no doubt, as a witness to his times.* The men of his day had little thought of the hereafter. At the very best the Jews had but vague notions of the other life. But here a convincing evidence was given that there was a spiritual world into which the righteous entered; and that, when the body sank in death, the spirit did not share its fate, but entered into a state of being in which its noblest instincts found their befitting environment and home—fire to fire; spirit to spirit; the man of God to God.

A similar testimony was given to the men of his time by the rapture of Enoch before the Flood, and by the ascension of our Lord from the brow of Olivet. Where did these three wondrous journeys end, unless there was a destination that was their befitting terminus and goal? And as the tidings spread, thrilling all listeners with mysterious awe, would there not break on them the conviction that they likewise would have to take that wondrous journey into the unseen, soaring beyond all worlds, or sinking into the bottomless pit?

b. *Another reason was evidently the desire on the part of God to give a striking sanction to His servant's words.* How easy it was for the men of that time to evade the force of Elijah's ministry by asserting that he was an enthusiast, an alarmist, a firebrand! And if he had passed away in decrepit old age, they would have been still further encouraged in their impious conjecturings. But the mouths of blasphemers and gainsayers were stopped when God put such a conspicuous seal on His servant's ministry. The translation was to the life work of Elijah what the resurrection was to that of Jesus—it was God's undeniable testimony to the world.

3. THE LESSONS OF THIS TRANSLATION FOR OURSELVES.

a. *Let us take care not to dictate to God.* This was the man who lay down on the ground and asked to die. How good it was of God to refuse him the answer he craved! Was it not better to pass away, missed and beloved, in the chariot his Father had sent for him?

This is no doubt one reason why our prayers go unanswered. We do not know what we ask. When next your request is denied, reflect that it may be because God is preparing something for you as much better than your request as the translation of Elijah was better than his petition for himself.

b. *Let us learn what death is*. It is a translation: we pass through a doorway; we cross a bridge of smiles; we flash from the dark into the light. There is no interval of unconsciousness, no parenthesis of suspended animation. "Absent from the body," we are instantly "present with the Lord." As by the single act of birth we entered into this lower life, so by the single act—which men call death, but which angels call birth (for Christ is the firstborn from among the dead)—we pass into the real life. The fact that Elijah appeared on the Mount of Transfiguration in holy communion with Moses and with Christ proves that the blessed dead are really the living ones, and they entered that life in a single moment, the moment of death.

Was it not some reference to this august event that was in the mind of the great Welsh preacher Christmas Evans who, when dying, majestically waved his hand to the bystanders, and looked upward with a smile, and uttered these last words, *"Drive on!"* "The chariots of God are twenty thousand."

18

A Double Portion of Elijah's Spirit
2 Kings 2

We are told that, after they had passed the Jordan, the two friends *went on and talked*. They must have discussed sublime themes as they stood on the very confines of heaven, and in the vestibule of eternity! The apostasy of Israel and its approaching doom; the ministry just closing, with its solemn warnings; the outlook toward the work on which Elisha was preparing to enter—these and cognate subjects must have occupied them.

It was in the course of this conversion that "Elijah said unto Elisha, Ask what I shall do for thee, before I be taken away from thee." It was a very wide door flung open by the elder to his younger friend.

1. ELISHA'S LARGE REQUEST. Elisha sought neither wealth, nor position, nor worldly power, nor a share in those advantages on which he had turned his back forever when he said farewell to home, and friends, and worldly prospects. "And Elisha said, I pray thee, let a double portion of thy spirit be upon me."

What did Elisha mean by this request? He was asking that he might be considered as Elijah's eldest son; the heir to his spirit, the successor to his work. There is a passage in the law of Moses that clearly proves that the "double portion" was the right of the firstborn and heir (Deut. 21:17). This the prophet sought; and this he certainly obtained.

It was a noble request! Elisha was evidently called to carry on Elijah's work, but he felt that he dare not undertake its responsibilities or face its inevitable perils unless he were especially equipped with spiritual power.

We need not shrink from attempting Elijah's work if first we have received Elijah's spirit. There is no work to which God calls us for which He has not prepared us to qualify. Let it never be forgotten that Elijah himself did what he did, not by inherent qualities, but because through faith he had received such gracious bestowments of the Spirit of God; and what he did we may do again—the weakest and humblest may do—if only we are prepared to wait, and watch, and pray, until our Pentecost breaks on us with or without its sound of rushing wind and its tongues of flaming fire.

2. LET US CLEARLY UNDERSTAND THE TWO CONDITIONS IMPOSED ON ELISHA.

a. *Tenacity of purpose.* Elijah tested it severely at every step of that farewell journey. Repeatedly he said, "Tarry here." But Elisha knew what he sought; he read the meaning of the discipline to which he was being exposed; and his heroic resolution grew with the ordeal, as the waters of a stream grow against an arresting dam until they overleap it and rush forward on their way.

How often we persuade ourselves that we can acquire the greatest spiritual blessings without paying the equivalent price! Thus James and John thought that they could obtain a seat each on the throne for the asking. They did not realize that the cross preceded the crown; and that the bitter cup of Gethsemane lay between them and the coronation anthem. We must pass through the Jordan; we must daily take up the cross and follow Jesus; we must be conformed to Him in the likeness of His death, and in the fellowship of His sufferings; the divine will must be lovingly accepted, though it cost tears of blood and bitter sorrow. Then, having evinced the steadfastness of our purpose, we will prove ourselves worthy to be the recipients of God's supreme gift.

b. *Spiritual insight.* "If thou see me when I am taken from thee, it shall be so unto thee; but if not, it shall not be so." There was nothing arbitrary in this demand. To see the transactions of the spirit world requires a spirit of no ordinary purity, and of no ordinary faith. No mere mortal eye could have beheld that fiery cortege. To senses dulled with passion, or blinded by materialism, the space occupied by the flaming seraphim would have seemed devoid of any special interest, and bare as the rest of the surrounding scenery. Perhaps there was not another individual in all Israel with heart pure enough, or spiritual nature sharp enough, to have been sensible of that glorious visitation. But since Elisha saw it all, it is clear that his passions were under control; his temper refined; and his spiritual life healthy.

3. THE ANSWER. "He took up also the mantle of Elijah that fell from him." Ah, that falling mantle! How much it meant! It is said that the bestowal of the mantle has always been considered by Eastern people an indispensable part of consecration to a sacred office. When therefore Elijah's mantle fluttered to Elisha's feet, he knew at once that heaven itself had ratified his request. He believed that he was anointed with Elijah's power.

If, in patience and faith, we claim of our Father the filling of the Holy Ghost, we must never ask ourselves *if we feel full.* We must believe that God has kept His word with us, and that we are filled, though no celestial sign accompanies the entering glory of that power. But others will become aware of the presence of something that we never had before, as they see us stand by some tameless Jordan and behold the turbulent waters part here and there before our stroke.

As soon as we receive some great spiritual endowment, we may expect to have it tested. It was so with Elisha. "He went back, and stood by the bank of Jordan." Did he hesitate? If so, it was but for a moment. He had seen Elijah go; and he believed that therefore the double portion of his spirit had fallen to him. He therefore acted on the assurance of his faith. "He took the mantle of Elijah that fell from him, and smote the waters, and said, Where is the LORD God of Elijah? and when he also had smitten the waters, they parted hither and thither: and Elisha went over. And when the sons of the prophets which were to view at Jericho saw him, they said, The Spirit of Elijah doth rest on Elisha."

"Where is the LORD God of Elijah?" That cry has often been raised when the church, bereft of its leaders, has stood face to face with some great and apparently insuperable difficulty. And sometimes there has been more of despair than hope in the cry. But though Elijah goes, Elijah's God remains. He takes His weary workers home; but He is careful to provide replacements, and to anoint others to carry on their work. Catch up the mantle of the departed. Emulate their lives. Seek their spirit. Smite the bitter waves of difficulty in unwavering faith: and you will find that the Lord God of Elijah will do as much for you as for the saints who have been swept to their reward, and are now mingling with the great cloud of witnesses that are watching your conflicts, your triumphs, and your joys.

19

The Transfiguration
Luke 9

Wearied with His toils, and requiring time for private intercourse with His friends, to prepare them for the approaching tragedy of which they were strangely unconscious, Jesus traveled northward with His disciples, avoiding the larger towns, until they reached one of the smaller villages, nestled on the lower slopes of Mount Hermon.

After eight days, Jesus took with Him Peter, James, and John; and as the evening shadows darkened over the world, He led them up to some neighboring summit, removed from the sight and sound of men. He went to brace Himself for the coming conflict by prayer, and perhaps for the earlier part of the night the favored three provided Him fellowship. But they soon grew weary; and presently, as afterward in Gethsemane, they were sound asleep—though dimly conscious of their Master's presence as He poured out His soul with strong cryings and tears. We do not know how many hours elapsed before they were suddenly startled from their slumbers—not by the gentle touch of morning light, but beneath the stroke of the unbearable glory that streamed from their Master's person. The fashion of His countenance was altered; "His face did shine as the sun." It was not lit up as that of Moses was by reflection from without; but was illumined from within as if the hidden glory of Shekinah, too long concealed, were bursting through the frail veil of flesh. "His raiment"—the common homespun of the country—"became white and [dazzling]." It was more resplendent than the glistening snow above, and was as though angels had woven it of light. But perhaps the greatest marvel of all was the presence of the august pair, "which were Moses and [Elijah]; who appeared in glory, and spake of his decease [His exodus] which he should accomplish at Jerusalem."

1. CONSIDER THE PROBABLE REASONS WHY THESE TWO, AND ESPECIALLY ELIJAH, WERE CHOSEN ON THIS SUBLIME OCCASION.

a. *The first reason might have been that they should attest the dignity of the Lord Jesus.* He was approaching the darkest hour of His career, when His son would set in an ocean of ignominy and shame; heaven itself was astir to assure His friends and to convince the world of His intrinsic worth. Should seraphs be commissioned? No; for men would simply be dazzled. Better far to send back some of the human family, whose illustrious deeds still lived in the memory of mankind, giving weight to their witness. Yet who should be selected?

There might have been good to send the first Adam to attest the supreme dignity of the second; or Abraham, the father of those who believe. But their claims were waived in favor of these two, who might have more weight with the men of that time, as representing the two great departments of Jewish thought and Scripture: Moses the founder of the Law; Elijah the greatest of the prophets.

It is impossible to exaggerate the prominence given to Elijah in the Jewish mind. At the circumcision of a child, a seat was always placed for him; and at the annual celebration of the Passover in each home, wine was placed for him to drink. It was universally believed that he was to come again to announce the advent of the Messiah. It would therefore have great weight with these disciples, and through them to later ages, to feel that he had stood beside Jesus of Nazareth offering Him homage and help. And it was partly the memory of the allegiance given by Elijah to his Master that led Peter to say, years later, that he had been an eyewitness of His majesty.

b. *Another reason may be found in the peculiar circumstances under which they left the world.* Moses died, not by disease, or by natural decay, but beneath the kiss of God. His spirit passed painlessly and mysteriously to glory, while God buried his body. Elijah did not die. Disease and old age had nothing to do in taking down the fabric of his being. We may not penetrate into the secrets of that mysterious border these two passed and repassed in their holy ministry to the Savior's spirit; but we feel that there was something in the method of their departure from our world that made that passage easier.

c. *Yet another reason is suggested in the evident fulfillment of their ministry.* They had been originally sent to prepare for Christ. "We have found him," said Philip, "of whom Moses in the law and the prophets did write." "Moses," said Jesus, "wrote of me." But the Jews were in danger of forgetting this, and of attaching more importance to the messengers than was justifiable. It was the death warrant of Stephen, that he seemed to them to slight the Old Testament, by hinting that it would be abrogated and superseded by the New. Peter himself was quite prepared to treat Moses and Elijah on an equality with his Master, by building three tabernacles. Therefore Moses and Elijah were swept away by a cloud, and "Jesus only" was left; and the voice of God was heard insisting that Peter and the two other disciples should listen to Him alone. It was as though God had said: "As you have listened to the Law and the Prophets, so now listen to My Son. Do not put yourselves again under the law, or rest content with the prophets, however lofty their ideals and burning their words; but pass from the anticipation to the reality; from the type to the perfect fulfillment."

2. CONSIDER THE THEME ON WHICH THEY SPOKE. They spoke not of the latest tidings of heaven, nor of their own wondrous past; nor of the distant future. They spoke of the decease (exodus) He was to experience so soon at Jerusalem.

Heaven was full of this theme. Angels were absorbed in wonder, awe, and love, as they watched each step toward the destined goal. May we not imagine all the life of heaven arrested and pausing before that stupendous tragedy? It was natural then that these latest comers from those shores should talk of the one all-engrossing topic in the land they had left.

Their own salvation depended on the issue of that wondrous death. If ever there were men who might have stood a chance of being accepted on their own merits, surely these were such. But they had no merits of their own. Their only hope of salvation lay where ours does—in His overcoming the sharpness of death, and opening the kingdom of heaven to all believers.

And surely our Lord would lead them to dwell on a theme so constantly present to His mind. He had always anticipated the hour of His death. It was for this He had been born. But now it seemed very near. He stood within the shadow of the cross. And it must have been an encouragement to Him to talk with these lofty spirits of the various aspects of the joy that was set before Him. Moses might remind Him that if, as God's Lamb, He must die, yet as God's Lamb He would redeem countless souls. Elijah might dwell on the glory that would be given to the Father.

Let us learn how men view the work of Christ in the light of eternity. They do not dwell primarily on the mystery of the holy Incarnation, or on the philanthropy of His life, or on the insight of His teachings. All these things are dwarfed by comparison with His death. That is His masterpiece. Here the attributes of God find their most complete and most harmonious exemplification. Here the problem of human sin and salvation are met and solved. The nearer we get to the cross, and the more we meditate on the death accomplished at Jerusalem, the closer we will come into the center of things; the deeper will be our harmony with ourselves, and all other noble spirits, and God himself. Climb that mountain often, in holy reverie; and remember that in all the universe there is no spirit more deeply interested in the mysteries and meaning of our Savior's death than that noble prophet who now seeks no higher honor than to stand forever near to the beloved Master, as he did, for one brief space, on the Transfiguration Mount.

20

"Filled With the Holy Ghost"
Luke 1:15, 17

What can we do in our brief life, if we are willing to be simply living pipes through which the power of God may descend to others? There is no limit to the possible usefulness of such a life. All that is required is a channel of communication between the two; why should you not be such a channel?

There is a splendid illustration of this in the life of Elijah, of which we are now taking our farewell. For more than a hundred years the tide had been running strongly against the truth of God. Idolatry had passed from the worship of Jeroboam's calves to that of Baal and Astarte; with the licentious orgies and hideous rites that gathered around the ancient worship of the forces of Nature. The system was maintained by an immense organization of crafty priests who had settled down upon the national life like a fungus growth, striking its roots into the heart.

Into such a state of things Elijah came, unarmed, from his native trans-Jordanic hills; a highlander, unkempt, unpolished; unaccustomed to the manners of a court or the learning of the schools. And at once the progress of idolatry received a decisive check. The existence and power of Jehovah were vindicated. New courage was infused into the timid remnant of true-hearted disciples. Altars were rebuilt; colleges were opened for the training of the godly youth; a successor was appointed; and an impetus given to the cause of truth, which was felt for many generations.

Perhaps the greatest tribute to Elijah's power with his contemporaries is in the fact that his name and work stood out in bold and clear outline for nine hundred years after his death, surpassing the whole school of Jewish prophets, and furnishing a model for the forerunner of our Lord. Malachi, the last of the prophets, could find no better symbol of the pioneer of the Christ than to compare Him with the famous prophet who, centuries before, had swept to heaven in the chariot of flame: "Behold, I will send you Elijah the prophet before the coming of the great and dreadful day of the LORD" (Mal 4:5). Gabriel found no easier method of conveying to the aged priest the type of the wondrous son that was to gladden his old age, than to liken him to Elijah. "He shall go before His face in the spirit and power of [Elijah]."

Whenever a notable religious movement was stirring through the land, the people were accustomed to think that the prophet of Carmel had again returned to earth; and thus the deputation asked John the Baptist, saying, "Art thou Elijah?" And when a mightier than John had set all men musing in their hearts, as the disciples told our Lord, many of the common people believed that the long expectation of centuries was realized, and that Elijah was risen again.

All these things are evidences of the towering greatness of Elijah's character and work. He was a great man, and did a noble work. And the secret of all was to be found in the fact that he was filled with the Holy Ghost.

God will take young men and women, old men and children, servants and hand-maidens, in the waning days of this era, and will fill them with the Spirit. Then when, like John the Baptist, we are filled with the Holy Ghost, like John the Baptist we will go "before his face in the spirit and power of Elijah."

1. THIS FILLING OF THE HOLY GHOST WAS THE CHARACTERISTIC OF THE CHURCH. On the day of Pentecost they were *all* filled with the Holy Ghost—women as well as men; obscure disciples as well as illustrious apostles. New converts, like Saul of Tarsus, were told to expect this blessed filling. Deacons called to do the secular business of the church must be men filled with the Holy Ghost. That he was a good man, full of the Holy Ghost, was a greater recommendation of Barnabas than that he had parted with his lands. And even churches, like those in the highlands of Galatia, were no sooner brought into existence by the labors of the apostle Paul than they were filled with the Holy Ghost. In point of fact, the Christians of the first century were taught to expect this blessed filling. And the early church was a collection of Holy-Ghost-filled people. It was probably the exception, rather than the rule, *not* to be filled with the blessed presence of God the Holy Ghost.

There is no formal conclusion to the Acts of the Apostles because God meant the story to be prolonged, through the ages, after the same manner. Pentecost was simply meant to be the specimen and type of all the days of all the years of the present age. And if our times seem to have fallen far below this blessed level, it is because the church has neglected this holy doctrine. She has been simply paralyzed for want of the only power that can avail her in her conflict against the world—a power that was distinctly pledged to her by her ascending Lord. No doubt He is in us if we are Christians, but we must never be content until He is in us in power—not a breath, but a mighty wind; not a rill, but a torrent; not an influence, but a mighty, energizing Person.

2. WE MUST COMPLY WITH CERTAIN CONDITIONS, IF WE WOULD BE FILLED

a. *We must desire to be filled for the glory of God.* A lady once told me that she had long been seeking the power of the Spirit, but in vain until she came to see that she was seeking Him for the joy that He would bring, rather than for the glory that would accrue to God. Ah, we must seek for the Spirit's power, not for our happiness or comfort, but that "Christ shall be magnified in my body, whether it be by life or by death" (Phil. 1:20).

b. *We must bring cleansed vessels.* God will not deposit His most precious gift in unclean receptacles. And we need cleansing in the precious blood before we can presume to expect that God will give us what we seek. We cannot expect to be free from indwelling sin, but we may at least be washed in the blood of Christ from all conscious filthiness and stain.

c. *We must be prepared to let the Holy Spirit do as He will with and through us.* There must be no reserve, no holding back, no contrary purpose. The whole nature must be unbarred, and every part yielded. Let us present no resistance to the working of the Holy Ghost. God gives the Holy Ghost to those who obey Him (Acts 5:32).

d. *We must appropriate Him by faith.* The Holy Spirit *has been given* to the church. We need not struggle and agonize; we have simply to take what God is waiting to impart. As soon as you ask, you do receive, though you experience no rush of transcendent joy; go your way considering yourself filled, whether you feel so or not: and as the days go on, you will find that you have been filled, and are being filled, with new power, and joy, and wealth.

3. TIME WOULD FAIL TO ENUMERATE ALL THE BLESSINGS THAT WILL ENSUE. The presence of the Holy Ghost in the heart, in all His glorious fullness, cannot be hid. This conception of His work is clearly taught by the word selected by the apostle to describe the results of His indwelling. He speaks of them as the *"fruit* of the Spirit," and what deep suggestions of quiet growth, and exquisite beauty, and spontaneousness of life lie in that significant phrase!

a. *There is victory over sin.* The law of the Spirit of life in Christ Jesus makes us free from the law of sin and death; just as the law of elasticity of the air makes the bird free from the predominating power of the down-pull of gravitation.

b. *There is the indwelling of the Lord Jesus.* Christ dwells in the heart by the Holy Ghost. And this is not figurative or metaphorical, but a literal and glorious reality.

c. *There is the quickening of the mortal body.* This is an expression that certainly points to the Resurrection, but which may mean some special strength and health imparted to our present mortal bodies.

d. *There are all the graces of the Spirit* that come with linked hands; love brings joy, and joy peace, and peace longsuffering, and similarly through the whole series; so that the heart becomes filled with angels.

e. *There is also power for service.* No longer timid and frightened, the apostles give their witness with great power. The gospel comes in power and demonstration through consecrated lips and lives. The devils are exorcised, and great crowds are brought to the feet of Christ.

This and much more is awaiting the moment in your life when you shall definitely avail yourself of your privilege and become filled with the Holy Ghost.

Amid the myriads of stars that will shine forever in the firmament of heaven, not one shall shine with more brilliant or more steady glory than Elijah; a man of like passions with ourselves, who was swept to heaven unhurt by death, and stood beside Christ on the Transfiguration Mount. Prophet of fire, till then, Farewell!

JEREMIAH

1

"The Word of the Lord Came Unto Me"
Jeremiah 1:4, 12–13

If the days of David and Solomon may be compared to spring and summer in the history of the kingdom of Israel, it was late autumn when our story opens. The influence of the spiritual revival under Hezekiah and Isaiah, which had for a brief interval arrested the process of decline, had spent itself; and not even the reforms of the good king Josiah, which affected rather the surface than the heart of the people, would avail to avert inevitable judgment. King and court, princes and people, prophets and priests, were infected with abominable vices.

Every high hill had its thick grove of green trees, within whose shadow the idolatrous rites and abominable license of nature worship were freely practiced. The face of the country was thickly covered with temples erected for the worship of Baal and Astarte and all the host of heaven, and with lewd idols. In the cities, the black-robed chemarim, the priests of these unhallowed practices, flitted to and fro in strange contrast to the white-stoled priests of Jehovah.

But it was in Jerusalem that these evils came to a head. In the streets of the holy city, the children were taught to gather wood, while the fathers kindled the fire and the women kneaded dough to make cakes for Astarte, "the queen of heaven," and to pour out drink offerings to other gods.

In such a Sodom God's voice must be heard. Yet if God speaks, it must be through the yielded lips of you and me. He seeks such today. We are still the vehicles of His communications to others. In the call of Jeremiah we may discover the sort of person whom God chooses as the medium for his speech. It is not to be expected that a superficial gaze will comprehend the special qualifications that attracted the divine choice to Jeremiah. There are several reasons why Jeremiah might have been passed over.

1. HE WAS YOUNG. How young we do not know, but young enough for him to hold back at the divine proposal with the cry, "Ah, Lord GOD! behold I cannot speak: for I am a child."

God has often selected the young for posts of eminent service: Samuel and Timothy; Joseph and David; Daniel and John the Baptist; Calvin, who wrote his *Institutes* before he was twenty-four; and Wesley, who was only twenty-five when he inaugurated the great system of Methodism.

2. HE WAS NATURALLY TIMID AND SENSITIVE. By nature he seemed cast in too delicate a mold to be able to combat the dangers and difficulties of his time. The bitter complaint of his later years was that his mother had brought him into a world of strife and contention. And it was in allusion to the natural shrinking of his disposition that Jehovah promised to make him a "defenced city, and an iron pillar, and a brasen wall against the whole land."

Many are molded on this type. Yet such, like Jeremiah, may play a heroic part on the world's stage, if only they will let God lay down the iron of His might along the lines of their natural weakness. Happy is the soul who can look up from its utter helplessness, and say with Jeremiah, 'O LORD, my strength . . . in the day of affliction."

3. HE ESPECIALLY SHRANK FROM THE BURDEN HE WAS SUMMONED TO BEAR. His chosen theme would have been God's mercy—the boundlessness of His compassion, the tenderness of His pity. In the earlier chapters, when he pleads with the people to return to God, there is a tenderness in his voice, and pathos in his speech, which proves how thoroughly his heart was in this part of his work.

But to be charged with a message of judgment; to announce the woeful day; to oppose every suggestion of heroic resistance; to bring charges on the prophetic and the priestly orders, to each of which he belonged, and the anger of each of which he incurred, the crimes by which they were disgraced—this was the commission that was furtherest from his choice.

4. HE WAS CONSCIOUS OF HIS DEFICIENCY IN SPEECH. Like Moses, he could say, "O LORD, I am not eloquent, neither heretofore, nor since thou hast spoken unto thy servant: but I am slow of speech, and of a slow tongue."

Do not then despair because of apparent disqualifications. Notwithstanding all, the Word of the Lord shall come to you. The one thing that God demands of you is absolute consecration to His purpose, and willingness to go on any errand on which He may send you. If these are yours, all else will be given you. He will assure you of His presence—"I am with thee, to deliver thee." He will equip you—"Then the LORD put forth his hand, and touched my mouth. And the LORD said unto me, Behold I have put my words in thy mouth." Oh, for the circumcised ear, and the loyal, obedient heart!

2

"I Formed Thee"
Jeremiah 1:5

God has a plan for each of His children. The path has been prepared, it is for us to walk in it. There is no emergency in the path for which there has not been provision made in our nature; and there is no faculty stored in our nature which, sooner or later, will not have its proper exercise and use. From the earliest inception of being, God had a plan for Jeremiah's career, for which He prepared him. Before the dawn of consciousness, in the very origin of his nature, the hands of the great Master Workman reached down out of heaven to shape the plastic clay for the high purpose He had in view.

1. THE DIVINE PURPOSE. "I knew thee . . . I sanctified thee . . . I have appointed thee a prophet." In that degenerate age the great Lover of souls needed a spokesman; and the divine decree determined the conditions of Jeremiah's birth, and character, and life.

It is wise to discover, if possible, while life is yet young, the direction of the divine purpose. There are four considerations that will help us. First, the indication of our natural aptitudes, for these, when touched by the divine Spirit, become talents or gifts. Second, the inward impulse or energy of the divine Spirit, working in us both to will and to do His good pleasure. Third, the teaching of the Word of God. Fourth, the evidence of the circumstances and demands of life. When these concur and focus in one point, there need be no doubt as to the divine purpose and plan. It was thus that God disclosed to Samuel, and Jeremiah, and Saul of Tarsus, the future for which they were destined. Perhaps the noblest aim for any of us is to realize that word which was addressed by God to Jeremiah, when He as much as said to him, "On whatsoever errand I shall send thee, thou shalt go; and whatsoever I shall command thee, thou shalt speak."

2. FORMATIVE INFLUENCES. It is interesting to study the formative influences that were brought to bear on the character of Jeremiah. There were the character and disposition of his mother, and the priestly office of his father. There was the near proximity of the holy city, making it possible for the boy to be present at all the holy festivals, and to receive such instruction as the best seminaries could provide. There was the companionship and association of godly families. His uncle, Shallum, was the husband of the illustrious and devoted prophetess, Huldah; and their son Hanameel shared with Baruch, the grandson of Maaseiah, the close friendship of the prophet, probably from the days they were boys together. There were also the prophets Nahum and Zephaniah, who were burning as bright constellations in that dark sky, to be soon joined by Jeremiah himself.

His mind was evidently very sensitive to all the influences of his early life. His speech is saturated with references to natural emblems and national customs, to the life of men, and the older literature of the Bible. Many chords made up the music of his speech.

It is thus that God is ever at work, forming and molding us. The plan of God threads the maze of life. The purpose of God gives meaning to many of its strange experiences. Be brave, strong, and trustful!

3. THERE WAS ALSO A SPECIAL PREPARATION AND ASSURANCE FOR HIS LIFE'S WORK. "The LORD put forth his hand, and touched my mouth. And the LORD said unto me, Behold, I have put my words in thy mouth." In a similar manner the seraph had touched the lips of Isaiah years before. Words are the special gift of God. They were the endowment of the church at Pentecost. And it is always an evidence of a Spirit-filled man when he begins to speak as the Spirit gives him utterance.

God never asks us to go on His errands (1:7) without telling us what to say. If we are living in fellowship with Him, He will impress His messages on our minds, and enrich our life with the appropriate utterances by which those messages will be conveyed to others. If only God's glory is our object, His hand will touch our mouth, and He will leave His words there.

Two other assurances were also given. First, "Thou shalt go to all that I shall send thee." This gave a definiteness and directness to the prophet's speech. Second, "Be not afraid of their faces: for I am with thee to deliver thee, saith the LORD." An assurance that was remarkably fulfilled, as we shall see, in the unfolding of this narrative.

As long as we are on the prepared path, performing the appointed mission, He is with us. We may defy death. We bear a charmed life. Men may fight against us, but they cannot prevail; for the Lord of Hosts is with us, the God of Jacob is our refuge (1:19).

4. LAST, GOD PROMISED A TWOFOLD VISION TO HIS CHILD. On the one hand, the swift-blossoming almond tree assured him that God would watch over him, and see to the swift performance of His predictions; on the other, the seething cauldron, turned toward the north, indicated the breaking out of evil. So the pendulum of life swings to and fro; now to light, and then to darkness. But happy is the man whose heart is fixed, trusting in the Lord. Men may fight against him, but they will not prevail; he is encircled in the environing care of Jehovah. As God spoke to Jeremiah, so He addresses us: "They shall fight against thee; but they shall not prevail against thee; for I am with thee, saith the LORD, to deliver thee" (1:19).

There was a period in Jeremiah's life when he seems to have swerved from the path of complete obedience (15:19), and to have turned from following the God-given plan. But as he returned again to his allegiance, these precious promises were renewed, and again sounded in his ears.

It may be that you have stepped back before some fearful storm of opposition, as a fireman before the belching flames. Thus Cranmer signed his recantation. Yet return again to your post; the old blessing will flood your soul; God will bring you again that you may stand before Him, and you shall be as His mouth. Thus it was with Peter on the day of Pentecost.

3

Cistern Making
Jeremiah 2:13

There was probably but little interval between Jeremiah's call and his entrance on his sacred work. We are told that to this young ardent soul "the word of the LORD came" (2:1). Coming, it thrilled him.

He dwelled lightly on the ominous mention of the inevitable conflict which the divine voice predicted. He did not stay to gauge the full pressure of opposition indicated in the celestial storm signal. He had been told that kings and princes, priests and people, would fight against him; but in the first blush of his young faith he thought more of the presence of Jehovah, who had promised to make him "a defenced city, and an iron pillar, and brasen walls against the whole land."

1. THE PROPHET'S TWOFOLD BURDEN. When Jeremiah began his ministry, going from Anathoth to Jerusalem for that purpose (2:2), Josiah, though only twenty-one years of age, had been on the throne for thirteen years. He was beginning those measures of reform that were used to postpone, though not to avert, the doom of city and nation. "They brake down the altars of Baalim in his presence; and the images, that were on high above them, he cut down; and the groves and the carved images, and the molten images, he brake in pieces, and made dust of them, and strowed it upon the graves of them that had sacrificed unto them. And he burnt the bones of the priests upon their altars, and cleansed Judah and Jerusalem" (2 Chron. 34:4–5).

For seventy years the grossest forms of idolatry had held almost undisputed sway. The impious orgies and degrading rites, which licensed vice as a part of religion, were in harmony with the depraved tastes of the people.

The result was first, that the work of reform was largely superficial; it did not strike beneath the surface nor change the trend of national choice. And second, this policy compacted together a strong political party, determined to promote a closer alliance with Egypt, which had just asserted her independence against the king of Assyria. In these two directions the young prophet was called to make his influence felt.

a. *He protested against the prevalent sin around him.* The one thought of the people was to preserve the outward acknowledgment of Jehovah by the maintenance of the temple services and rites. If these were rigorously observed, they figured that there was no sufficient cause for charging them with the sin of apostasy. They insisted that they were not polluted (2:23); and reiterated with wearisome monotony, "The temple of the LORD, The temple of the LORD, The temple of the LORD, are these" (7:4). This accounts for the plain denunciations of sin that came burning from the lips of the young prophet. He included the priests and expounders of the law, pastors and prophets, in his scathing words (2:8). Every metaphor is adopted that human art can suggest to bring home to the people their infidelity to their great Lover and Redeemer, God (3:20).

b. *He also protested against the proposal to form an Egyptian alliance.* The little land of Canaan lay between the vast rival empires founded on the Nile and the Euphrates. It was therefore constantly exposed to the transit of immense armies, like locusts, destroying everything, or to the hostile incursions of one or other of its belligerent neighbors. It had always been the policy of a considerable party at the court of Jerusalem to cultivate alliance with Egypt or Assyria. In Hezekiah's and Manasseh's time the tendency had been towrad Assyria; now it was toward Egypt, which had a remarkable way thrown off the yoke that the great King Esarhaddon in three terrible campaigns had sought to rivet on its neck. The prophet strenuously opposed these overtures. Why should his people bind themselves to the fortunes of any heathen nation whatsoever? Was not God their King? Surely their true policy was to stand alone, untrammelled by foreign alliances, resting only on the mighty power of Jehovah.

This, then, was Jeremiah's mission—to stand almost alone; to protest against the sins of the people, which were covered by their boasted reverence to Jehovah; and to oppose the policy of the court, which sought to cultivate friendly relations with the one power that seemed able to give aid to his fatherland in the awful struggle with the northern kingdom that he saw to be imminent (1:15). And this ministry was carried out in the teeth of the most virulent opposition. Here was a priest denouncing the practices of priests, a prophet the lies of prophets. Small wonder therefore that the most powerful parties in the state conspired against him.

2. THE IMAGERY HE EMPLOYED. It is a scene among the mountains. In that green glade a fountain rises icy cold from the depths, and pours its silver stream downward through the valley. It is flowing in abundance, but its banks are unvisited, neither cup nor bucket descends into its crystal depths; for all practical purposes it might as well cease to flow.

Far away from that verdant valley you hear the clink of the chisel, and presently discover people of every age and rank engaged in making cisterns to supply their homes. Each man has his own scheme, his own design. After years of work he may achieve his purpose, and wait expectantly for the shower. It soon descends, and he is filled with price and pleasure to think of the store of water that he has been able to secure. But lo! it does not stay. He finds that with the utmost care the cisterns made in the quarry can hold no water.

What an infinite mistake to miss the fountain freely flowing to quench the thirst, and cut out the broken cistern in which is disappointment and despair! Yet this, said the prophet, was the precise position of Israel. In resorting to false religions and heathen alliances, they were cutting out for themselves broken cisterns that would fail them in their hour of need.

3. ITS APPLICATION TO OURSELVES. Many cistern makers may read these words—each with soul-thirst craving satisfaction; each within easy reach of God, but all attempting the impossible task of satisfying the thirst for the infinite and divine, with men and things.

There is the cistern of *pleasure*, the cistern of *wealth*, the cistern of *fame*, and the cistern of *human love*, which, however beautiful as a revelation of the divine love, can never satisfy the soul that rests in it alone—all these, made at infinite cost of time and pain, deceive and disappoint. They are "broken cisterns that can hold no water." And in the time of trouble they will not be able to save those who have constructed and trusted them.

At your feet, O weary cistern-cutter, the fountain of God's love is flowing through the channel of the divine Man! Stoop to drink it. "The Spirit and the bride say, Come. And him that heareth say, Come! And let him that is athirst come: And whosoever will, let him take the water of life freely" (Rev. 22:17).

4

The Second Discourse
Jeremiah 3:6

We do not know how Jeremiah's first address was received. It was impossible for Jerusalem to have heard the eager pleadings of the young preacher, protesting so earnestly against the policy of its priests, without becoming aware that a new force had entered the arena of its public life. And from that moment, through the forty-four years that followed, the influence of his holy example and fervent words was destined to make itself mightily felt. Another voice was audible through which God could utter his pleadings and remonstrances.

In his second discourse, lasting from the third to the sixth chapters inclusive—and which perhaps is preserved as a specimen of Jeremiah's words at this period—there is an added power and pathos. The flame burns higher; the sword has a keener edge; yet the tone is more tremulous and tender. In his own touching words, Jeremiah was as a gentle lamb led to the slaughter (11:19); but he was also strong as a lion, in the vehemence with which he strove to avert the doom, threatening to devastate his beloved fatherland. If any pure and holy soul could have saved Judah by its pleadings, tears, and warning, Jeremiah would have done it.

But it was not to be. The evil that Manasseh had sown had too thickly impregnated the soil. This, however, did not appear in those early days of Jeremiah's ministry; and with all the hopefulness of youth, he thought that he might yet avert the disaster.

This discourse is occupied with a clear prevision of the Chaldean invasion; with plaintive expressions of pity and pain; and with eloquent assertions of the redeeming grace of God.

The Second Discourse

1. THE PROPHET'S PREVISION OF APPROACHING JUDGMENT. At the opening of Jeremiah's ministry, as we have seen, the land was rejoicing in a brief time of peace; and it appeared probable that it might last. Assyria was weakened by internal dissension; Babylon was becoming a formidable rival of Nineveh; the Medes, under Cyaxares, were beginning to descend the western slopes of the Taurus; while in Egypt Psammetichus was too deeply engaged in expelling the Assyrian garrisons and founding his dynasty, to have leisure or desire to interfere with the tiny neighboring kingdom.

Thus Josiah was able to pursue his reforms in peace, and there was no war cloud on the horizon. It was on one of these days of Josiah the king (3:6) that the newly appointed prophet startled the men of Jerusalem and Judah, as he made known what he had seen on his watchtower.

He had heard the trumpet summoning the peasantry from the open country to the fenced cities, leaving their crops at the mercy of the invader, to save their lives. He had caught the cries of the watchers as they announced the advent of the invader. He had beheld the desolation of the land, the hurried retreat of the defenders of the holy city herself.

So real was the whole scene to him that we find him turning to his brother Benjamites, who had fled for shelter to the metropolis, urging them to flee still further south. He beholds the preparations for the siege, and the chargrin of her assailants that the evening shadows of declining day interpose between them and her inevitable capture. He describes the invader as a mighty and ancient nation, gleaning Israel as men gather the last grapes into their basket; cruel and merciless as evening wolves.

It has been supposed that these words referred to the invasion of the Scythians, who about this time poured in countless hordes over Western Asia. But these barbarian hordes do not fulfill the entire scope of the prophet's words. They do not appear to have entered Palestine, but to have passed down on the eastern or western frontier, skirting the territory of Josiah. It is better, therefore, to refer these ominous words to the invasion of Judah by Babylon, which was to take place in thirty years, but of which the people were amply warned, that they might put away their abominations and return to the Fountain of Living Waters.

2. HIS PLAINTIVE EXPRESSION OF PITY AND PAIN. The tender heart of Jeremiah was filled with the utmost sorrow at the heavy tidings he was called to announce—the impending destruction of the holy city.

He identifies himself with his land; he struggles against uttering his message of judgment until he can no longer contain himself, and becomes weary with holding in (6:11).

He had no alternative but to announce the judgments that he saw on their way; but there was a sob in the voice that predicted them. So far from desiring the evil day, gladly would he have laid down his life to avert it. The chalice of his life was full of that spirit that led the Master in following years to weep as he beheld the guilty and doomed city.

Such preaching will always be a convincing and irresistible argument to turn sinners from the error of their ways. Nothing is more awful than to speak of the great mysteries of life and death, without that compassion of heart that is borrowed from close communion with the Savior of the world.

3. HIS ASSERTION OF REDEEMING GRACE. Few of the sacred writers have had truer or deeper views of the love of God. It is to the earlier chapters of Jeremiah that backsliders

must always turn for comfort and assurance of abundant pardon. The word "backslide" is characteristic of this prophet.

a. *To Jeremiah's thought, sin could not quench God's love.* Though our sin be fixed, it cannot cut off that love that is from everlasting to everlasting. Sin may hide the manifestation of the love of God, but can never make God abandon his love to us (Jer. 3:1).

b. *The love of God goes forth in forgiving mercy.* He only asks that the people acknowledge their iniquity and confess to having perverted their way and forgotten their God. It would be enough if they would accept the terms of the confession he himself suggested: "Behold we come unto thee, for thou art the LORD our God"; and he assures them that though their sin and iniquity were sought for, there would be none (4:1; 50:20).

c. *The love of God does not deal with us after our sins.* He gives showers immediately on repentance. He does not keep his anger forever. He waits to receive us back, saying, "If thou wilt return, O Israel, unto me, thou shalt return."

What true and delightful conceptions of the love of God were guaranteed the young prophet! His living spirit had taken deep drinks of the everlasting, forgiving, pitiful love of God. Oh, blessed love!—through which backsliding hearts may be admitted again to the inner circle, and have restored the years that the cankerworm has eaten.

5

At the Temple Gates
Jeremiah 7:10

We must read the records given in the Books of the Kings and Chronicles, to understand the remarkable movement that was on foot during the time covered by the first twelve chapters of the Book of Jeremiah. He scarcely refers to the great reforms being introduced by his friend, the King Josiah, and he is scarcely mentioned in the historical records. But there is no doubt that he was in constant and close communication with the king and the little group of earnest reformers that clustered around him, which included Shaphan, Hilkiah, the prophet Zephaniah, the prophetess Huldah, and his own friend, Baruch.

Josiah promoted measures of reform from the earliest years of his reign, but at first he was opposed by the dead weight of national apathy to the cause he espoused. The worship of idols had so many fascinations that the mass of the people had no desire to revert to the purer worship of their forefathers.

A wonderful and horrible thing had come to pass in the land; the prophets prophesied falsely, and the priests bare rule by their means; and the people loved to have it this way.

The cooperation of Zepahniah and Jeremiah was therefore exceedingly valuable. While Josiah worked from without, pursuing a career of uncompromising iconoclasm, they worked from within, appealing to the conscience and heart.

Notwithstanding their united efforts, the cause of reform moved slowly, or might even have come to a standstill—as an express train when buried in an avalanche of soft snow—had not the discovery, made in the eighteenth year of Josiah's reign, given a new and unexpected impetus to the ancient religion of Israel. And though it is not exactly an incident in the life of Jeremiah, he was so closely associated with the men who were principally concerned, and his third discourse is so evidently suggested by the reforms to which it led, that we must briefly touch on it.

1. THE FINDING OF THE LAW. At the time to which this incident refers, the temple was under repair. The fabric was probably showing signs of disintegration and age, for two and a half centuries had elapsed since it had been completely restored by Joash.

The work was entrusted to the superintendence of Hilkiah, the high priest, who was assisted by a small group of Levites; and the cost was contributed by the people who passed through the temple gates. On one occasion the king sent Shaphan, his secretary and chancellor, the father of Gemariah and a good man—who afterward defended Jeremiah (36:10–19, 25)—to take an account with Hilkiah of the money that had been gathered by the doorkeepers. When they had attended to this and delivered the money into the hands of the workmen who had the oversight of the work, Hilkiah, the high priest, said to Shaphan, the scribe, "I have found the book of the law in the house of the LORD."

It was a very startling discovery. There has been much discussion as to what that roll of ancient manuscript contained; some holding that it was the entire Pentateuch, others that it was the Book of Deuteronomy. We are disposed to think that the Book of Deuteronomy is referred to here. It seems unquestionable that this portion alone of the Pentateuch was ordained to be written out by each king on his accession, and was read before the assembled congregation once every seven years. The terms of the covenant made afterward by Josiah and his people are precisely those with which the Book of Deuteronomy abounds.

Its discovery by Hilkiah made a great sensation. Shaphan read parts of it before the king, among them probably chapter 28. "And it came to pass, when the king had heard the words of the book of the law, that he rent his clothes." In hot haste he sent a deputation of his most trusty friends to one of the suburbs of the city, where the prophetess Huldah dwelt. Jeremiah may have been at this time at Anathoth, or he may have been too inexperienced in his work to be recognized as an authority in so grave a crisis. The question to be asked was whether the nation was expected to suffer all the awful curses those words predicted; and the answer was an uncompromising "Yes," though their infliction might be postponed for a brief space.

The king immediately summoned a mighty convocation of all the men of Judah and all the inhabitants of Jerusalem, and from a platform erected in the entrance of the inner court, he read aloud all the words of the book of the covenant that had been found in the house of the Lord. And further, he solemnly renewed the covenant between Jehovah and the people, that they would walk after the Lord, and keep His commandments, testimonies, and statutes.

Then the work of reform broke out afresh, and outwardly at least, Israel again became true to its allegiance to the God of their fathers, and free from the taint of idolatry.

2. THE DIVORCE BETWEEN RELIGION AND MORALITY. The influence of the court, the finding and reading of the law and success of the great Passover that Josiah instituted, and the glow of the crusade against the old idolatries, all sufficed for a time to effect

widespread reform, and the fickle populace gave an outward adherence at least to the service of Jehovah. The temple courts were thronged; the rites and forms of the Levitical code were rigorously maintained; every point of cereminial allegiance to the institutions of Moses was punctiliously observed. But there was no real change in disposition. The reformation was entirely superficial.

Jeremiah was deeply disappointed at the result of a movement that had promised so well. He detected its true character, and sought an opportunity to show its insufficiency to avert the wrath of God. Taking up his position in the gate of the temple, on the occasion of some great festival, he poured forth a torrent of remonstrance and appeal.

He was not unaware of the attention paid by the nation to outward ritual, which they mistook for religion. Against every accusation that the prophet laid at the nation's door, they pointed to the order and beauty of the restored ritual, of their splendid temple, of their privileged condition as the chosen of God. But alongside this outward decorum, the grossest sins were permitted with unblushing shame.

There was an evident divorce between religion and morals, and whenever that comes into the life of a nation or an individual, it is fatal! Satan himself has no objection to a religion that consists in postures, and ceremonies, and rites. Indeed, he fosters it; for the soul of man demands God, and craves religion; and it is the art of the great enemy of souls to substitute the counterfeit for the reality. The soul of man is too apt to be enticed by that which is not bread, and which does not satisfy.

3. THE EXCUSES BENEATH WHICH THE SOUL OF MAN SHELTERS ITSELF.

a. *Ritualism.* It was the old belief that God was bound to help a nation or person that steadfastly complied with the outward forms of religion; as if He had no alternative but to help his devoted worshiper. In one form or another this conception has appeared in every nation and age.

The incessant remonstrance of the Bible is against such protestations. "What doth the LORD require of thee," says Micah, "but to do justly, and to love mercy, and to walk humbly with thy God?" (Mic. 6:8). "To what purpose is the multitude of your sacrifices unto me?" saith the Lord, in one of Isaiah's earliest sentences; and here Jeremiah takes up the same strain.

Where the heart is right with God, it will find proper expression in the well-ordered worship of the sanctuary; but the outward can never be a substitute for the inward. The soul must know God, and worship Him as a Spirit. There must be faith, repentance, inward grace.

b. *Destiny.* Men often say, as the Jews did, "we are swept forward by an irresistible current, which we cannot control" (see 7:10). So many lay the blame of their sin on their Creator, alleging that it is only the outworking of the natural tendencies with which he was endowed! Whatever truth there may be in the doctrine of predestination, there is more than enough grace in God to counteract the drift of the current, and the strength of passion.

c. *Special Privilege.* Many a soul has presumed on being a favorite of heaven. Soul beware! you are not indispensable to God. Before you were, He was well served; and if you fail Him, He will call others to minister to Him. See what He did to Shiloh (7:14) and to Jerusalem! How bare the site; how woeful the overthrow! "If God spared not the natural branches, take heed lest He aslo spare not thee!" (Rom. 11:21).

6

The Swelling of Jordan
Jeremiah 12:5

Between the incidents already described and the subject of the present chapter, a crushing calamity had befallen the kingdom of Judah. In the face of urgent remonstrances, addressed to him from all sides, Josiah, perhaps desirous of emulating the heroic faith of Hezekiah and Isaiah, led his little army down from the mountain to attack Pharaoh Necho, who was marching up the coast route to participate in the scramble for the spoils of Nineveh, then in her death throes. The two armies met at Megiddo, at the foot of Carmel, on the extreme border of the plain of Esdraelon, which has so often been a decisive battlefield. The outcome didn't keep people in suspense long. Josiah's army was routed, and he was mortally wounded. His death was the signal for an outburst of grief throughout the land.

The next king, Josiah's son Jehoahaz, reigned only three months, and then was led off with a ring in his nose, like some wild beast, to Egypt, where he died. Necho placed his brother Jehoiakim in his stead, as his nominee and tributary. But the four last kings of Judah reversed the policy of Josiah. They did evil in the sight of the Lord, and of Jehoiakim it is recorded that he committed abomination (2 Chron. 36:1–8).

At the death of Josiah, the large party that favored idolatry again asserted itself. Of what use was a religion that had not saved its chief promoter from such a disaster? The reformation promoted by the good king had never struck its roots deeply in the land; and the vigor with which he had carried out his reforms now led to a corresponding reaction. The reformers fell under the popular hate, and Jeremiah came in for a large share of it.

The symptoms of this rising storm were less likely to reach him because he had been commanded to travel among the cities of Judah, as well as the streets of Jerusalem; and had probably started on a prolonged tour throughout the land, standing up in the principal market places and announcing everywhere the inevitable retribution that must follow on the breach of the divine covenant (11:8). The issue of that tour was profoundly disappointing, and the prophet was convinced that intercession itself was useless for a people so deeply and resolutely set on sin. They had sinned the sin to death, for which prayer is in vain (11:14; 1 John 5:16).

Disappointed and heartsick, Jeremiah retired to his native place, Anathoth. But there was treachery in the little village. The priestly houses had winced beneath the vehement denunciations of their young relative, and could bear it no longer. A plot was set on foot, and they conspired to take the prophet's life. He had not known of his danger except for divine illumination: "The Lord hath given me knowledge of it, and I know it; then thou shewedst me their doings" (11:18). Stunned with the sudden discovery, Jeremiah turned to God, with remonstrance and appeal.

1. The appeal of the maligned and persecuted soul.

a. *He was conscious of his own integrity.* Without doubt, Jeremiah was profoundly conscious of his unworthiness. No one could have lived as close to God as he did without an overwhelming sense of uncleanness. But in respect to this special outburst of hatred, he knew of nothing for which to blame himself. The sins of the people had procured the evils he predicted; and he had sought only to warn the reckless mariners of the rocks that lay straight in their course.

b. *He was perplexed at the inequality of human lot.* He had never swerved from the narrow path of obedience; at all hazards he had dared to stand alone, bereft of the comforts and alleviations that come to most people. But he was hated, persecuted, threatened with death.

It is the question of all ages, to be answered only by remembering that this world is upside down; that the course of nature has been disturbed by sin; that the prince of the power of the air is god of this world; and that the servants of righteousness fight, not against flesh and blood, but against principalities and powers, against the rulers of the darkness of this world, the wicked spirits in heavenly places.

c. *He was anxious for God's character.* There is a touch of apparent vindictiveness in his cry. "Let me see thy vengeance on them . . . pull them out like sheep for the slaughter and prepare them for the day of slaughter" (Jer. 11:20; 12:3). We contrast these words with those Jesus breathed for His murders from the cross, and that Stephen uttered as the stones crashed on him.

But he was concerned with the effect that would be produced on his people if Jehovah passed by the sin of his persecutors and intending murderers. It was as though the prophet feared lest his own undeserved sufferings might lead men to reason that wrongdoing was more likely to promote their prosperity than integrity and holiness. Josiah was the one God-fearing monarch of his time, but he was slain in battle; *he* was the devoted servant of God, and his life was one long agony. Was it the best policy then to fear God? Might it not be wiser, safer, better, to worship the gods of the surrounding peoples, who seemed well able to defend their adherents, and to promote the prosperity of the great kingdoms that maintained their temples? As Jeremiah beheld the destroying influence of sin, his heart misgave him. He saw no limit to the awful evil of his times, so long as God seemed indifferent to its prevalence. Therefore he cried for vengeance—not for the gratification of his own feeling, but for the sake of Israel.

d. *He also rolled his cause on God.* So might 11:20 be rendered: "On thee have I rolled my cause." Ah, this was wise! And it is our only safety in times of great anguish of soul. In his steps we must plant our feet. When men malign and plot against us, when friends forsake, we must roll our anxieties from ourselves onto the blessed Lord, our burden-bearer, and leave them with Him. We need have no further cause for fear.

2. THE DIVINE REPLY. God said: "Do you not remember when I first called you to be my prophet that I foreshadowed the loneliness and isolation, the difficulty and persecution, which were in store? Do you not remember that I told you that you would have to be a brazen wall against the whole people? Have you already lost heart? Are you so soon discouraged? You have as yet run with footmen; presently you will encounter horses: you are now in the land of comparative peace, your native village, and yet you are dismayed; but how will you do when a tide of sorrow comes on this land, as when the Jordan leaps its banks, and swells over the low-lying land around, and drives the wild beasts from their lair—how then?"

Be sure that whatever your sorrows and troubles are at this hour, God has allowed them to come to afford you an opportunity to prepare for future days. Do not be discouraged, or give up the fight, or be unfaithful in the very little. Do not say you cannot bear it. You can! Trust in God, and remember that when He brings you to the swelling of Jordan, He cleaves the path through the heart of the river.

7

The Drought
Jeremiah 14–15

The reign of Jehoiakim was still young. Necho was back in Egypt; Nineveh was tottering to her fall; Babylon was slowly growing on the horizon as the rival of each great empire, and as the future desolator of Judah. Meanwhile, the chosen people were corrupted by innumerable evils. As a premonition of coming destruction, a terrible drought cast its dry mantle over the land.

The vines on the terraced hills were withered, the cornfields were covered with stubble, and the pasture was yellow and scorched. The very dew seemed to have forsaken the land; where the river had poured its full tide, there were only a few trickling drops. The beds of the water-courses were filled with stones. And the bitter cry of Jerusalem ascended.

Let us draw near, and overhear the discussion between Jeremiah and the Almighty. It may be that we shall discover arguments that we may take on our own lips when days of drought visit the church at large, or that area of work in which we are called especially to labor.

1. THE PLEADINGS OF THE INTERCEDING SOUL. "My God, I come into Your presence to acknowledge my own sin, and especially the sins of my people. I stand before You as their priest, to confess the sins that have separated You and them. Our iniquities testify against us, and our backslidings are many. Once You seemed to abide in our midst; Your smile a perpetual summer; but of late Your visits have been few and far between. You have tarried for a night, and been away again at dawn, and we sorely miss You. You have not really changed; You are our Savior; You are in the midst of us. We bear Your name. What You could not do for any merit of ours, do for the credit of Your name. Leave us not, nor let that foreboding prediction of Ezekiel be realized, when he saw the glory of the Lord recede by stages from the holy place, until it stood outside the city walls" (see 14:7–9).

The answer of the divine Spirit. There are times when God seems to speak this way to the soul—if we may dare put our impression of His words in our own phrase: "It is useless, my servant, to pray. My grace is infinite; my mercy endures forever; my fullness waits to pour forth its tides, to make the wilderness rejoice and blossom as the rose. I have no pleasure in the parched wilderness; I would that it were springs of water. I have no liking for the glowing sand; I would that it might become a pool. But as long as men cling to their sins, it is impossible for Me to cause rain or give showers. Your work just now is not that of the intercessor, but of the reformer; not yet to plead with Elijah on the brow of Carmel, but, like Elijah, to extirpate the lurking evil of the people, as when he dyed the waters of Kishon with the blood of Ahab's priests" (see 14:10–12).

2. THE LAMENT OF THE TRUE SHEPHERD. "Ah, Lord God! True, too true, sadly too true, are Your words. Your people deserve all that You have said. There is grievous fault; but

surely it lies at the door of those who mislead the fickle, changeful crowd. They cry Peace! peace! when there is none. The very remonstrances of conscience are scattered because the shepherds have failed in their high commission" (see 14:13).

The answer of the divine Spirit. In our pleadings for men, we sometimes obtain a glimpse of the inevitableness of the divine judgments and the injury that false teachers may do to others. Better be mute and not able to speak, than to say words that may destroy the faith of childhood, or start questionings that may shatter by one fell blow the construction of years. It was in this strain that God replied to the prophet.

"The doom of false prophets will be terrible. Their fate will be the more awful, because they have run without being sent; and prophesied without having seen a vision. There has been no divine impulse energizing their words. Position, bread, power, have been the incentives of their office; but the people have loved to have it so. Their corrupt morals have produced a corrupt priesthood, and a crop of false prophets. My people would not endure the simple truth of the divine word; until the people themselves have put away their sin, and returned to me in penitence and consecration, they must be held guilty before my sight, and suffer the outworking of their sin. 'I will pour their wickedness upon them'" (see 14:14–16).

3. THE INTERCEDING SOUL "Granted, Great God, that You are just, and right: yet You cannot utterly reject. Your smiting cannot be to death. You must heal. There is a tie between You and us that our sin cannot break. Remember the covenant; remember the word on which You have caused us to hope—therefore we will still wait on You" (see 14:17–22).

The answer of the divine Spirit. It is as though the Lord said, "I am wearied with repenting. I have tried every means of restraining them, and turning them to better things. They have appeared to amend, but the improvement was only superficial. Now My mind is thoroughly made up. My methods must be more drastic, My discipline more searching and thorough. I will turn My hand on My people, and thoroughly purge away their dross, and take away all their sin; and I will restore their judges as at the first, and their counselors as at the beginning. Thus I will answer Your pleadings on their behalf. The destruction of the city, the decimation of the people by sword and famine, the awful sorrows of captivity will act as purging fires, through which they will pass to a new and blessed life. For My love of them I cannot spare them, since only thus can My eternal purpose of redemption be realized" (see 15:1–9).

4. THE CRY OF THE INTERCESSOR. Here the prophet falls into a muse. "Why, O God, did You make me so gentle and sympathetic; so naturally weak and yielding? Would not some stronger, rougher nature have done Your bidding better? Even now, have You not some man of ruder make to whom You can entrust this mission? There are skins more impervious to the scorching heat than mine; may they not go into these flames? Why this stammering lip, this faltering heart, this thorn in my flesh?" (see 15:10).

The answer of the divine Spirit. "My grace is sufficient for you. I have summoned you with all your weaknesses, to perform My will, because My strength is only perfected in this way. I need a low platform for the exhibition of My great power. O frail, weak soul, you are likeliest to be the channel and organ for the forthputting of My energy. Only yield yourself to Me, and let Me have My way with you; then you shall be as the northern iron and brass that man cannot break" (see 15:11–14).

5. THE RESPONSE OF THE SOUL. "O Lord, You know. And yet sometimes a dark foreboding comes that You will be to me as a deceitful brook, whose intermittent waters fail, which is dry when its flow is most needed. I know it cannot be, since You are faithful; and yet what could I do if, after having made me what I am, You should leave me to myself?" (see 15:15–18).

The answer of the divine Spirit. "Renounce Your forebodings," God seems to say. "Consider not your frailty, but My might; not your foes, but My deliverances. Divest yourself of all that is inconsistent with your high calling. Then you shall be as My mouth; you shall stand amid the surging crowd as a fenced brazen wall; I will be with you to save and deliver. And I will deliver you out of the hand of the wicked and redeem you out of the hand of the terrible" (see 15:19–21).

8

On the Potter's Wheel
Jeremiah 18:4

One day, beneath the impulse of the divine Spirit, Jeremiah went beyond the city precincts to the Valley of Hinnom, on the outskirts of Jerusalem, where he found a potter, busily engaged at his handicraft.

As the prophet stood quietly beside the potter, he saw him take a piece of clay from the mass that lay beside his hand, and having kneaded it to rid it of the bubbles, place it on the wheel, rapidly revolving at the motion of his foot driving the treadle. From that moment his hands were at work, within and without, shaping the vessel with his deft touch, here widening, there leading it up into a more slender form; opening out the lip, so that from the shapeless clay there emerged a fair and beautiful vessel. When it was nearly complete, and the next step would have been to remove it, to await the kiln, through a flaw in the material it fell a shapeless ruin, some broken pieces on the wheel, and others on the floor of the house.

The prophet naturally expected that the potter would immediately take another piece of clay. Instead, the potter with scrupulous care gathered up the broken pieces of the clay and pressed them together as he had first done, and placed the clay where it had lain before, and *made it again* into another vessel.

O vision of the long-suffering patience of God! O bright anticipation of God's redemptive work! O parable of remade characters, and lives, and hopes! "Cannot I do with you as this potter? saith the LORD. Behold, as the clay is in the potter's hand, so are ye in mine hand, O house of Israel."

The purpose of Jeremiah's vision seems to have been to give his people hope that even though they had marred God's fair ideal, yet a glorious and blessed future was within reach; and that if only they would yield themselves to the touch of the Great Potter, He would undo the results of years of disobedience that had marred and spoiled His fair purpose, and would make the chosen people a vessel to honor, sanctified and meet for the Master's use.

The same thought may apply to us all. Who is there who is not conscious of having marred and resisted the touch of God's molding hands? Who is there that would not like to be made again as seems good to the Potter?

1. THE DIVINE MAKING OF MEN.

a. *The Potter has an ideal.* Floating through His fancy there is the vessel that is to be. He already sees it hidden in the shapeless clay, waiting to evoke His call. His hands achieve as far as they may the embodiment of the fair conception of His thought.

So of God in nature. The pattern of this round world and of her sister spheres lay in his creative thought before the first beam of light streamed across the abyss. All that exists embodies with more or less exactness the divine ideal—sin alone excepted. I do not know if we will ever be permitted, amid the archives of heaven, to see the transcript of God's original thought of what our life might have been had we only yielded ourselves to the hands that reach down from heaven molding men; but it is sure that God foreordained and predestinated us, each in his own measure and degree, to be conformed to the image of His Son.

b. *The Potter achieves His purpose by means of the wheel.* In the discipline of human life this surely represents the revolution of daily circumstance; often monotonous, common place, trivial enough, and yet intending to effect, if it may, ends on which God has set His heart.

Do not therefore seek to change, by some rash and willful act, the setting and environment of your life. Stay where you are until God as evidently calls you elsewhere as He has put you where you are. Throw on Him the responsibility of indicating to you a change when it is necessary for your development. In the meanwhile, look deep into the heart of every circumstance for its special message, lesson, or discipline.

You complain of the monotony of your life. Yet remember that the passive virtues are even dearer to God than the active ones. They need more courage and evince greater heroism than those qualities the world admires most. But they can be acquired only in just that monotonous and narrow round of which many complain as offering so scant a chance of acquiring saintliness.

c. *The bulk of the work is done by the Potter's fingers.* How delicate their touch! How fine their sensibility! And in the nurture of the soul, these represent the touch of the Spirit of God working in us to will and to do of His good pleasure.

But we are too busy, too absorbed in many things, to heed the gentle touch. Sometimes, when we are aware of it, we resent it, or stubbornly refuse to yield to it. Hence the necessity of setting apart a portion of every day, or a season in the course of the week, in which to seclude ourselves from every other influence, and expose the entire range of our being to divine influences only.

Therefore, whenever you are in doubt as to the meaning of certain circumstances through which you are called to pass, and which are strange and inexplicable, be still; refrain from murmuring; and listen until there is borne in on your soul a persuasion of God's purpose; and let His Spirit within cooperate with the circumstance without.

2. GOD'S REMAKING OF MEN. "He made it again." How often He has to make us again! He made Jacob again, when He met him at the Jabbok ford. He found him a supplanter and a cheat, but after a long wrestle He left him a prince with God. He made Simon again, on the resurrection morning, when He found him somewhere near the open grave, and left him Peter, the man of the rock, the apostle of Pentecost. He made Mark again, between his impulsive leaving of Paul and Barnabas, as though frightened by the first touch of seasickness, and the times when Peter spoke of him as his son, and Paul from the Mamertine prison described him as being profitable.

Are you conscious of having marred God's early plan for you? His ideal of a life of earnest devotion to His cause has been so miserably lost sight of! Into the soul the conviction is burned: "I had my chance, and missed it; it will never come to me again." It is here that the gospel comes with its gentle words for the outcast and lost. The bruised reed is made again into a pillar for the temple of God. The feebly smoking flax is kindled to a flame.

3. OUR ATTITUDE TOWARD THE GREAT POTTER. Yield to Him! Each particle in the clay seems to say "Yes" to wheel and hand. And in proportion as this is the case the work goes merrily on. If there is rebellion and resistance, the work of the potter is marred. Let God have His way with you.

We cannot always understand His dealings, because we do not know what His purpose is. We fail to recognize the design; the position that we are being trained to fill; the ministry we are to exercise. What wonder, then, that we get puzzled and perplexed!

There is special comfort in these thoughts for the middle-aged and old. Do not look back regretfully on the wasted springtide and summer, gone beyond recall. Even though it is autumn, there is yet chance for you to bear some fruit, under the care of the great Husbandman. Only let Him have a free hand. Trust in God: and according to your faith it will be done to you.

When the clay has received its final shape from the potter's hands, it must be baked in the kiln to keep it; and even then its discipline is not complete, for whatever colors are put in must be rendered permanent by fire. It is said that what is to become gold in the finished article is a smudge of dark liquid before the fire is applied; and that the first two or three applications of heat obliterate all trace of color, which has to be renewed again and again. So in God's dealings with His people. The molding Hand has no sooner finished its work than it plunges the clay into the fiery trial of pain or temptation. But let patience have her perfect work. You shall be compensated when the Master counts you fair and meet for His use.

9

The Fire of Holy Impulse
Jeremiah 20:9

Jeremiah's nature reminds us of the Aeolian harp, which is so sensitive to the passing breeze that one moment it wails with sorrow, and the next it is jubilant with song.

There are many indications of this in the chapters before us. For instance, there is the exclamation: "Cursed be the day wherein I was born. . . . Cursed be the man who brought tidings to my father, saying, A man child is born unto thee. . . . Wherefore came I forth out of the womb to see labour and sorrow?" (20:14–18). But in the same breath there is the heroic outburst, "The LORD is with me as a mighty terrible one; therefore my persecutors shall stumble, and they shall not prevail" (20:11). How great the contrast between these moods!

The same contrast appears in this verse. There we find the half-formed resolution to make no further mention of God, and to speak no more in His name. Then Jeremiah is instantly aware of his inability to control the passionate outbursts of the Spirit within.

"But his word was in mine heart as a burning fire shut up in my bones, and I was weary with forbearing, and I could not stay." It is good for us when we learn to distinguish between the life of our emotions and that of our will; and resolve to live no more in mood or emotion, but to build the edifice of our life on the granite of the obedient will.

1. THE CIRCUMSTANCES OUT OF WHICH THESE WORDS SPRANG.

Jeremiah's half-formed resolution. "I will not make mention of him, nor speak any more in his name." It is probable that by this time Nineveh had fallen. For six hundred years she had ruled surrounding nations with a rod of iron tyranny, exerting an imperial sway with merciless cruelty. At last her time had come. A vast host gathered from Asia Minor and surrounded her; for two years the siege had lasted under the direction of the trusted general of the last king of Nineveh, Nabopolassar, whose son, Nebuchadnezzar, was destined to be the "hammer of God."

At this time, Egypt was in the zenith of her power. Amid the weakening of Nineveh, Pharaoh had seized the opportunity to extend his empire to the banks of the Tigris. The kingdom of Judah, like all neighboring nations, owned, at least nominally, the king of Egypt as sovereign. Confidence in the proximity and prowess of his great ally encouraged Jehoiakim in his career of shameless idolatry and sin. The whole land, as we have seen, was corrupt.

Jeremiah, the foremost of the little band that remained true to the best traditions of the past, never lost an opportunity of striving to resist the downward progress of his people. In doing this, he aroused an ever-growing weight of opposition. He sat alone, cast out by prophet and priest, by court and people. He was a laughing-stock to all. Everyone mocked him.

Matters culminated finally in the episode of chapters 19 and 20. Beneath a divine impulse he procured a common earthen bottle, and gathering a number of the elders, led them into the valley of Hinnom, beside the gate of the potsherds. On this spot the refuse of the city was perpetually exposed to the foul birds and the wild dogs. There he uttered a long and terrible indictment of the sins of his people, accompanying it with predictions of the certain and irrevocable doom to which they were hurrying. To emphasize his words he broke the potter's vessel, pouring forth its contents in token that the blood of his countrymen would be shed to saturate the soil.

Not satisfied with this, he returned from Tophet and stood in the court of the temple, perhaps on the steps that led up to the court of the priests. Crowds of people were probably at the time engaged in some sacred rite; it may have been the time of one of the great feasts. When his voice was heard, a large crowd must have gathered, whose angry faces and vehement gestures indicated the intensity of their dislike. The endurance of one of them at least had at last reached its limit. Pashur, the chief governor of the temple, gathering a band of Levites, or temple servants, seized the prophet, threw him on the pavement, scourged him, and finally thrust him into the stocks, leaving him there all night to the ridicule and hatred of the populace, to the cold night and the prowling dogs.

In the morning Pashur appears to have repented of his harsh treatment, and to have released the prophet, whose strong spirit was not for a moment intimidated by the indignity and torture to which he had been exposed. Turning on his persecutor, he told him that he would live to be a terror to himself and all his friends; that all Judah would be given into the hand of the king of Babylon; that the people would be carried captives to Babylon, and slain there with the sword; and that all the riches of the city would be given into the hand of their enemies to carry to Babylon.

Set free, Jeremiah went to his home, and there poured forth that marvelous combination of heroic faith and wailing grief, which is recorded for us that we may know the weakness of his nature, and learn how earthen was the vessel in which God had placed His heavenly treasure. He was no brazen wall, but a reed shaken by the wind.

Then came a suggestion to his heart that he should relinquish his labors, and renounce public for private life. Why struggle anymore against the inevitable? Why set himself to convince those who would not be convinced, and who repaid his love with hate?

Not dissimilar have been the appeals of God's servants in every age, when they measured their weakness against the strength of the evils they combated, and marked their limited success. They have felt like crying, with the greatest of the prophets, "It is enough, let me die!"

2. THE IRRESISTIBLE IMPULSE. "But his word was in mine heart as a burning fire shut up in my bones, and I was weary with forbearing, and I could not stay." "O LORD, thou art stronger than I, and hast prevailed." Three things interest us here.

a. *The prophet's habit of turning from man to God.* Throughout the book there are so many indications of the close fellowship in which he lived with Jehovah. God seemed always near at hand. He poured into the ear of God every thought as it passed through his soul. He spread his roots by the river of God, which is full of water.

Let us seek this attitude of soul, which easily turns from man to God. Talk over each detail of your life with God, tell Him all things, and find the many needs of the soul satisfied in Him.

b. *The burning fire.* Within Jeremiah's heart a fire had been lit from the heart of God, and was kept aflame by the continual fuel heaped on it. The difficulty with him therefore was not in speaking, but in keeping silent—not in acting, but in refraining.

Our desire is to know how we may have this heart on fire. We are tired of a cold heart toward God. We complain because of our sense of effort in Christian life and duty. The source of the inward fire is the love of God; not primarily our love to God, but our sense of His love to us. If we set ourselves with open face toward the cross which, like a burning lens, focuses on the love of God and if, at the same time, we depend on the Holy Spirit—well called the Spirit of Burning—to do His will, we will find the ice that cakes the surface of our heart dissolving in tears of penitence; and presently the sacred fire will begin to glow. Then the love of Christ will constrain us; His almighty Spirit will destroy the fire of self-esteem, and replace it with the sacred fire of passionate devotion.

When that love has once begun to burn within the soul, when once the baptism of fire has set us aglow, the sins and sorrows of men will only incite in us a more ardent spirit. To see the multitudes rushing to destruction will be enough to fan the smoldering embers until they break out in the least emotional; as when Jeremiah said that he felt an inner impulse to restrain what was a weariness, and to stop obeying what was a sin.

c. *The prophet's safety.* "The LORD is with me as a mighty terrible one: therefore my persecutors shall stumble, and they shall not prevail." The presence of God is salvation. When Ezekiel describes the plot of Edom to possess herself of the land of the chosen people, he indicates by a single phrase the futility of the attempt, saying significantly, "Whereas the LORD was there" (Ezek. 35:10). It was enough, though Israel was in exile, that God's Spirit was brooding over their desolate land.

Jeremiah might be the weakest of the weak, having neither might, nor wisdom, nor power of speech, apparently the easy prey of Pashur and Jehoiakim; but since God was with him, he was invulnerable.

O weak and trembling soul, if you are true to God, He is with you, besetting you behind and before, and covering you with the shadow of His wing.

10

Afflictions, Distresses, Tumults
Jeremiah 26

Jehoiakim was, perhaps, the most despicable of the kings of Judah. Josephus says that he was unjust in disposition; an evildoer; neither pious toward God nor just toward men. Something of this may have been due to the influence of his wife Nehushta, whose father, Elnathan, was an accomplice in the royal murder of Urijah.

Jeremiah appears to have been constantly in conflict with this king; and probably the earliest manifestation of the antagonism that could not but subsist between two such men occurred in connection with the building of Jehoiakim's palace. Though his kingdom was greatly impoverished with the heavy fine of between forty and fifty thousand pounds imposed by Pharaoh Necho, after the defeat and death of Josiah, and though the times were dark with portents of approaching disaster, yet he began to build a splendid palace for himself, with spacious chambers and large windows, floors of cedar and decorations of vermilion. As Elijah confronted Ahab, so did Jeremiah confront the young king with his terrible woes: "Woe unto him that buildeth his house by unrighteousness, and his chambers by wrong; that useth his neighbour's service without wages, and giveth him not for his work; . . . thine eyes and thine heart are not but for thy covetousness . . . and for oppression, and for violence."

Clearly such a monarch must have entertained a mortal hatred toward the man who dared to raise his voice in denunciation of his crimes; and, like Herod with John the Baptist, he would not have hesitated to quench in blood the light that cast such strong condemnation on his oppressive and cruel actions. Little attention then, could be expected by Jeremiah. But it would appear that this time, at least, his safety was secured by the interposition of influential friends among the aristocracy, one of whom was Ahikam the son of Shaphan (26:20–24).

1. THE DIVINE COMMISSION. Beneath the divine impulse, Jeremiah went up to the court of the Lord's house and took his place on some great occasion when all the cities of Judah had sent their populations to worship there. Not one word was to be kept back. The heart of man may become the medium through which God can pour his thoughts on men.

2. THE MESSAGE AND ITS RECEPTION. There was a twofold appeal in the words Jeremiah was commissioned to deliver on this great occasion, when the whole land seemed eager to listen. On the one side, by his lips, God entreated His people to

repent, and turn from their evil ways; on the other, He bade them know that their obduracy would compel Him to make their great national shrine as complete a desolation as the site of Shiloh, which for five hundred years had been in ruins. It is impossible to realize the intensity of passion that such words evoked. They seemed to insinuate that Jehovah could not defend His own, or that their religion had become so heartless that He would not. Prophets and priests had assured the people that the very presence among them of Jehovah's temple was a guarantee of their safety; and to suggest that a fate might overtake them like that which in the days of Samuel made the ears of every listener to tingle seemed the height of impertinence. There is little doubt that Jeremiah would have met his death had it not been for the prompt interposition of the princes.

3. WELCOME INTERPOSITION. The princes were seated in the palace, and instantly on receiving tidings of the outbreak, came up to the temple. Their presence stilled the excitement, and prevented the infuriated people from carrying out their plans on the life of the defenseless prophet. They hastily constituted themselves into a court of appeal, before which prophet and people were summoned. The priests and prophets acted as the exponents of the people's wish, and demanded sentence of death, turning from the court to the people, to ask their concurrence. Then Jeremiah stood on his defense. His plea was that he could not but utter the words with which the Lord had sent him. He acknowledged that he was in their hands, but he warned them that innocent blood would bring its own nemesis on them all; and at the close of his address he reaffirmed his calling from Jehovah.

This bold and ingenuous defense seems to have turned the scale in his favor. The princes gave their verdict: "This man is not worthy to die: for he hath spoken to us in the name of the LORD our God." And the fickle populace, swept here and there by the wind, appear to have passed over *en masse* to the same conclusion; so that princes and people stood in a body against the false prophets and priests. The conclusion thus gained was further confirmed by the voice of certain of the elders of the land, who had come from all the cities of Judah, and who reminded the people that the good king Hezekiah had acted very differently to the prophet Micah in listening to his remonstrances, entreating the favor of the Lord, and securing the reversal of the divine sentence.

Thus does God hide His faithful servants in the hollow of His hand. No weapon that is formed against them prospers.

HISTORICAL CONNECTION. We have no narrative in Scripture of the fall of Nineveh, except the prophecy by Nahum. On her ruins arose the Babylonian empire, first under the government of Nabopolassar, and afterward of his greater son, Nebuchadnezzar.

In a previous chapter we saw that Egypt was mistress of all lands from the Nile to the Euphrates. But as soon as the Chaldeans had established their kingdom on the ruins of Nineveh, they turned their attention to wrest from Pharaoh Necho some portion of his vast empire. Jeremiah had depicted in graphic imagery the scene and issue of the awful battle at Carchemish, by the Euphrates, where the two mighty peoples wrestled for the supreme power of the world.

He heard the call to arms. He beheld the horses heavily armed, and the horsemen with flashing spears and coats of mail. Egypt never rallied again, nor dared to do more than strive against the yoke that Nebuchadnezzar, with imperial might, fastened on her.

After this there was nothing to stop the onset of Nebuchadnezzar, who probably had been associated in the kingdom with his aged father, and the first year of whose reign would therefore coincide with the fourth year of Jehoiakim (25:1). Like a leopard, to use the expression of Habakkuk, the young king leaped on the peoples who had been subject to Egypt, and had aided in her expedition. And as the tidings of his prowess spread through the world, Jeremiah foretold that he would be the scourge of God, to punish the abounding wickedness of the people.

In his first invasion of Judah, the king of Babylon contented himself with binding Jehoiakim in chains to carry him to Babylon, though he seems afterward to have changed his intention, and to have restored him to this throne as his vassal, taking an oath of allegiance (Ezek. 17:12–13). He stripped the temple of its precious vessels to enrich the house of his god at Babylon, and carried into captivity several of the mighty of the land, among them Daniel and his three friends (Dan. 1:1–2). He then hastened back to Babylon, summoned there by the news of the death of his father, Nabopolassar.

For three years Jehoiakim remained faithful to his oath (2 Kings 24:1); then he was deluded by the hope of independence, based on the hope of forming a confederation of neighboring peoples. Messengers went to and fro between himself and Pharaoh, negotiating for horses and people; though all this time Ezekiel and Jeremiah protested that Jehovah would certainly punish him for violating his pledge to the king of Babylon. The prophets of Jehovah did their utmost to avert a political mistake, founded on a moral delinquency and sure to incur terrible vengeance (Ezek. 17:15–21).

It befell as they feared. Nebuchadnezzar, who was not prepared to brook such infidelity on the part of a subject king, soon put his forces in motion, and prepared to advance across the desert to punish the weak and faithless Jehoiakim. It was during his march on Jerusalem that the incidents narrated in the two following chapters took place, the one the proclamation of a fast, the other the gathering of the Rechabites, with other fugitives, into the shelter of the city.

We have no certain clue to the prophet's history during these three or four years. His heart must have been filled with the patriot's anguish as he saw the coils of invasion drawn closer around the devoted city.

11

The Indestructible Word
Jeremiah 36:23

We are admitted to the prophet's private chamber, where he is keeping close that he may not excite the acute animosity and hatred of the people. Baruch, his trusted friend, a man of rank and learning, sits writing with laborious care at the dictation of the prophet.

When the roll was filled Jeremiah, not venturing to go into places of public assembly, entrusted it to Baruch, and urged him to read it to the assembled crowds. Jerusalem just then was unusually full. From all parts of Judah people had come to observe the great fast that had been proclaimed in view of the approach of the Babylonian army.

Choosing a position in the upper court at the entry of the new gate to the Lord's house, Baruch began to read, while the people stood densely massed around him. Amid the awestruck crowd was a young man, Micaiah, the grandson of Shaphan, who was so impressed and startled by what he heard that he hastened to inform the princes, then sitting in council in the chamber of the chief Secretary of State, in the royal palace. They in turn were so aroused by what he told them that they sent him back to the temple, and asked Baruch to come without delay and read the prophet's words to them. He came at their request, and sitting among them, began to read.

A great fear fell on them as they heard those ominous words, which were probably closely similar to those recorded in the twenty-fifth chapter of this book. It seemed their plain duty was to acquaint the king with the contents of the roll.

Before doing so, however, they counseled Baruch and Jeremiah to conceal themselves, for they well knew the despotic and passionate temper of Jehoiakim; and the roll was left in the chamber of Elishama. It would appear that in the first instance they thought a verbal statement of the words they had heard would suffice. This, however, would not satisfy the king, who urged Jehudi to get the roll itself. It was winter, the month of December; the king was occupying the winter quarters of his palace, and a fire was burning brightly in the brazier. It is a vivid picture—the king sitting before the fire; the princes standing around him; Jehudi reading the contents of the roll; consternation and panic reigning throughout the city and darkening the faces of the prostrate crowds in the temple courts. As Jehudi began to read, the royal brow knit, and after the scribe had read three or four columns, Jehoiakim snatched the roll from his hand and, demanding the penknife he carried as symbol and implement of his calling, began to cut the manuscript in pieces, which he flung contemptuously into the fire. Nothing could stop him until the whole roll was cut to pieces, and every fragment consumed. Not content with this flagrant act of defiance, he gave orders for the immediate arrest of Jeremiah and Baruch; an order which his emissaries attempted to execute, but in vain.

The destruction of the roll did not however cancel the terrible doom to which the ship of state was hurrying. On another roll all the words of the book that he had burned were written again; and others were added foretelling the indignity and insult to which the dead body of the king would be exposed. "His dead body shall be cast out in the day to the heat, and in the night to the frost."

1. EYES OPENED TO SEE. There was a vast difference between Baruch, whose heart was in perfect sympathy with Jeremiah, and Jehudi or the princes. But there was almost as much between the faithful scribe and the heaven-illumined prophet. The one could write only as the words streamed from those burning lips; he saw nothing, he realized nothing; to him the walls of the chamber were the utmost bound of vision: while the other beheld the whole landscape of truth outspread before him. Men may be seers still.

It is very important that all Christians should be alive to and possess this power of vision. It is deeper than intellectual, since it is spiritual; it is not the result of reasoning or learning, but of intuition; it cannot be acquired in the school of earthly science, but is the gift of Him who alone can open the eyes of the blind. If you lack it, seek it at the hands of Jesus; be willing to do His will, and you will know. If you have the opened eye, you will not need books of evidences to establish to your satisfaction the truth of our holy religion; the glory of the risen Lord; the world of the unseen. They who see these things are indifferent to the privations of the tent life or, as in Jeremiah's case, rise superior to the hatred of man and the terrors of a siege.

2. THE USE OF THE PENKNIFE. Men use the knife to the Bible in varied ways. *Teachers of error do this.* They have done it. They will do it again. They are wise to do it—I mean, wise in their own interests. For when once the Bible is in the hands of the

people, the false teacher, who has deluded them for selfish purposes, must pack.

The next that follows Jehoiakim's practice is *the infidel*, who uses the sharp blade of bitter sarcasm and miscalled reason to destroy the Scriptures. The hostility that manifested itself in the winter palace among the princes of this world, has wrought in the halls of earthly learning and science, instigating similar acts to theirs. The Bible is cut up regularly once in each generation by men like these.

The next are the *higher critics* of our time, who surely have gone beyond the necessities of the case in their ruthless use of the knife. There is room for the honest examination of the fabric of sacred Scripture, its language, the evidence furnished in its texture of the successive hands that have reedited its most ancient documents; but this is altogether different to ruthless vandalism.

We are all tempted to use Jehudi's penknife. It is probably that no one is free from the almost unconscious habit of evading or toning down certain passages that conflict with the doctrinal or ecclesiastical position in which we were reared, or which we have assumed.

In our private reading of the Scripture, we must beware of using the penknife. Whole books and tracts of truth are practically cut out of the Bible of some earnest Christians—passages referring to the Second Advent, the inevitable doom of the ungodly; those who describe the types and shadows of the ancient law; or those who build up massive systems of truth and doctrine, as in the epistles. But we can only eliminate these things at our peril. It is a golden rule to read the Bible as a whole. Of course each will have his favorite passages but, beside these, there should be the loving and devout study of all Scripture, which is given by inspiration of God.

3. THE INDESTRUCTIBLE WORD. Men may destroy the words and the fabric on which they are written, but not the Word itself. It must sometimes be an uncomfortable reflection to those who refuse the testimony of the Word of God, that their attitude toward the message cannot affect the reality to which it bears witness.

Jeremiah wrote another roll. The money spent in buying up copies of the Bible to burn at St. Paul's enabled Tyndale to reissue the Scriptures in a cheaper form and a better type. And perhaps the most remarkable fact in this connection is that, in spite of all that has been done to stamp out the Bible, it exists in millions of copies, and is circulated among all the nations of the world; it is with us today in unimpaired authority.

And the facts to which Jeremiah bore witness all came to pass. Neither knife nor fire could arrest the inevitable doom of the king, city, and people. The drunken captain may cut in pieces the chart that tells of the rocks in the vessel's course, and put in irons the sailor who calls his attention to it; but neither will avert the crash that must follow unless the helm is turned. You may tamper with and destroy the record, but the stubborn facts remain.

12

The Rechabites
Jeremiah 35:6–10

The march of Nebuchadnezzar on Jerusalem was anticipated by invasions of Syrians, Moabites, and the children of Ammon. They swept up the valley, massacred the peasantry, devoured the crops, and spread terror on every hand. The inhabitants, eager to save their lives and some relics of their property, left their houses and lands to the mercy of the invader, and fled for protection to the metropolis; figuring that within the massive walls of Zion they would find safety. What a stir there must have been as day by day the motley groups pressed in under the old gateways, gray with age, and sought accommodation and food in the already overcrowded tenements of the city!

Among the rest came a tribe that excited much curiosity by reason of its strange and antique manners. The sheikh's name was Jaazaniah—"he whom Jehovah hears"; and his brethren and sons and the heads of other households were with him. They refused to seek shelter in the houses or permanent buildings of the city, but pitched their dusky tents in some open space within the walls, and there awaited the turn of events.

Their record was an honorable one, and reached far back into the early days of Hebrew history. When Israel was passing through the wilderness of Sinai, the tribe of the Kenites showed them kindness; and this laid the foundation of perpetual friendliness between the two peoples. It was of this tribe that the Rechabites, for such was the name of this strange tent-loving people, had sprung (Judg. 4:17–24; 1 Sam. 15:6; 1 Chron. 2:55).

About the time of Elijah, and perhaps largely influenced by him, the sheikh, or leader of one branch of the Kenites, was Jonadab the son of Rechab. He was dismayed at the abounding corruption and iniquity of the time, and especially of the northern kingdom, then under the fatal spell of Jezebel's and Ahab's influence. This noble man bound his people under a solemn pledge to drink no wine forever; nor to build houses, nor sow seed, nor plant vineyards, but to dwell in tents. Two hundred and fifty years had passed since then, but when they arrived in Jerusalem they were still true to the traditions of their race; living representatives of the noblest and purest days of Hebrew story.

1. JEREMIAH'S TEST OF THE RECHABITES. As soon as their arrival was noised abroad, and had come to the ears of Jeremiah, he was seized by a divine impulse to use them as a striking object lesson for his own people. Taking the leaders of the Rechabites with him, he went into the temple, to a room belonging to the sons of Hanan.

It is probable that a small group of Jews, arrested by the prophet's association with these strange-looking men, followed them in to watch the proceedings. They were curious witnesses of the prophet's action, as he had bowls of wine set before the tribesmen, and cups offered to them, that they might dip in them and drink. They also heard the blunt unqualified refusal of these quaint old-fashioned Puritans, "We will drink no wine," followed by an explanation of the solemn obligation laid on them centuries before.

The moral was obvious. Here were men loyal to the wish of their ancestor. How great a contrast to the people of Jerusalem! If the people could not heed words of expostulation, of entreaty, and warning, taking them to be exaggerated and vain, they should at least be compelled to admit that not one of God's threats of vengeance fell impotent on the air or missed its aim.

On the other hand, such devotion to principle; such persistent culture of simplicity, frugality, and abstinence; such literal adherence to the will of the father of their house had to receive the signature and blessing of the Almighty. "Therefore thus saith the LORD of hosts, the God of Israel; Jonadab the son of Rechab shall not want a man to stand before me for ever."

2. THE ELEMENTS OF A STRONGLY RELIGIOUS LIFE. The phrase "to stand before God" designates a deep religious life, and includes the knowledge of God, the faculty of executing His commands, and the power of interceding for others. Oh, to stand always before Him, on whose face the glory of God shines as the sun in His strength! But if this is to be something more than an idle dream, three things should be remembered.

a. *There must be close adherance to great principles.* They stood on the principles that Jonadab had laid down to guide them; and they did not hesitate to keep them; let those ridicule who would.

In contrast to this, we drift with the current. Let me urge my readers not to do or permit things simply because custom, or taste, or public opinion advocates them; but to bring their entire life to the touchstone of the kingdom of heaven.

What a revolution would come to us all if it became the one fixed aim and ambition of our lives to always do those things that are pleasing in His sight! It would not make us less tender in our friendships, or less active in our service. It would not take the sparkle from the eye, the nerve from the grasp, or the warm glow from the heart. But it would check many a vain word, stop many a silly act, stop much selfish and vainglorious deeds, and bring us back to whatever things are true, honorable, just, pure, lovely, and of good report.

b. *Abstinence from the spirit of the age.* Their abstinence was not only a protest against the evils that were honeycombing their age, but was a sure safeguard against participation in them. In these days, the same principles apply. Surely, then, we will do well to say with the Rechabites, "We will drink no wine."

But wine may stand for the spirit of the age, its restlessness, its constant thirst for novelty, for amusement, for fascination. It is easier to abstain from alcohol than from this insidious spirit of our time. We might well refer to this the wise words of the apostle: "Be not drunk with wine, wherein is excess; but be filled with the Spirit" (Eph. 5:18). You cannot exorcize Satan by a negation. It is only those who are filled by the Holy Spirit, in His blessed energy, who are proof against the intoxicating cup of this corrupt world.

c. *We must hold lightly to the things around us.* The Rechabites dwelt in tents. They drove their large flocks from place to place, and were content with the simple life of the wandering shepherd. It was in this way that the great patriarchs had lived before them (Heb. 11:8, 13). And ever since their days the tent life has been the chosen emblem of the life that is so strongly attacted to the other world as to be lightly attached to this.

All of us are conscious of ties that hold us to the earth. It may be name, fame, notoriety, pride of fashion, rank, money. But whatever it is, if it is a weight that impedes our speed heavenward; it should be laid deliberately on God's altar, that He may do with it as He will, and that we may be able, without hindrance, to be wholly for God.

13

Hidden But Radiant
Jeremiah 36:26

After Jehoiakim had deliberately cut in pieces the prophet's roll, and so rejected his warnings and expostulations; and when in addition to this he had threatened the lives of

God's faithful servants—it became clear that no further good could be gained by reiterating his messages. Thus the prophet's voice was hushed, apparently for the remainder of the reign of this bad and infatuated king.

Into that new and beautiful palace of Jehoiakim, whose spacious halls were ceiled with cedar from Lebanon, lighted by wide windows, and painted with bright colors, the one presence never entered which at that time would have saved the ship of state—as the timely arrival of a pilot may save an ocean steamer from the fatal ignorance of an incompetent captain. The false prophets might beguile the ears of king and people with predictions. The strong Egyptian partisans might urge on the king alliance with Pharaoh as the certain cure for the difficulties of their position. But Jeremiah's voice, during the dark and troublesome days that succeeded that scene in the palace, and until Jehoiakim's body was cast forth, unburied and unwept, was still. How did it fare with the prophet during those eventful years?

1. THE LORD HID HIM. Jeremiah was hidden in the cover of the divine presence from the plottings of man, and was kept secretly in a pavilion from the strife of tongues.

There is a literal sense also, O tried and tempted believer, in which God will hide you. On one occasion when the dragoons of Claverhouse were scouring the mountains of Scotland in search of the Covenanters, a little party of these godly folk, gathered on the hillside for prayer, would have fallen into their hands had not a cloud suddenly settled on them, effectively concealing them from their pursuers. Thus the Son of God still interposes for His own. Live to Him alone. Abide in Him.

2. HE REEDITED HIS PROPHECIES. To this period we may refer the divine injunction: "Thus speaketh the LORD God of Israel, saying, Write thee all the words that I have spoken unto thee in a book" (30:1–2). It may be that throughout this period Baruch continued to act as his faithful amanuensis and scribe. He, at least, was certainly included in the divine hidings (36:26–32). It was at great cost to his earthly prospects. He came of a good family, and he cherished the ambition of distinguishing himself among his colleagues. But he was reconciled to the lot of suffering and sorrow to which his close identification with Jeremiah led him, by a special revelation, assuring him of the speedy overthrow of the state; and that, in the general chaos, he would escape with his life (chap. 45).

By the aid of this faithful friend, Jeremiah gathered together the prophecies that he had uttered on various occasions, and put them in order, especially elaborating the predictions given in the fourth year of Jehoiakim against the surrounding nations. The word of the Lord came to him concerning the Philistines, and Moab, and the children of Ammon and Edom, Damascus and Kedar. And the devout student may well pause to read again the marvelous paragraphs that foretell the fate of these nations, beneath the all-desolating incursions of Nebuchadnezzar and his ruthless soldiers. "Thou art my battle axe and weapons of war," said the prophet, addressing the great king in Jehovah's name; "with thee will I break in pieces that nations, and with thee will I destroy kingdoms" (see 47 to 49:33).

This time of Jeremiah's seclusion was therefore not lost to the world. Unseen, the prophet busied himself, as the night settled down on his country, in kindling the sure light of prophecy that should cast its radiant beams over the dark waters of time, until the day should dawn, and the daystar die out in the eastern sky.

3. HE MADE A DOUBLE JOURNEY TO BABYLON. To this period we must also refer the incident of the linen girdle, because the discourse on it was delivered during the three months' reign of Jehoiachin, which was altogether too brief to admit of so long a journey as was necessary for the purposes on which the prophet was set (chap. 13; notably verse 18).

The Israelite was extremely particular as to cleanliness, and especially of linen. It therefore attracted universal notice that Jeremiah, at a certain period, wore a newly-purchased linen girdle without washing it. When it was soiled and filthy, he took it, under divine direction, to the river Euphrates, and there buried it in a hole of the rock.

After his return from Babylon, "many days" passed. Indeed, his second journey, to recover his marred girdle, may have been so timed by almighty Providence as to insure his absence from the city during the last scene of Jehoiakim's sad and tragic history; and to bring him there again as Jehoiachin began his brief reign. But that rotted piece of linen, held up before the eyes of his people, told its own sad story. Judah and Jerusalem might have been to Jehovah for a name, a praise, and a glory; but they went after other gods. Therefore they were destined to be cast aside as worthless and unprofitable.

The lesson of this double journey, which must have meant about a thousand miles on foot, teaches us that no exertion on our part should be considered excessive, if we can execute the commissions of our King. It is enough if He has said, "Go to Euphrates." When once we are sure of this, we must imitate the prophet, who says, with charming simplicity, "So I went to Euphrates."

4. HE HAD VISIONS OF THE NEW COVENANT. There is much reason for supposing that it was in this time of seclusion that Jeremiah's eyes were opened to see a spiritual truth, which was far in advance of any contemporary revelation, and was destined to become the mold into which some of the richest ore of gospel truth should be poured.

The exquisite poem to which we must now turn is found in chapters 30 and 31, and consists of some seven stanzas. The prophet is no longer concerned with Judah alone; his thought embraces the ten tribes also—"Israel" he calls them, or "Ephraim," which one hundred and seventy years before had been carried away captive to Nineveh. But his heart exults as he anticipates the return of the entire people from the land of the north, baptized through suffering, into a purer, nobler life.

> Fear thou not, O my servant Jacob, saith the LORD,
> Neither be dismayed, O Israel;
> For, lo, I will save thee from afar,
> And thy seed from the land of their captivity.
>
> I will restore health unto thee,
> And I will heal thee of thy wounds, saith the LORD.
>
> Yea, I have loved thee with an everlasting love:
> Therefore with loving-kindness have I drawn thee.
> Again will I build thee,
> And thou shalt be built, O virgin of Israel;
> Thou shalt again be adorned with thy tabrets,
> And shalt go forth in the dances of them that make merry.
>
> My people shall be satisfied with my goodness, saith
> the LORD.

Transported by words like these, as he lay in prophetic trance, it is no wonder that Jeremiah experienced an ecstatic joy. "Upon this I awaked and beheld; and my sleep was sweet unto me" (31:26).

But the more stupendous revelation was to follow. God unveiled the glory of the new covenant, a covenant that would no longer depend on man's obedience to "Thou shalt," and "Thou shalt not"; but would glisten with the seven times repeated, "I will" of God (31:31–34; Luke 22:20; Heb. 8:8–12).

That the law of God should not be *without* as a precept, but *within*, as though worked into the very structure of the heart and will; this was the vision that illumined the prophet's heart, and is realized in Christ for all who belong to Him by faith. This blessed covenant will yet gather Israel within its provisions, and then our heart will go out in the dance; our mourning will be turned into joy; our soul will be as a watered garden; and God will comfort us, making us rejoice from our sorrow, and enabling us to reap in joy what we sowed in tears (31:10–14).

14

The Ministry of Destruction
Jeremiah 27:2–9

When Jeremiah was first summoned to the work of prophet, it was divided under six distinct divisions. He was set over nations and kingdoms to pluck up, and to break down, and to destroy, and to overthrow; to build and to plant (1:10). Two-thirds of his work was therefore in the direction of destruction. It is not pleasant or easy work. Before the sowing of the seed, there must be the plowing, before the ourburst of the spring, the stern disintegration of winter, rubbing the soil to powder in its mighty hands. Such was the work that fell to the lot of Jeremiah.

1. THE WORK OF DEMOLITION.
   a. *Jehoiakim.* When Josiah died, the whole land mourned. Each citizen felt personally bereaved. But Jeremiah foretold that at the death of Jehoiakim there should be no such expression. "He shall be buried with the burial of an ass, drawn and cast forth beyond the gates of Jerusalem." And again, when the king in impious defiance had burned the roll, the prophet said, "He shall have none to sit upon the throne of David: and his dead body shall be cast out in the day to the heat, in the night to the frost" (22:13–19; 36:29–31).

The words of the prophet carried with them the imprimatur of Jehovah. They pronounced the inevitable sentence that He executed. There are several traditions as to his death—one that he was assassinated in the streets of Jerusalem; another that he fell in a skirmish with raiders; another that he was enticed to the camp of the king of Babylon, and there treacherously murdered; but he died as he lived, dishonorably and miserably.

   b. *Jeconiah.* His was a reign, like Napoleon's after his return from Elba, of one hundred days. He was eighteen when he was called to the throne, and he occupied it for three months and ten days (2 Chron. 36:9); but in that brief time he was able to show the drift of his character. "He did evil in the sight of the LORD." His mother, Nehushta, and the strong heathen party who dominated the policy of the court, between them molded the young monarch to their will.

Jeremiah uttered the words of awful significance. Passing through the streets he showed the marred linen girdle, and foretold the doom of the king and queen mother. "Sit down," he cried, "in the dust; for the crown of royalty shall be rolled from your brow to the ground." He said that Coniah would be given into the hands of those who sought his life, and of those of whom he was afraid; that Jehovah would cast his mother and himself, like a despised broken vessel, into another country, where they were not born; that there they should die (13:18–21; 22:28–30).

And so it happened. Such was the bitter fierceness of the Chaldeans, who were again besieging the city to punish Jehoiakim's treachery, that nothing would appease them but the surrender of the persons of the king and his mother. There was no alternative; the king, his mother, the nobles and officials, all went to the Chaldean camp and sat down on the ground, robed in black, and their faces veiled. By this time Nebuchadnezzar had returned from fighting against Pharaoh Necho, who had marched to the relief of his ally, but had finally been stopped; and he received in person the submission of the royal fugitives (2 Kings 24:7).

The spoliation of the city followed. The temple was stripped of its gold and treasures. All the princes, and the mighty men of valor, the craftsmen and the smiths, the king's harem and court officials, were manacled in long lines, and torn from their beloved country, the majority of which were never again to be seen. Ezekiel was one of that sad procession; and it seemed as though a pitiful wail arose from the whole country as the exiles wended their way to their distant destination. And the prophet wept deeply, because the Lord's flock was taken captive.

c. *The prophets.* The prophets were a large and influential class. Dating from the days of Samuel, their schools had sent forth a succession of men hwo occupied a unique position in the land as the representatives of God. But in the degenerate days of which we are now writing, when the kingdom of Judah was rapidly tottering to its fall, they seemed to have been deeply infected by the prevailing vices of their time. Greedy and drunken, lazy and dissolute, dreaming, lying down, and loving to slumber, they denied the Lord and said, when Jeremiah spoke, "It is not He" (Isa. 56:9–12; Jer. 5:12).

It must have been very painful for Jeremiah to oppose them and counteract their influence on the people, but he had no alternative. Listen to these terrible words, spoken in the name of Jehovah, "I have seen in the prophets of Jerusalem an horrible thing: they commit adultery, and walk in lies; they strengthen also the hands of evildoers, that none doth return from his wickedness: they are all of them unto me as Sodom, and the inhabitants thereof as Gomorrah" (23:9–14). Jeremiah urged his people not to listen to these men, who spoke the vision of their own heart, and not out of the mouth of the Lord.

Matters came to pass shortly after the deportation of Jeconiah. Hananiah, of Gibeon, which was one of the priestly settlements, rose up and publicly contradicted Jeremiah when he was speaking in the temple, in the presence of the priests and of all the people. Using the holy name of Jehovah, he declared it had been divinely revealed to him that in two years Jeconiah, and all the captives, and all the sacred vessels, which Nebuchadnezzar had taken away, would be returned. Jeremiah instantly spoke up from amid the crowd. "Amen," he cried; "would that it might be so; would that Jehovah might return the captives; but it shall not be. No, it cannot be, without cancelling words that have been spoken by Him through the prophets before me, and even before."

Not content with his words, however, the false prophet snatched from Jeremiah's shoulders the wooden yoke that he carried for the purpose of perpetually reminding his people and the neighboring nations that they must serve the king of Babylon until the appointed time had gone. He broke it in two, saying that in this way God within two years would break Nebuchadnezzar's yoke. Jeremiah did not prolong the altercation; but privately told Hananiah that the yoke of wood would be replaced by one of iron, and that he was causing the people to trust a lie. "This year thou shalt die," he said, as he turned away; and two months later the false prophet was a corpse.

d. *The surrounding nations.* On two occasions Jeremiah protested agains a combination of the surrounding nations to resist the growing power of Babylon, which without doubt was fostered by the neighboring power of Egypt (chs. 25, 27).

All this must have laid the prophet open to the charge of the lack of patriotism; his words weakened the people; his influence withheld them from joining a great league of emancipation. He had no alternative, however, but to be spokesman of that great word of Jehovah, "I will overturn, overturn, overturn."

e. *The exiles.* The false prophets had suffered the fate of their nation and were with the rest in captivity; they at once endeavored to raise the hopes of the exiles by prophesying a speedy return. "It is of no use," they said in effect, "to build houses, or plant gardens, or enter into marriage relations. In a short time we will be back in Jerusalem again." The ringleaders were Zedekiah and Ahab, men of grossly immoral life, who were made an example of by being roasted alive (29:21–23). Still the ferment continued, and the people refused to settle down into contentment with the conditions of their captivity.

Jeremiah therefore wrote a letter, which was entrusted to two men of high rank, who were friends, whom Zedekiah, the uncle and successor of Jeconiah, sent to Babylon with assurances of his fidelity. "Yield to the will of God" was the burden of the letter. "Build, plant, settle." "Seek the peace of the city where God has caused you to be carried away captives, and pray to the Lord for it: for in its peace you shall have peace." When Shemaiah, one of these false prophets, heard this letter, he hurriedly wrote to Zephaniah, who was now high priest, and demanded that the prophet be put into stocks, and his head into a collar, as a madman. The high priest, however, read the letter to Jeremiah, who replied by sending a second letter to the exiles, assuring them that God would punish Shemaiah and his seed, so that he would not have a son to perpetuate his name, and would not see the good that could come at the end of the predestined time (chap. 29).

These denunciations were filled with terror; and equally terrible was the fate that befell these men.

2. His COADJUTOR. While Jeremiah was exercising this ministry of destruction in utter loneliness and isolation, his heart must often have misgiven him. Remember that he loved his country with all the passionate patriotism of which the Jewish nature was capable. It was just because he loved so much that he suffered so much.

Suppose that Jeremiah had put aside the heavenly summons, and had lived in the sequestered ease of Anathoth: he might have secured a respectable and peaceable life, but Jehovah would never have spoken to him.

God sent him an ally and comrade in the heart of the exiles, Ezekiel arose, uttering the same messages, though he was clothed in the superb imagery of his gorgeous imagination. He too denounced his people's sins; advised them to settle in the land of exile; and spoke of the certain doom of the people and city. In the mouth of these two witnesses every word was established. Like well-attuned instruments, they harmonized. Theirs was no easy task, for they were hated by those whom their words tormented. But God has long since called them to His throne, where they stand in the foremost rank of those who, having fulfilled the will of God, have received His welcome and reward.

3. THE NEED OF THIS MINISTRY.

a. *It must be fulfilled with the unconverted.* One of the most important ministries of the servant of God is to destroy false confidence, and to show the utter futility of venturing on the sea of entry in any other craft than that which Christ launched from the cross of Calvary.

b. *It must be fulfilled with those who lack assurance.* When men say that they cannot believe, it is probably because they are harboring some evil thing in their hearts, or are conscious of some unrepaired wrong in their lives. The inability to realize acceptance with God often points to something that is grieving the Spirit; and at such times the searching ministry of probing and testing and demolition is invaluable.

c. *It must be fulfilled in the higher attainments of the divine life.* As our obedience grows, our light will grow. The Holy Spirit will lead us to discriminate between the wrong and the right, and reveal what may be hindering us. Then as He destroys one subterfuge after another, ploughs up the fallow ground, disinters the buried secrets, reveals us to ourselves—we may gratefully accept His ministry; which destroys to build that He may minister eternal life.

15

Jeremiah's Grandest Ode
Jeremiah 51

It was a very deserted Jerusalem in which Jeremiah lived, after king Jehoiachin, his household and court, princes and mighty men of valor had been carried off to Babylon. Still, the fertility and natural resources of the land were so considerable as to give hope of its comparative prosperity, as a trailing vine dependent on Babylon (Ezek. 17).

Mattaniah, the third son of Josiah—who was now in his twenty-first year—was called to the throne by the conqueror, and required to hold it under a solemn oath of allegiance which was affirmed and sanctioned by an appeal to Jehovah Himself. It was as though the heathen monarch thought to make insubordination impossible on the part of the young monarch, since his word of honor was ratified under such solemn and august conditions—conditions that under similar circumstances the heathen king would probably have felt binding and final.

At the urging of his conqueror, the young king took the name Zedekiah, "the righteousness of Jehovah." It was an auspicious sign; every encouragement was given him to follow in the footsteps of his illustrious father. And throughout his reign he gave evident tokens of desiring better things, but he was weak and irresolute, lacking strength of purpose. He respected Jeremiah, but did not dare to espouse his cause publicly, showing him his royal favor by stealth.

Meanwhile the kingdom was violently agitated by rumors from every side, which encouraged the hope that before long the power of Babylon would be broken and the exiles returned. These thoughts were rife among the exiles themselves, as we have seen; they were diligently fostered by the false prophets.

About this time there was a revolt in Elam against Babylon. What if this should spread until the empire itself became disintegrated! But Jeremiah, by the voice of God, said: "It shall not be; the bow of Elam shall be broken; her king and princes destroyed, her people scattered toward the four winds of heaven" (see 49:34–39).

Then there was the seething discontent of the neighboring peoples who, though they had accompanied the invader as allies, were eager to regain their independence, and desired to draw Judah into one vast confederacy, with Egypt as its base. "No," said Jeremiah; "it must not be; Nebuchadnezzar is doing the behest of Jehovah; all the nations are to serve him, and his son, and his son's son" (see 27:6–7). Perhaps it was at Jeremiah's suggestion that Zedekiah at this time made a journey to Babylon to pay homage to his king, and assure him of his fidelity.

All through the troubles that followed, Jeremiah pursued the same policy; and his policy was so well known among the Chaldeans that in the final overthrow they gave him his life, and allowed him to choose where he would dwell (chap. 40).

It must have seemed to his choicest friends as though his advice was often wanting in the courage of faith. Did he really favor Babylon above Jerusalem? Was he traitorous to the best interests of his people? But if they ever entertained such questions, they must have been suddenly and completely disillusioned when he summoned them to hear the tremendous indictment he had composed against Babylon in the early months of Zedekiah's reign, together with the graphic description of its fall. A copy of this prophecy was entrusted to Seraiah, the chief chamberlain, who went in the train of Zedekiah to Babylon, with instructions that he should read it privately to the exiles; and then, weighting it with a stone, cast it into the midst of the Euphrates, with the solemn words, "Thus shall Babylon sink, and shall not rise from the evil that I will bring upon her! and they shall be weary" (51:59–64).

1. THE PROPHECY OF THE FALL OF BABYLON

a. *The glory of Babylon.* In glowing imagery Jeremiah depicts her glory and beauty. She had been a golden cup in the hand of Jehovah; his battle axe and weapons of war. Her influence was carried far and wide. She dwelt by many waters, rich in treasure, and the wonder of the earth. Like a mighty tree, she stretched her branches over the surrounding lands.

b. *The divine controversy.* The Almighty had used her, but she had abused, for unrighteous and selfish ends, the power that God had entrusted to her. And therefore Jehovah opened his armory and brought out the weapons of his wrath.

But God was especially against Babylon for her treatment of His people. "As Babylon hath caused the slain of Israel to fall, so at Babylon shall fall the slain of all the earth . . . for the LORD God of recompenses shall surely requite."

c. *The summons to her foes.* The standard is raised, and around it, at the sounding of the trumpet, the nations gather. "Behold!" the prophet cries, "a people shall come from the north; and a great nation, and many kings shall be raised up from the coasts of the earth. They shall hold the bow and the lance; they are cruel, and will show no mercy; their voice shall roar like the sea, and they shall ride upon horses, every one put in array, like a man to the battle, against thee, O daughter of Babylon" (50:41–42).

d. *The attack.* The archers surround the city on every side, so that none may escape. They are commanded to shoot at her, and not spare their arrows. Now the battle shout is raised, and an assault is made against her walls. Lo, the fire breaks out amid her dwelling places. The messengers, running with similar tidings from different quarters of the city, come to show the king of Babylon that the fords are in the hand of the foe, and that the city is taken.

e. *The overthrow of the city.* Then the captured city is given up to the savage soldiery. There is plunder enough to satisfy the most rapacious. Her granaries are ruined; her treasuries ransacked; her stores of grain blown away. All the captive peoples are set free, and especially the Jews. "Let us forsake her," they cry, "and let us go every one into his own country; for her judgment reacheth unto heaven, and is lifted up even to the skies."

And now her cities become a desolation, a dry land; it lies waste from generation to generation.

Such were the predictions of Jeremiah. Seventy years were to pass before his words would be fulfilled, but history itself could hardly be more definite and precise. Those who can compare this prophecy with the story of the fall of Babylon, and with the researches of Layard, will find how exactly every detail was repeated.

"They drank wine, and praised the gods of gold, and of silver, of brass, or iron, of wood, and of stone. In the same hour came forth fingers of a man's hand, and wrote over against the candlestick upon the plaster of the wall of the king's palace. . . . In that night was Belshazzar the king of the Chaldeans slain, and Darius the Mede took the kingdom" (Dan. 5:4–5, 30–31).

2. BABYLON THE GREAT. In every age of the world, Babylon has had its counterpart. Where God has built up His kingdom, the devil has always counterfeited it by some travesty of his own.

Jeremiah comforted his heart amid the desolations that fell thick and heavily on his beloved fatherland, by anticipating the inevitable doom of the oppressor. Let us strengthen our confidence in the certain prevalence of good over evil, of the church over the world, and of Christ over Satan, as we consider the precise fulfillment of Jeremiah's predictions concerning the fall of Babylon. "So let all thine enemies perish, O Lord: but let them that love thee be as the sun when he goeth forth in his might."

3. OUR OWN BABYLON. Each heart has its special form of sin, to which it is liable, and by yielding to which it has been perpetually overthrown. How bitter have been your tears and self-reproach! How you have chafed and fumed beneath the strong iron bit of your tyrant!

But there is a deliverance for you, as for those weak in misguided but suffering Jews. How exactly your life history is delineated in theirs! They were the children of God; so are you. They might have lived in an impregnable fortress of God's covenant protection; so might you. They forfeited this by their disobedience and unbelief; so have you. But as God saved them by his own right hand, so will He save you.

Accept these rules, if you would have this blessed deliverance.

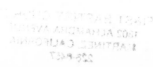

1. Put out of your life all known sin. Be willing to be set free, and deliberately tell God so.

2. Entrust the keeping of your soul to God. You cannot control it, but He can. He made you, and must be able to keep you. Put the case deliberately, thoughtfully, calmly into His hand. Do not cry, "Help me!" for that implies that you are going to do some and He some, and your part will inevitably destroy all; but cry, "Keep me!" thus throwing the entire responsibility on Him.

3. Believe that the almighty Savior accepts your deposit at the moment of your making it. As it leaves your hand, it passes into His. Be sure that He has undertaken it all for you. Do not try to *feel* that He has, but *believe* that He has. You may have no glad emotion, no feeling of victory, no share of ecstasy; never mind, lie still, and trust Him.

16

How a Reed Stood As a Pillar
Jeremiah 24; 34; 37

To a sensative nature it is an agony to stand alone. To many, the sense of being esteemed and loved is the very breath of life. They are so constituted as to require an atmosphere of sympathy for the full efforts of their powers.

Jeremiah, tender, shrinking, sensitive, with a vast capacity for emotion, strong to hate, and therefore to love, was not constituted by nature to stand alone. But in this let us adore that grace that stepped into his life and for forty years made him a defensed city, and an iron pillar, and brazen walls against the whole land—against princes, priests, and people. He outlasted all his foes, and maintained the standard to life's end. And this marvelous endurance and steadfastness of spirit was nowhere so conspicuous as during the last months of his nation's independence.

1. JEREMIAH'S ATTITUDE TOWARD THE KING. We gain much information concerning the situation at Jerusalem, during the reign of Zedekiah, from the pages of Ezekiel who, though resident in the land of the exile, faithfully reflected and in prophetic vision anticipated what was transpiring in the beloved city, to which his thoughts were incessantly directed.

Zedekiah, as we have seen, on ascending the throne bound himself under the most solemn sanctions to be loyal to the supremacy of Babylon; and there is no doubt that at the time he fully intended to be faithful, the more especially as, at Nebuchadnezzar's command, he took the oath of allegiance in the sacred name of Jehovah. But he was weak and young, and wholly in the hands of the strong court party that favored an alliance with Egypt, and the casting off of the Chaldean yoke.

Two years before the catastrophe took place, Ezekiel clearly foretold what was about to happen. He foresaw the embassy sent to Pharaoh requesting horses and people, and asked indignantly, "Shall he prosper? shall he escape that doeth such things? or shall he break the covenant, and be delivered?" And he followed up his bitter remonstrances by the awful words, "As I live, saith the Lord GOD, surely in the place where the king dwelleth that made him king, whose oath he despised, and whose covenant he brake, even with him in the midst of Babylon he shall die. Neither shall

Pharaoh with his mighty army and great company make for him in the war" (Ezek. 17:11–21).

Jeremiah, as we know, earnestly dissuaded both king and princes from entering into the alliance that was being advocated between Judah and the neighboring states (chap. 27). Notwithstanding all these remonstrances, however, the confederacy was formed; and in a fatal moment Zedekiah renounced his allegiance to the king of Babylon.

Then it took place precisely as Ezekiel had foreseen. Stung to the quick by the treachery and ingratitude of the Jews, who had so persistently and obstinately outraged him, Nebuchadnezzar gathered around him a vast army, and resolved to make a public example of them to surrounding peoples by the swiftness and mercilessness of his vengeance (Ezek. 21:8–17).

The king of Babylon comes to the junction of the ways—this to Jerusalem, that to Rabbah, the chief city of Ammon. He consults the usual signs of divination that point him to the assault of Jerusalem with battering rams, and mounts, and forts.

At last, in December, 591 B.C., the siege began. On the approach of Nebuchadnezzar the confederacy had melted away, and Jerusalem was left alone, an islet amid the roaring waves of Chaldean armies. But the citizens had laid in a good store of provisions, and were expecting daily the advance of Pharaoh Hophra, with the chivalry of Egypt, to raise the siege.

At this juncture, Zedekiah sent two well-known men to Jeremiah, to ask whether Jehovah would not interpose for His people, as He had done in the great days of the past. It must have been a trying ordeal to the prophet. Why should he not be the Isaiah of this new siege? Why not arouse and encourage his people to indomitable resistance and heroic faith? Why not blend his voice with those of the prophets that foretold a certain deliverance, and so acquire an influence over them, which might be used ultimately for their highest good?

It is not impossible that such considerations passed before his mind. But if so, they were immediately dismissed. "Then said Jeremiah unto them, Thus shall ye say to Zedekiah: Thus saith the Lord God of Israel; Behold, I will turn back the weapons of war that are in your hands, wherewith ye fight against the king of Babylon, and against the Chaldeans, which besiege you without the walls, and I will assemble them into the midst of this city. And I myself will fight against you with an outstretched hand and with a strong arm, even in anger, and in fury, and in great wrath."

He followed up these terrible words by saying that the only way of safety was to go forth to the Chaldeans, who were now surrounding the city on every side. Those who went forth and surrendered themselves to the king of Babylon would save their lives (21; 22:1–9; 24).

Yet once again, when the siege of Jerusalem was in progress, and every day the air was full of the cries of the combatants, the heavy thud of the battering rams against the walls, and the cries of wounded men borne from the ramparts to the care of women— Jeremiah went fearlessly to Zedekiah with the heavy tidings that nothing could stop the sack and burning of the city, since God had given it into the hands of the king of Babylon; and that he would surely be taken, and behold Him face to face. "He shall speak with thee mouth to mouth, and thou shalt go to Babylon" (34:1–7).

2. His attitude toward the slave-owning Jews. It is not impossible that Jeremiah's vehement words of reproof aroused the deeply-drugged conscience of his people; and

they resolved, at the suggestion of Zedekiah, to make some atonement for their sins, and at the same time strengthen their garrison by setting their slaves free. This was done at a solemn convocation, specially summoned in the temple, and the national resolve was ratified before God with the most sacred rites.

Great joy spread through hundreds of hearts—a body of stalwart defenders was raised for the beleaguered city. Best of all, the nation had done right in the eyes of the Lord. Two months or so passed when, to the unbounded joy of the citizens, the attacks of Nebuchadnezzar became less frequent; the lines of the besieging army thinned; and the tents were struck and the whole host moved off. This diversion was caused by the approach of Pharaoh's army. The Jews thought that they would never see their foes again, and must have derided Jeremiah mercilessly. They also repealed the edict of emancipation, and caused the servants and handmaidens whom they had let go to return to their former condition.

It must have needed uncommon faith and courage to raise a bold and uncompromising protest. But their treachery to their pledged oath compelled him to speak out.

His opponents would be proportionately indignant as the voice of conscience, not yet quite silenced, protested that he was speaking the very word of Jehovah.

3. His attitude during the interval of respite. The city was delirious with joy. The Chaldeans had withdrawn, Pharaoh would prove more than a match for them and they would not return. The thunder cloud had broken and there was nothing to fear. But Jeremiah never changed his word. When the king sent another deputation to inquire through him of Jehovah, he gave this terrible reply: "Deceive not yourselves, saying, The Chaldeans shall surely depart from us: for they shall not depart. For though ye had smitten the whole army of the Chaldeans that fight against you, and there remained but wounded men among them, yet should they rise up every man in his tent, and burn this city with fire" (37:1–10).

God's prophets had too clear a vision of the issue of the duel between Chaldaea and Egypt, to be able to buoy up their people with hopes of deliverance. Jeremiah had already foreseen that the daughter of Egypt would be put to shame and delivered into the hand of the people of the north; he had even asked that the tidings of invasion might be published in her principal cities (46:13–28). Ezekiel was not less decisive: "Thus saith the Lord God. . . . I will strengthen the arms of the king of Babylon, and put my sword in his hand: but I will break Pharaoh's arms and he shall groan before him with the groanings of a deadly wounded man" (Ezek. 30).

Shortly after this, the prophet resolved to take the opportunity, offered by the withdrawal of the Chaldeans, to visit his inheritance at Anathoth. As he was passing through the gate of Benjamin, he was recognized by a captain whose family had long been at odds with him; and it didn't take him long to turn the occasion to advantage (37:13). He therefore laid hold on the prophet, saying, "Thou fallest away to the Chaldeans." Jeremiah was dragged with violence into the presence of the princes.

When he had been in a similar plight in the previous reign, Ahikam the son of Shaphan had rescued him; but he was now dead or in exile. Zedekiah was too weak to intercede to rescue the prophet from the fury of his lords, even if he were acquainted with his peril. So they sentenced him to be beaten; forty stripes save one fell from the scourge on his bare back; and he was then thrust into a dark, underground, unhealthy dungeon, where he remained many days at the peril of his life.

After awhile Zedekiah, perhaps pricked by remorse, or alarmed at the tidings that came from the frontier, sent for him. "Is there any word from the LORD?" the king asked anxiously. But again there was no compromise. "And Jeremiah said, There is: for said he, thou shalt be delivered into the hand of the king of Babylon."

He then pleaded with the royal clemency for a lessening of the severity of his sentence, with such good success that he was committed, at the king's command, to the court of the guard, in the immediate vicinity of the palace; and fed daily with a loaf of bread out of the baker's street, until all the bread in the city was used up. Meanwhile the army of the Chaldeans, having defeated Pharaoh, returned; and again formed their thick-set lines around the city, like a fence of iron, to be drawn closer and closer until Jerusalem fell like a snared bird into their grasp.

It is impossible to recite or read this story without admiration for the man who dared to stand alone with God against a nation in arms. Our sole duty is to see that we are in God's plan and doing His work. Then we will leap barrier walls, pass unscathed through troops of foes, and stand as pillars in His temple, never to be removed.

17

Into the Ground, To Die
Jeremiah 32

While shut up in the court of the prison, perhaps fastened by a chain that restrained his liberty, Jeremiah received a divine intimation that his uncle would come to him shortly with a request for him to purchase the family property at Anathoth. The divine command quite staggered him, and may have made him for a moment question whether there had not been some mistake in the message he had so constantly reiterated in the ears of his people.

He gave no outward sign of his perplexities however; but when his uncle's son entered the courtyard with his request, the prophet at once assented to the proposal, and purchased the property for seventeen shekels (about seven ounces).

In addition to this, Jeremiah took care to have the purchase recorded and witnessed with the same elaborate pains as if he were at once taking possession. Not a single form was omitted or slurred over; and ultimately the two deeds of contract—the one sealed with the more private details of price; the other open, and bearing the signatures of witnesses—were deposited in the charge of Baruch, with the injunction that he put them in an earthen vessel and preserve them. They were probably not opened again until the return from the captivity; but we can well imagine how strong a rush of emotion and confidence must have been inspired as the men of that day perused the documents.

But Jeremiah was not a participant in that glad scene. He did as God bade him, though the shadow of a great darkness lay on his soul.

1. HOURS OF MIDNIGHT DARKNESS. Jeremiah could never regret that he had given the strength and measure of his days to the service of others. If he had not done so, but had shrunk back from the high calling of his early life, his misery would have been in proportion to the royal quality of his nature, and his power to enrich the life of man.

But none can give themselves to the service of others, except at bitter cost of much that this world holds dear. In the case of every true life there must be death to the attractions and indulgences of the self-life. This will explain the privations and sorrows to which Jeremiah was subjected. Death took place in him that life might work in Israel, and in all who would read the book of his prophecy.

a. *He died to the dear ties of human love.* "Thou shalt not take thee a wife, neither shalt thou have sons or daughters in this place," was said to him early. The men of Anathoth, of the house of his father, conspired against him. The friends with whom he took sweet counsel, and in whose company he walked to the house of God, betrayed him.

b. *He died to the goodwill of his fellowmen.* None can be indifferent to this. But it was his bitter lot to encounter from the first an incessant stream of verbal abuse and dislike. We have no record of one voice being raised to thank or encourage him.

c. *He died to the pride of national patriotism.* No patriot allows himself to despair of his country. But Jeremiah found himself compelled to speak in such a fashion that the princes proposed, not without show or reason, to put him to death because he weakened the hands of the men of war.

d. *He died to the sweets of personal liberty.* A large portion of his ministry was exerted from the precincts of a prison. We read repeatedly of his being shut up, and not able to go about. His friend Baruch had to act constantly as his intermediary and interpreter. This too must have been bitter to him. The iron fetters of restraint must have eaten deeply into the tender flesh of his gentle heart.

e. *He died also to the meaning he had been placing on his own prophecies.* Up to the moment when Jehovah bade him purchase the property of Hanameel, he had never questioned the impending fate of Jerusalem. It was certainly and inevitably to be destroyed by sword, famine, pestilence, and fire. But now the word of God seemed to indicate that the land was to remain under the cultivation of the families that owned it.

2. JEREMIAH'S BEHAVIOR. To very few men has it been given to walk so closely along the path that the Redeemer walked during his early life. He was stripped of almost everything that men prize most. But amid it all he derived solace and support in three main directions.

a. *He prayed.* There is no help to the troubled soul like that which comes through prayer. You may have no clear vision of God. Nevertheless, pray; pray on your knees; "in everything, by prayer and supplication, let your requests be made known unto God"; and the peace of God will settle down on, and enwrap your weary, troubled soul.

b. *He rested on the Word of God.* The soul of the prophet was nourished and fed by the divine word. How often have God's people turned to the Bible and found a psalm or a chapter the balm of Gilead, the tree of life with healing leaves!

c. *He faithfully kept to the path of duty.* "And I bought the field." It does not always happen that our service to men will be met by rebuff, ill-will, and hard treatment; but when it does, there should be no swerving, or flinching, or drawing back. Often when the lonely soul has reaped nothing but disgrace and opposition, has been borne to a cross and crucified as a malefactor, it has comforted itself with the prospects of the harvests of blessing that were to accrue to those who had rejected its appeals.

Such are the resorts of the soul in its seasons of anguish. It casts itself on the ground crying, "Father, Abba, Father."

3. COMPENSATIONS. To all valleys there are mountains, to all depths heights; for all midnight hours there are hours of sunrise; for Gethsemane, an Olivet.

So Jeremiah found it. His compensations came. God opened to him the vista of the future, down whose long aisles he beheld his people planted again in their own land. He saw men buying fields for money, and subscribing deeds and sealing them, as he had done; he heard the voice of joy and the voice of gladness; the voice of the bridegroom and the voice of the bride; the voice of those who bring the sacrifices of joy into the Lord's house. There was compensation also in the confidence with which Nebuchadnezzar treated him, and in the evident reliance that his decimated people placed in his intercessions, as we shall see.

So it will be with all who fall into the ground to die. God will not forget or forsake them.

18

The Fall of Jerusalem
Jeremiah 38–39

During those long dark months of siege, probably the only soul in all that crowded city that was in perfect peace, and free in its unrestrained liberty, was Jeremiah's. And amid the cries of assailants and defenders, unbroken by the thud of the battering rams, deep as the blue Syrian sky that looked down on him, was the peace of God that passed the understanding of those that thronged in and out, between the city and the royal palace.

1. THE HORRORS OF THE SIEGE. It lasted in all for about eighteen months, with the one brief respite caused by the approach of Pharaoh's army; and it is impossible for us to estimate the amount of human anguish that was crowded into that fateful space.

Imagine for a moment the overcrowded city into which the peasantry and villagers had gathered from all over the country. Who, with such of their valuables as they had been able to hastily collect and transport, had sought refuge within the gray old walls of Zion from the violence and outrage of the merciless troops. This mass of fugitives would greatly add to the difficulties of the defense by their demands on the provisions that were laid up in anticipation of the siege, by overcrowding the thoroughfares and impeding the movements of the soldiery.

So much for the earlier months of the siege; but as the days passed on darker shadows gathered. It was as though the very pit of hell added in human passion the last dread horrors of the scene. The women became cruel and refused to spare from their breast for their young the nutrition they needed for themselves. Young children asked for bread, and asked in vain. The nobles lost their portly mien, and walked the streets like animated mummies. The sword of the invader without had fewer victims than that which hunger wielded within; and, as a climax, pitiful women murdered their own children for food. Finally, pestilence began its ravages; and the foul stench of bodies that men had no time to bury, and that fell thick and fast each day in the streets of the city, caused death that mowed down those that had escaped the foe and privation. Ah, Jerusalem! who stoned the prophets, and shed the blood of the just, this was the day of the overflowing wrath and fury of Jehovah! You, O God, have slain them in the day of Your anger; You have slaughtered and not pitied.

And as Jeremiah waited day after day, powerless to do anything else than listen to tidings of woe that converged to him from every side, he resembled the physician who, unable to stay the slow progress of some terrible form of paralysis in one he loves better than life, is compelled to listen to the news of its conquests, knowing surely that these are only stages in an assault that ultimately must capture the citadel of life—an assault that he can do nothing to stay.

2. THE PROPHET'S ADDED SORROWS. In addition to the discomfort he shared in common with the rest of the crowded populace, Jeremiah was exposed to aggravated sorrows. He lost no opportunity of asserting that Jerusalem should surely be given into the hands of the king of Babylon, and that he would take it. As these words passed from lip to lip, they carried dismay throughout the city, and the fact that Jeremiah had so often spoken as the mouthpiece of Jehovah gave an added weight to his words.

It was quite natural therefore that the princes, who knew well enough the importance of keeping up the courage of the people, should demand the death of one who was not only weakening the hands of the people generally, but especially of the men of war. The young king was weak rather than wicked, a puppet and toy in the hands of his princes and court. He therefore yielded to their demand, saying, "Behold, he is in your hand; for the king is not he that can do any thing against you."

Without delay Jeremiah was flung into one of those rock-hewn cisterns that abound in Jerusalem, and the bottom of which, because the water was exhausted during the extremities of the siege, consisted of a deep sediment of mud, into which he sank. There was not a moment to be lost. Help was sent through a very unexpected channel. An Ethiopian eunuch—who is probably anonymous, since the name Ebed-melech simply means "the king's servant"—with a love to God's cause, hastened to the king and urged him to take immediate steps to save the prophet from imminent death.

Always swayed by the last strong influence brought to bear on him, the king bade him take a sufficient number of men to protect him from interference, and at once release the prophet. There was great gentleness in the way this noble Ethiopian executed his purpose. He was not content with merely dragging Jeremiah from the pit's bottom, but placed on the ropes old castoff cloths and rotten rags, gathered hurriedly from the house of the king; thus the tender flesh of the prophet was neither cut nor chafed. It is not only what we do, but the way in which we do it that most quickly indicates our real selves. Many might have hurried to the pit's mouth with ropes; only one of God's own gentlemen would have thought of the rags and cloths.

From that moment until the city fell the prophet remained in safe custody; and on one memorable occasion the king sought his counsel, though in strict secrecy. Once more Zedekiah asked what the issue would be: and once more received the alternatives that appeared so foolish to the eye of sense—defeat and death by remaining in the city; liberty and life by going forth.

"Go forth?" said Zedekiah, in effect; "Never! It would be unworthy of one in whose veins flows the blood of kings."

"Obey, I beseech thee, the voice of the LORD," said Jeremiah, "which I speak unto thee: so it shall be well with thee, and thy soul shall live." Finally, in graphic words he painted the picture of the certain doom the king would incur if he stayed until the city fell into the captor's hands.

The weakness that was the ruin of Zedekiah came out in his request that Jeremiah would not inform the princes of the nature of their communications, and would hide the truth beneath the semblance of truth. It is difficult to pronounce a judgment on the way in which the prophet veiled the content of his conversation with Zedekiah from the inquisitive questions of the princes. He shielded the king with a touch of chivalrous devotion and loyalty that was probably the last act of devotion to the royal house, to save what he had poured out his heart's blood in tears and entreaties and sacrifices for nearly forty years.

3. THE FATE OF THE CITY. At last a breach was made in the old fortifications and the troops began to rush in. The terrified people fled from the lower into the upper city; and as they did so, their homes were filled with the desolating terror of the merciless army.

A hundred different forms of anguish gathered in that devoted city, like vultures to the dead camel of the desert. Woe, then, to the men who had fought for their very life! but woe more agonizing to the women and girls, to the children and little babes. "All the princes of the king of Babylon came in, and sat in the middle gate," from which they gave directions for the immediate prosecution of their success on the terrified people, who now crowded the upper city, prepared to make the last desperate stand.

Everything had to be done to preserve the royal house. It was therefore arranged that, as soon as night fell, Zedekiah and his harem would go forth under the protection of all the men of war, through a breach to be made in the walls of the city to the south; and exactly as Ezekiel had foretold, so it came to pass.

A long line of fugitives, each carrying property of necessities, stole silently through the king's private garden, and so toward the breach; and, like shadows of the night, passed into the darkness between long lines of armed men, who held their breath. If only by dawn they could reach the plains of Jericho, they might hope to elude the fury of their pursuers. But all night Zedekiah must have remembered those last words of Jeremiah: "Thou shalt not escape; but shalt be taken by the hand of the king of Babylon." This was not the first time, nor the last, that man has sought to elude the close meshes of the Word of God.

Somehow the tidings of the flight reached the Chaldeans. The whole army arose to pursue. What happened the next morning in Jerusalem, and what befell her a month later, when the upper city also fell into the hands of the conqueror, is told in the Book of Lamentations. The street and houses were filled with the bodies of the slain, after having been outraged with nameless atrocities; but those who perished could be considered better off than the thousands who were led off into exile, or sold into slavery, to suffer in life the horrors of death. Then the wild fury of fire engulfed temple and palace, public building and dwelling-house, and blackened ruins covered the site of the holy and beautiful city that had been the joy of the whole earth; and the ear of the prophet heard the spirit of the fallen city crying,

> Is it nothing to you, all ye that pass by?
> Behold, and see if there be any sorrow like unto my sorrow,
>   which is done unto me,
> Wherewith the LORD hath afflicted me in the day of his fierce
>   anger!

As for Zedekiah, he was taken to Riblah where Nebuchadnezzar was at this time, perhaps not expecting so speedy a downfall of the city. With barbarous cruelty he slew the sons of Zedekiah before his eyes, so that the last scene he beheld might be of their dying agony. He was also compelled to witness the slaughter of all his nobles. Then as a coup de grâce, with his own hand probably, Nebuchadnezzar struck out Zedekiah's eyes with his spear.

It is indeed a subject for an artist to depict, the long march of the exiles on the way to their distant home. Delicate women and little children forced to travel day after day, irrespective of fatigue and suffering; prophets and priests mingled together in the overthrow they had done so much to bring about; rich and poor marching side by side, manacled, and urged forward by the spear-point or scourge. All along the valley of the Jordan, past Damascus, and then for thirty days through the inhospitable wilderness, retraveling the route taken in the dawn of history by Abraham, their great progenitor, the Friend of God, while all the nations around them clapped their hands. In later years the bitterest recollection of those days was the exultation of the Edomites in the fall of their rival city. "Remember, O LORD , against the children of Edom, the day of Jerusalem!"

Thus God brought on His people the king of the Chaldeans, who slew their young men with the sword in the house of their sanctuary, and had no compassion on young man or woman, or old person, but gave them all into his hand. And all the vessels of the house of God, great and small, and the treasures of the house of the Lord, and the treasures of the king and his princes, all these he brought to Babylon. And they burned the house of God, and broke down the wall of Jerusalem; and burned all the palaces with fire, and destroyed all the goodly vessels in them. And those who had escaped from the sword he carried away to Babylon, and they were servants to him and his sons.

19

A Clouded Sunset
Jeremiah 40–44

If the closing verses of the Book of Jeremiah were written by his own hand, he must have lived for twenty years after the fall of Jerusalem; but they were filled with the same infinite sadness as the forty years of his public ministry. It would appear that as far as his outward lot was concerned, the prophet Jeremiah spent a life of more unrelieved sadness than has perhaps fallen to the lot of any other, with the exception of the divine Lord.

His sufferings may be classed under three divisions—those recited in the Book of Lamentations, and connected with the fall of Jerusalem; those connected with the murder of Gedaliah, and the flight into Egypt; and those of the exile there. But amid the salt brine of these bitter experiences, there was always welling up a spring of hope and peace.

1. THE DESOLATE CITY. It is only in later years that any question has been raised as to the authorship of the Book of Lamentations. The cave in which Jeremiah is said to have written them is still shown on the western side of the city; and every Friday the Jews assemble to recite as his these plaintive words, at their wailing-place in Jerusalem,

where a few of the old stones still remain. There is no good reason therefore for disassociating the Book of Lamentations from the authorship of Jeremiah.

This being so, what a flood of light is cast on the desolate scene when Nebuzaradan had completed his work of destruction, and the long lines of captives were already far on their way to Babylon! How many went into exile we have no means of knowing; the number would probably amount to several thousand, principally of the wealthier classes. Only the poor of the people were left to cultivate the land that it might not revert to an absolute desert. But the population would probably be very sparse—a few peasants scattered over the sites that had teemed with crowds.

The city sat solitary, which once had been full of people She had become as a widow. The holy fire was extinct on her altars; pilgrims no longer traversed the ways of Zion to attend the appointed feasts; her gates had sunk into the ground and her habitations were pitilessly destroyed by fire. How often would Jeremiah pass mournfully amid the blackened ruins!

2. GEDALIAH'S MURDER. Nebuchadnezzar and his chiefs had evidently been kept closely informed of the conditon of certain people during the siege of Jerusalem; and the king gave definite instructions to his chief officers to take special precautions for the safety of Jeremiah. When the upper city fell into their hands they sent and took him out of the court of the guard; and he was brought in chains along with the other captives to Ramah, about five miles north of Jerusalem.

In a remarkable address that the captain of the guard made to Jeremiah, he acknowledged the retributive justice of Jehovah—one of the many traces of the real religion that gave a tone and bearing to these men by which they are altogether removed from the category of ordinary heathen. "The LORD thy God hath pronounced this evil upon this place. Now the LORD hath brought it, and done according as he hath said: because ye have sinned against the LORD, and have not obeyed his voice, therefore this thing is come upon you."

The chains were then struck from off his fettered hands, and liberty was given him either to accompany the rest of the people to Babylon, or to go where he chose throughout the land. Ultimately, as he seemed to hesitate as to which direction to take, the Chaldean general urged him to make his home with Gedaliah, to strengthen his hands, and give him the benefit of his counsel in the difficult task to which he had been appointed. Thus again he turned from rest and ease to take the rough path of duty.

Gedaliah was the grandson of Shaphan, King Josiah's secretary, and son of Ahikam, who had been sent to inquire of the prophetess Huldah concerning the newly found book of the law. On a former occasion the hand of Ahikam had rescued Jeremiah from the nobles. Evidently the whole family was bound by the strongest, tenderest ties to the servant of God, imbued with the spirit, and governed by the policy that he enunciated. These principles Gedaliah had consistently followed; and they marked him out in the judgment of Nebuchadnezzar as the fittest to be entrusted with the reins of government, and to exert some kind of authority over the scattered remnant. To him, therefore, Jeremiah came with an allowance of supplies and other marks of the esteem in which the conquerors regarded him.

For a brief interval all went well. The new governor took up his residence at Mizpah, an old fort that Asa had erected three hundred years before, to check the invasion of Baasha. The town stood on a rocky eminence, but the castle was supplied with water from a deep well. Chaldean soldiers gave the show of authority and stability to Gedaliah's rule. To Mizpah the scattered remnant of the Jews began to look with hope. The captains of the forces that were in the fields still holding out, as roving bands, against the conqueror, hastened to swear allegiance to the representative of the Jewish state, and the Jews who had fled to Moab, Edom, and other surrounding peoples returned from every place out of which they had been driven, and they came to the land of Judah to Gedaliah, to Mizpah.

How happy Jeremiah must have been to see this nucleus of order spreading its influence through the surrounding chaos and confusion; and with what eagerness he must have used all the energy he possessed to aid in the establishment of Gedaliah's authority! The fair dream, however, was rudely dissipated by the treacherous murder of Gedaliah—who seems to have been eminently fitted for his post—by Ishmael, the son of Nethaniah. In the midst of a feast given by the unsuspecting governor, he was slain with the sword, together with all the Jews who were with him and the Chaldean garrison. On the second day after that, the red-handed murderers, still thirsting for blood, slew seventy pilgrims who were on their way to weep amid the ruins of Jerusalem, and lay offerings on the site of the ruined altar. The deep well of the keep was choked with bodies, and shortly afterward Ishmael carried off the king's daughters and all the people who had gathered around Gedaliah, and started with them for the court of Baalis, the king of the children of Ammon, who was an accomplice in the plot. It was a bitter disapointment; and to none would the grief of it have been more poignant than to Jeremiah.

The people themselves appear to have lost heart, for though Johanan and other of the captains of roving bands pursued Ishmael and delivered from his hand all the captives he had taken, and recovered the women and the children, yet none of them dared to return to Mizpah; but like shepherdless sheep, harried by dogs, driven, draggled, panting, and terrified, they resolved to quit their land, and retire southward, with the intention of fleeing into the land of Egypt, with which during the later days of their national history they had maintained close relations.

They carried Jeremiah with them. They had confidence in his prayers and in his veracity, since his predictions had been verified so often by the event. They knew he stood high in the favor of the court of Babylon. They believed that his prayers prevailed with God. And, therefore, they regarded him as a shield and defense.

Halting at the inn at Chimham, the people earnestly debated whether they should go forward or return. They also came to Jeremiah and asked him to give himself to prayer. They professed their willingness to be guided entirely by the voice of God, though in this they were probably not sincere; in fact, they were determined to enter into Egypt.

For ten days Jeremiah gave himself to prayer. Then the word of the Lord came to him, and he summoned the people around him to declare it. Speaking in the name of the Most High, he said: "If ye will still abide in this land, then will I build you, and not pull you down; and I will plant you, and not pluck you up. . . . Be not afraid of the king of Babylon . . . for I am with you to save you, and to deliver you from his hand." If, on the other hand, they persisted in going into the land of Egypt, then they would be overtaken there by the sword, the famine, and the pestilence, and they would never again see their native land. As he spoke he seems to have been sadly aware that during the ten days devoted to intercession on their behalf the prepossession in favor of Egypt had been growing, and that his words would do nothing to stop the strong current that was bearing them there.

So it befell. When he had finished speaking, the chiefs accused him of speaking falsely, and of misrepresenting the divine word. So the terrified people pursued their way to Egypt, and settled at Tahpanhes, which was ten miles across the frontier. Almost the last ingredient of bitterness in Jeremiah's cup must have been furnished by this pertinacious obstinacy.

3. EGYPT. His life of protest was not yet complete. No sooner had the people settled in their new home than he was led to take great stones in his hand and lay them beneath the mortar in some brickwork that was being laid down at the entry of Pharaoh's palace in Tahpanhes. "On these stones," he said, "the king of Babylon shall set his throne, and spread out his royal pavilion upon them. He shall smite the land of Egypt, and kindle a fire in the houses of its gods, and array himself in her spoils, as easily as a shepherd throws his outer garment around his shoulders. The obelisks of Heliopolis will be also burnt with fire. To have come here, therefore, is not to escape the dreaded foe, but to throw yourselves into his arms."

Some years must have followed of which we have no record, and during which the great king was engaged in the siege of Tyre, and therefore unable to pursue his plans against Pharaoh. During this time the Jews scattered over a wide extent of territory, so that colonies were formed in Upper as well as Lower Egypt, all of which became deeply infected with the prevailing idolatries and customs around them. Notwithstanding all the bitter experiences that had befallen them in consequence of their idol worship, they burned incense to the gods of Egypt, and repeated the abominations that had brought such disaster and suffering on their nation.

Taking advantage therefore of a great convocation at some idolatrous festival, Jeremiah warned them of the inevitable fate that would overtake them in Egypt, as it had befallen them in Jerusalem. The faithful prophet told them that God would punish Jerusalem, by "the sword, by the famine, and by the pestilence; so that none of the remnant of Judah, which are gone into the land of Egypt to sojourn there, shall escape or remain, that they should return into the land of Judah . . . to dwell there."

A severe altercation then followed. The men indignantly protested that they would still burn incense to the queen of heaven as they had done in the streets of Jerusalem; and they even ascribed the evils that had befallen them to their discontinuance of this custom. Jeremiah, on the other hand, gray with age, his face marred with suffering, did not hesitate to insist in the name of the God he served so faithfully that the sufferings of the people were due, not to their discontinuance of idolatry, but to their persistence in its unholy rites. He went on to predict the invasion of Egypt by Nebuchadnezzar, which took place in the year 568 B.C. and which resulted, as Josephus tells us, in the carrying off to Babylon of the remnant of Jews who had, against Jeremiah's advice, fled there for refuge. So it was proved whose word should stand, God's or theirs.

Through all these dark and painful experiences, the soul of Jeremiah quieted itself as a weaned babe. He looked far away beyond the mist of years and saw the expiration of the sentence of captivity; the return of his people; the rebuilding of the city; the holy and blessed condition of its inhabitants; the glorious reign of the Branch, the scion of David's stock; the new Covenant, before which the old should vanish away. Therefore his days were probably not all dark; but aglow with the first rays of the Sun of Righteousness.

If these words should be read by some whose life, like Jeremiah's, has been draped with curtains of somber hue, let them know that to none does the infinite One stoop so closely as to those that are severely broken on the wheel of affliction. It is only when we fall into the ground and die that we cease to abide alone, and begin to bear much fruit. Do not try to feel resigned. *Will* resignation. Submit yourself under the mighty hand of God. If you can say nothing else, fill your nights and days with the cry or sob of "Father, not my will, but Thine be done." Never doubt the love of God. Never suppose for a moment that He has forgotten or forsaken.

Scripture says nothing about the death of Jeremiah. Whether it took place, as Christian tradition affirms, by stoning in Egypt, or whether he breathed out his soul beneath the faithful care of Baruch, in some quiet chamber of death, we cannot tell.

But how gladly did the prophet close his eyes on the wreck that sin had wrought on the chosen people, and open them in the land where neither sin, nor death, nor the sight and sound of war can break the perfect rest! What a look of surprise and rapture must have settled on the worn face, the expression of the last glad vision of the soul as it passed out from the body of corruption, worn and weary with the long conflict, to hear the "Well done!" and welcome of God.

JOHN THE BAPTIST

1

The Interest of His Biography

The morning star is the fittest emblem that Nature can supply of the herald who proclaimed the rising of the Sun of Righteousness—answering across the gulf of three hundred years to his brother prophet, Malachi, who had foretold that Sunrise and the healing in His wings.

Every sign attests the unique and singular glory of the Baptist. Not that his career was signalized by the blaze of prodigy and wonder, for it is expressly said that "John did no miracle." Not that he was a master of a superb eloquence like that of Isaiah or Ezekiel; for he was content to be only "a cry"—short, thrilling, piercing through the darkness, ringing over the desert plains. Yet, his Master said of him that "among them that are born of women there hath not risen a greater than John the Baptist" (Matt. 11:11); and in six brief months the young prophet of the wilderness had become the center to which all the land went forth. We see Pharisees and Sadducees, soldiers and publicans, enthralled by his ministry; the Sanhedrin forced to investigate his claims. He has left a name and an influence that will never cease.

But there is a further feature; he was ordained to be "the clasp" of two covenants. In him Judaism reached its highest embodiment, and the Old Testament found its noblest exponent. It is significant therefore that he who caught up the torch of Hebrew prophecy with a grasp and spirit unrivalled by any before him, should have it in his power and in his heart to say: "The object of all prophecy, the purpose of the Mosaic law, the end of all sacrifices, the desire of all nations, is at hand."

John and the Lord were born at the same time; they were surrounded from their birth by similar circumstances; drank in from their earliest days the same patriotic aspirations, the same sacred traditions, the same glowing hopes.

In each case, life was strenuous and short—an epoch being inaugurated, in the one case in about six months, in the other some three years. In each case, at first, there was abounding enthusiasm, but also unconcealed hatred of the religious world of their time. In each case, the brief sunny hours of service were soon succeeded by the rolling up of the thunderous clouds, and these by the murderous tempest of deadly hatred, even to death. In each case, there was a little handful of detached disciples who bitterly mourned their master's death and took up the desecrated corpse to lay it in the tomb.

But there the parallel ends. The life purpose of the one culminated in his death; with the other, it only began. When the axe of Herod's executioner had done its deadly work in the dungeons of Machaerus, the bond that knit the disciples of John was severed also, and they were absorbed in the followers of Christ; but when the Roman soldiers thought their work was done, his disciples met together in the upper room, and continued there for more than forty days until the descent of the Holy Spirit formed them into the strongest organization that this world has ever beheld.

John's influence on the world has diminished, but Jesus is King of the ages. John, then, was "a burning and shining torch," lifted for a moment aloft in the murky air; but Jesus was *that light.*

To read the calm idyllic pages of the Gospels, apart from some knowledge of contemporary history, is to miss one of their deepest lessons—that such piety and beneficence were set in the midst of a most tumultuous and perilous age.

Herod was on the throne—crafty, cruel, sensual, imperious, and magnificent. The gorgeous temple that bore his name was the scene of priestly service and sacramental rites. The great national feasts of the Passover, of Tabernacles, and of Pentecost, were celebrated with solemn pomp, and attracted large crowds from all the world. In every part of the land synagogues were maintained with punctilious care, and crowds of scribes were perpetually engaged in a microscopic study of the law and in the instruction of the people. In revenue, and popular attention, and apparent devoutness, that period had not been excelled in the most palmy days of Solomon or Hezekiah. But beneath this decorous surface the rankest, foulest, most desperate corruption thrived.

The aged couple in the hill-country of Judæa, as to Mary and Joseph at Nazareth, must have groaned beneath the grinding oppression by which Herod extorted from the poorer classes the immense revenues that he squandered on his palaces and fortresses and on the creation of new cities. That he was introducing everywhere Gentile customs and games; that he had dared to place the Roman eagle on the main entrance of the temple; that he had pillaged David's tomb; that he had set aside the great council of their nation; that the religious leaders, men like Caiaphas and Annas, were willing to wink at the crimes of the secular power, so long as their prestige and compensation were secured; that the national independence for which Judas and his brothers had strived, during the Maccabean wars, was fast being laid at the feet of Rome, which was only too willing to take advantage of the chaos that followed immediately upon Herod's hideous death—such tidings must have come, in successive shocks of anguish, to those true hearts who were waiting for the redemption of Israel. Still, they made their yearly journeys to Jerusalem, and participated in the great convocations which, in outward splendor, eclipsed memories of the past; but they realized that the glory had departed. When the feasts were over, these pious hearts turned back to their homes among the hills, tearing themselves from the last glimpse of the beautiful city, with the cry, "O Jerusalem, Jerusalem!"

The darkest hour precedes the dawn, and it was just at this point that Old Testament predictions must have been so eagerly scanned by those who watched and waited. That the Messiah was nigh, they could not doubt. Even the Gentile world was penetrated with the expectation of a King. Sybils in their ancient writings, hermits in their secret cells, magi studying the dazzling glories of the eastern heavens, had come to the conclusion that He was at hand who would bring again the Golden Age.

And so those loyal and loving souls must have felt that as the advent of the Lord was near, that of His messenger must be nearer still. At any moment might a voice be heard crying, "Cast up, cast up the highway; gather out the stones; lift up a standard for the people. . . . Say ye to the daughter of Zion, Behold, thy salvation cometh" (Isa. 62: 10–11). Those anticipations were realized in the birth of John the Baptist.

2

The House of Zacharias
Luke 1

To the evangelist Luke we are indebted for details of those antecedent circumstances that ushered John the Baptist into the world. What were the sources from which the third evangelist drew his information? Why should we not attribute them to "the Mother" herself? Mary had kept all things, pondering in her heart those wonderful circumstances that had left so indelible an impression on her life.

The story of John the Baptist was so clearly part of that of Jesus, that Mary could hardly recall the one without the other. And besides, Elisabeth, as the angel said, was her kinswoman—perhaps her cousin—to whom she naturally turned in the hour of her maidenly astonishment and rapture. Though much younger, Mary was united to her relative by a close and tender tie, and it was only natural that what had happened to Elisabeth should have impressed her almost as deeply as her own memorable experiences. So it is possible that from the lips of the mother of our Lord we obtain these details of the house of Zacharias.

1. THE QUIET IN THE LAND. God has always had His hidden ones; and while the world has been rent by faction and war, ravaged by fire and sword, and drenched with the blood of her sons, these have heard His call to enter their chamber.

It was eminently so in the days of which we write. Darkness covered the earth, and gross darkness the people. Herod's infamous cruelties, craft, and bloodshed were at their height. The country questioned with fear what new direction his crimes might take. The priesthood was submissive to his whim; the bonds of society seemed dissolved. Theudas and Judas of Galilee, mentioned by Gamaliel, were but specimens of the bandit leaders who broke into revolt and harried the country districts for the maintenance of their followers.

Is it to be wondered that the godly remnant would meet in little groups and secluded hiding places to comfort themselves in God? The gloom of their times only led them more eagerly to study the predictions of their Hebrew prophets, and desire their accomplishment.

We are not drawing on our imagination in describing these true-hearted watchers for the rising of the Day-star. They are fully indicated in the gospel story. There was Simeon, righteous and devout, unto whom it had been revealed by the Holy Spirit that he would not see death before he had seen the Lord's Christ; and Anna, the prophetess, who did not depart from the temple, worshiping with fastings and supplications night and day. There were guileless Nathanael, an Israelite indeed, and the peasant maiden Mary, and last, but not least, Zacharias and his wife Elisabeth, who were "both righteous before God, walking in all the commandments and ordinances of the Lord blameless " (Luke 1:6).

This attitude of spirit, which dwells in the unseen and eternal, which counts on the indwelling of the Son of God by faith, and which ponders deeply over the sins and sorrows of the world around, is the temper of mind out of which the greatest deeds are wrought for the cause of God on the earth. The Marys who sit at Christ's feet arise to anoint Him for His burial. Those who wait on God renew their strength. The world ignores them, but there presently steps one who, like John the Baptist, opens a new chapter in the history of the race, and accelerates the advent of the Christ.

2. THE PARENTAGE OF THE FORERUNNER. As the traveler emerges from the dreary wilderness that lies between Sinai and the southern frontier of Palestine—a scorching desert—he sees before him a long line of hills, which is the beginning of "the hill country of Judaea" (Luke 1:39). Among these, a modern traveler has identified the site of Juttah, the village home of the priest Zacharias and his wife Elisabeth.

To judge by their names, we may infer that their parents years before had been godly people. *Zacharias* meant *God's remembrance*, as though he were to be a perpetual reminder to others of what God had promised, and to God of what they were expecting from His hand. *Elisabeth* meant *God's oath*, as though her people were perpetually appealing to those covenant promises in which, since He could swear by no greater, God had sworn by Himself.

Zacharias was a priest, "of the course of Abia," and twice a year he journeyed to Jerusalem to fulfill his office, for a week of six days and two Sabbaths. There were, Josephus tells us, somwhat more than 20,000 priests in Judæa at this time. The general character of the priesthood was deeply tainted by the corruption of the times, and as a class they were blind leaders of the blind. However many were evidently deeply religious men, for we find that "a great number of the priests," after the crucifixion, believed on Christ and joined His followers. In this class we must therefore place Zacharias who, with his wife, herself of the daughters of Aaron, is described as being "righteous before God."

It is evident, from the apt and plentiful quotations from Scripture with which the song of Zacharias is replete, that the Scriptures were deeply pondered and reverenced in that highland home; and we have the angel's testimony to the prayers that ascended day and night. In all these things they were blameless and harmless, the children of God, without blemish, in the midst of a crooked and perverse generation.

But they lived under the shadow of a great sorrow. "They had no child, because that Elisabeth was barren, and they both were now well stricken in years." It seemed almost certain that their family would soon die out and be forgotten; and that by no link whatsoever could they be connected with the Messiah, to be the progenitor of whom was the cherished longing of each Hebrew parent.

"They had no child!" They would therefore count themselves under the frown of God; and the mother especially felt that a reproach lay on her. What a clue to the anguish of the soul is furnished by her cry: "Thus hath the Lord dealt me in the days wherein he looked on me, to take away *my reproach among men*" (Luke 1:25).

3. THE ANGEL'S ANNOUNCEMENT. One memorable autumn Zacharias left his home for his priestly service. Reaching the temple he would lodge in the cloisters, and spend his days in the innermost court, which none might enter save priests in their sacred garments. Among the various priestly duties, none was held in such high esteem as the offering of incense, which was presented morning and evening on a special golden altar, in the Holy Place at the time of prayer. "The whole multitude of the people were praying without at the time of incense." So honorable was this office that it was fixed by lot, and no one was allowed to perform it twice. Only once in a priest's life was he permitted to sprinkle the incense on the burning coals, which an assistant had already

brought from the altar of burnt-sacrifice, and spread on the altar of incense before the veil.

The silver trumpets had sounded. The smoke of the evening sacrifice was ascending. The worshipers who thronged the different courts, rising tier on tier, were engaged in silent prayer. The assistant priest had retired; and Zacharias, for the first and only time in his life, stood alone in the holy shrine, while the incense that he had strewn on the glowing embers arose in fragrant clouds, enveloping and veiling the objects around, while it symbolized the ascent of prayers and intercessions not only from his own heart, but also from the hearts of his people, into the presence of God.

What a litany of prayer poured from his heart! For Israel, that the chosen people should be delivered from their low estate; for the cause of religion, that it might be revived; for the crowds without, that God would hear the prayers they were offering toward His holy sanctuary; and perhaps for Elisabeth and himself that, if possible, God would hear their prayer, and if not, that He would grant them to bear patiently their heavy sorrow.

"And there appeared unto him an angel of the Lord standing on the right side of the altar of incense." Mark how circumstantial the narrative is. There could be no mistake. He stood—and he stood on the right side. It was Gabriel who stands in the presence of God, who had been sent to speak to him and declare the good tidings that his prayer was heard; that his wife would bear a son, who would be called John. He would be a Nazirite from his birth, would inherit the spirit and power of Elias, and would go before the face of Christ to prepare His way.

He tarried long in the temple, and what wonder! Presently he came out, but when he began to pronounce the customary blessing his lips were silent. He made signs as he reached forth his hands in the attitude of benediction, but that day no blessing fell on the upturned faces of the crowd. He continued making signs to them and remained silent. Silent, because he questioned the likelihood of so good and gracious an answer. Silent, that he might learn in solitude the full purposes of God, to set them presently to song.

With the light of that glory on his face, and those sweet notes of "Fear not" ringing in his heart, Zacharias continued to fulfill the duties of his ministration, and when his work was fulfilled, departed unto his house. But that day was long rememberd by the people.

3

His Schools and Schoolmasters
Luke 1

Zacharias and Elisabeth had probably almost ceased to pray for a child, or to urge the matter. It seemed useless to pray further. There had been no heaven-sent sign to assure them that there was any likelihood of their prayer being answered, and nature seemed to utter a final No; when suddenly the angel of God broke into the commonplace of their life, bringing the assurance that there was no need for fear, and that their prayer was heard.

On his arrival in his home, the aged priest, by means of the writing table later referred to, informed his wife of all that had happened, even to the name that the child was to bear. She at least seems to have found no difficulty in accepting the divine assurance, and during her five months of seclusion she nursed great and mighty thoughts in her heart, in the belief and prayer that her child would become all that his name is supposed to signify, *the gift of Jehovah.* It was Elisabeth also who recognized in Mary the mother of her Lord, greeted her as blessed among women, and assured her that there would be for her a fulfillment of the things that had been promised her.

Month followed month, but Zacharias neither heard nor spoke. His friends had to make signs to him. How different this time of waiting from the blessedness it brought to his wife's young relative, who believed the heavenly messenger. He was evidently a good man, and well versed in the history of his people. He could believe that when Abraham and Sarah were past age, a child was born to *them,* but he could not believe that such a blessing could fall to his lot.

During the whole period that the stricken but expectant priest spent in his living tomb, shut off from communication with the outer world, his spirit was becoming charged with holy emotion that waited for the first opportunity of expression. Such an opportunity came at last. His lowly dwelling was one day crowded with an eager and enthusiastic throng of relatives and friends. They had gathered to congratulate the aged pair, to perform the initial rite of Judaism, and to name the infant boy that lay in his mother's arms.

In their perplexity at the mother's insistence that the babe's name should be John—none of his kindred being known by that name—they appealed to his father, who with trembling hand inscribed on the wax of the writing tablet the verdict, "He shall be called John." As soon as he had broken the iron fetter of unbelief in this acknowledging the fulfillment of the angel's words, "his mouth was opened immediately, and his tongue loosed, and he spake, and praised God. And fear came on all that dwelt round about them." All these sayings quickly became the staple theme of conversation throughout all the hill country of Judæa. People laid them up in their hearts, saying, "What manner of child shall this be?"

"And the child grew, and waxed strong in spirit." "And the hand of the Lord was with him."

There were several remarkable formative influences operating on this young life.

1. THE SCHOOL OF HOME.

a. *His father was a priest.* John's earliest memories would register the frequent absence of his father in the fulfillment of his duties; and on his return with what eagerness would the boy drink in a recital of all that had transpired in the Holy City! No wonder that years later, as he looked on Jesus as He walked, he pointed to Him and said, "Behold the Lamb of God"; for, from the earliest, his young mind had been saturated with thoughts of sacrifice.

When old enough his parents would take him with them to one of the great festivals where, amid the thronging crowds, his boyish eyes opened for the first time on the stately temple, the order and vestments of the priests, the solemn pomp of the Levitical ceremonial. The young heart dilated and expanded with wonder and pride; but how little he realized that his ministry would be the first step to its entire subversal.

He would also be taught carefully in the Holy Scriptures. Like the young Timothy, he would know them from early childhood. The song of Zacharias reveals a vivid and realistic familiarity with the prophecies and phraseology of the Scriptures; and as the happy parents recited them to his infant mind, they would stay to emphasize them with impressive personal references. What would we not have given to hear Zacharias quote Isaiah 40 or Malachi 3, and see him turn to the lad at his knee and say—"These words refer to thee"—"And thou, child, shalt be called the prophet of the Highest: for thou shalt go before the face of the Lord to prepare his ways."

He would proceed to tell him the marvelous story of his Kinsman's birth in Bethlehem, and of His growing grace in Nazareth. Next the father would tell as much of the story of Herod's crimes, and of his oppressive rule, as the lad could understand; and would explain how there would soon be "salvation from their enemies, and from the hand of all that hated them." And his young soul would be thrilled by the hopes that were bursting in the bud, and so near breaking into flower.

Sometimes when they were abroad together in the early dawn, and saw the first peep of day, the father would say: "John, do you see that light breaking over the hills? What that dayspring is to the world, Jesus, your cousin at Nazareth, will be to the darkness of sin. See your destiny, my son: I am an old man, and shall not live to see you in your meridian strength; but you will shine for only a brief space, and then decrease, while He will increase from the faint flush of dayspring to the perfect day." And might not the child reply, "Yes, father, I understand; but I shall be satisfied if only I have prepared the way of the Lord."

b. *There were also the associations of the surrounding country.* The story of Abraham would often be recited in the proximity of Machpelah's sacred cave. The career of David could not be unfamiliar to a youth who was within easy reach of the haunts of the shepherd-psalmist. And the story of the Maccabees would stir his soul, as his parents recounted the exploits of Judas and his brethren, in which the ancient Hebrew faith and prowess had revived in one last glorious outburst.

2. THERE WAS THE SCHOOL OF HIS NAZIRITE-VOW. The angel, who announced his birth, foretold that he should drink neither wine nor strong drink from his birth, but that he should be filled with the Holy Spirit. "John," said our Lord, "came neither eating nor drinking" (Matt. 11:18). This abstinence from all stimulants was a distinct sign of the Nazirite, together with the unshorn locks, and the care with which he abstained from contact with death. The Nazirite held himself as peculiarly given up to the service of God.

"Mother, why do I wear my hair so long? You never cut it, as the mothers of other boys do."

"No, my son," was the proud and glad reply; "you must never cut it as long as you live: *you are a Nazirite.*"

"Mother, why may I not taste the grapes? The boys say they are so nice and sweet. May I not, next vintage?"

"No, never," his mother would reply; "you must never touch the fruit of the vine: *you are a Nazirite.*"

If, as they walked along the public way, they saw a bone left by some hungry dog, or a bird fallen to the earth to die, and the boy would approach to touch either, the mother would call him back to her side, saying, "You must never touch a dead thing. If your father were to die, or I, beside you, you must not move us from the spot, but call for help. Remember always that you are separated to God.

This would give a direction and purpose to the lad's thoughts and anticipations. He realized that he was set apart for a great mission in life. He would acquire self-restraint, self-mastery.

On each of us rests the vow of separation, by right of our union with the Son of God, who was holy, harmless, undefiled, and separate from sinners. His death has made a lasting break between His followers and the rest of men. They are crucified to the world, and the world to them. Let us not taste of the intoxicating joys in which the children of the present age indulge; let us have no fellowship with the unfruitful works of darkness, but come out and be separate, not touching the unclean thing.

But while we put away all that injures our own life or the lives of others, let us be very careful to discriminate, exaggerating and extenuating nothing. Christ has come to sanctify all life. Disciples are not to be taken out of the world, but kept from evil. Natural instincts are not to be crushed, but transfigured.

This is the great contrast between the Baptist and the Son of Man. The Nazirite would have felt it a sin against the law of his vocation and office to touch anything pertaining to the vine. Christ began His signs by changing water into wine, though of an innocuous kind, for the peasants' wedding at Cana of Galilee. John would have lost all sanctity had he touched the bodies of the dead, or the flesh of a leper. Christ would touch a bier, pass His hands over the seared flesh of the leper, and stand sympathetically beside the grave of His friend. Thus we catch a glimpse of our Lord's meaning when He affirms that, though John was the greatest born of women, yet the least in the kingdom of heaven is greater than he.

3. THERE WAS THE SCHOOL OF THE DESERT. "The child . . . was in the deserts till the day of his shewing unto Israel." Probably Zacharias, and Elisabeth also, died when John was quite young. But the boy had grown into adolescence, was able to care for himself, and "the hand of the Lord was with him."

Beneath the guidance and impulse of that hand he tore himself from the little home where he had first seen the light of day, and spent happy years, to go forth from the ordinary haunts of men, perhaps hardly knowing where. There was a wild restlessness in his soul.

Fatherless, motherless, brotherless, sisterless—a lone man, he passed forth into the great and terrible wilderness of Judæa, which is so desolate that the Jews called it the abomination of desolation. When Jesus was there some two or three years later, He found nothing to eat; the stones around mocked his hunger, and there was no company except that of the wild beasts.

In this great and terrible wilderness John supported himself by eating locusts—the literal insect, which is greatly esteemed by the natives—and wild honey, which abounded in the crevices of the rocks; while for clothing he was content with a coat of coarse camel's hair, such as the Arab women still make, and a girdle of skin about his loins. A cave, like that in which David and his men often found refuge, sufficed for a home, and the water of the streams that hurried to the Dead Sea for his beverage.

Can we wonder that under such a regimen he grew strong? In loneliness and solitude, wherein we meet God, we become strong. God's strong men are rarely clothed in soft raiment, or found in king's courts.

Yes, and there is a source of strength beside. He who is filled and taught, as John was, by the Spirit, is strengthened by might in the inner man. All things are possible to him who believers. They who know God are strong and do great things.

4

The Prophet of the Highest
Luke 1

"Thou, child, shalt be called the prophet of the Highest"—thus Zacharias addressed his infant son, as he lay in the midst of that group of wondering neighbors and friends. What a thrill of ecstasy quivered in the words! A long period, computed at four hundred years, had passed since the last great Hebrew prophet had uttered the words of the Highest. Reaching back from him to the days of Moses had been a long line of prophets. And the fourteen generations, during which the prophetic office had been discontinued, had gone wearily. But now hope revived, as the angel voice proclaimed the advent of a prophet. Our Lord corroborated His words when, months later, He said that John had been a prophet, and something more.

The Hebrew word that stands for *prophet* is said to be derived from a root signifying "to boil or bubble over," and suggests a fountain bursting from the heart of the man into whom God had poured it. It is a mistake to confine the word to the prediction of coming events, for so employed it would hardly be applicable to men like Moses, Samuel, and Elijah in the Old Testament, or John the Baptist and the apostle Paul in the New, who were certainly prophets in the deepest significance of that term. Prophecy means the forth-telling of the divine message. The prophet is borne along by the stream of divine indwelling and inflowing, whether he utters the truth for the moment or anticipates the future.

With Malachi, the succession that had continued unbroken from the very foundation of the Jewish commonwealth had terminated. But as the voice of Old Testament prophecy ceased, with its last breath it foretold that it would be followed, some time later, by a new and glorious revival of the noblest traditions of the prophetic office. "Behold," so God spoke by Malachi, "I will send you Elijah the prophet before the coming of the great and dreadful day of the LORD. And he shall turn the heart of the fathers to the children, and the heart of the children to their fathers" (Mal. 4:5–6).

1. THE FORMATIVE INFLUENCES BY WHICH THE BAPTIST'S PROPHETIC NATURE WAS MOLDED. Among these we must place in the foremost rank *the prophecies*, which had given a forecast of his career. From his childhood and upwards they had been reiterated in his ear by his parents, who would never tire of reciting them.

How often he would ponder the reference to himself in the great messianic prediction—"Comfort ye, comfort ye my people, saith your God. . . . The voice of him that crieth . . . Prepare ye the way of the LORD; make straight in the desert a highway for our God. . . ." There was no doubt as to the relevance of those words to himself (Luke 1:76; Matt. 3:3). And it must have influenced his character and ministry greatly.

There was also that striking anticipation by Malachi that we have already quoted, and which directly suggested Elijah as his model. Had not Gabriel himself alluded to it when he foretold that the predicted child would go before the Messiah, in the spirit and power of Elijah (Luke 1:17)? And again his statement was confirmed by our Lord later (Matt. 11:14).

Thus the great figure of Elijah was always before the mind of the growing youth, as his model and inspiration. He found himself perpetually asking, How did Elijah act, and what would he do here and now? And there is little doubt that his choice of the lonely wilderness, of the rough mantle of camel's hair, of the abrupt and arousing form of address, was suggested by that village of Tishbe in the land of Gilead, and those personal characteristics that were so familiar in the Prophet of Fire.

But the mind of the forerunner must also have been greatly affected by *the lawlessness and crime* that involved all classes of his countrymen in a common condemnation and discontent. The priests were hirelings; the Pharisees were hypocrites. "Brood of vipers" was apparently not too strong a phrase to use of the foremost religious leaders of the day—at least, when used, its relevance passed without challenge.

Tidings of the evil that was overflowing the land were constantly coming to the ears of this eager soul, filling it with horror and dismay; thus the pressure of the burden pressed on him until he was forced to give utterance to the cry it extorted from his soul: "Repent, for the kingdom of heaven is at hand."

But in addition to these we must add *the vision of God,* which must have been especially given to him while he wandered in those lonely wilds. He spoke once of Him "who sent him to baptize." Evidently he had become accustomed to detect His presence and hear His voice. Those still small accents that had fallen on the ear of his great prototype had thrilled his soul. He too had seen the Lord high and lifted up, had heard the chant of the seraphim, and had felt the live coal touch his lips, as it had been caught from the altar by the seraph's tongs.

This has ever been characteristic of the true prophet. He has been a seer. He has spoken, because he has beheld with his eyes, looked upon, and handled the very Word of God.

These are the three signs of a prophet: vision, a deep conviction of sin and impending judgment, and the gushing forth of moving and eloquent speech; and each of these was apparent, in an exalted and extreme degree, in John the son of Zacharias.

2. AN ILLUSTRATIVE AND REMARKABLE PARALLEL. As John came in the spirit and power of Elijah so, four hundred years ago, in the lovely city of Florence, a man was sent from God to testify against the sins of his age, who in many particulars so exactly corresponds with our Lord's forerunner that the one strongly recalls the other. And it may help us to bring the circumstances of the Baptist's ministry within a measurable distance of ourselves if we briefly compare them with the career of Girolamo Savonarola.

The physician's household at Ferrara, into which Savonarola was born on September 21, 1452, was probably no more distinguished than that of Zacharias and Elisabeth in the hill country of Judæa. And as we read of the invincible love of truth that characterized the intelligent young man, we are forcibly reminded of the Baptist, whose whole life was an eloquent protest on behalf of reality.

We cannot read of Savonarola's saintly life, over which even the breath of slander has never cast a stain—of his depriving himself of every indulgence, content with the hardest couch and roughest clothing, and just enough of the plainest food to support life—without remembering the camel's cloth, the locusts and wild honey of the Baptist.

If John's lot was cast on evil days, when religion suffered most in the house of her friends, so it was with Savonarola. The fourteenth and fifteenth centuries witnessed the increasing corruption and licentiousness of popes and clergy. The grossest immorality was prevalent in all ranks of the church, and without concealment. Even the monasteries and convents were often dens of vice.

As John beheld the fire and fan of impending judgment, so the burden of Savonarola's preaching was that the church was about to be chastised, and afterward renewed.

The herald of Jesus possessed a marvelous eloquence, beneath which the whole land was moved, and so it was with Savonarola. During the eight years that he preached in the cathedral, it was filled with vast crowds; and he pleaded for purity of life and simplicity of manners.

What Herod was to John the Baptist, the Pope and the magnificent Lorenzo de Medici were to Savonarola. The latter seems to have felt a strange fascination toward the eloquent preacher, tried to woo him to his court, was frequent in his attendance at San Marco, and gave large gifts to his ministry. To use the words of the New Testament, he feared him, "knowing that he was a just man, and an holy" (Mark 6:20). But Savonarola took care to avoid any sign of compliance or compromise; declined to pay homage to Lorenzo for promotion to high ecclesiastical functions; returned his gold; and when he was told that Lorenzo was walking in the convent garden, answered, "If he has not asked for me, do not disturb his meditations or mine."

Like John, Savonarola was unceasing in his denunciation of the hypocritical religion that satisfied itself with outward observances.

The fate of martyrdom that befell John was awarded also to Savonarola. Through the impetuosity of his followers, he was involved in a challenge to ordeal by fire. But by the maneuvering of his foes, the expectations of the populace in this direction were disappointed and their anger aroused. "To San Marco!" shouted their leaders. To San Marco they went, fired on the buildings, burst open the doors, dragged Savonarola from his devotions, and thrust him into a loathsome dungeon. After languishing there, amid every indignity and torture, for some weeks, on May 23, 1498 he was led forth to die. The bishop whose duty it was to pronounce his sentence, stumbled at the formula declaring—"I separate thee from the Church, militant and triumphant." "From the militant thou mayest, but from the triumphant thou canst not," was the martyr's calm reply. He met his end with unflinching fortitude. He was strangled, his remains hung in chains, burned, and the ashes flung into the river. When the commissioners of the Pope arrived at his trial, they brought with them express orders that he was to die, "even though he were *a second John the Baptist.*" It is thus that the apostate church has always dealt with her noblest sons. But Truth, struck to the ground, revives. Hers are the eternal years. Within a few years, Luther was nailing his theses at the door of the church at Wittenberg, and the Reformation was on its way.

The story recalls forcibly the words with which the evangelist John introduces his notice of the forerunner—"There was a man sent from God, whose name was John." Men are always coming, sent from God, especially adapted to their age, and entrusted with the message that the times demand. See to it that you too realize your divine mission; for Jesus said, "As the Father hath sent me, even so send I you." *Every true life is a mission from God.*

5

The First Ministry of the Baptist
Luke 3

Thirty years had left their mark on the forerunner. The aged priest and his wife Elisabeth had been carried to their grave by hands other than those of the young Nazirite. The story of his miraculous birth, and the expectations it had aroused, had almost died out of the memory of the countryside. For many years John had been living in the caves that indent the limestone rocks of the desolate wilderness that extends from Hebron to the western shores of the Dead Sea. By the use of the scantiest fare and roughest garb he had brought his body under complete mastery. From nature, from the inspired page, and from direct fellowship with God, he had received revelations that are bestowed only on those who can stand the strain of discipline in the school of solitude and privation. He had carefully pondered also the signs of the times, of which he received information from the Bedouin and others with whom he came in contact. Blended with all other thoughts, John's heart was filled with the advent of Him, His relative who was growing up, a few months his junior, in an obscure highland home, but who was soon to be manifested to Israel.

At last the moment arrived for him to utter the mighty burden that pressed on him; and "in the fifteenth year of the reign of Tiberius Caesar, Pontius Pilate being governor of Judæa, and Herod being tetrarch of Galilee and Annas and Caiaphas being the high priests, the word of God came unto John the son of Zacharias in the wilderness." The word was "Repent! the kingdom of heaven is at hand."

It was as though a spark had fallen on dry tinder. The tidings spread with wonderful rapidity that in the wilderness of Judæa one was to be met who recalled the memory of the great prophets, and whose burning eloquence was of the same order as of Isaiah or Ezekiel. People began to flock to him from all sides. The neighborhood suddenly became black with hurrying crowds. From lip to lip the tidings sped of a great leader and preacher who had suddenly appeared.

He seems finally to have taken His stand not far from the rose-clad oasis of Jericho, on the banks of the Jordan; and men of every tribe, class, and profession, gathered there, listening eagerly, or interrupting Him with loud cries for help.

1. MANY CAUSES ACCOUNTED FOR JOHN'S IMMENSE POPULARITY.

a. *The office of the prophet was almost obsolete.* We have seen how several centuries had passed since the last great prophet had finished his testimony. It seemed unlikely that another prophet should arise in that formal, materialistic age.

b. *John gave such abundant evidence of sincerity—of reality.* His independence of anything that this world could give made men feel that whatever he said was inspired by his direct contact with things as they literally are. It was certain that his severe and lonely life had rent the veil, and given him the knowledge of facts and realities hidden from ordinary men. When men see the professed prophet of the Eternal as eager after his own interests as any worldling, shrewd at a bargain, captivated by show, obsequious to the titled and wealthy; they are apt to reduce to a minimum their faith in his words. But there was no trace of this in the Baptist, and therefore the people came to him.

c. *Above all, he appealed to their moral convictions and, indeed, expressed them.*

The people knew that they were not as they should be. They flocked around the man who revealed themselves to themselves and indicated with unfaltering decision the course of action they should adopt. How marvelous is the fascination that *he* exerts over people who will speak to their innermost souls! Though we may shrink from the preaching of repentance, yet, if it tells the truth about us, we will be irresistibly attracted to hear the voice that harrows our soul. John rebuked Herod for many things; but still the royal offender sent for him again and again, and heard him gladly.

It is expressly said that John saw many Pharisees and Sadducees coming to his baptism (Matt. 3:7). Their advent appears to have caused him some surprise. "O generation of vipers, who hath warned you to flee from the wrath to come?" The strong epithet he used of them suggests that they came as critics; but it is quite likely that in many cases there were deeper reasons. The Pharisees were the ritualists and formalists of their day, but the mere externals of religion will never permanently satisfy the soul made in the likeness of God. Ultimately it will turn from them with a great nausea and an insatiable desire for the living God. As for the Sadducees, they were the materialists of their time. The reaction of superstition, it has been said, is to infidelity; and the reaction from Pharisaism was to Sadduceeism. Disgusted and outraged by the trifling of the literalists of Scripture interpretation, the Sadducee denied that there was an eternal world and a spiritual state. But mere negation can never satisfy. It was hardly to be wondered at then that these two great classes were largely represented in the crowds that gathered on the banks of the Jordan.

2. Let us briefly enumerate the main burden of the Baptist's preaching.

a. *"The kingdom of heaven is at hand."* To a Jew that phrase meant the reestablishment of the theocracy, and a return to those great days in the history of his people when God Himself was Lawgiver and King. The long-expected Messiah was at hand; but some misgiving must have passed over the minds of his hearers when they heard the young prophet's description of the conditions and accompaniments of that long-looked-for reign. Instead of dilating on the material glory of the messianic period, far surpassing the magnificent splendor of Solomon, he insisted on the fulfillment of certain necessary preliminary requirements, which lifted the whole conception of the anticipated reign to a new level, in which the inward and spiritual took precedence of the outward and material. It was the old lesson, which in every age requires repetition, that unless a man is born again, and from above, he cannot see the kingdom of God.

Be sure of this, that no outward circumstances, however propitious and favorable, can bring about true blessedness. Life must be centered in Christ if it is to be concentric with all the circles of heaven's bliss. It is only when we are right with God that we are blest and at rest. When all hearts are yielded to the King; when all gates lift up their heads, and all everlasting doors are unfolded for his entrance—then the curse that has so long brooded over the world will be done away.

b. Alongside the proclamation of the kingdom was the uncompromising insistence on *"the wrath to come."* John saw that the advent of the King would bring inevitable suffering to those who were living in self-indulgence and sin.

There would be careful discrimination. He who was coming would carefully discern between the righteous and the wicked; between those who served God and those who

179

did not serve Him. There will be a very careful process of discrimination before the unquenchable fires are lighted; so that none but chaff will be consigned to the flames—a prediction that was faithfully fulfilled. At first Christ drew all men to Himself; but as his ministry proceeded He revealed their quality. A few were permanently attracted to Him; the majority were as definitely repelled. So it has been in every age. Jesus Christ is the touchstone of trial. Our attitude toward Him reveals the true quality of the soul.

There would also be a period of probation. "The axe laid unto the root of the trees" is familiar enough to those who know anything of forestry. The lumberjack destroys some tree that seems to him to be occupying space capable of being put to better use. But when once that word is spoken, there is no appeal. The Jewish people had become sadly unfruitful; but a definite period was to intervene—three years of Christ's ministry and thirty years beside—before the threatened judgment befell.

For all such there must be "wrath to come." After there has been searching scrutiny and investigation, and every reasonable chance has been given to change, and still the soul is impenitent and disobedient, there must be "a certain fearful looking for of judgment and fiery indignation, which shall devour the adversaries" (Heb. 10:27).

The fire of John's preaching had its primary fulfillment in the awful disasters that befell the Jewish people, culminating in the siege and fall of Jerusalem. But there was a deeper meaning. The wrath of God avenges itself, not on nations but on individual sinners. "He that believeth not the Son shall not see life; but the wrath of God abideth on him" (John 3:36). The penalty of sin is inevitable. The wages of sin is death.

Even if we grant, as of course we must, that many of the expressions referring to the ultimate fate of the ungodly are symbolical, yet it must also be granted that they have counterparts in the realm of soul and spirit, which are as terrible to endure, as the nature of the soul is more highly organized than that of the body. Believe me that when Jesus said, "These shall go away into eternal punishment," He contemplated a retribution so terrible, that it would be good for the sufferers if they had never been born.

All the great preachers have seen and faithfully borne witness to the fearful results of sin, as they take effect in this life and the next. On the other hand, because God is not confined to any one method, the preaching of the late D. L. Moody was especially steeped in the love of God. It is for want of a vision of the inevitable fate of the godless and disobedient, that much of our present-day preaching is so powerless and ephemeral. And only when we modern preachers have seen sin as God sees it, and begin to apply the divine standard to the human conscience; only when we know the terror of the Lord, and begin to persuade men as though we would pluck them out of the fire by our strenuous expostulation and entreaties; only then will we see the effects that followed the preaching of the Baptist when soldiers, publicans, Pharisees, and scribes, crowded around him, saying, "What shall we do?"

All John's preaching therefore led up to the demand for repentance. The word that was most often on his lips was "Repent ye!" It was not enough to plead direct descent from Abraham, for God could raise up children to Abraham from the stones of the river bank. There had to be the renunciation of sin, the definite turning to God, the bringing forth of fruit meet for an amended life. In no other way could the people be prepared for the coming of the Lord.

6

Baptism to Repentance
Mark 1:4

At the time of which we are speaking, an extraordinary sect, known as the Essenes, was scattered throughout Palestine, but had its special home in the oasis of Engedi; and John must have been in frequent association with the adherents of this community. They were the recluses or hermits of their age.

The aim of the Essenes was moral and ceremonial purity. They sought after an ideal of holiness, which they thought could not be realized in this world; and therefore leaving villages and towns, they took to dens and caves and gave themselves to continence, abstinence, fastings, and prayers, supporting themselves by some odd jobs on the land. The cardinal point with them was faith in the inspired Word of God. By meditation, prayer and mortification, frequent ablutions, and strict attention to the laws of ceremonial purity, they hoped to reach the highest stage of communion with God. They agreed with the Pharisees in their extraordinary regard for the Sabbath. Their daily meal was of the simplest kind, and was partaken of in their house of religious assembly. After bathing, with prayer and exhortation, they went with veiled faces to their dining room, as to a holy temple. They abstained from oaths, despised riches, manifested the greatest abhorrence of war and slavery, faced torture and death with the utmost bravery, refused the indulgence of pleasure.

It is clear that John was not a member of this holy community, which differed widely from the Pharisaism and Sadduceeism of the time. But it cannot be doubted that he was in deep accord with much of the doctrine and practice of this sect.

John the Baptist however cannot be accounted for by any of the preexisting conditions of his time. He stood alone in his God-given might. That he was conscious of this appears from his own declaration when he said, "He that sent me to baptize with water, the same said unto me" (John 1:33). The distinct assertion of the Spirit of God, through the fourth evangelist, informs us: "There was a man sent from God, whose name was John. The same came for a witness, that *all* men through him might believe" (John 1:9–10).

1. THE SUMMONS TO REPENT. John represents a phase of teaching and influence through which we must needs pass if we are properly to discover and appreciate the grace of Christ. In proportion to our repentance will be our glad realization of the fullness and glory of the Lamb of God; but we must guard ourselves here, lest it be supposed that repentance is a species of good work that must be performed so that we may merit the grace of Christ. It must be made equally clear that repentance must not be viewed apart from faith in the Savior, which is an integral part of it. It is also certain that, though "God commandeth," Jesus is exalted "to *give* repentance and the remission of sins."

Repentance, according to the literal rendering of the Greek word, is "a change of mind." Perhaps we should rather say, it is a change in the attitude of the will. It no longer refuses the yoke of God's will, but yields to it, or is willing to yield. The habits may rebel; the inclinations and emotions may shrink back; the consciousness of peace and joy may yet be far away—but the will has made its secret decision, and has begun to turn to God.

It cannot be too strongly emphasized that repentance is an act of the *will*. In its beginning there may be no sense of gladness or reconciliation with God: it is the consciousness that certain ways of life are wrong, mistaken, hurtful, and grieving to God; and includes the desire, which becomes the determination, to turn from them.

Repentance may be accounted as the other side of faith. They are the two sides of the same coin. If the act of the soul that brings it into right relation with God is described as a turning round, then *repentance* stands for its desire and choice to turn from sin, and *faith* for its desire and choice to turn to God. We must be willing to turn from sin and our own righteousness—that is *repentance;* we must be willing to be saved by God, in His own way, and must come to Him for that purpose—that is *faith*.

We need to turn from our own righteousnesses as well as from our sins. Nothing apart from the Savior and His work can avail the soul, which must meet the scrutiny of eternal justice and purity.

Repentance is produced sometimes and especially by the presentation of the claims of Christ. We suddenly awake to realize what He is, how He loves, how much we are missing, the gross ingratitude with which we respond to His agony and bloody sweat, His cross and suffering, the beauty of His character, the strength of His claims.

At other times repentance is brought about by the preaching of John the Baptist. Then we hear of the axe laid at the root of the trees, and the heart trembles. It is at such a time that the soul sees the entire fabric of its vain confidences and hopes crumbling like a cloud palace, and turns from it all.

If John the Baptist has never brought about his work in you, be sure to open your heart to his piercing voice. Expose your soul to its searching scrutiny, and allow it to have free and uninterrupted course.

2. THE SIGNS AND SYMPTOMS OF REPENTANCE.

a. *Confession.* "They were all baptized of him in the river of Jordan, confessing their sins" (Mark 1:5). On that river's brink, men not only confessed to God, but probably also to one another. Lifelong feuds were reconciled; old quarrels were settled; frank words of apology and forgiveness were exchanged; hands grasped hands for the first time after years of alienation and strife.

Confession is an essential sign of a genuine repentance, and without it forgiveness is impossible. "If we confess our sins, he is faithful and just to forgive us our sins, and to cleanse us from all unrighteousness" (1 John 1:9).

Confess your sin to God, O troubled soul, from whom the vision of Christ is veiled. Excuse nothing, extenuate nothing, omit nothing. Do not speak of mistakes of judgment, but of lapses of heart and will. Do not be content with a general confession; be particular and specific. Drag each evil thing before God's judgment bar; let the secrets be exposed, and the dark, sad story told. To tell Him all is to receive at once His assurance of forgiveness, for the sake of Him who loved us and gave Himself a propitiation for our sins. As soon as the confession leaves our heart, nay, while it is in the process, the divine voice is heard assuring us that our sins, which are many, are put away as far as the east is from the west, and cast into the depths of the sea.

But such confession should not be made to God alone, when sins are in question that have injured and alienated others. If our brother has anything against us, we must find him out, while our gift is left unpresented at the altar, and first be reconciled to him. We must write the letter, or speak the word; we must make honorable reparation and amends; we must not be behind the sinners under the old law, who were instructed to add a fifth part to the loss their brother had sustained through their wrongdoing, when they made it good.

b. *Fruit worthy of repentance.* "Bring forth, therefore, fruit worthy of repentance," said John, as he saw many of the Pharisees and Sadducees coming to his baptism.

That demand of the Baptist probably accounted for the alteration in his life of which Zaccheus made confession to Christ, when He became his guest. The rich publican lived at Jericho, near where John was baptizing, and he was probably among the publicans who were attracted to his ministry. And something touched that hardened heart. A great hope and a great resolve sprang up in it. On his arrival at Jericho he was a new man. He gave the half of his goods to feed the poor; and if he had wrongfully exacted anything of any man, he restored it fourfold. Would any ask him the reason for it all, he would answer, "Ah, I have been down to the Jordan and heard the Baptist; I believe the kingdom is coming, and the King is at hand."

You will never get right with God until you are right with man. It is not enough to confess wrongdoing; you must be prepared to make amends as far as lies in your power. Sin is not a light thing, and it must be dealt with, root and branch.

c. *The baptism of repentance.* "They were baptized . . . confessing their sins." It was not baptism *unto remission,* but *unto repentance.* It was the expression and symbol of the soul's desire and intention, as far as it knew, to confess and renounce its sins, as the necessary condition of obtaining the divine forgiveness.

In John's hands the rite assumed altogether novel and important functions. It meant death and burial as far as the past was concerned; and resurrection to a new and better future.

It is easy to see how all this appealed to the people, and especially touched the hearts of young men. At that time, by the blue waters of the Lake of Galilee, there was a handful of ardent youths, deeply stirred by the currents of thought around them, who resented the Roman sway, and were on the tip-toe of expectation for the coming kingdom. When, one day, tidings reached them of this strange new preacher, they left all and streamed with all the world beside to the Jordan valley, and stood fascinated by the spell of his words.

One by one, or all together, they made themselves known to him, and became his loyal friends and disciples. We are familiar with the names of one or two of them, who afterward left their earlier master to follow Christ; but of the rest we know nothing, except that he taught them to fast and pray, and that they clung to their great teacher until they bore his headless body to the grave. After his death they joined themselves with Him whom they had once regarded with some suspicion as John's rival and supplanter.

How much this meant to John! He had never had a friend; and to have the allegiance and love of these noble, ingenuous youths must have been very grateful to his soul. But from them all he repeatedly turned his gaze, as though he were looking for someone whose voice would give him the deepest and richest fulfillment of his joy, because it would be the voice of the Bridegroom Himself.

7

The Manifestation of the Messiah
John 1:31

John's life, at this period, was an extraordinary one. By day he preached to the teeming crowds, or baptized them; by night he would sleep in some slight booth, or darksome cave. But the conviction grew always stronger in his soul, that the Messiah was soon to come; and this conviction became a revelation. The Holy Spirit who filled him, taught him. He began to see the outlines of His person and work.

He conceived of the coming King, as we have seen, as the Woodsman, laying his axe at the root of the trees; as the Husbandman, fan in hand to winnow the threshing floor; as the Baptist, prepared to plunge all faithful souls in his cleansing fires; as the Ancient of Days who, though coming after him in order of time, must be preferred before him in order of precedence, because He was before him in the eternal glory of his being (John 1:15–30). He insisted that he was not worthy to perform the most menial service for Him whose advent he announced.

John was not only humble in his self-estimate, but also in his modest appreciation of the results of his work. It was only transient and preparatory. It was given him to do; but it would soon be done. His course was a short one, and it would soon be fulfilled (Acts 13:25). His simple mission was to bid the people to believe on Him who would come after him (19:4).

1. OUR LORD'S ADVENT TO THE JORDAN BANK. For thirty years the Son of man had been about His Father's business in the ordinary routine of a village carpenter's life. He had found scope enough there for his marvelously rich and deep nature. Often He must have felt the strong attraction of the great world of men, which He loved. But He waited still, until the time was fulfilled that had been fixed in the eternal council chamber.

As soon as the rumors of the Baptist's ministry reached Him, however, He had to tear Himself away from Nazareth, home, and mother, and take the road that would end at Calvary.

Tradition locates the scene of John's baptism as near Jericho, where the water is shallow and the river opens out into large lagoons. But some, inferring that Nazareth was within a day's journey of this notable spot, place it nearer the southern end of the Lake of Galilee.

It may have been in the late afternoon when Jesus arrived; a sudden and remarkable change passed over the Baptist's face as he beheld his Kinsman standing there.

John said, "I knew him not" (John 1:31); but this need not be interpreted as indicating that he had no acquaintance whatever with his blameless relative. He knew enough of Him to be aware of His guileless, blameless life, as He presented Himself for baptism, John felt that there was a whole heaven of difference between Him and all others. These publicans and sinners, these Pharisees and scribes, these soldiers and common people—had every need to repent, confess, and be forgiven; but there was surely no such need for Him. He said, "I have need to be baptized of thee, and comest thou to me?" (Matt. 3:14).

There may have been, besides, an indescribable premonition that stole over that lofty nature. There was an indefinable majesty, a moral glory, a tender grace, an ineffable attractiveness in this Man.

2. THE SIGNIFICANCE OF CHRIST'S BAPTISM. "Suffer it to be so now; for thus it becometh us to fulfil all righteousness"—with such words our Lord overruled the objections of his loyal and faithful forerunner. This is the first recorded utterance of Christ, after a silence of more than twenty years; the first also of His public ministry. He does not say, "I have need to be baptized of thee"; nor does He say, "Thou hast no need to be baptized of Me."

John's baptism was the inauguration of the kingdom of heaven. In it the material made way for the spiritual. The old system, which gave special privileges to the children of Abraham, was in the act of passing away. It was the outward and visible sign that Judaism was unavailing for the deepest needs of the spirit of man, and that a new and more spiritual system was about to take its place.

With our race, in its sin and degradation, our Lord now formally identified Himself. His baptism was His formal identification with our fallen and sinful race, though He knew no sin for Himself, and could challenge the minutest inspection of His enemies: "Which of you convinceth me of sin?"

Was He baptized because He needed to repent, or to confess his sins? No! He was as pure as the bosom of God, from which He came; but He needed to be made sin, that we might be made the righteousness of God in Him.

A friend suggests that the Lord Jesus was here referring to the sublime prophecy of Daniel 9:24. That He might make an end of sin and bring in everlasting righteousness, it was essential that the Lamb of God should confess the sins of the people as His own (see Ps. 69:5). This was His first step on His journey to the cross, every step of which was in fulfillment of all righteousness, in order that He might bring in everlasting righteousness.

"Then he suffered him." Some things we have to *do* for Christ, and some to *bear* for Him. In all our human life, there is nothing more attractive than when a strong man yields to another, and is prepared to set aside his strong convictions of propriety before the tender pleadings of a still, soft voice. Yield to Christ, dear heart. Allow Him to have His way. Take His yoke, and be meek and lowly of heart—so shall you find rest.

3. THE DESIGNATION OF THE MESSIAH. It is not to be supposed that the designation of Jesus as the Christ was given to any but John. It was apparently a private sign given to him, as the Forerunner and Herald, through which he might be authoritatively informed as to the identity of the Messiah. He says, "I knew him not" (i.e., as Son of God), "but he that sent me to baptize with water, the same said unto me, Upon whom thou shalt see the Spirit descending, and remaining on him, the same is he which baptizeth with the Holy Ghost. And I saw, and bear record that this is the Son of God" (John 1:32–34).

What a theophany this was! As the Man of Nazareth emerged from the water, the sign for which John had been eagerly waiting and looking for was granted. He had believed he would see it, but had never thought to see it granted to a relative of his. He saw far away into the blue vault, which had opened into depth after depth of golden glory. The veil was torn to admit the coming of the divine Spirit, who seemed to descend in visible shape—as a dove might, with gentle, fluttering motion—and to alight on the head of the Holy One, who stood there fresh from His baptism.

The voice of God from heaven proclaimed that Jesus of Nazareth was His beloved Son, in whom He was well pleased; and the Baptist could have no further doubt that the Lord whom his people sought, the Messenger of the covenant, had come. "John bare record saying, I saw the Spirit descending from heaven like a dove, and it abode upon him" (John 1:32).

The Baptist knew that his mission was nearly fulfilled, that his office was ended. The Sun had risen, and the daystar began to wane.

8

Not that Light, but a Witness
John 1:8

The baptism and revelation of Christ had a marvelous effect on the ministry of the forerunner. Previous to that memorable day, the burden of his teaching had been in the direction of repentance and confession of sin. But afterward, the whole force of his testimony was toward the person and glory of the Shepherd of Israel. He understood that for the remainder of his brief ministry, which perhaps did not greatly exceed six months, he must bend all his strength to announcing to the people the prerogatives and claims of Him who stood among them, though they did not know Him.

Our subject therefore naturally divides itself into two divisions: John's admissions about himself and his testimony to the Lord. They were given on three successive days, as appears from the twofold use of the phrase, "The next day." "The next day (i.e., after he had met and answered the deputation from the Sanhedrin), John seeth Jesus coming unto him . . ." (1:29). "Again, the next day after John stood, and two of his disciples . . ." (1:35).

These events took place at Bethany, or Bethabara, on the eastern bank of the Jordan.

1. THE BAPTIST'S ADMISSIONS ABOUT HIMSELF. When the fourth evangelist uses the word "Jews" he invariably means the Sanhedrin. John had become so famous, and his influence so commanding, that he could not be ignored by the religious leaders of the time. His preaching of repentance, and his unmeasured denunciation of them as a brood of vipers, were not to be borne. But they bore it so they could meet him in the open field, and resolved to send a deputation that might extract some admission from his lips that would furnish them with ground for subsequent action. "The Jews sent priests and Levites from Jerusalem to ask him, 'Who art thou?' . . . 'Why baptizest thou?'" The first question was universally interesting; the second especially so to the Pharisee party, who were the high ritualists of their day, and who were reluctant that a new rite, which they had not sanctioned, should be added to the Jewish ecclesiastical system.

The deputation challenged the prophet with the inquiry, "Who art thou?" There was a great silence. Men were prepared to believe anything of the eloquent young preacher. "The people were in expectation, and all men mused in their hearts of John, whether he were the Christ or not" (Luke 3:15). "And he confessed, and denied not; but confessed, I am not the Christ."

If a murmur of voices burst out in anger, disappointment, and chagrin, it was immediately hushed by the second inquiry, "What then? Art thou Elias?" (alluding to the prediction of Mal. 4:5). If they would have worded their question rather differently, and put it this way, "Hast thou come in the power of Elias?" John would have had to acknowledge that it was so; but if they meant to inquire if he were literally Elijah returned again to this world, he had no alternative but to say, decisively and laconically, "I am not."

There was a third arrow in their quiver, since the other two had missed the mark: and amid the deepening attention of the listening multitudes, and in allusion to Moses' prediction that God would raise up a prophet like to Himself (Deut. 18:15; Acts 3:22, 7:37), they said, "Art thou that prophet?" and he answered, "No."

Their spokesman, for the fourth time, challenged him. "Then said they unto him, Who art thou? that we may give an answer to them that sent us. What sayest thou of thyself?" "He said, I am the voice of one crying in the wilderness, Make straight the way of the Lord, as said the prophet Isaias."

How infinitely noble! How characteristic of strength! What a mingling of strength and humility! Such humility always accompanies a true vision of Christ. To the crowds John may have seemed to fulfill all the essential conditions of the prophetic portraiture of the Messiah; but *he* knew how infinitely the Christ stood above him. This is apparent in his reply to the final inquiry of the Sanhedrin, "And they asked him, and said unto him, 'Why, baptizest thou then, if thou be not that Christ, neither Elias, neither that prophet?'" And John said in effect, "I baptize because I was sent to baptize, and I know very well that my work in this respect is temporary and transient; but what matters that? In the midst of you stands One whom ye do not know, even He who comes after me, the latchet of whose shoe I am not worthy to unloose. The Christ is come. Have I not seen Him, standing amid your crowds, yea, descending these very banks?"

The people must have turned one to another, as he spoke. What! Had the Messiah come! It could hardly be. There had been no prodigies in earth or sky worthy of His advent. How could He be among them, and they unaware! But it was even so, and it is so still. Ah, "the natural man receiveth not the things of the Spirit of God: for they are foolishness unto him: neither can he know them, because they are spiritually discerned" (1 Cor. 2:14). "There standeth one among you," said the Baptist, "whom ye know not."

2. THE BAPTIST'S WITNESS TO THE LORD. Six weeks passed by from that memorable vision of the opened heaven and the descending Spirit, and John had eagerly scanned every comer to the river bank to see again that divinely beautiful face. But in vain: for Jesus was in the wilderness, being tempted of the devil, for forty days and nights, the companion of wild beasts, and exposed to a very hurricane of temptation.

At the end of the six weeks, the interview with the deputation from the Sanhedrin took place, which we have already described; and on the day after, his eyes flashed, his face lit up, and he cried, saying: "This is he of whom I said, After me cometh a man which is preferred before me: for he was before me. Behold the Lamb of God, which taketh away the sin of the world."

Did all eyes turn toward the Christ? Was there a ripple of interest and expectancy through the crowd? We do not know. Scripture is silent, only telling us that on the following day when, with two disciples, he looked on Jesus as He walked, and repeated his affirmation, "Behold the Lamb of God," those two disciples followed Him, never to return to their old master—who knew it must be so and was content to decrease if only He might increase.

Let us notice the successive revelations that were made to John, and through him to Israel who, you remember, held him, as they had every warrant for doing, to be in the deepest sense a prophet of the Lord.

a. *He rightly conceived of Christ's preexistence.* "He was before me" (John 1:30). The phrase resembles Christ's own words, when He said: "Before Abraham was, I am." In John's case it developed soon after into another and kindred expression: "He that cometh from above, is above all" (John 3:31). With such words the Baptist taught his disciples. He insisted that Jesus of Nazareth had an existence anterior to Nazareth, and previous to his birth of the village maiden. It is not surprising, therefore, that one of his disciples, catching his Master's spirit, wrote: "In the beginning was the Word, and the Word was with God, and the Word was God. The same was in the beginning with God. All things were made by Him."

b. *He rightly apprehended the sacrificial aspect of Christ's work.* "Behold the Lamb of God, which taketh away the sin of the world." Was it that his priestly lineage gave him a special right to coin and use this appellation? His whole previous training, as the son of a priest, fitted him to receive and transmit. To the Jews who listened, the latter part of his exclamation could have but one significance. They would at once connect with his words, those of the Law, the Prophets, and the Psalms. "The goat shall bear upon him all their iniquities unto a land not inhabited" (Lev. 16:22). "He bare the sin of many" (Isa. 53:12). "He is brought as a lamb to the slaughter" (Isa. 53:7).

Dear soul, you may venture on Him. He is God's Lamb; on Him the sin of our race has been laid, and He stood before God with the accumulated load—"made sin"; the iniquity of us all was laid on Him; wounded for our transgressions; bruised for our iniquities; chastised for our peace; stricken for our transgression; bearing the sin of many. As the first Adam brought sin on the race, the second Adam has put it away by the sacrifice of Himself.

c. *He understood the baptism of the Holy Spirit.* "The same is he that baptizeth with the Holy Spirit." As Son of God, our Savior from all eternity was one with the Holy Spirit in the mystery of the blessed Trinity; but as "the one man," He received in His human nature the fullness of the divine Spirit.

We may all adopt the words of the Baptist, and tell our living Head that we need to be baptized of Him—need to be plunged into the fiery baptism; need to be cleansed from dross and impurity; need to be caught in the transfiguring, heaven-leaping energy of the Holy Spirit. The blood of the Lamb and the fire of the Holy Spirit are thus inextricably united.

d. *He beheld the mystery of the Holy Trinity.* For the first time this was made manifest to man. On the one hand there was the Father speaking from heaven; on the other the Spirit descending as a dove—and between them was the Son of Man who was proclaimed to be the Son of God, the beloved Son. Surely John might say that flesh and blood had not revealed these things, but they had been made known to him by a divine revelation.

The doctrine of the Holy Trinity is a profound mystery, hidden from the intellect, but revealed to the humble and reverent heart; hidden from the wise and prudent, and revealed to babes. Welcome Jesus Christ as John did; and, as to John, so the whole wonder of the Godhead will be made known to your heart.

e. *He appreciated the divine sonship of Christ.* "I saw and bare record that this is the Son of God." This witness counts for much. John knew men, knew himself, knew Christ. What though, when on the following day he repeats his exclamation, his whole congregation leaves him to follow the Man of Nazareth to his home? The heart of the forerunner is satisfied, for he has heard the Bridegroom's voice.

9

"He must Increase, but I must Decrease"
John 3:30

From the Jordan Valley our Lord returned to Galilee and Nazareth. The marriage feast of Cana, His return to Jerusalem, the cleansing of the temple, and the interview with Nicodemus, followed in rapid succession. And when the crowds of Passover pilgrims were dispersing homeward, He also left the city with His disciples, and began a missionary tour throughout the land of Judæa.

This tour is not dwelt on much in Scripture. We only catch a glimpse of it here in verse 22, and again in the address of the apostle Peter to Cornelius, where he speaks of Christ preaching good tidings of peace throughout all Judæa (Acts 10:36–37). How long it lasted we cannot tell; but it must have occupied some months, for He tarried from time to time at different points.

It is not likely that our Lord unfolded His messianic character, or taught with the same clearness as He did later. For the most part, He would adopt the cry of the Baptist. Of the commencement of his ministry it is recorded: "Jesus came . . . preaching the gospel of the kingdom of God, and saying, The time is fulfilled, and the kingdom of God is at hand: repent ye, and believe the gospel" (Mark 1:14–15). But His deeds declared His royalty.

During all this time the Baptist was continuing his preparatory work in the Jordan Valley, though now driven by persecution to leave the western bank for Ænon and Salim on the eastern side, where a handful of followers still clung to him. "John was not yet cast into prison," but the shadow of his impending fate was already gathering over him; so he was baptizing in Ænon, near Salim, where the Jordan sweeps out into broad sheets of water, eminently suitable for his purpose. There many came and were baptized.

It would appear from verse 25 that a Jew, probably an emissary of the Sanhedrin, brought tidings to that little circle of true-hearted disciples of the work that Jesus was doing in Judæa, and drew them into a discussion as to the comparative value of the two baptisms. It was acknowledged that Jesus did not, with His own hands, perform the rite of baptism, but it would be administered by His disciples, at His direction, and with His countenance. Therefore it could be reported to the Baptist by his disciples, who came to him with eyes flashing with indignation, and faces heated with the excitement of the discussion: "Rabbi, he that was with thee beyond Jordan, to whom thou barest witness, behold, the same baptizeth, and all men come to him" (v. 26).

But there was no tinder in that noble breast which these jealous sparks could kindle. Nothing but love dwelled there. His reply will always rank among the greatest utterances of mortal man. The Lord said that of those born of woman none was greater than John; and, if by nothing else, by these words his moral stature and superlative excellence were vindicated.

1. JOHN COUNTED INFLUENCE AND POSITION AS DIVINE GIFTS. It was for this reason that the Baptist reasoned: "Whatever success and blessing I had are due to the appointment of Him who sent me to preach His gospel and announce the advent of his Son. If this new Teacher meets with such success, we have no right to be jealous of Him, lest we sin against God, who has made Him what He is. And if we have not the same crowds as we once did, let us be content to take this, too, as the appointment of heaven, glad to do whatever is assigned to us, and to leave all results with God."

Here is the cure of jealousy, which more than anything else blights the soul of the servant of God. "A man can receive nothing, except it be given him from heaven. I had my glad hours of meridian glory, and have still the mellow light of a summer sunset. It was God's gift to me, as rest is now; and I will rejoice that He raises up others to do His work."

2. JOHN CAUGHT SIGHT OF A FULLER AND RICHER IDEAL THAN HIS OWN. Tidings had, without doubt, been brought to him of our Lord's first miracle in Cana of Galilee. We know that it had made a great impression on the little group of ardent souls, who had been called to share the village festivities with their newly-found Master; and we know that some of them were still deeply attached to their old friend and leader. From these he would learn the full details of that remarkable inauguration of this long-expected ministry. How startled he must have been at the first hearing! He had announced the husbandman with his fan to thoroughly winnow his floor; the Baptist with his fire; the Lamb of God, holy, harmless, and separate from sinners. But the Messiah opens His ministry among men by mingling with the simple villagers in their wedding joy, and actually ministers to their innocent mirth, as He turns the water into wine! The Son of Man has come "eating and drinking"! What a contrast to the austerity of the desert, the coarse raiment, the hard fare! "John the Baptist came neither eating nor drinking." Could this be He? And yet there was no doubt that the heaven had been opened above Him, that the dove had descended, and that God's voice had declared Him to be the "beloved Son." But what a contrast to all that he had looked for!

Further reflection, however, on that incident in which Jesus manifested forth His glory, and the cleansing of the temple that immediately followed, must have convinced the Baptist that this conception of holiness was the true one.

John saw beneath the illuminating ray of the Holy Spirit that this was the divine Ideal; that the Redeemer could not contradict the Creator; that the kingdom was consistent with the home; and the presence of the king with the innocent mirth of the village feast. This he saw, and cried in effect: "That village scene is the key to the Messiah's ministry to Israel. The bridegroom is here. He who has the bride is the Bridegroom. As for me, I am the Bridegroom's friend, blessed with the unspeakable gladness of hearing the Bridegroom's speech. Do you tell me that He is preaching, and that all come to Him? That is what I have wanted most of all. This my joy, therefore, is fulfilled. 'He must increase, but I must decrease.'"

3. JOHN HAD AN ENLARGED PERCEPTION OF THE TRUE NATURE OF CHRIST. Consider, then, the Baptist's creed at this point of his career. He *believed* in the heavenly origin and

divinity of the Son of Man—that He was from heaven and above all. He *believed* in the unique and divine source of His teaching: "For he whom God has sent speaketh the words of God." He *believed* in his copious enduement with the Holy Spirit. He recognized that when God anointed Jesus of Nazareth with the Holy Spirit there was no limit, no measurement. He *believed* in His near relationship to God, using the well-known Jewish phrase of sonship to describe His possession of the divine nature in a unique sense. Last, he *believed* in the mediatorial function of the Man of Nazareth—that the Father had already given all things into His hand; and that the day was coming when He would sit on the throne of David, yea, on the mediatorial throne itself, King of kings, and Lord of lords, the keys of death and hades, of the realms of invisible existence and spiritual power, hanging at his girdle.

There are two concluding thoughts. First, the only hope of a decreasing self is an increasing Christ. There is too much of the self-life in us all; but how can we be rid of this accursed self-consciousness and pride? Ah! we must turn our back on our shadow, and turn our face toward Christ.

Second; we must view our relationship to Christ as the betrothal and marriage of our soul to our Maker and Redeemer, who is also our husband. "Wherefore, my brethren," says the apostle, "ye also are become dead to the law by the body of Christ; that ye should be married to another, even to him who is raised from the dead, that we should bring forth fruit unto God" (Rom. 7:4).

The Son of God is not content to love us. He cannot rest until He has all our love in return.

10

The King's Courts
Mark 6

Our story brings us next to speak of the Baptist's relations with Herod Antipas, son of the great Herod, a contemptible princeling who inherited a fourth part of his father's dominions (hence known as the Tetrarch), ruling over Galilee and part of Perea. For the most part he lived at Tiberias, in great state, which he had imported from Rome, where he had spent part of his early life. From an early age he had been entrusted with despotic power and, as the natural and inevitable result, had become sensual, weak, capricious, and cruel.

It is of the conflict between this man, whom our Lord compared to a fox, and John the Baptist, that we now want to discuss.

1. THE CAUSE OF THE CONFLICT. All the world had flocked to see and hear John the Baptist. Marvelous stories were being told of the effect he had produced on the lives of those who had come under his influence. All this was well known to Herod.

For some months, also, Herod had watched the career of the preacher. He felt that John was a true man. He observed him, and was satisfied that he was a just and holy man. Reasons of state forbade the king from going in person to the Jordan Valley, but he was extremely eager to see and hear this mighty man of God: and so, one day, Herod "sent for him."

Another reason probably motivated Herod. He knew that the land was filled with the fame of the Baptist, and it seemed an easy path to popularity. It seemed likely to divert attention from his private sins, which had made much scandal, to partronize the religion of the masses.

One interpretation of Mark 6:20 suggests that the Baptist's first sermon before Herod was followed by another, and yet another. The Baptist dealt with general subjects, urged on the king's attention some minor reforms, which were not too personal or drastic, and won his genuine regard. We are told that he used to hear (the imperfect tense) him gladly, and "did many things." But John knew that his duty to Herod, to truth, to public morality, demanded that he should go further, and therefore on one memorable occasion he accosted the royal criminal with the crime of which men were speaking secretly everywhere, and uttered the memorable sentence that could not be forgiven: "It is not lawful for thee to have thy brother's wife."

We are told that "Herod sent forth and laid hold upon John" (Mark 6:17). Herodias gave her paramour no rest; and a handful of soldiers arrested him, bound him, and led him off to the strong castle of Machærus.

2. JOHN'S IMPRISONMENT AND ITS OPPORTUNITIES. The castle of Machærus was known as "the diadem," or "the black tower." It lay on the east side of the Dead Sea, almost on a line with Bethlehem. The ruins of the castle are still to be seen, in great masses of squared stone, on the top of a lofty hill, surrounded on three sides by unscaleable precipices, descending to such depths that Josephus says the eye could not reach their bottom. This was the scene of John's imprisonment.

The evangelist says expressly that they "bound" the child of the desert wastes, with his love for dear liberty—sensitive to the touch of the sunshine and the breeze, to the beauty that lay over the hills, accustomed to go and come at his will—as though it were the last indignity and affront to fetter those lithe and supple limbs, and place them under constraint. What a sin to bind the preacher of righteousness and imprison him in sunless vaults—what an agony! What a contrast between the gay revelry that reigned within the palace, and the slow torture that the noble spirit of the Baptist was doomed to suffer through those weary months!

From time to time it would seem as though the strictness of John's imprisonment was relaxed. His disciples were permitted to see him, and tell him of what was happening in the world without; but stranger than all, he was summoned to have audiences with Herod himself.

Herod had been deeply incensed; and he had beside him a Lady Macbeth, a beautiful fiend and temptress, who knew that while the Baptist lived, and dared to speak as he had done, her position was not safe. She knew Herod well enough to dread the uprising of his conscience at the appeals of truth. "Herodias set herself against him, and desired to kill him; but she could not."

On the other side, Herod was in fear. He feared John, "knowing that he was a just man and an holy." He feared the people, because they held him for a prophet. And, beneath all, he feared God, lest He should step in to avenge any wrong perpetrated against His servant.

Between these two influences he was "greatly puzzled" (Mark 6:20 NIV). When he was with Herodias, he thought as she did, and left her, almost resolved to give the fatal order; but when he was alone, the other influence made itself felt, and he would send for John.

Might not Herod attempt to induce the prophet to take back his ruthless sentence? "Come," he might say, "if you unsay that sentence, I will set you free. One word of apology, and you may go your way."

If such an offer were made, it must have presented a strong temptation to the emaciated captive, whose physique had already lost the elasticity and vigor of his early manhood, and was showing signs of his grievous privation. But he had no alternative; and, however often the ordeal was repeated, he met the royal solicitation with the same unwavering reply: "I have no alternative. It is not lawful for you to have your brother's wife. I would betray my God, and act treacherously to you, if I were to take back one word that I have spoken; and you know that it is so." And as he reasoned of righteousness, temperance, and a judgment to come, the royal culprit trembled.

How many men are like Herod! They resemble the superficial ground on which the seed springs into rapid and unnatural growth; but the rock lies close beneath the surface. Now they are swayed by the voice of the preacher, and moved by the pleadings of conscience, allowed for one brief moment to utter its protests and remonstrances; and then they feel the fascination of their sin, that unholy passion, that sinful habit, that ill-gotten gain—and are sucked back from the beach, on which they were almost free, into the sea.

So John was left in prison. Month after month he languished in the dark and stifling dungeon, wondering a little, now and again, why the Master, if He were the Son of God, did not interpose to work His deliverance.

3. HEROD'S INEVITABLE DETERIORATION. Again and again John was remanded to his cell. Probably twelve months passed; but each time the king failed to act on the preacher's remonstrances; he became more impervious to his appeals, more liable to the sway of passion. Thus, when a supreme moment came, in which he was under the influence of drink and unholy appetite, it is not to be wondered that Herodias had her way, so he gave orders that it should be as she desired.

The story does not end here. Herod not only murdered John the Baptist, but he inflicted a deadly wound on his own moral nature, from which it never recovered.

Is it wonderful that our Lord was speechless before such a man? What else could He be? The deterioration had been so awful and complete. For the love of God can say nothing to us, though it be prepared to die on our behalf, as long as we refuse to repent of, and put away, our sin. We remember some solemn words, which may be applied in all their fearful significance to that scene: "There is a sin unto death; not concerning this do I say that he should make request."

11

"Art Thou He?"
Matthew 11

It is very touching to notice the tenacity with which some of John's disciples clung to their great leader. The majority had dispersed: some to their homes; some to follow Jesus. Only a handful still lingered, not alienated by the storm of hate that had broken on thier master, but drawn nearer, with the unfaltering loyalty of unchangeable affection. They could not forget that he had taught them to pray; that he had led them to the Christ. So they dare not desert him now, in the dark, sad days of his imprisonment and sorrow. They did not hesitate to come to his cell with tidings of the great outer world, and especially of what *He* was doing and saying, whose life was so mysteriously bound up with his own. "The disciples of John [told] him all these things" (Luke 7:18).

It was to two of these friends that John confided the question that had long been forming in his soul, "And John calling unto him two of his disciples sent them to Jesus, saying, Art thou he that should come? or look we for another?"

1. JOHN'S MISGIVINGS. Can this be he who, but a few months ago, had stood in his rock-hewn pulpit, in radiant certainty? He pointed to Christ with unfaltering certitude, saying, This is He, the Lamb of God, the Son of the Father, the Bridegroom of the soul. How great the contrast between that and this sorrowful cry, "Art thou he?" He was for a brief spell under a cloud, involved in doubt, tempted to let go the confidence that had brought him such ecstatic joy when he first saw the dove descending and abiding.

Yes, let us believe that, for some days at least, John's mind was overcast, his faith lost its foothold, and he seemed to be falling into bottomless depths. "He sent them to Jesus, saying, Art thou he that should come?" We can easily trace this lapse of faith to three sources.

a. *Depression*. He was the child of the desert. The winds that swept across the waste were not freer. As he found himself cribbed, cabined, and confined in the narrow limits of his cell, his spirits sank. He yearned with the hunger of a wild thing for liberty—to move without the clanking fetters; to drink of the fresh water of the Jordan; to breathe the morning air; to look on the expanse of nature. Is it hard to understand how his deprivations reacted on his mental and spiritual organizations, or that the depression of his physical life cast a shadow on his soul?

b. *Disappointment*. When first consigned to prison, he had expected every day that Jesus would in some way deliver him. Surely He would not let His faithful follower lie in the despair of that dark dungeon! In that first sermon at Nazareth, of which he had been informed, was it not expressly stated to be part of the divine program for which He had been anointed, that He would open prison doors, and proclaim liberty to captives?

But the weeks grew to months, and still no help came. It was inexplicable to John's honest heart, and suggested the fear that he had been mistaken after all.

c. *Partial views of Christ*. "John heard in the prison the works of Jesus." They were wholly beneficent and gentle.

"What has He done since last you were here?"

"He has laid His hands on a few sick folk, and healed them; has gathered a number of children to His arms, and blessed them; has sat on the mountain, and spoken of rest and peace and blessedness."

"Yes; good. But what more?"

"A woman touched the hem of His garment, and trembled, and confessed, and went away healed."

"Good! But what more?"

"Well, there were some blind men, and He laid His hands on them, and they saw."

"Is that all? Has He not used the fan to winnow the wheat, and the fire to burn up the chaff? This is what I was expecting, and what I have been taught to expect by Isaiah and the rest of the prophets. I cannot understand it. This quiet gentle life of benevolence is outside my calculations. There must be some mistake. Go and ask Him whether we should expect *another,* made in a different mold, and who will be as the fire, the earthquake, the tempest, while He is as the still small voice."

John had partial views of the Christ—he thought of Him only as the Avenger of sin, the Maker of revolution, the dread Judge of all; and for want of a clearer understanding of what God by the mouth of His holy prophets had spoken since the world began, he fell into this slough of despond.

It was a grievous pity; yet let us not blame him too vehemently, lest we blame ourselves. Is not this what we do? We form a notion of God, partly from what we think He ought to be, partly from some distorted notions we have derived from others; and then because God fails to realize our conception, we begin to doubt.

2. THE LORD'S REPLY. "In that hour he cured many of their infirmities and plagues, and evil spirits; and unto many that were blind he gave sight." Through the long hours of the day, the disciples stood in the crowd, while the sad train of sick and demon-possessed passed before the Savior, coming in every stage of need, and going away cleansed and saved. Even the dead were raised. And at the close the Master turned to them, and with a deep significance in his tone, said, "Go your way, and tell John what things ye have seen and heard; how that the blind see, the lame walk, the lepers are cleansed, the deaf hear, the dead are raised, to the poor the gospel is preached. And blessed is he, whosoever shall not be offended in me."

a. *It was indirect.* He did not say, "I am He that was to come, and there is no need to look for another." Had He done so, He might have answered John's intellect, but not his heart. After a few hours the assurance would have waxed dim and he would have questioned again. He might have wondered whether Jesus were not Himself deceived.

b. *The answer was mysterious.* Surely, if He were able to do so much, he could do more. The power that healed the sick and lame and blind, and cast out demons, could surely deliver John. It made his heart the more wistful, to hear of these displays of power. He had to learn that the Lord healed these people so easily because the light soil of their nature could not bear the richer harvests; because their soul could not stand the cutting through which alone the brilliant facets that were possible to his could be secured. It was because John was a royal soul, the greatest born of woman, because his nature was capable of yielding the best results to the divine culture, that he was kept waiting, while others caught up the blessing and went away healed. Only three months remained of life, and in these the discipline of patience and doubt had to do their perfect work.

c. *The answer was sufficient.* The Lord strived to convince the questioner that his views were too partial and limited, and to send him back to a more comprehensive study of the old Scriptures. It was as though Jesus said, "Go to your master, and tell him to take again the ancient prophecy and study it. He has taken the sterner predictions to the neglect of the gentler, softer ones. It is true that I am to proclaim the day of vengeance; but first I must reveal the acceptable year. It is true that I am to come as a Mighty One, and my arm shall rule for Me; but it is also true that I am to feed my flock like a Shepherd, and gather the lambs in my arm."

We make the same mistake. We have but a partial view of Christ, and need to get back to the Bible afresh, and study anew its comprehensive words; then we will come to understand. We have not yet seen the end of the Lord: we do not have all the evidence. But our Savior is offering us every day evidences of His divine and loving power. The world is full of evidences of His gracious and divine power. And these are sufficient, not only because of the transformations that are effected, but because of their moral quality, to show that there is One within the veil who lives in the power of an indissoluble life.

3. A NEW BEATITUDE. "Blessed is he, whosoever shall not be offended in me." Our Lord put within the reach of his noble forerunner the blessedness of those who have not seen and yet have believed; of those who wait the Lord's leisure; and of those who cannot understand His dealings, but rest in what they know of His heart. This is the beatitude of the unoffended, of those who do not stumble over the mystery of God's dealings with their life.

This blessedness is within our reach also. There are times when we are overpowered with the mystery of life and nature. The world is so full of pain and sorrow, the litany of its need is so sad and pitiful, strong hearts are breaking under an intolerable load.

God's children are sometimes the most bitterly tried. For them the fires are heated seven times; days of weariness and nights of pain are appointed them; they suffer, not only at the hand of man, but it seems as though God Himself were turned against them, to become their enemy. The waters of a full cup are wrung out in days like these; and the cry is extorted, "How long, O Lord, how long?"

You and I have been in this plight. We have said, "Has God forgotten to be gracious? Has He in anger shut up His tender mercies?" We are tempted to stumbling. We are more able than ever before to appreciate the standpoint occupied by Job's wife, when she said to her husband, "Curse God, and die."

Then we have the chance of inheriting a new beatitude. By refusing to bend under the mighty hand of God—questioning, chafing, murmuring—we miss the door that would admit us into rich and unalloyed happiness. We fumble about the latch, but it is not lifted. But if we will quiet our souls, light will break in on us as from the eternal morning; the peace of God will keep our hearts and minds, and we will enter on the blessedness that our Lord unfolded before the gaze of his faithful forerunner.

12

"None Greater than John the Baptist, yet . . ."
Matthew 11

While John's disciples were standing there, our Lord said nothing in his praise; but as soon as they had departed, the floodgates of his heart were thrown wide open, and He began to speak to the multitudes concerning His faithful servant. It was as though He would give him no cause for pride by what He said. He desired to give His friend no additional temptation during those lonely hours.

1. THE TIME CHOSEN FOR THE LORD'S COMMENDATION OF THE BAPTIST. It was when John had fallen beneath his usual level, below high-water mark, that Jesus uttered His

warmest and most generous words of appreciation—"Among them that are born of woman there hath not risen a greater than John the Baptist."

Heaven judges, not by a passing mood, but by the general tenor and trend of a man's life; not by the expression of a doubt, caused by accidents that may be explained, but by the soul of man within him, which is much deeper than the emotion.

Yes, the Lord judges us by that which is deepest, most permanent, most constant and prevalent with us; by the ideal we seek to apprehend; by the decision and choice of our soul.

There is a remarkable parallel to this incident in the Old Testament. When we are first introduced to Gideon, the youngest son of Joash the Abiezrite, he is not in a very dignified position. He is threshing wheat by the wine press, to hide it from the hosts of Midian, which devoured the produce of the entire country. There was no moral wrong in trying to elude the vigilance of the Midian spies, but there was nothing especially heroic or inspiring in the spectacle. Yet, when the angel of the Lord appeared to him, he said, "The LORD is with thee, thou mighty man of valour."

"Mighty man of valour!" At first there is an apparent incongruity between this high-sounding salutation and the bearing of the man to whom it was addressed, yet subsequent events prove that every syllable of it was deservedly true. Gideon was a mighty man of valor, and God was with him. The heavenly messenger read beneath the outward passing incident.

Is not this, in fact, the meaning of the apostle, when he says that faith is counted to us for righteousness? Faith is counted to us for righteousness, is the seed germ from which is developed in due course the plant, the flower, the bud, the seed, and reproduction of the plant in unending succession. God counted to Abraham all that his faith was capable of producing, which it did produce, and which it would have produced had he possessed all the advantages that pertain to our own happy lot. God gives to us all that blessed flowering and fruitage of which our faith will be capable, when patience has had its perfect work and we are perfect and entire, wanting nothing.

2. THE OUTSTANDING FEATURES OF JOHN'S CHARACTER AND MINISTRY TO WHICH OUR LORD DREW ATTENTION.

a. *His independence.* "What went ye out into the wilderness to see? A reed shaken with the wind?" The language of the Bible is so picturesque, so full of natural imagery, that it appeals to every age, and speaks in every language of the world. It employs natural figures and parables which the wayfaring man, though a fool, comprehends at a glance.

Thus, when our Lord asked the people whether John resembled a reed shaken by the wind, and implied their answer in the negative, could He have more clearly indicated one of the most salient characteristics of John's career—his daring singularity, his independence of mere custom and fashion, his determination to follow out the pattern of his own life as God revealed it to Him? In the singularity of his dress and food; in the originality of his message and demand for baptism; in his independence of the religious teachers and schools of his time; in his refusal to countenance the flagrant sins of the various classes of the community, and especially in his uncompromising denunciation of Herod's sin—he provoked himself to be as a sturdy oak in the forest of Bashan, or a deeply-rooted cedar in Lebanon, and not as a reed shaken by the wind.

Many a saintly soul has followed him since along this difficult and lonely track.

Indeed, it is the ordinary path for most of the choicest spirits of these Christian centuries.

You, my reader, admire, but feel you cannot follow. When your companions and friends are speaking depreciating and ungenerous words of some public man whom you love; when unkind and scandalous stories are being passed from lip to lip; when a storm of hatred is being poured on a cause, which in your heart you favor and espouse—you find it easier to bow before the gale, with all the other reeds around you, than to enter your protest, even though you stand alone. Christ can take the most pliant and yielding natures, and make them, as He made Jeremiah, "a defenced city, and an iron pillar, and brasen walls, against the whole land" (Jer. 1:18). You cannot; but He can. He will strengthen you; yea, He will help you.

b. *His simplicity.* A second time the Master asked the people what they went forth into the wilderness to behold; and by His question implied that John was no Sybarite clothed in soft raiment, and feasting in luxury, but a strong, pure soul, who had learned the secret of self-denial and self-control. Too many of us are inclined to put on the soft raiment of self-indulgence and luxury. The real happiness of life consists not in increasing our possessions but in limiting our wants.

So with service. It is not right to depend on others. If it is part of our lot to be surrounded by servants, let us accept their offices with grace and kindliness, but never allow ourselves to lean on them. We should know how to do everything for ourselves, and be prepared to do it whenever it is necessary. Of course, nothing would be more unfortunate than that those who are highly gifted in some special direction should fritter away their time and strength in doing trifles that others could do for them equally well. To think of a physician whose consulting room was crowded with patients needing help which he alone, of all men living, could give, spending the precious morning hours polishing his boots, or preparing his food! Let these things be left to those who cannot do the highest work to which he is called.

This is the secret of making the best of your life. Discover what you can do best. Set yourself to do this, devolving on voluntary or paid helpers all that they can do as well as, and perhaps better than, yourself. It was in this spirit that the apostles said, "It is not reason that we should leave the word of God and serve tables. Look ye out among you seven men . . . whom we may appoint over this business. But we will give ourselves continually to prayer, and to the ministry of the Word" (Acts 6:2–4). It is good to look carefully into our life from time to time, lest almost insensibly its strong energetic spirit may not be in process of deterioration as the soldiers of Hannibal in the plains of Capua. If so, resolve to do without, not for merit's sake, but to conserve the strength and simplicity of your soul.

c. *His noble office.* "But what went ye out for to see? A prophet? yea, I say unto you, and more than a prophet." Subsequent ages have only confirmed our Savior's estimate of His forerunner. We are able to locate him in the divine economy. He was a prophet, yes, and much more. He was Jehovah's messenger, the herald of that new and greater era, whose gates he opened, but into which he was not permitted to enter.

But our Lord went further, and did not hesitate to class John with the greatest of those born of woman. He was absolutely in the front rank. He may have had peers, but no superiors; equals, but no overlords. Who may be classed with him, we cannot, dare not, say. But "there hath not risen a greater than John the Baptist."

There was a further tribute paid by our Lord to His noble servant. Some two or three centuries before, Malachi had foretold that Elijah, the prophet, would be sent before the great and terrible day of the Lord came, and the Jews were always on the outlook for his coming. This is what was meant when they asked the Baptist, at the commencement of his ministry, if he were Elijah. He shrank, as we have seen, from assuming so great a name, and declared, "If ye will receive it, this is Elias, which was for to come."

3. THE MASTER'S RESERVATION. Let us again quote His memorable words: "Among them that are born of women there hath not risen a greater than John the Baptist; notwithstanding, he that is least in the kingdom of heaven is greater than he" (Matt. 11:11).

The greatness of John the Baptist shone out in conspicuous beauty in his meek confession of inferiority. His greatness was revealed in the lowliness of his self-estimate.

When the Lord Jesus summarized His own character He said, "I am meek and lowly in heart." The greatness of John was proved in this, that like his Lord he was meek and lowly in heart. No sublimer, no more God-like utterance ever passed the lips of man than John's answer to his disciples: "A man can receive nothing, except it be given him from heaven. He must increase, but I must decrease" (see the whole passage, John 3:27–36). The same spirit of meekness was speaking in John as acted in his Lord. There was no man, not even the apostle John or Paul, whose spirit accorded more exactly with the Master's than His faithful and self-effacing herald and forerunner, John the Baptist.

But what was in our Lord's thought when He made the reservation, *"He that is least in the kingdom of heaven is greater than he"*? It has been suggested that the Lord was speaking of John not only as a man, but as a prophet, and that this declaration applies more particularly to John as a prophet. John could say, "Behold the Lamb of God"; but the least of those who, being scattered abroad, went everywhere proclaiming the word of the kingdom, preaching "Jesus and the resurrection."

But there is another way of interpreting Christ's words. John ushered in the kingdom, but was not in it. He proclaimed a condition of blessedness in which he was not permitted to have a part. And the Lord says that to be in that kingdom gives the opportunity of attaining to a greatness that the great souls outside its precincts cannot lay claim to. The least instructed in the kingdom of heaven is privileged to see and hear the things that prophets and kings longed and waited for in vain.

And may there not be even more than this? The character of John was strong, grand in its wild magnificence. He had courage, resolution, an iron will, a loftiness of soul that could hold commerce with the unseen and eternal. But is this the loftiest ideal of character? Assuredly not; there is something better, as is manifest in our Lord's own perfect manhood. The balance of quality; the power to converse with God, mated with the tenderness that enters the homes of men, wipes the tears of those who mourn, and gathers little children to its side; that has an ear for every complaint, and a balm of comfort for every heartbreak; that pities and soothes, teaches and leads; that is able not only to commune with God alone in the desert, but brings Him into the lowliest deeds and commonplaces of human life—this is the type of character that is characteristic of the kingdom of heaven. It is described best in those inimitable beatitudes which canonize, not the stern and rugged, but the sweet and tender, the humble and meek; and stamp heaven's tenderest smile on virtues that had hardly found a place in the strong and gritty character of the Baptist. Truly, "He that is least in the kingdom of heaven is greater than he."

13

A Burning and Shining Lamp
John 5:35

Our Master, Christ, was on trial. He was challenged by the religious leaders of the people because He had dared to heal a man and to command him to carry his bed—his straw pallet—on the Sabbath day. He was therefore accused and, so to speak, put on defense.

Of course we must not for a moment think that our Lord was lax in His observance of the Sabbath, but simply that He desired to emancipate the day from the intolerable burdens and restrictions with which the Jewish leaders had surrounded it. He was the Emancipator of the Sabbath day from foolish and mistaken notions of sanctity.

It is of the greatest importance that we should do what we may to conserve one rest day in seven to our country and our world. Let your rest on the one rest day consist, not in lolling idly and carelessly, but in turning your faculties in some other direction; because the truest rest is to be found, not in luxurious ease, but in using the fresh vigor of your life in other compartments of the brain than those that have been worn by the demands of the six days. Then, fresh from the Sunday school class, the worship of the church, and the sermon, you will return to the desk or office, or whatever may be your toil, with new and rejuvenated strength.

The light cannot shine unless it burns. The candle that gives light wastes inch by inch as it gives it. The very wick of your lamp, that conducts the oil to the flame, chars, and you have to cut it off bit by bit until the longest coil is at length exhausted. Too many of us want to shine, but are not prepared to pay the cost that must be faced by every true man who wants to illuminate his time. We must burn down until there is but an eighth of an inch left in the candlestick, until the light flickers a little and drops, makes one more eager effort, and then ceases to shine—"a burning and a shining light."

Obviously, then, we have first the comparison between John and the candle, or lamp; then we have the necessary expenditure, burning to shine; and, third, we have the misuse that people may make of their opportunities.

1. THE LORD'S COMPARISON. John "was a burning and a shining light." In the original a great contrast is suggested between "lamp" and "light." The King James Version says: "He was a burning and a shining light"; but some newer versions use "lamp"; and there is a considerable difference between the two.

You may have a candle with a wick, but it gives no light. The air may be full of luminousness, but as yet it has found no point on which to kindle and from which to irradiate. All of a sudden the light touches the candle wick, which had stood helpless and useless, and it begins to shine with a light not its own. It is borrowed light, caught from some burning cone of flame.

Men are born into the world like so many unlighted candles. Jesus Christ, the Light of men, waits with yearning desire and, as each successive generation passes across the stage of human life, He is prepared to illumine the spirits that are intended to be the candles of the Lord. In these ages He illumines us with the gospel; He, who as the true Light lights every person coming into the world. Whenever and wherever someone has flamed up with unusual fervor and spiritual power, with a desire to help others, and has shone like a torch, we must believe that that person was illumined by the Son of God, whom he may not have known, but whom he would recognize as soon as he crossed the portal of the New Jerusalem. He lights every person, He is willing to illumine every person who comes into the world.

What is the process of lighting? The wick of the candle is simply brought into contact with the flame, and the flame leaps to it, kindles on it, without parting with any of its vigor or heat, and continues to burn, drawing to itself the nourishment that the candle supplies. So let Jesus Christ touch you. Believe in the Light, that you may become a child of Light. Take off the extinguisher; cast away your prejudice; let Jesus kindle you.

We are kindled that we might kindle others. I would like, if I might have my choice, to burn down steadily, with no guttering waste, and as I do so to communicate God's fire to as many unlit candles as possible, so that as one expires they may begin burning and spreading light that shall shine until Jesus comes. Get light from Christ, then share it; and remember that it is the glory of fire that one little candle may go on lighting hundreds of candles—one insignificant taper may light all the lamps of a cathedral church, and yet not be robbed of its own little glow of flame. Andrew was lit by Christ Himself, and passed on the flame to Simon Peter, and he to three thousand more on the Day of Pentecost. Every Christian soul illumined by the grace of God thus becomes, as John the Baptist was, a lamp. But there is always the same impassable chasm between these and the Lord. They are derived; He is original.

2. THE INEVITABLE EXPENDITURE. "He was a burning and a shining lamp."

a. *If you would shine, you must burn.* The ambition to shine is universal; but all are not prepared to pay the price by which they alone can acquire the right to give the true light of life. There are plenty of students who would win all the prizes, and wear all the honors, apart from days and nights of toil; but they find it a vain ambition. Before a man can become Senior Wrangler he must have burned, not only the midnight oil, but also some of the very fiber of his soul. Conspicuous positions in the world are less the reward of genius than of laborious toil. The great chemist will work sixteen hours out of twenty-four. The illustrious author acquires, by profound research, the materials that he weaves into his brilliant page. Such men shine because they burn.

But this is preeminently the principle in the service of Christ. It was so with the Lord Himself. He shone, but ah, how He burned! The disciples remembered that it was written of Him: "The zeal of thine house hath eaten me up" (Ps. 69:9). He suffered, that He might serve. He would not save Himself, because He was bent on saving others. He ascended to the throne because He did not spare Himself from the cruel tree. He shone because of the fire that burned within Him.

It was so with the great apostle Paul, who gave freely of his best. He shone because he never hesitated to burn.

All the saints have passed through similar experiences. They knew, as Cranmer said, that they could never hope to kindle a fire that would never be put out, unless they were prepared to stand steadily at the stake and give their bodies to be burned. The men and women who shine as beacon lights across the centuries are those whose tears were their meat day and night, whose prayers rose with strong cryings and tears.

Every successful worker for God must learn that lesson. You must be prepared to suffer; you can help men only when you die for them. If you desire to save others you cannot save yourself; you must be prepared to fall into the ground and die, if you would not abide alone: there must be with you, as with Paul, the decaying of the outward man, that the inward man may be renewed day by day. You must be prepared to say with him, "Death worketh in us, but life in you" (2 Cor. 4:12).

b. *If you burn, you will shine.* The burning and the shining do not always go together; often the burning goes on a long time without much illumination resulting from the expenditure. In many cases the saints of God have burned down to the last film of vital energy and expired, and there has been no shining that the world has taken cognizance of. Their bitter complaint has been, "I have labored in vain; I have spent my strength for nothing." But even these shall shine. They shall shine as the stars forever and ever in that world where all holy and faithful souls obtain their due.

Let us see to the burning; God will see to the shining. It is ours to feed the sacred heaven-enkindled flame with the daily fuel of the Word of God and holy service; and God will see to it that no ray of power or love is wasted. It is ours to keep in company with the risen Lord, listening to Him as He opens to us the Scriptures, until our hearts burn within us. Then, as we hasten to tell what we have seen, tasted, and handled of the Word of Life, there will be a glow on our faces, whether we know it or not; and men will say of us: "They have been with Jesus." If we think only of the shining, we will probably miss both it and the burning. But if we devote ourselves to the burning, even though it involve the hidden work of the mine, the stoke hole, the furnace room, there will be the raying forth of a light that cannot be hid.

c. *For the burning and the shining, God will provide the fuel.* Be of good cheer; He who has begun a good work in you will perfect it unto the day of Jesus Christ. All grace will be made to abound toward you, that you may have all sufficiency for all things, and abound to every good work.

It is a wonderful thing how often God puts his lighted candles in the cellar. We would have supposed that He would have placed a man like John on a pedestal or a throne, that his influence might reach as far as possible. Instead of that He allowed him to spend the precious months of his brief life in prison. And the lamp flickered somewhat in the pestilential damp. It may be that this is your place also. It seems such a waste. Loneliness and depression are hard to endure; but the consciousness of accomplishing so little, though at such cost, is very painful. This is your cellar life, your dungeon experience. Remember that Joseph and Rutherford, John Bunyan and Madame Guyon, have been there before you. Probably, because the cellar is so very dark, God wants to station a candle there, and has placed you there because you can accomplish a work for Him, and for others, of priceless importance. Where is the light needed as much as on a dark landing or a sunken reef? Go on shining, and you will find some day that God will make that cellar a pedestal out of which your light will stream over the world; for it was out of his prison cell that John illuminated the age in which his lot was cast, quite as much as from his rock pulpit beside the Jordan.

3. CHRIST'S WARNING AGAINST THE MISUSE OF OPPORTUNITIES. "Ye were willing for a season to rejoice in his light." The Greek word rendered "rejoice" has in it the idea of moths playing around a candle, or of children dancing around a torch light, as it burns lower and lower. It is as though a light were given to men for an hour, for them to use for some high and sacred purpose; but they employ it for dancing and foolish recreation, instead of girding up their loins to serious tasks.

The ministry of the gospel is but for "an hour," and the proclamation of the good news from God occupies but a very limited space.

With what eager care men should prize these fleeting opportunities taking heed to hear for eternity, receiving in meek and retentive hearts the precious grain as it falls from the sower's hand, and giving diligence that the best possible results may accrue.

14

Set at Liberty
Mark 6:27

The evangelist Mark tells us, in the twenty-first verse of this chapter, that Herod on his birthday made a supper for his lords, and the high captains, and the chief men of Galilee. Now Galilee, over which Herod had jurisdiction, and where, for the most part, he dwelt, in the beautiful city of Tiberias, was a considerable distance from the Castle of Machærus which, as we have seen, was situated in the desolate region on the eastern side of the Dead Sea. There would probably therefore have been a martial and noble procession from Galilee, which followed the course of the Jordan to the oasis of Jericho, and then branched off to the old, grim fortress.

The days that preceded the celebration of Herod's birthday were probably filled with merry-making and carousing. Archery, jousts, and other sports would fill the slowly-moving hours. Jests, light laughter, and buffoonery would fill the air. And all the while, in the dungeons beneath the castle, lay that mighty preacher, the confessor, forerunner, herald, and soon to be martyr.

But this contrast was more than ever accentuated on the evening of Herod's birthday, when the great banqueting chamber was especially illuminated; the tables decked with flowers and gold and silver plate; laughter and mirth echoing through the vaulted roof from the splendid company. Servants, in costly liveries, passed to and fro, bearing the rich dainties on massive platters, one of which was to be presently besprinkled with the martyr's blood.

In such a scene I would have you study the beginning of a great crime, because you must remember that in respect to sin, there is little to choose between the twentieth century and the first; between the sin of that civilization and of ours. This chapter is therefore written under more than usual solemnity, because one is so sure that, in dealing with that scene and the passions that met there in a foaming vortex, words may be penned that will help souls that are caught in the drift of the same black current, and are being swept down. Perhaps this page will utter a warning voice to arrest them, before it be too late. For there is help and grace in God by which a Herod and a Judas, a Jezebel and a Lady Macbeth, may be arrested, redeemed, and saved.

In this, as in every sin, there were three forces at work: first, the predisposition of the soul, which the Bible calls "lust," and the "desire of the mind." Second, the suggestion of evil from without. Finally, the act of the will by which the suggestion was accepted and finally adopted.

It is in this latter phase that sin especially comes in. That which is of the essence of sin is in the act of the will, which allows itself to admit and entertain some foul suggestion, and ultimately sends its executioner below to carry its sentence into effect.

John the Baptist

1. THE PREDETERMINATION TOWARD THIS SIN. In dealing with temptation and sin, we must always take into account the presence in the human heart of that sad relic of the Fall, which biases men toward evil. Such a bias has come to us all: first, from our ancestor Adam; and, second, by that law of heredity that has been accumulating its malign and sinister force through all the ages. God alone can compute the respective strength of these forces; but He can, and He will, as each separate soul stands before His judgment bar.

Herod was the son of the great Herod, a voluptuous, murderous tyrant; and, from some source or other, he had inherited a very weak nature. If he had perhaps come under strong, wholesome influences, he would have lived a passably good life; but it was his misfortune to fall under the influence of a beautiful fiend, who became his Lady Macbeth, his Jezebel, and brought about the ruin of his soul.

The influences that suggest and make for sin in this world are so persistent that if my readers have no other failing than that they are weak, I am bound to warn them, in God's name, that unless they succeed in some way, directly or indirectly, in linking themselves to the strength of the Son of God, they will inevitably become wicked. The men, and especially the women, who are filling our prisons as criminals, were, in most cases, only weak, but they therefore drifted before the strong, black current that flows through the world. If you are conscious of your weakness, do what the sea anemone and the limpet do, which cling to the rock when the storms darken the sky. "Be strong in the Lord, and in the power of his might."

Herod was reluctant to take the course to which his evil genius urged him, but she finally had her way, and dragged him to her lowest level.

Beware, then, of yourself. Take heed, to guard against anything in your life that may open the gates to a temptation that you may not be able to withstand. If you are weak in physical health, you guard against a draft and fatigue, against impure atmosphere and contagion—how much more should you guard against the scenes and company that may act prejudicially on the health of your soul? Of all our hours, none are so filled with danger as those of recreation.

It was the most perilous thing that Herod could do, to have that banquet. Lying back on his divan, lolling on his cushions, eating his rich food, quaffing the sparkling wine, exchanging conversation with his obsequious followers, it was as though the heart of his soul was open to receive the first insidious spore of evil that might float past on the sultry air.

2. TEMPTATION. In the genesis of a sin we must give due weight to the power of the Tempter, whether by his direct suggestion to the soul or by the instrumentality of men and women whom he uses for his evil purpose. In this case Satan's accomplice was the beautiful Herodias—beautiful as a snake, but also as deadly. She knew the influence that John the Baptist wielded over her weak paramour, that he was accustomed to attach unmeasured importance to his words. She realized that his conscience was uneasy, and therefore the more liable to be affected by his words when he reasoned of righteousness, temperance, and judgment to come. She feared for the consequences if the Baptist and Herod's conscience should make common cause against her. She was not safe as long as John the Baptist breathed. Herod feared him, and perhaps she feared him with more abject terror, and was bent on removing him from her life.

She watched her opportunity, and it came on the occasion we have described. The ungodly revel was at its height. The strong wines of Messina and Cyprus had already done their work. Toward the end of such a feast it was the custom for immodest women to be introduced, who, by their gestures, imitated scenes in certain well-known mythologies, and still further inflamed the passions of the banqueters. But instead of the usual troupe, Salome herself came in and danced a wild gyrating dance. What must we think of a mother who could expose her daughter to such a scene? The girl, alas, was as shameless as her mother.

She pleased Herod, who was excited with the meeting of the two strong passions, which have destroyed more victims than have fallen on all the battlefields of the world; and in his frenzy, he promised to give her whatever she might ask, though it were to cost half his kingdom. She rushed back to her mother with the story of her success. "What shall I ask?" she cried. The mother had perhaps anticipated such a moment as this, and had her answer ready. "Ask," she replied instantly, "for John the Baptist's head." Back from her mother she tripped into the banqueting hall, her black eyes flashing with cruel hate, lighted from her mother's fierceness. A dead silence fell on the buzz of conversation, and every ear strained for her reply. "And she came in straightway with haste unto the king, and asked, saying, I will that thou give me by and by in a charger the head of John the Baptist." The imperious demand of the girl showed how eagerly she had entered into her mother's scheme.

It is thus that suggestions come to us; and as far as I can understand, we may expect them to come as long as we are in this world. There seems to be a precise analogy between temptation and the microbes of disease. These are always in the air; but when we are in good health they are absolutely innocuous, our nature offers no hold or resting place for them. So temptation would have no power over us, if our souls were filled with God. It is only when the vitality of the inward man is impaired, that we are unable to withstand the fiery darts of the wicked one.

This shows how greatly we need to be filled with the life of the Son of God. If you have the victorious nature of the living Christ in you, you must be stronger than the nature that He bruised beneath His feet.

3. THE CONSENT OF THE WILL. "The king was exceeding sorry." The girl's request sobered him. His face turned pale, and he clutched convulsively at the cushion on which he reclined. On the one hand, his conscience revolted from the deed; on the other, he said to himself, "I am bound by my oath. My words were spoken in the audience of so many of my chief men, I dare not go back, lest they lose faith in me." "And immediately the king sent an executioner, and commanded his head to be brought."

Isn't it amazing that a man who did not refrain from committing incest and murder, should be so scrupulous about violating an oath that ought never to have been sworn? You have thought that you were bound to go through with your engagement, because you had pledged yourself, although you know that it would condemn you to lifelong misery and disobedience to the law of Christ. But wait a moment. Looking back, can you not see that you ought never to have bound yourself, and do you not feel that if you had your time again you would not bind yourself? Then be sure that you are not bound by that "dead hand." You must act in the clearer, better light, which God has communicated. You had no right to pledge half the kingdom of your nature. It is not yours to give, it is God's. And if you have pledged it, through mistake, prejudice, or passion, dare to believe that you are absolved from your vow, through repentance and faith.

"And he went and beheaded him in prison." Had the Baptist heard anything of the unseemly revelry? Perhaps so. Those old castles are full of strange echoes. His cell was perfectly dark. Was his mind glancing back on those never-to-be-forgotten days, when the heaven was opened above him, and he saw the descending dove? Was he wondering why he was allowed to lie there month after month, silenced and suffering? Ah, he did not know how near he was to liberty!

There was a tread along the corridor. It stopped outside his cell. The light gleamed under the door; the heavy wards of the lock were turned: in a moment more he saw the gleam of the naked sword, and guessed the soldier's errand. There was no time to spare; the royal message was urgent. Perhaps one last message was sent to his disciples; then he bowed his head before the stroke; the body fell helpless here, the head there, and the spirit was free. Forerunner of the Bridgroom here, he was his forerunner there also; and the Bridegroom's friend passed homeward to await the Bridegroom's coming, where he will ever hear the voice he loves.

"And [the soldier] brought his head in a charger, and gave it to the damsel, and the damsel gave it to her mother." There probably was not much talking while the tragedy was being consummated. When the soldier entered, carrying on the platter that ghastly burden, they beheld a sight that was to haunt some of them to their dying day. Often Herod would see it in his dreams. It would haunt him, and fill his days and nights with anguish that all the witchery of Herodias could not dispel.

Months afterward, when he heard of Jesus, the conscience-stricken monarch said: "It is John, whom I beheaded: he is risen from the dead." And still afterward, when Jesus Himself stood before him, and refused to speak one word, he must have associated that silence and his deed together, as having a fatal and necessary connection.

So the will, which had long played around with the temptress, at last took the fatal step, and perpetrated the crime that could never be undone.

If you have taken the fatal step, and marred your life by some sad and disastrous sin, dare to believe that there is forgiveness for you with God. Men may not forgive, but God will.

But if we have not yet come to this, let us devoutly thank God, and be on the watch against any influences that may cause us to drift there. We may yet disentangle ourselves. We may yet receive into our natures the living power of the Lord Jesus. We may yet cut off the right hand and right foot, and pluck out the right eye, which is causing us to offend. Better this, and go into life maimed, than be cast, as Herod was, to the fire and worm of unquenchable remorse.

15

The Grave of John, and Another Grave
Matthew 14:12

We have beheld the ghastly deed with which Herod's feast ended—the golden platter, on which lay the freshly-dissevered head of the Baptist, borne by Salome to her mother, that the two might gloat over it together. John's disciples heard of the ghastly tragedy, and they came to the precincts of the castle to gather up the body as it lay dishonored on the ground, or ventured into the very jaws of death to request that it might be given to them. In either case, it was a brave thing for them to do; an altogether heroic exploit.

The headless body was then borne to a grave, either in the grim, gaunt hills of Moab, or in that little village, away on the southern slopes of the Judæan hills where, some thirty years before, the aged pair had rejoiced over the growing lad. God knows where that grave lies; and some day it will yield up to honor and glory the body that was sown in weakness and corruption.

Having performed the last sad rites, the disciples "went and told Jesus." Every mourner should go along the path they trod, to the same gentle and tender Comforter; and if any who read these words have placed within the narrow confines of a grave the precious remains of those dearer than life, let them follow where John's disciples have preceded them, to the one Heart of all others in the universe that is able to sympathize and help. Go, and tell Jesus!

It is not on these details however that we desire to dwell, but to use the scenes before us as a background and contrast to magnify certain features in the death, grave, and abiding influence of Jesus of Nazareth.

1. CONTRAST THE DEATH OF JOHN AND THAT OF JESUS. There were many points of similarity between their careers. These two rivers sprang from the same source, in a quiet glen far up among the hills; lay in deep lagoons during their earlier course; leaped down in the same mighty torrent when their time had come; and for the first few miles watered the same tract of country.

It would be possible to enumerate a large number of identical facts of the life courses of the two cousins. Their births were announced, and their ministries anticipated, under very special circumstances; Mary was unmarried, and Elisabeth past age—and an angel of the Lord came to each. John seemed, to the superficial view, the stronger and mightier of the two; but Jesus followed close behind and took up a similar burden, as he bade the people repent and believe the gospel. They attracted similar attention, gathered the same crowds, and protested against the same sins. Rearing the same standard, they summoned men from formality and hypocrisy to righteousness and reality. They incurred the same hatred on the part of the religious leaders of their nation, and suffered violent deaths—the one beneath the headsman's blade in the dungeons of Herod's castle; the other on the cross, at the hand of Pilate and the Roman soldiers. Each suffered a death of violence at the hand of men whom he had lived to nourish; each died when the life blood throbbed with young manhoods prime; each was loved and mourned by a little handful of devoted followers.

But there the similarity ends, and the contrast begins. With John, it was the tragic close of a great and epoch-making career. When he died men said, Alas! a prophet's voice is silenced. Such men are rare! Ages flower in this way but once, and then years of barrenness! But as we turn to the death of Jesus, other feelings master us. We do not recognize that there is in any sense an end of His work—rather it is the beginning. Here, at the cross, is the head of waters, rising from unknown depths, which are to heal the nations; here the sacrifice is being offered that is to expiate the sin of man, and bring peace to myriads of penitents; here the last Adam at the tree undoes the deadly work wrought by the first at another tree. This is no mere martyr's last agony; but a sacrifice, premeditated, prearranged, the effects of which have already been prevalent in securing the remission of sins committed earlier. This is an event for which millenniums have been preparing, and to which millenniums shall look back. John's death affected no destiny but his own; the death of Jesus has affected the destiny of our race. As His forerunner explained, He was the Lamb of God who bore away the sin of the world. The Lord has laid on Himself the iniquity of us all.

The there is another contrast. In the case of John, the martyr had no control on his destiny; he could not order the course of events. As he stood boldly at his rock-hewn pulpit, and preached to the eager crowds, do you suppose that the idea ever flashed across his mind? But, from the first, Jesus meant to die. If, eight centuries ago, you had seen the first outlines drawn of Cologne Cathedral, you would have been convinced that the completed fabric would enclose a cross; so the life of Jesus, from the earliest, portended Calvary. He had received power and commandment from the Father to lay down His life. Others die because they have been born: Jesus was born that He might die.

In his great picture of the carpenter's shop, Millais depicts the shadow of the cross, flung back by the growing lad, on the wall, strongly defined in the clear oriental light. Mary beholds it with a look of horror on her face. The thought is a true one. From the earliest, the cross cast its shadow over the life of the Son of Man. He was never deceived as to His ultimate destiny. He told Nicodemus that He had to be lifted up. He knew that as the Good Shepherd He would have to give His life for the sheep. He assured His disciples that He would be delivered up to the chief priests and scribes, who would condemn Him to death, crucify, and slay Him. Man does not need primarily the teacher, the example, nor the miracle worker; but the Savior who can stand in his stead, and put away his sin by the sacrifice of Himself.

What answer and explanation can be given to account for the marvelous spell that the cross of Christ exerts over the hearts of men? No other death affects us thus or effects so immediate a transformation.

2. CONTRAST THE GRAVE OF JOHN AND THAT OF JESUS. Men have alleged that the Lord did not really rise from the dead, and that the tale of His resurrection, if it were not a fabrication, was the elaboration of a myth. But neither of these alternatives will bear investigation. It is absurd to suppose that the temple of truth could be erected on the quagmire and morass of falsehood; and it is a demonstrated impossibility that a myth could have found time to grow into the appearance of substantial fact during the short interval that elapsed between the death of Christ and the first historical traces of the church.

In this connection, it is interesting to consider one sentence dropped by the sacred chronicler. He tells us, that when Herod heard of the works of Jesus, he said immediately, "This is John the Baptist; he is risen from the dead." Why, then, did that myth not spread, until it became universally accredited? There was the grave of John the Baptist to disprove it. If Herod had seriously believed it, or the disciples of John attempted to spread it, nothing would have been easier than to exhume the body from its grave, and produce the ghastly but indubitable refutation of the royal delusion.

When the statement began to spread and gain credence that Christ had risen from the dead; when Peter and John stood up and affirmed that He was living at the right hand of God; if it had been a mere surmise, the fond delusion of loyal and faithful hearts, a hallucination of two or three hysterical women, would it not have been easy for the enemies of Christianity to go immediately to the grave in the garden of Joseph, and produce the body of the crucified, with the marks of the nails in hands and feet? Why did they not do it? If it is said that it could not be produced, because it had been taken away, let this further question be answered. Who had taken it away? Not his friends; for they would have taken the wrappings with which Jospeh and Nicodemus had covered it. Not his enemies; for they would have been only too glad to produce it. What glee in the grim faces of Caiaphas and Annas, if at the meeting of the Sanhedrin, called to deal with the new heresy, there could have been given some positive proof that the body of Jesus was still buried, if not in Joseph's tomb, yet somewhere else, to which their emissaries had conveyed it!

The disciples did not expect Jesus to rise. They stubbornly held that the women were mistaken, when they brought to them the assurance that it was even so. But as the hours passed, the tidings of the empty grave were corroborated by the vision of the risen Lord, and they were convinced that He who was crucified in weakness was living by the power of God. There could henceforth be no hesitation in their message to the world. Thank God, we have not followed cunningly-devised fables.

3. THE CONTRAST BETWEEN THE EFFECTS OF THEIR TWO DEATHS ON THE FOLLOWERS OF JOHN THE BAPTIST AND OF JESUS RESPECTIVELY. What a picture for an artist of sacred subjects is presented by the performance of the last rites to the remains of the great forerunner! Devout men bore him to his grave, and made great lamentation over him.

The little band broke up at his grave. Farewell! they said to him; farewell to their ministry and mission; farewell to one another. "Goodbye!" "Goodbye!" And so they separated, never to meet in a common corporate existence again.

When Jesus lay in His grave, this process of disintegration began at once among His followers also. The women went to embalm Him; the men were apart. Peter and John broke off together—at least they ran together to the sepulcher; but where were the rest? Two walked to Emmaus apart; while Thomas was not with them when Jesus came on the evening of Easter Day. Soon Peter would have been back in Gennesaret; Nathanael beneath his fig tree; Luke in his dispensary; and Matthew at his toll booth.

What arrested that process and made it impossible? Why was it that they who had been like timid deer, before He died, became as lions against the storm of Pharisaic hate, and stronger as the weeks passed?

There is only one answer to these questions. The followers of Jesus were convinced by positive proofs that their Master was living at the right hand of power; nay, that He was with them all the days—nearer them than ever before, as much their Head and leader as at any previous moment. When the shepherd is smitten, the flock is scattered; but this flock was not scattered because the Shepherd had recovered from His mortal wound, and was alive forever.

And surely the evidence that sufficed for them is enough for us. Let us follow Him. It is not for us to linger around the grave: even John's disciples didn't do this. Let us join ourselves by faith with our Prince and Captain, sure that where He is, we too shall be; but in the meanwhile we are assured that He is not in the grave, but risen, ascended, glorified—our Emmanuel, our Love and Life. "The Lord is my Shepherd . . . Though I walk through the valley of the shadow of death . . . Thou *art* with me."

16

Yet Speaking
John 10:40–42

"Beyond Jordan!" To the Jews who dwelled at Jerusalem that was banishment indeed. There were some tracts of fertile country, dotted by a few scattered villages, but there our Lord spent His last few months.

But why? Why did the Son of Man banish Himself from the city He loved so dearly? The religious leaders of the age were pursuing Him with relentless malice, and would have taken His life before the predestined hour had arrived, had He not gone away "beyond Jordan into the place where John at first baptized; and there he abode: and many resorted unto him."

There was a peculiar fascination to the Lord Jesus in those solitudes, because of their connection with the forerunner. Those banks had witnessed the baptism of thousands of people who, in the symbolic act of baptism, had put away their sins.

Probably our Lord would resume His ministry of preaching the good tidings, and to Him they probably brought the lame, the blind, the sick, and paralyzed—and He healed them all. People could not help contrasting the two ministries. "They said, John did no miracle." It was quite true—John had done no miracle.

But there was a generous tribute and acknowledgment. "But all things that John spake of this man were true." He said that He was the Lamb of God; *and it was true.* He said that He would use His fan, separating the wheat from the chaff; *and it was true.* He said that He would baptize with fire; *and it was ture.* John did no miracle, but he spoke strong, true words of Jesus, and they have been abundantly verified. And these simple-hearted people of Perea did what the Pharisees and scribes, with all their fancied wisdom, had failed to do: they put the words of the Baptist and the life of Jesus together, and reasoned that since these had fit, as a key fits the lock, therefore Jesus was indeed the Son of God and the King of Israel; and "many believed on him there."

1. LIFE WITHOUT MIRACLES. The people were inclined to disparage the life of John because there was no miracle in it. But surely his whole life was a miracle; from first to last it vibrated with divine power. And did he work no miracle? If he did not open the eyes of the blind, did not multitudes, beneath his words, come to see themselves sinners, and the Eternal as alone enduring and desirable? If he did not lay his priestly hand on leprous flesh, as Jesus did, did not many a moral leper go from the waters of his baptism, with new resolves and purposes, to sin no more? If he did not raise dead bodies, did not many, who were confined in the graves of pride, and lust, and worldliness, hear his voice, and come forth to the life—which is life indeed? No miracles! Surely his life was one long pathway of miracle.

This is still the mistake of men. They allege that the age of miracles has passed. No miracles! But last summer He made the handfuls of grain, which the farmers cast on the fields, to feed the people of the world—as easily as He made five barley loaves provide a full meal for more than ten thousand persons. No miracles! But last autumn, in ten thousand vineyards, He turned the dews of the night and the showers of the morning into the wine that rejoices man's heart; as once, in Cana, He changed the water drawn from the stone jars into the blushing wine. No; it is still the age of miracles.

a. *Let us not disparage the age in which we live.* To look back on the Day of Pentecost with a sigh, as though there were more of the Holy Spirit on that day than today; and as though there were a larger presence of God in the upper room than in the room in which you sit, is a distinct mistake and folly. We may not have the sound as of a rushing mighty wind, nor the crowns of fire, but the Holy Spirit is with the church in all His fullness.

If there is any failure it is with ourselves. We have not believed in the mighty power and presence of God because we have missed the outward and visible sign of His working. We have become so accustomed to associate the startling and spectacular with the divine, that we fail to discover God, when the heaven is brilliant with stars, and the earth carpeted with flowers: as though the lightning were more to us than starlight, and the destructive than the peaceful and patient constructive forces, which are ever at work building up and repairing the fabric of the universe.

Do not look back on the Incarnation, or forward to the Second Advent, as though there were more of God in either one or the other than is within our reach. God is; God is here; all of God is present at any given point of time or place. He may choose to manifest Himself in outward signs, that impress the imagination more at one time than another; the faith of the church may be quicker to apprehend and receive in one century than the next: but every age is equally His workmanship and equally full of His wonder-working power. How sad for us that we don't see this.

b. *Let us not disparage the ordinary and commonplace.* We are all taught to run after the startling and extraordinary—we like miracles! Whatever appeals to our love for the sensational and unexpected is likely enough to displace our appreciation of the simple and ordinary. When the sun is eclipsed, we all look heavenward; but the golden summer days may be filled with sunlight, which is dismissed with a commonplace remark about the weather. Thus our tastes are vitiated and blinded.

It is good to cultivate simple tastes. It is a symptom of a weak and unstable nature to be always in search for some new thing, for some greater sensation, for some more startling sign. All life is so interesting; but we need eyes to see, and hearts to understand.

c. *Let us not disparage ourselves.* We know our limitations; we are not capable of working miracles. But if we cannot work miracles, we can speak true words about Jesus Christ; we can bear witness to Him as the Lamb of God; we can urge men to repent and believe the gospel. The world would have been in a sorry plight if it had depended entirely on its geniuses and miracle workers. It probably owes less to them than to the untold myriads of simple, commonplace people, whose names will never be recorded in its roll call, but whose lives have laid the foundations on which the superstructure of good order, and government, and prosperity, has been reared.

Remember that God made you what you are, and placed you. Dare to be yourself—a simple, humble, sincere follower of Jesus. Be content to find out what God made you for, and be that at its best. You will be a bad copy, but a unique original, for the Almighty always breaks the pattern from which He has made one vase. Above all, speak out the truth, as God has revealed it to you, and long after you have passed away, those who remember you will gather at your grave and say, "he did no miracle, but he spoke true things about Jesus Christ, which we have tested for ourselves, and are undeniable. Indeed, they led us to believe in Him for ourselves."

2. THE WAYS IN WHICH WE MAY BEAR TESTIMONY TO THE LORD JESUS. There is no miracle in your life, my reader. As you look daily into the common routine of your lot, it seems ordinary enough. Be it so; there is at least one thing you can do, as we have seen—like the Baptist, you may witness for Jesus.

a. *Speak to others privately.* When only two disciples were standing beside him, John preached the same sermon as he had delivered to the crowd the day before, and both of them went to the frail lodging where Jesus was making His abode. There is nothing that more deeply searches a man than the habit of speaking to individuals about the love of God. We cannot do it unless we are in living union with God Himself. To speak to another about Christ demands that there should be an absolutely clear sky between the speaker and the Lord of whom he speaks. But as this practice is the most difficult, it is the most blessed in its reflex influence. To lead another to Jesus is to get nearer Him. Whether by letters addressed to relatives or companions, or by personal and direct appeal, let each one of us adopt the sacred practice which Mr. Moody followed and commended, of allowing no day to pass without seeking to use some opportunity given by God for definite, personal dealings with others.

The apostle Andrew seems to have specially consecrated his life to this. On each of the occasions he is referred to in the Gospels he is dealing with individuals. He brought his own brother; was the first to seek after a boy to bring to the Savior's presence; and at the close of our Lord's ministry he brings the seeking Greeks. Did he not learn this blessed art from his master, the Baptist?

It is required that there should be the deliberate resolution to pursue this holy habit; definite prayer for guidance as we rise from the morning hour of prayer; abiding fellowship with the Son of God, that He may give the right word at the right moment; and a willingness to open the conversation by some manifestation of the humble, loving disposition begotten by the Holy Spirit, which is infinitely attractive and beautiful to the most casual passer-by.

b. *Speak experientially.* Be content to say, "I was lost, but Jesus found me; blind, and he gave me sight; unclean, and He cleansed my heart." Nothing goes so far to convince another as to hear the accent of conviction on the lips of one whose eyes survey the landscape of truth to which he allures, and whose ears are open to the eternal harmonies that he described.

c. *Speak from a full heart.* The lover cannot but speak about his love; the painter can do no other than transfer to canvas the conceptions that entrance his soul; the musician is constrained to give utterance to the chords that pass in mighty procession through his brain. "We cannot but speak the things that we have seen and heard."

Does it seem difficult to always have a full heart? Yes, it is difficult, and impossible, unless the secret has been acquired of abiding always in the love of God, of keeping the entire nature open to the Holy Spirit, and of nourishing the inward strength by daily meditation on the truth. We must have deep and personal fellowship with the Father and the Son by the Holy Ghost. We must live at first-hand on the great essentials of our faith. We will speak true things about Jesus Christ.

Thus, some day, at your burial, as people turn homeward from the new-made grave, they will say, "He will be greatly missed. He was no genius, not eloquent nor profound; but he used to speak about Christ in such a way that he led me to know Him for myself: I owe everything to him. He did no miracle; but whatever he said of Jesus was true."

3. THE POWER OF POSTHUMOUS INFLUENCE. John had been dead for many months, but the stream he had set flowing continued to flow. How many voices are speaking still in our lives—voices from the grave! Voices from dying beds! Voices from books and sermons! Voices from heaven! "Being dead, they yet speak." Let us live so that, when we are gone, our influence shall tell, and the accents of our voice linger. No one lives or dies to himself or herself. Each of us is affecting the lives of all who are now existing with us in the world, or will exist. To untold ages, what we have been and said will affect all other beings for good or ill. We may be forgiven for having missed our opportunities, or started streams of poison instead of life; but the ill effect can never be undone.

Parents, put your hands on those young childish heads, and speak words of Christ, which will return to memory and heart long after you have gone to your reward! Ministers of religion, and Sunday school teachers, remember your tremendous responsibility to use to the uttermost the opportunity of saying words that will never die! Friend, be true and faithful with your friend; he may turn away in apparent thoughtlessness or contempt, but no right word spoken for Christ can ever really die.

17

The Spirit and Power of Elijah
Luke 1:17

Great men are God's greatest gifts to our race; and it is only by their interposition that we are able to step up to higher and better levels of life. We believe that at distinct points in the history of the universe there has been a direct interposition of the will and hand of God; and it is remarkable that in the first chapter of Genesis that august and majestic word "create" is introduced three times, as though the creation of matter, the creation of the animal world, and the creation of man, were three distinct stages at which the direct interposition of the will and workmanship of the Eternal was especially manifest. Similarly, we believe that there have been great epochs in human history that cannot be accounted for by the previous evolution of moral and religious thought, and which must be due to the fact that God Himself stepped in, and by the direct raising up of a man, who became the apostle of the new era, lifted the race to new levels of thought and action. It is in this light that we view the two illustrious men who were the apostles of new epochs in human history—Elijah in the old Covenant, and John the Baptist in the new.

It is remarkable that the prophet Malachi tells us that the advent of the Messiah should be preceded and heralded by Elijah the prophet; and that Gabriel, four hundred years after, said that John the Baptist, whose birth he announced, would come in the spirit and power of Elijah. And, indeed, there was a marvelous similarity between these two men.

1. LET US INSTITUTE A COMPARISON BETWEEN ELIJAH THE TISHBITE, AND JOHN THE BAPTIST. They resembled each other in dress. We are told that Elijah was a hairy man—an expression that is quite as likely to refer to the rough garb in which he was habited, as to the unshorn locks that fell on his shoulders. And John the Baptist wore a coarse dress of camel's hair.

Each of them lived for awhile in Gilead. In the remarkable sentence which, for the first time, introduces Elijah to the Bible and the world, we are told that he lived in Gilead, that great tract of country, thinly populated, and largely given over to shepherds and their flocks, which lay upon the eastern side of the Jordan. And we know that it was there that John the Baptist waited, fulfilled his ministry, preached to and baptized the teeming crowds.

Each of them learned to make the body subservient to the spirit. Elijah was able to live on the sparse food brought by ravens, or provided from the meal barrel of the widow. He was able to outstrip the horses of Ahab's chariot in their mad rush across the valley of Jezreel; and after a brief respite, given to sleep and food, went in the strength of it for forty days and nights through the heart of the desert until he came to Horeb, the Mount of God. His body was but the vehicle of the fiery spirit that dwelled within; he always handled it as the weapon to be wielded by his soul. And what was true in his case, was so of John the Baptist, whose food was locusts and wild honey.

We remember also that each of these heroic spirits was confronted by a hostile court. In the case of Elijah, Ahab and Jezebel, and in the case of John the Baptist, Herod, Herodias, and the whole drift of religious opinion, dogged his steps, and ultimately brought him to a martyr's end.

Also, in each case we see distinctly the consciousness of the presence of God. This consciousness of the divine presence in his life revealed itself in his great humility, when he cast himself on the ground with his face between his knees; and in the unflinching courage that enabled him to stand like a rock on Mount Carmel, when king, and priest, and people, were gathered in their vast multitudes around him, sufficient to daunt the spirit that had not beheld anyone greater. This God-consciousness was especially manifest in the Baptist, who referred so frequently to the nearness of the kingdom of God. "The kingdom of heaven," he said, "is at hand." And when Jesus came, unrecognized by the crowds, John's high spirit prostrated itself, and his very visage was shadowed with the veil of intense modesty and humility, as he cried: "In the midst of you stands One whom you know not, the latchet of whose shoes I am not worthy to stoop down and unloose."

Coupled with this sense of God, there was, in each case a marvelous fearlessness of man. When Obadiah met Elijah, and was astonished to hear that the prophet was about to show himself to Ahab, Elijah overbore his attempts to disuade him, saying: I will certainly show myself to thy master: go, tell him Elijah is here. This fearlessness was also conspicuous in the forerunner, who dared to defy the king in his palace, asserting that he must be judged by the same standard as the meanest of his subjects, and that it was not lawful for him to have his brother's wife.

To each there came moments of depression. In the case of Elijah, the glory of his victory on the brow of Carmel was succeeded by the weight of dark soul anguish. And did not John the Baptist from his prison cell send the inquiry to Jesus, as to whether his hopes had been too glad, his anticipations too great, and that perhaps after all He was not the Messiah for whom the nation was waiting?

Both Elijah and John the Baptist had the same faith in the baptism of fire. We never can forget the scene on Carmel when Elijah proposed the test that the God who answered by fire should be recognized as God. John the Baptist passed through no such ordeal as that; but it was his steadfast faith that Christ should come to baptize with the Holy Ghost and fire.

Both of them turned the hearts of the people back. It would be impossible for one man to turn back a whole army in mad flight—he would necessarily be swept away in their rush; but this is precisely what the expression attributes to the exertions of Elijah and John. The one turned Israel back to cry, Jehovah, He is God; the other turned the whole land back to repentance and righteousness, so that publicans and soldiers, Sadducees and Pharisees, began to confess their sin, put away their evil courses, and return to the God of their fathers.

Each prophet was succeeded by a gentler ministry. Elijah was sent from Horeb to anoint Elisha who, for the most part, passed through the land like genial sunshine—a perpetual benediction to men, women, and children; while John the Baptist opened the door for the Shepherd, Christ, who went about doing good, and whose holy, tender ministry fell on His times like rain on the mown grass.

From the solitudes beyond the Jordan, as he walked with Elisha, talking as they went, the chariot and horses of fire from heaven bore him homeward. In those same solitudes, or within view of them, the spirit of John the Baptist swept up in a similar chariot. As the headsman, with a flash of his sword, put an end to his mortal career, though no mortal eyes beheld them, and no chronicler has told the story, there must have been horses and chariots of fire waiting to convey the noble martyr spirit to its God.

What these men did far back in the centuries, it is probably that others will have to do before this dispensation passes away completely. A man, or men, shall again rise up, who will tower over others, who will speak and act in the spirit and power of Elijah. Perhaps some young life may be inspired by this page to yield itself to God, so that it may be sent forth to turn the heart of the fathers to their children, and the heart of the children to their fathers, to make ready a people prepared for the Lord.

2. NOTICE THE INFERIORITY OF THESE GREAT MEN TO THE LORD. Neither of these dared to offer himself as the Comforter and Savior of men. It was never suggested for a moment that Elijah could act as mediator between God and men, though he might be an intercessor. And John the Baptist, could only point to One who came after him, and say: "Behold the Lamb of God, which taketh away the sin of the world" (John 1:29). But Jesus says: "The Son of Man hath authority on earth to forgive sins" (Matt. 9:6); and presently: "This is my blood of the new testament, which is shed for many, for the remission of sins" (Matt 26:28); and again: "The Son of man came . . . to give his life a ransom for many" (Mark 10:45). Tell me of anything, either in the story of Elijah or of John the Baptist, to compare with these words. Does that not indicate that He stood in a relationship to God and man that has never been realized by another?

O Christ, You stand preeminent in Your unparalleled glory! Let Elijah and John the Baptist withdraw, but oh, may you stay! To whom shall we go? You have the words of eternal life. To have You is to have all that is strong, and wise, and good, gathered up into the perfect beauty of a man, with the divine glory of the Infinite God.

3. HOW MAY WE HAVE THAT SAME SPIRIT? John the Baptist came in the spirit and power of Elijah: that spirit and power are for us too. Just as the dawn touches the highest peaks of the Alps, and afterward as the morning hours creep on, the tide of light passes down into the valley, so the Spirit that smote that glorious pinnacle Elijah, and that nearer pinnacle the Baptist, is waiting to descend on and empower us.

We are all believers in Jesus, but did we receive the Holy Spirit when we believed? (Acts 19:2). This power of the Holy Spirit is for us all. Of course we could not believe in Jesus in the remission of sin, or the quickening of our spiritual life, apart from the work of the Holy Spirit; but there is something more than this—there is a power, an anointing, a gracious endowment of fitness for service which are the privilege of every believer. The Holy Spirit waits to empower us to witness for Jesus, to endure the persecution and trial that are inevitable to the exercise of a God-given ministry, and to bring other people to God. It would be well to tarry and receive it. Stop your work for a little, and wait on the ascended, glorified Redeemer, in whom the Spirit of God dwells. Ask Him to impart to you that which He received on your behalf. Never rest until you are sure that the Spirit dwells in you fully, and exercises through you the plenitude of His gracious power. We cannot seek Him at the hand of Christ in vain. Dare to believe this: dare to believe that if your heart is pure, and your motives holy, and your whole desire fervent—and if you have dared to breathe in a deep, long breath of the Holy Spirit—that according to your faith so it has been done to you; and that you may go forth enjoying the same power that rested on the Baptist, though you may not be conscious of any divine inspiration, though there may have been no stroke of conscious power, no crown of flame, no rushing as of the mighty wind.

God is still able to grant to us as large a portion of His Spirit as He gave to the disciples on the day of Pentecost. The power of His grace is not passed away with the primitive times; Christ waits to lead His church to greater triumphs than she has ever known. O that He would take His throne as Prince of the kings of the earth! Creation travails; the mind of man has tried all possible combinations of sovereignty, and in vain.

"O Lord Jesus Christ, who at Your first coming did send Your messenger to prepare the way before You: grant that the ministers and stewards of Your mysteries may likewise so prepare and make ready Your way, by turning the hearts of the disobedient to the wisdom of the just; that, at Your second coming to judge the world, we may be found an acceptable people in Your sight, who lives and reigns with the Father and the Holy Spirit, ever one God, world without end. Amen."

PETER

1

Introductory
Matt. 3:1–12; Mark 1:1–8; John 1:35–42

The leader of the apostolic band was drawn from the ranks of very ordinary people, and the story of his life opens in the obscure village of Bethsaida, at the northwest corner of the Lake of Galilee. The unadorned and simple homes of its fishermen were in striking contrast to the marble palaces of the neighboring proud city of Capernaum.

1. THE COMING OF THE SON OF ZACHARIAS. The native population probably held aloof from the manners and habits of the conquerors, though they were quite ready to take advantage of their wealthy patronage and custom. Under their breath they spoke together of the great days of Judas Maccabæus and of Judas of Galilee, before whom even the mighty Roman legions had on more than one occasion been compelled to give way. To these echoes of the memorable past were added a strange anticipation and hope, which stirred in the breast of many, that the hour was near when the invader would be driven beyond the waters of the Great Sea, and the kingdom would once more be restored to Israel. Some told that the aged Simeon before his death bore witness to have held the Lord's Messiah in his arms; some spoke of visions of angel choirs. "The people were in expectation, and all men mused in their hearts" (Luke 3:15).

Suddenly the land was startled and shaken. A company of pilgrims, crossing the Jordan by the fords of Jericho, had been stopped by a strange figure, gaunt and sinewy, the child of desert solitudes, who had accosted them with the cry: "Repent, for the kingdom of heaven is at hand." It was a strange figure, half Bedouin and half prophetic! A voice that rang with trumpet note! He had no lodging but a cave! His food consisted of locusts dipped in water and baked on the hot coals, with wild honey to make them palatable! Without wife or child! These things gripped the national imagination.

The tidings spread everywhere, as by a mysterious telepathy. The whole country rose en masse. The confluent streams of people poured down the Jordan Valley in eager crowds. "Then went out to him Jerusalem, and all Judæa, and all the region round about Jordan" (Matt. 3:5). Multitudes were baptized in the Jordan—confessing their sins; among whom we may surely include the brothers Andrew and Peter, and their lifelong companions, James and John.

2. THE BAPTIST'S INFLUENCE ON PETER. Peter was in the prime of his manhood. Strong, vehement, impulsive and self-assertive, he could by no means be accounted a saint. He was doubtless attentive to the duties and formalities of his religion, attended the temple feasts, paid his dues, and was morally respectable.

From his youth he was an ardent patriot. Like all his friends and companions, he was prepared to sacrifice everything he possessed to see David's throne. Therefore, when he and others heard the tidings of the Baptist's appearance, they hailed them as heralding the new era.

Peter, his brother, and their friends bade goodby to home and craft and "went forth to see." They crossed the Jordan by the fords of Bethabara and joined the crowds who were streaming down the Jordan Valley to the scene of the Baptist's ministry.

The Baptist, selecting a ledge of rock for his pulpit, stood to address the awestruck throne, gathered from all the land to listen. Clearly enough, as our Lord suggested, he was no reed shaken by the wind of popular favor. He spoke what he knew and testified what he had seen. He penetrated the hollow pretensions of Pharisee and Scribe; compared them to the rock vipers; threatened them with the woodsman's axe, the smelter's furnace, and the harvester's fan. In his stern outlook there was short shrift for the sinner who refused to repent. Truly he was a light that burned as well as shone!

Beneath such preaching, Peter must have been deeply moved. It raked his soul. He felt then, as he confessed afterward, that he was "a sinful man." He was later probably baptized by the Baptist, confessing his sins. He had thus been born of water, as later he was to be born of the Holy Spirit.

3. PETER'S FIRST INTERVIEW WITH THE LORD. Andrew and John had spent some hours in Jesus' holy company. They had been welcomed to His dwelling, had listened with rapt attention while He spoke of heavenly things. As they listened their hearts had burned within them. They knew, with absolute conviction, that they had found the Messiah; and they rejoiced with a joy exceeding all their experience.

Leaving Christ's presence, they said each to the other, "We must tell Simon all about this, as soon as we can find him"; and, as was befitting, Andrew found him first and brought him to Jesus, saying, "We have found the Messiah."

Peter was immensely impressed by that interview. Perhaps the hardy fisherman may have been less attracted to Him than to John, the sinewy son of the desert. He may not have been immediately susceptible to the grace and truth, and gentleness and purity, the humility and selflessness of the Lamb of God. But if this was his first impression, it was instantly succeeded by one of awe and wonder, as those searching eyes looked into the depths of his nature, and Jesus said, "Thou shalt be called Cephas" (the Aramean equivalent for the Greek "Peter").

"Ah," said Peter to himself, at the close of that interview, "He little realizes how fickle and wayward I am. Why should I not, with His help, resolve to attain and apprehend that for which I have been apprehended?"

Thus our Savior deals with us still. He tells us what we can become by the proper development of our temperament and the exercise of divine grace; and as He speaks he imparts all needed help. We become possessed with the divine ideal, and laid hold of by divine strength; the reed becomes a pillar in the temple, the stone becomes a rock, and the chief of sinners the mightiest of saints.

It is said that Michelangelo saw in the blocks of marble, which others had refused, the forms that his genius would call into being; so in very unlikely souls our Lord descries qualities of unusual strength and beauty, which He sets Himself to elicit; and His first act often is to reveal the fair hidden image and to impute it. He saw Peter in Simon, Israel in Jacob, Paul in Saul—and told them so!

2

Early Days in the Master's College
John 1:43, 3:30; Matt. 4:23–25

The wonder of that first interview with the Lord must have almost dazed the mind of Simon, the son of John. The Baptist's ministry had already stirred his soul to the depths, but this fresh and gracious personality, so full of grace and truth, had revealed possibilities for his manhood that had never occurred to him. It seemed incredible that *he* could become a man of rock!

The incongruity of his nature with that name seemed an unbridged chasm. But nothing was impossible with God. Already Peter's heart had opened to Christ's knock, never to close to Him again. His soul had turned to Him with passionate devotion.

1. WALKS AND TALKS. Whatever may have been the fisherman's reverie, he was soon made aware that Jesus had decided to go into Galilee, and he resolved to accompany Him. Apparently they had hardly left the scene of the Baptist's ministry when they encountered Philip, and the fact that it is expressly recorded that he was a native of Bethsaida, "the city of Andrew and Peter," suggests that the two brothers had something to do with the Master's discovery of him and his immediate response.

This first journey in such company was the beginning of many similar experiences, as these newly-found disciples walked with Him, and heard Him open the Scriptures, their hearts burned within them, and emotions were aroused too tumultuous for words.

When they came within sight of the little village of Cana, Philip seems to have hastened forward to announce his discovery to a devout friend of his—Nathanael. Apparently he found him pondering the story of the ladder that Jacob saw as he slept and dreamed. The guileless Israelite little thought that the ladder was to be literally reared again on his lawn, that the angel ministry was actually in operation, and that he might begin to climb the scale of ascent that would presently land him in the divine presence-chamber.

It was at the marriage feast to which they were all invited on the following day that Peter drank in the deepest lessons of the Master to whom he had given his allegiance. At first he must have been greatly startled. Until he had come under the influence of the Baptist, his highest ideal of religion had been the curator of the synagogue, the Pharisee with his phylacteries, and the priests in the temple; but their inconsistencies had only enhanced the commanding splendor of the holiness of John. John's rigid asceticism, that he seemed to have no need of a woman's love or a little child's caress, that he was absorbed in face-to-face fellowship with God, that he was absolutely fearless and unyielding—these qualities enthralled their loyalty and respect. When, therefore, John introduced them to Jesus, as being incomparably greater than himself, they expected the same type of holiness, in its awful, lonely splendor.

2. THE MARRIAGE FEAST OF CANA. But Jesus led them to a village festival, where a group of simple peasants were celebrating a wedding. He sat there among young and old, the life of the party; His face beaming with joy, His words adding to the pleasure of the company, His presence welcomed by the children and greeted by the young men and women. This was an altogether new and unexpected type of holiness. Peter and the

rest watched it closely, as they reclined with Jesus at the feast. What would the Baptist have done? Would he approve? Certainly this was not the religion of the synagogue or the temple! But as they came more and more under the spell of their wonderful Friend and Teacher, they became more profoundly convinced that this was the religion that the world was waiting for. They could not all imitate the asceticism of the Baptist; Peter at least was already married. But they could all follow in the steps of their new Master in the sweet amenities of the home.

And Peter learned many things beside. That though the Lord addressed His mother with perfect respect, He was under direction from a higher source. That only a hint of need was necessary—*He* would know exactly how to meet it. That those who were called to cooperate with Him must always give Him brimfull obedience. That what His servant drew as water would blush beneath His word into wine. That He would always lead from good to better, from better to better still. These were wonderful discoveries: and it was a happy group that left Cana when the feast was over. What a story the brothers had to tell to their father, and Peter to his wife and her mother!

3. GROWING INFLUENCE OF THE MASTER. Though probably the Master and His disciples traveled with their own families to the feast, they met again in the precincts of the Holy City. Peter and the rest beheld with wonder their gentle and lowly Master cleanse the temple courts as though girded with the power of an Elijah. They watched the rising wrath of the Jewish magnates as they challenged the Nazarene's authority over the holy places. They pondered His affirmation that He would build the temple in three days, though not until He was risen from the dead did they understand that cryptic utterance. Since Peter, in his subsequent address in the house of Cornelius, expressly states that God preached peace by Jesus Christ throughout all Judæa, we may fairly infer that he at least accompanied the Master in that first great itinerary, through the very regions where Æneas, Tabitha, and Simon the Tanner, in later years, greeted him again.

Nine months were spent this way. For a further period of nine months our Lord seems to have been unattended. Finally, when the fate of the Baptist was sealed, and no advantage could be gained by further delay, the Master went forth alone, throughout all Galilee, "teaching in their synagogues, and preaching the gospel of the kingdom, and healing all manner of sickness and all manner of disease among the people. And his fame went throughout all Syria . . . and there followed him great multitudes of people from Galilee, and from Decapolis, and from Jerusalem, and from Judæa, and from beyond Jordan" (Matt. 4:23–25).

Peter was aware of this mighty movement, and found it irksome to stay with his boats and nets. He dreamed of Christ by night, and watched for His coming by day. Presently the morning broke, and the Master came along the shore. That day changed the entire direction of his career.

3

The Settlement as to the Supreme Control
Mark 1:14–20; Luke 5:1–11

Nine busy. months had passed. Time after time, as Jesus returned to His home at Capernaum, where His friends and disciples seem now to have settled, He devoted

Himself to their further instruction in the great principles on which His life was based, and to their preparation for the decisive moment when He should bid them leave all, rise up, and follow Him. That decisive moment came in this way:

1. THE SCENE. It was the early morning of an autumn day that provided the setting for the supreme event in the lives of the four fishermen who were destined to influence all the history.

They had been friends from boyhood. They were partners in their fishing business. They were ardent disciples and friends of Him who was moving the whole country. His life, deeds, and words were always on their lips, as they floated together over the fishing areas, while the stars kept vigil overhead. Probably they had been speaking of Him, as they drew to shore, after a night of fruitless toil.

They had disembarked, were rinsing out their seine nets, and spreading them on the shore to dry, when they became aware of the approach of a vast crowd, that was thronging and pressing on the person of their beloved Teacher and Friend. In a moment they had forgotten their weariness and disappointment, their hunger, and the call of their homes, and were on the alert to welcome Him. He made straight for Peter's boat and asked that it might be moored within one of the rock-lined inlets that indented the shore. There He sat and spoke to His congregation, many seated on the blocks of basalt, others standing but all rapt and wondering at the gracious words that proceeded from His lips.

2. THE INEXORABLE COMMAND. When our Lord is about to fashion a vessel unto honor, there can be no discussion or argument, no hesitancy or holding back. The disciple must leave all and follow Him.

Peter and the others probably knew this generally. They were prepared to give Him their loyal allegiance in the realms of morals and duty but it was altogether startling and unexpected when, invading their own sphere, He assumed their prerogative, and said to Peter: "Launch out into the deep, and let down your nets for a draught." Peter expressed his hesitation in the reply: "Master, we have toiled all the night, and have taken nothing."

Peter had fished these waters from boyhood. There was nothing in the craft with which he was not familiar. The habits of the fish; the hours and spots most suitable for taking them; the effect of climatic conditions: in all he was proficient. He would have hotly resented any interference on the part of other fishermen of his acquaintance; and now he found himself suddenly confronted with a bidding which was contradicted by his experience, by the universal maxims and practice of generations, and by the bitter failure of the preceding night, which had left him jaded, weary, and out of heart.

He would be prepared to obey the slightest precept that came from the Master's lips; but how could One who had spent His day in the carpenter's workshop of a mountain village be competent to take command of a boat and direct the casting of a net! The morning was no time for fishing; the glare of light revealed the meshes of the nets, and the fish were to be found, not in the deep, but the shallower part of the lake. All the fishermen who might see his boat putting out at such an hour, laden with nets, and evidently prepared for fishing, would laugh and call him crazy. Is it not thus with all who have been greatly used by Christ? There is no escaping the test. At a certain moment in our experience, often long after we have become disciples, the Master comes on board the ship of our life and assumes supreme control. For a moment or an hour there may be question and hesitation. We have been used to making our own plans, following our own chart, taking our own course, and being masters in our own crafts; shall we—may we, dare we—hand over the entire command to Christ? Happy are we if, after such a moment of hesitation we reply: "Nevertheless, at your command I will put out even to the deep, and let down the nets for a catch."

So it has been all through the ages. His word often speaks in the teeth of ordinary experience and convention, and asks us to leave the beach, which we have been hugging too long. It generally offers the acid test to our faith and exposes us to the ridicule of our associates. But it is endorsed in the depths of our soul by an answering assent. To disobey is to become a castaway. To yield obedience is to enter on a vast and lasting inheritance.

Christ must be Master. There cannot be two captains in the boat, if it is to make a successful voyage and return at last filled to the water's edge with fish. Today and now, let that question be decided! He has a place and a use for you, but you must surrender yourself to His disposal. Make Christ Captain, while you take to the oars! At His bidding, launch out into the deep and the unbroken net shall be dragged to shore, "full of great fishes, one hundred and fifty and three."

3. OBEDIENCE LEADS TO THE DEEP. As soon as the Lord takes control, He steers toward the deep. The deep of the eternal council-chamber, where we were chosen in Christ before the world began. The deep of the eternal love that loved us when we were yet sinners. The deep of fellowship and unity with God, like that between the Father and the Son. The deep workings of providence that underlie all human history. The deep bliss of eternity into which our restless souls will enter.

But here we are especially concerned with *the deep of divine partnership*. To Peter's surprise the boat, propelled by oar or sail, had passed over many well-known fishing grounds, and had kept its course to the midst of the lake, before our Lord told them to let down the nets. The necessary preparations were hardly completed when it was evident that they had netted a great catch of fish. So much so that the nets were strained to breaking point. The beads of perspiration were thick on his forehead, and his muscles stood out as whipcord, as Peter strived to cope with the bulging nets. His boat was lurching dangerously, and he made urgent signals to his partners, who apparently had put out in expectation that something of this kind would take place. And they came and filled both the boats, so that the gunwales were almost level with the water. Then Peter realized for the first time what partnership with Christ means, and how absolute obedience on our part secures absolute cooperation on His.

What a lesson is here for us all! We know only too well what it is to toil through long dark seasons and take nothing. Again and again we have returned to shore with only a minnow or two. But as soon as we enter into fellowship, or partnership, with the Son of God, to which indeed we have been called, we discover that all we have to do is to have washed and mended nets, to trust the Master to indicate the grounds where the fish lie, and to believe that He will do the rest.

On the Day of Pentecost Peter again let down his net, this time into the vast excited crowds, and again the Lord repeated the miracle of the Galilean lake, and filled his net with three thousand souls. In the house of Cornelius his net had hardly touched the water, when the catch filled the net. Surely on each occasion the apostle must have looked into the face of Jesus with a happy smile, and said: "Ah, Lord, here is the Lake of Galilee over again."

This experience might be ours, on similar conditions. If it is not so, let us inquire as to the reason. It lies, not with the Master, but with ourselves, our obedience, or our nets. If our nets are our addresses, sermons, or methods, we must make and mend them by careful study and earnest prayer. The meshes must be so closely articulated that no fish shall get through them. No pains shall be spared to present the Gospel so that our hearers may be without excuse. Mend your old nets, or make new ones.

Be sure also that they are clean. Wash out the gritty sand or weed that may have accumulated. Especially eliminate self. There must be nothing to attract your hearers from your message to yourself; and when you have done all, dare to believe that your Lord is still working with His servants and confirming their word by the power of the Holy Spirit.

4

A Fisher of Men
Luke 5:8–11

The Master's purpose for His disciples is disclosed in the words recorded by Matthew and Mark, and which were probably addressed to them on the shore, when they had again beached their boats: "Come ye, after me, and I will make you to become fishers of men." We can combine this form of the summons with that especially addressed to the impulsive, vehement, warm-hearted son of Zebedee, and which is recorded in Luke 5. It should be noticed that here, as generally in the Gospels, our Lord addresses him by the more intimate name of "Simon," as though "Peter" was reserved until, through the months of discipline that awaited him, he was fitted to take the foremost place among his fellow apostles.

The summons came while they were engaged in their usual occupation. David was summoned from the sheepfold to shepherd the chosen race. Paul was called from making the goat's-hair tents to teach the church. The eternal springs were revealed to the woman as she rested her pitcher on the edge of Jacob's Well. It was quite befitting, therefore, that our Lord should explain to His fisher friend the momentous and glorious ministry that awaited him, through the calling in which he had been engaged from boyhood, and which had so many points of resemblance with the work of winning souls. The one difference being brought out in the Greek word translated "catch," should be expanded to read, as in 2 Timothy 2:26, "Thou shalt catch, *in order to keep alive.*"

In every subsequent era sincere and earnest souls have lingered wistfully over these words, longing to extract from them the precious secret of successful soul-winning.

Many a godly minister with a perfectly-appointed church, and surrounded by a devoted people—the boat, the company, and the fishing-tackle being all of the best—has watched, almost enviously, the success of some simple evangelist who, apart from all adventitious aid, has lifted netfuls of fish from the great depths of human life into his creel. The study of this narrative may bring us still further into the heart of the matter and the mind of our Lord.

1. Successful soul-winning is generally based on a deep consciousness of personal sin. The untiring and extraordinary labors of the great apostle of the Gentiles laid the foundations of the Gentile church, but as he reviews the past and considers his natural condition, he does not hesitate to speak of himself as the chief of sinners and the least of saints. We all once lived "in the lusts of our flesh, fulfilling the desires of the flesh and of the mind; and were by nature the children of wrath, even as others" (Eph. 2:3).

Those who have had deep experiences of the exceeding sinfulness of sin are the better qualified to be tender and pitiful to such as are sold under sin. "Alas, poor souls!" they cry, "such were some of us." The ringleaders in the devil's army make great soldiers for Christ. Their knowledge of Satan's stratagems and wiles is invaluable. The sinner knows the bitterness of the wages of sin, as an unfallen angel or an innocent child cannot. We need not be surprised, therefore, at this preparatory revelation the Lord gave of Himself to Peter.

He and the rest had known the Lord for at least eighteen months, but were unaware of His true majesty and glory. For them He was the carpenter of Nazareth, the holy man, the marvelous teacher and wonder-worker. Then most suddenly and unexpectedly this shaft of His essential being struck into their ordinary commonplace, and left a trail of supernatural glory. As Peter felt the tug and pull of the bursting net, threatening to break beneath its sudden burden, he realized that his Teacher and Friend must have put forth a power that no mortal could resist. God was in the place, and he had not known it. At once the nakedness and sinfulness of his own heart were laid bare, and he cried: "I am a sinful man, O Lord." Note the significant exchange! When the boat left the shore it was *Master,* now, as this revelation has broken on him, it is *Lord.* Immediately following this Jesus said: "From henceforth thou shalt catch men."

There is a striking analogy between Peter's experience and Job's. The suffering analogy between Peter's experience and Job's. The suffering patriarch had persistently and successfully maintained his integrity. Then into his life God let fall visions of the Creation. He recited instance after instance of His almighty power, wisdom, and skill. As Peter's eyes were unveiled that he might behold Christ's wonders in the deep, so were Job's; and he exclaimed, as the divine glory shone on his soul, "I have heard of thee by the hearing of the ear: but now mine eye seeth thee. Wherefore I abhor myself, and repent in dust and ashes" (Job 42:5–6).

Whenever this experience befalls us, it may be considered as preparatory to new success in soul-winning. Expect to hear the Lord answer your confession of lowly sinfulness with a new summons to take your boat and net for a catch.

2. Failure and sin do not necessarily exclude from the divine partnership in soul-winning. "Depart from me," cried the conscience-stricken disciple. We can almost see him, when the well of the boat was heaped high with the slippery silver cargo, clambering across from prow and stern on his bare feet, falling at Jesus' knees as He sat near the tiller, clasping them, with the heaving sobs of a strong man torn with conflicting emotions.

"No," said our Lord in effect, "that need not be. Stay with Me, I will cleanse, heal, and save you, and make you the instrument of saving thousands of sinners like yourself."

It is impossible to exaggerate the comfort that these words afford to those who would want to serve Christ, but who are conscious of their profound unworthiness. "I am not worthy to bear the message of salvation to others, because I am such a sinful man! How employ me, who has hosts of unfallen angels at Your command? Let me stand in the outer circle and see You now and again. I cannot ask for more, for You know, and I know, that I am a sinful man."

But Jesus has only one reply: "Fear not; from henceforth thou shalt catch men." "I have blotted out your transgressions as a cloud, and will remember your sins no more. I have loved you with an everlasting love. Depart from Me! It is unthinkable. You are dearer to Me than all the stars in their galaxies. I have obtained from the Father that you should be with Me, where I am. After you have had your Pentecost, and fulfilled your ministry and finished your course, you shall be accounted worthy to stand in My presence chamber, that you may behold My glory, and you shall share it."

"Lord, it is too much; let me kiss Your feet!"

3. SOUL-WINNING, TO BE SUCCESSFUL, MUST BE THE ABSORBING OF OUR LIVES. It cannot be one interest among many. The apostle said truly, "One thing I do." "They left all and followed him."

May we indulge our imagination here? A friendly fisherman informs his wife that the well-known boat will soon be "in." His food has been waiting for him since early dawn. She hastens to the shore; her husband leaps into the shallow water and lifts Jesus from boat to beach. He then approaches her wistfully, and with an unwonted tenderness that startles her, "Can you share me for a little?" he inquires. "The Master has asked me to go with Him. He says that I am not to fear, and that He will provide for us. He has promised to teach me how to fish for men."

And she replies: "Husband, go with Him. Mother and I will get along somehow until you get back. Stay with Him as long as He needs you. Mother and I were saying only this morning that you have been a different man since you knew Him."

She came to believe also, and traveled everywhere with her husband, helping him, as Paul bears witness (1 Cor. 9:5). We cannot suppose that Peter at once entered into the Master's passion for the souls of men. At first he was content to follow Him, to listen to His words, to become His companion and helper. But it could not have been long before he and his companions began to be imbued with the same passion, until it became the master motive of their existence.

So it will be with ourselves. As we walk with Christ, we shall become identified with His interests, and with no backward look on ourselves. Our life will be spent as that of Peter, who by his love for Christ was qualified to feed His sheep and lambs.

Let us ask that we may become partners with Christ in His great passion for men. Oh, to be a living flame for Jesus Christ.

5

Primer Lessons
Mark 1:21–39

The Ephesian church was reminded by the apostle of having been taught by the Lord Himself, "as the truth is in Jesus." Everyone who desires to be a soul winner should sit in this lowest form in the Master's school.

1. THE FIRST LESSON WAS THAT ASSOCIATION WITH HIMSELF WOULD INEVITABLY INVOLVE THEM IN SPIRITUAL WARFARE. And so it happened. On what was probably not the first Sabbath after their final resolve to identify themselves with Jesus, the little group of fishermen accompanied Him to the synagogue. When the customary exercises were concluded, their Leader and Friend was invited to address the congregation, and the sharp contrast between His address and the dull deliverances of the scribes to which they were accustomed struck them with astonishment. "He taught them as one that had authority." Their hearts and consciences answered back with an echoing response.

The hush of the enthralled assembly was suddenly broken by the cry of a man's voice. It seemed as though a captive and unwilling soul was made the organ of an alien and compelling spirit. "Let us alone," was the demand. "What have we to do with thee, thou Jesus of Nazareth? . . . I know thee who thou art." This unclean spirit, or demon, may have resided in that man's body and mind for years, unsuspected by his most intimate associates. But the near presence of the divine holiness, though curtained by the unrent veil of His flesh, extorted an involuntary but irresistible outcry.

The disturbance caused by that wailing cry from the abyss must have been startling. The man may, up to that moment, have been regarded as a respectable member of society. No one suspected the duality of his nature; but Peter must have suddenly realized that his Master had to arouse and call into hostility the whole kingdom of evil spirits. The warfare for which he had enlisted was not against flesh and blood, but against the wicked spirits that rule the darkness of this world.

It was an infinite relief to know that his Lord was equal to the emergency. When He commanded the unclean spirit to hold his peace and come out of this tormented nature, it could do no other than obey, though he convulsed his victim with malignant rage and cried again with a loud unearthly voice. The disciples shared in the general amazement, but they saw clearly the necessity of a new piece of spiritual equipment.

The scene in that synagogue gave Peter food for profound thought. He realized, as when a lightning flash illumines a midnight landscape, that there was a vast underworld of evil spirits. He realized also that these would be violently perturbed if any attempt was made to rescue their victims; that they were constrained to bear witness to His superlative holiness; that, however much they strived against it, they could not resist His power.

It was not difficult for Peter to understand the effect produced on them by the Lord's purity. He also had cried, only a few hours before, "Depart from me, for I am a sinful man, O Lord." But all his fear had passed, since he had yielded his will to obey, and had submitted to Christ's undisputed authority. The presence of Jesus for him now meant joy unspeakable and full of glory. Thus he was being prepared to hear the Master say: "Heal the sick, cleanse the lepers, raise the dead, *cast out demons*. Nothing shall by any means hurt you."

2. THE SECOND LESSON WAS THE NEED FOR GENTLENESS IN MINISTRY. Peter was strong, forceful, vehement. His touch was not gentle enough for straightening bruised reeds. A considerable amount of training would have to be expended on him before he could commend, as he does in his epistles, compassion, pity, and courtesy (1 Peter 2:3; 3:4, 8). The first lesson in this art was given in his own home.

After the amazing scene witnessed in the synagogue the Lord accepted the invitation of Peter and Andrew to come to the home, which they occupied in common, for rest and refreshment. James and John were included in the invitation. However, when the guests reached the door of the fishermen's home Peter's wife hurriedly whispered that her mother was down with "a great fever." She was lying on a couch in the inner chamber, with a dangerously high temperature. It was an unfortunate incident to occur on such a day! But inconvenient incidents, in the hand of Christ, become radiant memories.

"They told him of her." Luke says that "they besought him for her." But next to the marvel of her immediate recovery so that she was able to take her part in ministering, they wondered at the tender gentleness with which the Master took her by the hand and raised her up. How little he realized that years later he would do the same for a lame man on the temple steps, and for the beloved Dorcas at Joppa.

The world needs tenderness as well as strength. Probably strength is never perfected until it is tender. Christlike tenderness is needed to touch the bleared eye of the blind, the seared flesh of the leper, and the feverish hand of a fever-stricken mother. The child's hymn addressed to Jesus as the *tender* shepherd is exact in its epithet. Strong men must combine tenderness and strength.

3. THE THIRD LESSON WAS A GLIMPSE INTO THE ANGUISH OF THE WORLD. It had for long lain heavy on the Master's heart, and was constant incentive to the putting forth of the saving strength of His right hand. Nothing less could sustain His disciples, and especially Peter, in all future trials and disappointments. It was therefore arranged that the fronts should be taken off the households of this one city, that their compassion might be moved by the vision of the anguish of a single community. All who were diseased and possessed, together with their agonized friends, were gathered at sunset in the humble street where Peter lived. He could not have believed that so vast a mass of misery and pain was concealed so near his home; but it was easier to pass from that heartbreaking spectacle to plumb the fathomless anguish of the world. The veil was lifted for a few hours on that Sabbath evening while the stars came out one by one to watch sadly in heaven's vault. Behind doors and windows there is a heavy weight of pain; and we need to know that, as with our Lord, so with His servants, we may sigh as we look up, and say Ephphatha.

Whether it was a single leper or a crowd, He was always moved with compassion in the presence of human need. The broken heart breaks and heals hearts!

The greatest of soul winners in any age testified that he travailed in birth for his converts, and was willing to be accursed from Christ for his kinsmen according to the flesh. He preaches best who loves most. If we are content to labor without conversions, we need not expect any. But if our soul breaks with longing, the answer will not be long in coming. Give us Your tears, O Christ, as we behold the city!

4. THE FOURTH LESSON WAS AS TO THE SOURCE OF POWER. In the early morning the household sought for their beloved guest, but the chamber was empty. In vain they searched the house. Where was He? The inquiry and search became general. In a sheltered dimple of the hillside, the awe-struck search party beheld the Master's kneeling or prostrate form. He had risen long before daybreak and departed into a solitary place, where He prayed.

He could cast out demons and heal a crowd of sick people, but (speaking after the manner of men) he was conscious of the expenditure of spiritual force. "He perceived that virtue had gone out of him." His human nature required to be recharged. Better leave some of the city woe unremedied than forfeit that recharging.

Peter never forgot his Master's prayer habit, and he clearly determined to follow in those blessed footsteps. Pentecost came to him and the rest because they continued with one accord in prayer and supplication. The Sanhedrin was powerless to hurt because the whole company lifted up their voice to God with one accord. Prayer opened his way from his prison cell on the eve of execution. The vision of the Gentile world, cleansed and sanctified, was given as he prayed on the roof of the tanner's house.

Brothers and sisters, let us pray. John Wesley told his preachers that their prime business is to win souls, and he ended saying: "Why are we not more holy? Why do we not live for eternity and walk with God all the day long? Do we rise at four or five in the morning to be alone with God? Do we recommend and observe the five o'clock hour for prayer at the close of the day? Let us fulfill our ministry."

6

The Second Primer
Luke 4:1–13; John 6:1–21; Matt. 14:22–23

The divine Spirit is prepared to cooperate with any who will faithfully fulfill His conditions. The poor, the weak, the despised, the nobodies of this world, can command and enjoy the greatest manifestations of the divine energy equally with the cultured and refined. Indeed, the simple and childlike dispositions can often make most of God, because they are most lowly and helpless in their self-estimate.

It is therefore very necessary, not only for apostles, for us all, to learn the conditions on which spiritual power operates; and these are clearly set forth in the threefold temptation through which our Lord passed at the opening of His ministry. Let us adopt the order of the Third Gospel.

1. We must refuse to employ divine power for selfish uses.

2. True rulership is won by service, sacrifice, and suffering to death.

3. Divine power is granted, never for purposes of vainglory or ostentation, but for the help and blessing of others.

The statement of these three principles may vary, but their essence is as invariable as Newton's law of motion. By an evident prearrangement of divine providence they were all compressed into experiences narrated by all the evangelists, but especially in John 6.

1. TRUSTEESHIP FOR OTHERS DEPENDS ON THE DENIAL OF SELF. At the given time and place, the apostles gathered again with the Master to tell Him what things they had done and taught. Almost immediately on their return to Him the news reached them that John the Baptist—known, honored, and loved by them all—had been treacherously murdered by the royal command in the dungeons of the Castle of Machærus, on the edge of the eastern desert. It was clear that the tide of opposition was rising against the new movement. Wisdom suggested a temporary retirement from the public eye, and grief required seclusion in order to recover from the hurricane of desolation. "And he said unto them, Come ye yourselves apart into a desert [i.e., an uninhabited] place,

and rest awhile: for there were many coming and going, and they had no leisure so much as to eat" (Mark 6:31).

Entering the boat, they directed its course to the northeast corner of the lake, where the shore sloped up from the beach to a grassy plain of considerable expanse. The people had noticed the course taken by the boat and, hastening in a vast concourse around the head of the lake, presented an audience that appealed to Christ as the spectacle of a harried flock of sheep would appeal to the heart of a true shepherd.

"He was moved with compassion, and healed their sick." "He began to teach them many things." But the most astounding experience of any was that which closed the day. With five barley loaves and two small fishes, which Peter's brother, Andrew, had discovered in a basket of a small boy—who with great pride and love had surrendered them, and whose faith perhaps afforded our Lord the human element that He always required—Jesus fed the vast crowd. "They did all eat, and were filled: and they took up the fragments that remained, twelve baskets full."

Peter and the rest of the apostles must have been fairly staggered by that experience. They were confronted by the extraordinary contrast between their Master's poverty and His hospitality. They had heard, probably from His own lips, the story of His forty days' fast, when He was tempted to use His power to turn the stones of the desert into bread. Why had He not used it for His own need? Why had He not given them banquet upon banquet?

The paradox contained at its heart a vital truth. God will trust no one with His power who will use it for his own satisfaction and indulgence.

2. RULERSHIP DEPENDS ON SELF-GIVING. After the meal the crowd seems to have been swept by a sudden impulse to make Jesus their leader in a determined revolt against their Roman oppressors. Here was a greater than Judas Maccabæus! But He would have none of it. He had already fought this question out in the wilderness, when the devil had offered Him the kingdoms of this world and the glory of them. He did not swerve by a hairbreadth of deviation from that position. The kingdoms of this world could never become His by force of arms, but at the price of agony and bloody sweat, of the cross and passion and of the death on Calvary.

We note how precisely the Master carried out the original program formed as the Son of man on the threshold of His public career. What significance this lesson has for us all! It is by service such as the Moravians gave to lepers; by sufferings like those of the martyrs in every age, not least in our own; by the sacrifice of tears and blood, the kingdom comes and the Father's will is done.

3. DIVINE POWER MUST NEVER BE USED FOR PURPOSES OF VAINGLORY OR DISPLAY. It is supposed by some that our Lord had appointed His disciples to meet Him at some well-known part of the coast, and that this made them toil so hard at the oar when the storm suddenly hurled itself down on the lake. He saw them toiling in rowing, and about the fourth watch of the night—i.e., as the gray dawn began to spread through the story scene—"He went unto them, walking on the sea." So often the storms that threaten us are permitted that we may learn to appreciate more truly the wonderful resources of His nature.

But Peter was animated by the spirit of adventure. It was not in him to remain quietly seated with all the others in the boat until the Lord entered it.

He asked to be *commanded* to come to Him on the water; our Lord simply invited him to step out. He stepped forth, but his faith was imperfect, and he began to sink.

In the Lord's grave hour of temptation it had been suggested to Him that He should cast Himself down from the temple portico to the depths of the valley, treading the air as Peter now attempted to tread the water. He had refused to act on the suggestion because His Father had not so told Him to do this. But there was another moment afterward when He received from the Father the commandment to lay down His life, and descend the dark valley of shadow. As soon as He knew this to be His unmistakable duty, there was no hesitation; He became obedient to death, even the death of the cross. And the everlasting arms of the Father bore Him down in His descent, so that later He might ascend far above all heavens.

There might come times years later when in like manner the clear command would come to Peter to step out of the boat of ordinary experience on to the storm waves of persecution and martyrdom, but that hour had not yet come. His motives, which were now full of self-confidence, must become purified and clear. Then it would not be needful to await the command to step out, because his duty would be unmistakable.

He began to sink. Immediately the Lord stretched forth His hand and caught him, and they went together to the boat. No rebuke fell from those wise and gentle lips, except the question: "Wherefore didst thou doubt?" Obviously, one reason for his failure was that he watched the turbulence of the elements rather than the face and presence of his Lord. But there was a deeper reason for the failure. His faith was imperfect. There was a flaw in it. The slightest ingredient of pride invalidates faith's action. The step you are making, and which you think to be good and right, is likely to fail because, almost unconsciously, the element of pride, vainglory, boastfulness, or selfness is deteriorating your soul life. Get rid of it by the incessant reference to the cross. Say what our Lord said under similar suggestions: "Get thee hence, Satan . . . thou savourest not the things that be of God, but those that be of men."

Thus Peter learned the third lesson of his second primer; and it was with the undying impression of that hour that he wrote years later the notable advice: "Humble yourselves under the mighty hand of God, that he may exalt you" (1 Peter 5:6).

7

To Whom If Not to Christ?
John 6:22–71

When at last the crowds had dispersed, our Lord walked to the edge of the mountains, and began the ascent. His pulse quickened its beat, as ours does when we climb. The gathering storm reverberated through the funnels of the mountains and hurled itself on the lake. Did not that storm portend an ever greater one which, on the following day, was to break on the little band, who even then were fighting their way through the angry water?

A crisis was upon Him. He was becoming surrounded by a mixed crowd, who only desired to live on His bounty, and thought to exploit Him to gratify their wild passions for independence and revenge. He must clearly undeceive them, else they would wreck His great purpose of redemption and make Him the tool of a political party. Not a day could be lost. On the morrow He would make such statements of the spiritual nature of His kingdom as would effectually quench these incendiary sparks. Therefore, in fellow-ship with His Father, He gathered strength to free His followers of their earthbound views. He knew quite well how much it would cost, but there was no alternative.

The following morning, on the farther side, witnessed a renewal of the excitement of the preceding evening, so our Lord withdrew into the synagogue and delivered that marvelous discourse of John 6 which, were it not for the further disclosures of Calvary, would be the high water-mark of the New Testament. And it changed the whole tenor of His career.

In the evangelist's narrative we can detect the effect that our Lord's deeply spiritual words had on the crowded audience. In verse 41 they murmured at Him. In verse 52 they discussed among themselves. In verse 60 many, even His disciples, confessed aloud that His sayings were hard and difficult to understand. In verse 66 many of those who had bowed their allegiance renounced Him, and quietly withdrew. "They walked no more with him." By ones and twos, and then by groups, the crowd thinned away. First in order, the hot-headed politicians; then those who hoped for another meal; then the good-hearted but narrow-minded people who were shocked at His demand that they should eat His flesh and drink His blood which, even if it were taken spiritually, arrogated for the speaker the claims of deity. Finally, the synagogue was entirely emptied, except for the little group of aghast apostles who had been the sorrowful witnesses of the shattering of the Master's popularity and of the fabric of their private ambitions. It was then that He looked at them and put the question, "Will *ye* also go away?" which drew from Peter the unhesitating reply: "Lord, to whom shall we go? Thou hast the words of eternal life. And we believe and art sure that thou art the Son of the living God."

1. THE URGENCY OF THE QUESTION. To whom shall we go? The question presses on us, as on Peter. He knew that the soul of man must go somewhere. To whom else could he go?

To whom shall we go at this time of world weariness? To whom shall we go when our souls have suddenly awakened to the majesty of the eternal presence? To whom shall we go when in the light of the great white throne we suddenly find that snow water can never cleanse hearts and consciences, on which sin has laid its defiling hand? To whom shall we go when one by one the lights that we have trusted die out in the sky, and neither sun nor stars shine for many days. To whom shall we go in the loneliness of age, in the pains of mortal sickness, in the hour of death, in the day of account, amid the splendor of a holiness that angels cannot face, and a purity before which the heavens are not clean?

2. THE ALTERNATIVES TO CHRIST. Let us understand clearly what we want. We want life, eternal life.

Shall we go to the sceptic? He will deride our demands as the phantasms of dis-ordered minds. It is as though we were to assure a hungry man that the sense of hunger was an absurd mistake.

Shall we go to the ritualist? He will offer us rites which, though fragrant with all that satisfies our sense of beauty or gratifies our reverence for the past, are inadequate to quench the soul's passion for the living God and allay the fever of remorse.

Shall we go to the great religions of the East? Has Confucious, or Buddha, or Mohammed, or the ancient Vedas, a medicine for the soul, that has seen in Christ the Holy One of God, and in whom the Spirit of Christ has started infinite desires for assured forgiveness, for acceptance with God?

Try every door! Each opens on despair. There is no satisfaction but in Christ.

3. THE IMPERISHABLE SUPREMACY OF JESUS. What are the grounds of His imperishable supremacy?

a. *Though all-holy, He satisfactorily deals with the grave question of sin.* Sin is a terrible reality to the awakened soul. It has extorted from the saintliest books of bitter confession. It has been the energizing cause of religious movements that have moved the world. We have sought to ignore and stifle it. We have suggested palliatives. Jesus alone has put sin away, has satisfied the sense of justice and the plea for mercy, and has supplied from His blood and righteousness the one all-satisfying answer to the inquiry, "Can God forgive me righteously?"

b. *Though man in His incarnation, He communicates and is the bread of God.* We know that bread nourishes us. No amount of argument or chemical demonstration could make us more sure than we are. So with our Lord. We know and are sure, because we have handled, tasted, and felt. The deep of our nature finds a response in the deep of His. He satisfies. Oh, my heart, with your heights and depths, and insatiable longings, you have found more than your match in Jesus! To whom else can you go?

8

"I Give Unto Thee the Keys"
Matt. 16:13–20

For two years and a half our Lord had lived among His apostles. Only six months of education remained before He was taken from them—a period during which His teaching must become much more intensive; and as a preliminary it was necessary to ascertain what conclusions they had arrived at as the result of their observations and experiences. If, notwithstanding His reticence, they had discovered His intrinsic glory, "the glory of the only begotten of the Father," it would serve as the common platform from which to ascend to higher revelations. But if not, it would be clear that He must go elsewhere for the heralds of His gospel and the foundation stones of His church.

In order to secure the necessary privacy for this all-important inquiry, our Lord journeyed to the extreme edge of the northern frontier of Palestine, where Mount Hermon lifts its mighty mass beyond the snow-line. The Jordan issues from one of the cliffs near the ancient town of Banias, known at that time as Cæsarea Philippi. This was the setting of the memorable conversation which more than any of our Lord's discourses has affected the life of Christendom.

1. THE MASTER'S SEARCHING QUESTION. "Whom do men say that I the Son of man am?" The answers were various. It was universally acknowledged that He was no ordinary man. But their views were as various as the speakers. Some, with Herod at their head, expressed the belief—not without a shudder—that the Baptist had risen

from his lonely grave beside the Castle of Machærus. Others said that Elijah, whom Malachi had taught them to expect, had come to them in the "day of the Lord." Others traced a resemblance between Jesus and one of the old prophets. But these inquiries were only intended to lead up to the second and all-important question: "But whom say ye that I am?"

The reply came instantly, emphatically, and decisively from the lips of Peter, always the spokesman for the rest: "Thou art the Christ, the Son of the living God." In a most significant manner it combined the hope of the Jew for the Anointed One, with the recognition of the unique and essential nature of our Lord, as the only begotten of the eternal God. It filled the heart of Jesus with ecstasy. "Blessed art thou, Simon Bar-Jona [son of Jonas or John]: for flesh and blood hath not revealed it unto thee, but my Father which is in heaven."

2. THE FOUNDATION OF THE CHURCH. Then for the first time our Lord spoke of His church. Notice the strong possessive pronoun "my." *My* church! From eternity Christ loved her. By His blood He redeemed her. Through His Spirit and by His Word He is cleansing her; and one day He will present her to Himself a glorious church, "having neither spot, nor wrinkle, nor any such thing."

The church is the special object of hatred to the dark underworld of fallen spirits, whom our Lord refers to as "the gates of hell." Long and sore the conflict may be, but the issue is not doubtful. *"They shall not prevail."* There will break on the ear of a startled world the voice of a great multitude, as they announce—first that the church has emerged victorious; and second, that the marriage of the Lamb has come, and His Bride has made herself ready. Her foundation doctrine is the deity of our Lord, as "the Son of the everliving God." The Greek phrasing of our Lord's reply leaves no doubt as to His meaning. Two Greek words are here. *Petros,* Simon's new name, signifying in Greek, as Cephas did in Syriac, a stone, or bit of rock, broken or hewn from its parent bed; and *petra,* the rock-bed itself. Our Lord carefully makes the distinction. If He had intended Peter to be the foundation of the church, He would naturally have shaped His sentence thus: "Thou art Peter, and on *thee* I will build my church." But carefully selecting His words, He said: "Thou art Peter, a stone, a fragment of rock, who under the power of God's Spirit hast spoken with strength and certainty; but I cannot build on thee, for the foundation of my church I must turn from *petros* to *petra,* from a fragment to the great truth, which for the moment has inspired thee. The truth of My eternal relationship to the Father is the only foundation, against which the waves of demon and human hatred will break in vain. No stone shall give. No bastion shall even rock."

3. THE GIFT OF THE KEYS. It must be carefully noted that our Lord used the same words that He addressed to Peter also to individual believers in Matthew 18:18, and again to His assembled apostles *and others* who were gathered with them in the Upper Room on the evening of the Resurrection Day. (See Luke 24:33, and John 20:22 and 23.)

In the light afforded by these references we may extend the significance of this gift of the keys to include all who live and act in the power of the Holy Spirit. If we have received that blessed gift of the Comforter, as they did on whom the Master breathed that Easter evening, we also may wield the power of the keys that will open closed doors, and emancipate prisoners from their cells.

This is the secret of the quest of the blessed life. Go through the world opening prison doors, lifting heavy burdens, giving light, and joy, and peace to the oppressed, proclaiming the Lord's Jubilee year. Close doors opening out on the dark waters of despair. Unlock and open those that face toward the sunrise, for this is a work that angels might envy. "Receive ye the Holy Ghost."

9

"With Him on the Holy Mount"
Matt. 17:1–9; 2 Peter 1:16–18

On the afternoon of the last day of our Lord's sojourn at Cæsarea Philippi He proposed to His three chief apostles that they should accompany Him for a season of retirement to the upper slopes of Hermon. In his last days Peter referred to it as affording the outstanding evidence of his Master's divine nature and mission. For him it was "the Holy Mount," where he and the others had been eyewitnesses of Christ's majesty, when He received from the Father honor and glory. There could be no doubt about it. They had not followed nor promulgated cunningly devised fables!

1. THE ACCESSORIES OF THE TRANSFIGURATION.

a. *The place was clearly Mount Hermon.* The previous days had been spent at its foot. Mount Tabor, which formerly was supposed to have been the chosen spot for this sublime spectacle, was at that time the site of a Roman fort and garrison, which would have been totally incongruous with the mystic beauty of heavenly glory. And the vivid comparison, in Peter's special Gospel of Mark, between the Master's appearance and the snow, is an additional confirmation that Mount Hermon's snow-capped heights were in his thought. Here only in Palestine is there the permanent presence of snow.

b. *The time was almost certainly the night.* Our Lord was accustomed to spend nights on the mountains. The overpowering sleep that mastered the apostles, until the transfiguration glory was on the point of passing, also suggests the night season. The background of the night afforded additional beauty and luster to the radiant glory that enwrapped the person and garments of the Lord.

c. *It is noticeable that the glory passed on Him as He prayed.* The glory that the disciples beheld—which streamed through His garments, so that His ordinary dress became shining, exceeding white as snow—was the shining from within of the glory of the only begotten of the Father.

d. *The appearance of Moses and Elijah added greatly to the impressiveness of the spectacle.* They were the representative leaders of the Hebrew theocracy. Moses was the embodiment of the law, Elijah of the prophets. Their advent, was due to the special encouragement they were able to afford the Redeemer at this great crisis.

Only a few days before our Lord had unfolded, with graphic minuteness, the scenes of His approaching death. Peter, speaking for the rest, had immediately sought to dissuade Him. "Be it far from thee, Lord," he said; "this shall not be unto thee." They were not able to understand or sympathize. It was necessary, therefore, that redeemed humanity should furnish two of its strongest and noblest ambassadors to reinforce and strengthen our Lord, on the human side, before He set His face steadfastly to go up to Jerusalem to die.

2. THE THEME OF THE CELESTIAL VISITANTS. "They spake of his *decease* which he should accomplish at Jerusalem" (Luke 9:31). The Greek word is "exodus"—a term that struck Peter's imagination. Years later he used it of his own death (2 Peter 1:14).

It must have been a startling rebuke to Peter and his companions. To them the death of the cross seemed as unthinkable as it appeared unnecessary. But now, to their surprise, they discovered that heaven could speak of nothing else! It was apparently the one subject about which Moses and Elijah cared to speak. As soon as the opportunity presented intercourse with Jesus, they fell to talking on it.

Moses would speak of the Passover Lamb, the slaying of which preceding the Exodus by which his people passed to liberty, and would assure our Lord that His death would mean emancipation and victory, when the ransomed hosts of the redeemed would sing the song of Moses and the Lamb.

Elijah would remind Him that the spirit of prophecy was testimony, and that it was written in the prophets and the psalms that the Christ should suffer and should enter into His glory.

Moses would testify that each victim that had bled on the altars of Israel had no intrinsic virtue to put away sin; and that if He were now to fail, all their suffering would be worthless, and that the redemption that the saints were already enjoying must be revoked.

Elijah would assure Him that on the other side of the Jordan of death, the strong waters of which He would cleave as He passed, the chariot of the ascension cloud awaited Him.

Clearly, the death of the Cross, which our Lord saw awaiting Him on the horizon, is the theme of eternity. Can we wonder at the intense interest with which the great cloud of witnesses watched the Savior, as (so to speak) He stepped into the stadium to run the last lap in the great race, to fight the last fight in the stupendous struggle? The battlements of the Holy City were crowded with awestruck crowds, until the ascension hour called them to follow in the glad procession of the Victor.

3. THE ENFOLDING CLOUD. Peter had made a suggestion that was as ill-considered as it was hasty. In his account of this scene, communicated through Mark, he admits that he did not know what he was saying. It was the suggestion that our Lord should disregard the claims of the lost world, and spend His remaining years in a tabernacle on the mountain top, instead of coping with such scenes as that which awaited at the foot of the mountain! Peter had much to learn.

While he was speaking he and his fellow apostles beheld a cloud descending, which enveloped the radiant vision. They feared as they saw their Master and His celestial visitors cut off from them and hidden in the brightness of that mist of glory. It was no ordinary cloud, but was probably the Shekinah cloud that led the wilderness march, that filled Solomon's temple on its dedication, and that formed the Lord's ascension chariot. From its heart the voice of the eternal God was heard, bearing sublime witness to the Savior as the beloved Son, and demanding homage from all.

What might have been! As the sinless Man, the Second Adam need not have died. In a moment, in the twinkling of an eye, He might have passed with Moses and Elijah, through the open door of paradise. Such a translation might have been possible; but if, at any moment, it was presented to His mind, He thrust it away. For the joy that was set before Him—or instead of the joy set before Him—He turned his back on paradise for

Himself, that He might open paradise for the dying thief and for us. And when the cloud had passed, He was left alone with his apostles, and took the straight road to Calvary.

10

"For Me and Thee"
Matt. 17:24–27

The Master was on His way to Jerusalem. Capernaum, with Peter's home as the resting place, offered a convenient place to stop. But evidently its inhabitants were animated by a very different spirit from that of the earlier days of His blessed ministry. The streets were no longer crowded by sick people waiting for His healing touch; nor was the synagogue open to His ministry. The seeds of jealousy and suspicion that the Pharisees had sown with such lavish eagerness had produced a harvest of tares. The atmosphere was laden with the blight of mistrust. Faces were averted that used to smile.

One symptom of this changed attitude presented itself almost immediately on His arrival. The collectors of the temple tax, which was a voluntary levy on all Jews, encountered Peter with the challenge, "Doth not your Master pay the tribute?" This tax was of very ancient origin, dating from the days of Moses, and supplied the funds required for the maintenance of the temple services. Religious teachers, such as rabbis, were exempted from the payment of the temple tax by general consent; and the universal respect that was paid our Lord in the earlier days of His ministry gave Him complete immunity from any question as to His liability to pay it. But now that He had lost caste and was being hunted down by Herod and the rulers, Peter, as His representative, was accosted with a challenge that proved that the cordon of respect and reverence that had formerly surrounded Him was broken down.

Peter said at once that his Master would certainly pay the tribute; but when he reached the home he learned that Jesus knew all about the demand, for he was anticipated in his story by the question whether it was customary for kings to demand tribute from their sons.

This brief conversation made it clear that our Lord had noticed the change in the treatment that He might from now on expect, but He had no intention of standing on His rights. Lest the most scrupulous conscience should be offended, He declared that He was willing to meet the demand for them both.

1. CHRIST PAYS THE CHARGES FOR HIS PENNILESS DISCIPLES. At His bidding Peter had left all to follow Him. Boats, nets, and the fish market were forsaken. If Peter still kept his boat, it was only to assist his Master in His strenuous life. No income, therefore, accrued from his craft for the upkeep of his home; and without doubt the Master arranged that a certain amount should be allocated from the common purse for the maintenance of that home and its tenants.

The two women—Peter's wife and her mother—may have viewed this arrangement at first with a certain amount of distrust, and during the absence of the whole party thirty miles to the north their faith must have been put to the test, for clearly, on Peter's arrival home, there was not a single coin left to meet this tax.

Peter rightly felt that this burden was not for himself to carry alone. By his summons to leave all, his Master had clearly made Himself liable for such demands. It was an immense relief, therefore, to find himself anticipated before he could relate his case—Christ knew of it and was prepared with a reply.

With what awe Peter must have taken his disused fishing line from the nail and gone forth on the lake, wondering where to cast his hook, but sure that in the water some fish was being guided through "the path of the sea" toward him. The fish had earlier caught at a glittering coin, dropped by a passenger or a child over a boatside. It had carried its unwelcome burden until it was able to disgorge it into Peter's wondering hands. If not by such a miracle, yet somehow the Lord will always meet the need of His devoted servants. No one who trusts in Him will be desolate.

2. Our Master links Himself to a sinful man. "That take, and give unto them for me and thee." It should be noted that the fish yielded not two half-shekels, but one coin—the stater—which was their equivalent. The conjunction "and" should be noted also, as the golden link between the Savior and His weak and fallible disciple. This surely is the wonder of eternity—that He should call us brothers and sisters. He says, "This is for me and thee."

Thus He links Himself to a sinful man, and who shall separate what God has joined together? Neither life nor death, things present or to come, can snap that link.

3. Christ makes mortals His almoners. "Take and give for me and thee." He requires almoners to distribute to the crowd, as of old His apostles took from His hands the bread and fish, and gave to the five thousand men, together with women and children.

The tragic failure of innumerable multitudes is that they have not learned to take. They pray, and pray fervently, but they have not acquired the art of taking or receiving. Our Lord said, "All things whatsoever ye pray and ask for, believe that you have *taken* them, you shall have them." The apostle does not bid us *pray* for the abundance of grace, but calls on us to *take* it.

With many taking is a lost art. They pray, but fail to take. Herein is the source of bitter disappointment. We pray, agonize, and strive, but often fail to see that the cargo has already been delivered on the wharf, and is in the depôt, waiting to be claimed and carried away. We must be sure that we are not prompted by personal ambition, but are acting in the name (i.e., according to the nature) of our Lord, and are standing on the distinct warrant of a promise. When these conditions are fulfilled, we hear our Father's voice saying: "Child, you are ever with Me, and all that I have is yours; take, and go your way to give." We may not *feel* to have received. Ours is the reckoning of a naked faith on the unfailing faithfulness of God.

We cannot give unless we have learned to take; and we cannot take unless we are prepared to give. Let us go forth to give. There are aching hearts, marred lives, mute, outstretched, open hands on all sides. Let us be channels through whom God may answer prayers and almoners, to whom He will be able to make all grace abound. He will feed the stream from inexhaustible fountains. He will minister seed for sowing, and will provide bread for the sower. Therefore, "Take and give."

11

The Shepherd on the Watch
Matt. 18:1–22; 19:23–30; 21:18–22

In his high-priestly prayer recorded in John 17, our Lord, speaking specially of His apostles, said: "While I was with them in the world, I kept them in thy name: those that Thou gavest me I have kept, and none of them is lost, but the son of perdition" (v. 12). In this allusion to His keeping we have a glimpse into the cure of souls, in which the Master was and is constantly engaged. He was no hireling. When He saw the stealthy approach of the wolf, so far from fleecing, He went before the little flock (as He called the apostolic band) and encountered the foe. He knew that the shepherd would be smitten, and the sheep scattered; but He never ceased from warning them. He saw that Satan had desired to sift them as wheat and had obtained his desire, and He had especially prayed for the one whose temperament might belie him into momentary denial, but whose love He never doubted, and whose dementing agony of soul He foresaw.

We must never forget that our Lord dealt with His apostles, not only in a group, but as individuals; that He studied their idiosyncrasies, and administered special correction or instruction as each required.

It would appear that Judas and Peter gave Him most concern. The one because his nature was so secretive and subtle, the other because his fervid and impulsive temperament was constantly hurrying him into extreme positions, from which he needed to be extricated. At one moment he would say, "Depart from me"; at the next he would leave all to follow. Now he has won the high praise, "Blessed art thou"; and again he is addressed as Satan. In the same breath, "Thou shalt never wash my feet," and "not my feet only." Within a single hour he is ready to fight for the Master, whom he passionately loved, but also denies that he had ever known Him. Jesus never doubted the sincerity of his affection, but was sorely tried by its fitful and impulsive exhibitions.

There were several particulars in Peter's life to which he needed to be especially cautioned and strengthened:

1. IN THE STRUGGLE OF PREEMINENCE. Though Peter is not especially mentioned, we are not doing him an injustice to suppose that he took a prominent part in the hot disputes that broke out from time to time, especially after our Lord's award of the keys, the reference to the significance of his name, and his inclusion with two others in that memorable transfiguration scene. When our Lord reached Capernaum, on His return from Mount Hermon, on entering "the house" which, of course, was Peter's, He asked them, "What was it that ye disputed among yourselves by the way?" (Mark 9:33). At first they held their peace, for along the way they had argued among themselves as to who should be the greatest. Then He sat down, and called them around Him, and said: "The only way in which a man can become first in My kingdom is by being last of all and servant of all." Then He took a child—tradition says that it was one of Peter's own children, who afterward became the Bishop and Martyr Ignatius—folded the happy boy in His arms, and said: "Whoso shall receive one such little child in my name receiveth me."

This ambition first of all probably led Peter to insist that though all the others failed and forsook in the approaching hour of trial, certainly he might be counted on, though all men shall be offended because of thee, yet will I never be offended." And he meant every word he spoke.

Nothing could so effectually have burned out this love of preeminence as the denial and failure of the betrayal night. We find no traces of the old spirit in the subsequent references to our apostle. He takes the foremost place in the incidents related in Acts 1 and 2 without ostentation or affectation; but in the first council of the church, described in Acts 15, the presidency is occupied by James, while Peter contributes his opinion, as one among the rest.

2. IN RESPECT TO FORGIVENESS. On one occasion, when the Lord had been giving instruction on the duty of forgiveness, Peter broke in with the inquiry, "Lord, how oft shall my brother sin against me, and I forgive him?" and further suggested that seven times was the limit that he could not be expected to exceed. Our Lord swept away the suggestion as unthinkable. Calvary and Pentecost would open sluice gates of unlimited mercy. "Jesus saith unto him, I say not unto thee, Until seven times: but until seventy times seven."

May we not imagine Peter hurrying through the streets, on which the gray dawn was breaking sadly, and making for the garden, where only three or four hours before he had slept while his Master was in agony. How could he have said those terrible words? That he had failed where he had vowed to be strong, and had added oaths and cursings that had not soiled his lips for many years! That the Master had heard all! And that look! What could he say, or where could he go? Should he take his life? Remorse was choking his breath. Then there stole over his heart the words: "I say not unto thee, Until seven times: but Until seventy times seven." Did He not say that the lord of the servant was moved with compassion, released the poor debtor at his feet, and forgave a debt of ten thousand talents? Surely He must have meant *me!*

3. IN THE MATTER OF REWARD. When the young man, unable to pay the price of discipleship, had turned sorrowfully away, Peter broke in on the Savior's disappointment with the question: "Lo! we have left all, and have followed thee, what shall we have therefore?" Clearly the hope of reward was looming large on his vision. But bargain making after this fashion was clearly inadmissible in the kingdom of heaven, and therefore the parable of the laborers in the vineyard was uttered to teach that in the service of God a spirit of trust in His grace must eradicate and supersede a spirit of bargaining and barter.

The laborers had waited in the market place from early dawn. "No man had hired them." It was not until almost sundown that they had their chance. But when, after one brief hour they came to be paid, they received a whole day's pay for that brief spell. It was in happy mood that these "short-term" workers went home. Yes! What the owner of the vineyard had been heard saying to one of the grumblers, "Is thine eye evil, because I am good," was perfectly true—he *was* good.

It was as if our Lord had said, in answer to Peter's question: "It is true that you came early into the vineyard. You were among the first. But when you completed the task, you will only have done your duty, and your reward will be according to the riches of God's grace."

This also in coming days may have afforded the broken-hearted apostle some comfort, as he said to himself: "The Master said that the reward was not determined by service, but by grace. God be merciful to me the sinner, and in me first may the Master show all longsuffering."

4. IN REGARD TO FAITH. As Jesus and His disciples passed by one morning they saw a withered fig tree that had been cursed with barrenness on the previous day, as a warning to the apostles and to Israel. And Peter said to Jesus, "Master, behold, the fig tree which thou cursedst is withered away." And Jesus said to them, "Have faith in God." A better rendering of that remarkable injunction would be, "Hold on to God's faith;" or, "Trust in God's faithfulness."

We lay stress, and rightly so, on faith; but there are days in human life when our faith seems about to expire, like a tiny flame in a storm of wind. Then it is a source of infinite consolation to turn our thoughts away from our faith to God's faithfulness, to hold on to it, to reckon on it, and to cry: "If we do not believe, He abides faithful; He cannot deny Himself."

In that storm burst that broke on Peter's soul on that fateful night, with what comfort must he have rested on these precious words: "Hold on to God's faith; trust in God's faithfulness." His own faith had failed, but God's faithfulness was like the great mountains.

12

The Evening of the Denial
Matt. 26:17–20; Mark 14:12–17; Luke 22:7–16; John 13:1–20

The Mount of Olives, during the Passover, was covered by a large number of families, gathered from all parts of the country, and from many lands. Unable to find accommodation in the overcrowded city, they provided for themselves slight booths or tents, their cattle tethered alongside.

It would be pleasant to think that our Lord was the guest of the home at Bethany where Lazarus and his sisters loved to welcome Him; but it is more than likely that, after the supper in the house of Simon on the evening of his arrival, He deliberately stayed aloof, lest His friends might become entangled in the web that was being woven about Him. Already the chief priests were consulting to put Lazarus to death, because by reason of him many of the Jews believed on Jesus.

It is with Peter's share in the happenings of the last evening of Christ's earthly life that we are now dealing. Jesus knew that the hour had come when He should depart this world to the Father. It is practically certain, therefore, that He was more concerned for "his own," and especially for Peter, than for Himself. Hence the following precautions:

1. HE PROVIDED HIM WITH A FRIEND. The priceless worth of friendship was a matter of daily experience with the Lord. He made no secret of the tender intimacy that knit His soul with that of the disciple whom He loved, and who, more than any other, has interpreted to the world the secret workings of His heart. He realized therefore how much a friend of the right king would mean for Peter in his abandonment to a remorse that threatened despair.

Jesus could trust John utterly. The ultimate proof of His confidence was given when, from the cross, He committed His mother to the filial care of His beloved friend. Thus He knew what John would be to Peter in the hour of black darkness, and therefore threw them together in His last sacred commission. We are expressly told that He sent Peter and John, saying, "Go and prepare us the Passover, that we may eat." Thus He set His seal on their long friendship. They had been attracted to each other by an instinctive consciousness that each supplied what the other lacked. It is more than probable that each chose the other as companion when the twelve were sent out two by two. Our Lord had often noticed and rejoiced in this congenial comradeship. He therefore took special pains to cement and hallow it by this expression of confidence.

The result justified His fond anticipations. It was to John that Peter naturally turned when the storm was expending its full fury on his soul. Mary of Magdala found them together on Easter morning. Together they ran to the sepulcher. Much as John loved his friend, he could not help outrunning him, because of another love that had a prior claim, but he compensated for it shortly afterward by refusing to take advantage of the keener sight of his younger eyes that had discerned the Lord standing on the shore in the morning haze. In a whisper of reverent love he passed on the news to his friend, and was only glad to know, as he saw him plunge into the water and head swiftly to shore, that he had secured for him a moment of private fellowship and a further assurance of forgiveness from those gentle lips.

They were much together in the coming days. They went together to the temple at the hour of prayer. Peter spoke for them both when he said to the lame man, "Look on us." They stood side by side when arrested by the Sanhedrin, and spent a memorable night together in the prison. Together they returned to their own company, and like the diverse metals of a compensating balance, they directed the policy of the infant church. Events separated them in later years—John to Ephesus and Peter to Babylon—but that the old love remained is evident, if the slight and tender reference that John makes to the lapse of his friend is contrasted with the explicit and circumstantial account that Peter gives in the second Gospel.

2. HE ASSURED HIM OF A COMPLETE CLEANSING. Our Lord desired to eat that Supper with the chosen band before He suffered. It would be for His own comfort and strength, and for theirs. He therefore committed the necessary preparations to His two devoted friends. They secured the lamb, brought it early to the priest for killing, purchased the bitter herbs, passover cakes, and skin of wine, and hastened back to prepare the humble meal.

The city was too preoccupied and crowded to notice the famous Teacher and His companions as they passed through the Kedron gate and made for the appointed meeting place. The sky was already darkening, and the earlier stars were beginning to appear. Apparently the embers of jealous rivalry were still smoldering, and burst into a flame as soon as the large upper room, where Peter and John had been at work all the afternoon, was reached. The walk had been hot and dusty, and all would have been thankful for the customary ablutions, common to every Jewish home. In this case, however, they were wanting. Ewer, basin, and towel were provided, but no servant could be spared from the household at that busy season. Would no apostle perform this office for the rest, and especially for the Lord? Apparently none volunteered. To undertake menial duty would be equivalent to signing a deed of abdication from the throne of power, which each was claiming. There was also the question of precedence at the table to be considered. Even if the couch on the Lord's right hand was conceded to John, who should be on His left? Ought not Peter, to whom all were indebted for his efforts to prepare the feast? But Judas insisted as treasurer, on his superior claims. To arrest further discussion the Lord arose from the supper table, laid aside His outer garments, girded Himself with the towel, poured water into the basin, and began to wash His disciples' feet, wiping them carefully with the towel.

A sudden silence must have befallen them as He passed from one to another in this lowly ministry, until He came to Peter, who had been watching the process with shame and indignation. "Dost thou wash my feet?" he exclaimed; "thou shalt never wash my feet." "If I wash thee not, thou hast no part with me!" Evidently Peter caught his Master's meaning. The outward was symbolic of the inward, the physical of the spiritual; and he replied: "Lord, not my feet only, but also my hands and my head."

It was as though he requested that his entire being might be plunged into the fountain opened for sin and uncleanness. "Make sure work this time, my Lord; let me begin again, as I began at the first, with Thee in my boat!"

"No," said Jesus in effect, "that is not necessary. He who has recently bathed does not require entire immersion, if hands or feet are dirty. It is sufficient for the soiled member to be cleansed, and the body is all clean. It is enough if the particular sin is confessed and put away. Whenever that confession is made I will show Myself faithful and just to forgive the sin and cleanse from all unrighteousness."

There was therefore a double significance in our Lord's lowly act of feetwashing. He taught the royalty of service, and also that sin does not sever the regenerate soul from God. There must be confession, and there will be instant restoration.

What a wealth of comfort has been ministered by this lowly act of the Savior to those whose feet have become soiled by the dust of earth's highways! He knew that He had come from God, was going to God, and was God; but to wash the feet of these simple men did not seem incongruous with the throne to which He went. And now that He, as the Lamb slain, is on the throne, He will turn aside from the adoration of eternity, and "stay His ear for every sigh a contrite suppliant brings."

13

"Let Not Your Heart Be Troubled"
Matt. 26:21–25, 31–35; Luke 20:21–23; John 13:21–38, 14:1–2

On the appearance of the first three stars, a blast from the silver trumpets of the temple gave the signal for the Passover supper to begin in all parts of the city. On the table were the bread, wine, water and herbs; on the side table the roasted lamb. The swinging lamps were aglow above, and below, around the table, were the thirteen couches. Everything bespoke the preparation of the two apostles. For hundreds of years the same customs had been followed, the same explanations given, the same psalms sung, the same blessings and thanksgivings pronounced. But the apostles were conscious that a heavy cloud was on the Master's soul, to which He presently gave the clue when He said: "Verily I say unto you, that one of you shall betray me. It had been better for that man if he had not been born."

Each disciple, except Judas, seems to have suspected himself more than any of the others, and said distrustfully: "Lord, is it I?" But Peter, impatient of the uncertainty, made a secret sign to John to figure out to whom the Lord referred. In a whisper, as he leaned back on the Savior's bosom, John asked who the traitor would be. Jesus did not wish to utter his name, and replied, again in an undertone, which probably only Peter, John, and Judas caught: "He it is, to whom I shall give the sop when I have dipped it." Then placing some bitter herbs between slices of bread, He dipped the morsel into a special bowl of mixed fruits called "Charosheth," and passed it to Judas. The traitor then knew that the Master knew; but with brazen effrontery, he said: "Lord, is it I?" Under His breath our Lord replied: "It is as thou hast said"; and then louder, so that everyone around the table heard Him, "That thou doest, do quickly."

The traitor could no longer bear the white light of Christ's holy presence. Hastily wrapping his cloak around him, he went out into the night; but the revealing words had been spoken so gently that only Peter and John were in the secret. So well had Judas played his part, that the rest supposed that the Lord had commissioned him to buy some additional article for the feast, or that he had gone out to make some offering to the poor.

His absence was a great relief to Jesus. "Therefore, when he was gone out, Jesus said. . . ." And He poured forth a volume of golden speech for the warning and comfort of the immediate circle of "His own," and through them of the universal church. We must especially concentrate on the words addressed to Peter:

1. "LET NOT YOUR HEART BE TROUBLED!" "I HAVE PRAYED FOR THEE." Years later Peter must have had in mind the Master's warning, "Simon, Simon, behold, Satan hath desired to have you that he may sift you as wheat: but I have prayed for thee, that thy faith may fail not."

There is no fear for the wheat, when the husbandman, in Oriental fashion, throws up the grain that he has threshed against the evening breeze. Its weight brings it back to the floor, and only the chaff disappears. It is a distinct advantage to be rid of the encumbering chaff, as it is for the church to be freed from the presence of those who are not truly one with it.

None of the apostles were lost except Judas. They were proved to be wheat. Though they forsook the Master at first, they were all assembled in the upper room on the resurrection night, although the doors were shut for fear of the Jews. They all gathered around the Master on the mount of ascension. It is said that each, excepting John, went to heaven in a martyr's chariot of fire. And the name of each is inscribed on the foundations of the Holy City, the bride of the Lamb.

In the meanwhile the Savior's phrasing is full of comfort. Greater is He who is for us than all who are against us, and the Great High Priest, who is pledged to present us before the Father's presence with exceeding joy, is on the watch, measuring the fiery ordeal to our strength and praying that our faith may not fail. Is it not well that we have been tempted? Temptation reveals our own weakness and drives us in penitence and faith to Christ. We cannot help being tempted. There is no sin in being attacked by the evil one. Our Lord Himself suffered being tempted. All through the conflict we are conscious of our Savior's intercessions. "Thanks be to God, which giveth the victory through our Lord Jesus Christ" (1 Cor. 15:57).

2. "LET NOT YOUR HEARTS BE TROUBLED!" "I GO TO PREPARE A PLACE." The unfortunate

division of chapters has hindered the full appreciation of Christ's special reference in the memorable words with which John 14 opens. We love them, learn them, repeat them; but we fail to connect them with the words immediately preceding: "Peter said unto Him, Lord, why cannot I follow thee now? I will lay down my life for thy sake. Jesus answered him, Wilt thou lay down thy life for my sake? Verily, verily, I say unto thee, The cock shall not crow, till thou hast denied me thrice." *Then* He said, "Let not your heart be troubled . . . In my Father's house are many mansions. . . . I go to prepare a place for you."

The Father's House is the place where broken lives are received to be remade and refitted. Life becomes rhythmic to the music of eternity, and joy has no bounds. They who live there are ever face to face with God, and all that He has is theirs.

There also are "many mansions," which suggest not only spaciousness, but room for each character and individual to develop on its own particular lines. As the gardner "beds out" the crowded plants of his hothouse, so will the saints have room to be themselves, and each will have love enough, joy enough, space enough, opportunity enough together with his own share of fullness and service of Christ. Peter will still be Peter, and John, John. Each star will differ from all the rest. There will be many mansions, and no need to scramble or contend for room.

The significance of our Lord's promise is clearly defined when we remember that He had predicted, only a few minutes before, that we should deny and forsake all. "I go to prepare a place for you"—for you, My beloved John; for you, Peter, when the memory of your denial shall be as waters that pass away; for you, Thomas, though given to doubt and pessimism; for you, Philip, longing to be shown the Father. "Let not your heart be troubled . . . neither let it be afraid." Surely we may take courage, if only we are trusting Him for His justifying grace. In spite of our sins and failures, our sorrows and temptations, He will bring us through.

3. "Let not your heart be troubled!" "I will receive you unto myself." It was as though the Master particularized each as He spoke: *"James!* you will be the first of the noble army of martyrs. Herod will slay you with the sword, but you will have a royal reception. *Thomas!* you will be sawn in two, but I will receive you, and an abundant entrance will be given. *John!* you will linger on until all of your generation shall have passed away, but I will be waiting for you, and you will see again the dear faces that you have loved and lost awhile. *Peter!* you will stretch forth your hands and be borne to a cross, but as My Father will receive My Spirit into His hands, so My hands shall receive yours. Each of you will find Me waiting for him on the doorstep of the Father's house."

You believe that you are sons of God, that you will enter into His Presence, that you will sit down with Abraham, Isaac, and Jacob—continue to believe. If it were not so, I would have told you. Let not your heart be troubled, neither let it be afraid!"

14

". . . and Peter"
Matt. 28:1–8; Mark 16:1–8; Luke 24:1–8; John 20:1–10

Matthew records the angel's words to the women at the tomb thus: "Go quickly, and tell his disciples," but Mark makes the significant addition, "and Peter." With the others, those words might be obliterated by tides of times and change, but they were engraven on the rock of Peter's character and inlet with gold.

In the Song of Solomon three traits are assigned to a perfect love, and each of these was notably present in our Lord's remarkable treatment of His apostle and friend, who had been warned three times, had denied Him three times, and on three different occasions was restored.

1. LOVE IS STRONG AS DEATH. Much had happened to our Lord since that hour in the judgment hall when He turned and looked on Peter. But His love was unimpaired. Neither death nor the grave had made any change in it. Peter's case had been on His heart when He closed His eyes in death, and it was present to Him when He stopped for a moment to speak with the angel sentinel, whom He charged with this message.

The first words of the risen Savior proved that His love is strong as death. Having loved His own, who were in the world, He loved them to the end. His love is strong as well as tender. He is immortal love, but He is the strong Son of God.

What death and the grave could not do, the lapse of time and the glories of heaven have not done. He loves us still, as He loved Peter and Mary, John and Thomas, in the days of His flesh. Still, He breaks the silence, uttering our names, understanding our failures, and calling us back from the far country into which we have wandered.

2. MANY WATERS CANNOT QUENCH LOVE. Like Greek fire, Christ's love burns under water; for surely in this case, as in myriads of others, it was beset by floods of ingratitude, indifference, waywardness, denial, and sin.

a. *Peter had failed Him in the garden, but He sent for him.* Jesus led His disciples across the Kedron, and up the lower slopes of Olivet, till they reached the upland lawns, studded by olive trees. An enclosure there had apparently been placed at His disposal by the owner, to which He frequently resorted. His disciples were somewhat startled, when He told eight of them to await His coming at the entrance, while only three were invited to advance farther along the grassy path. Even they had to stay while He went the distance of a stone throw. He had to tread the winepress alone, and no one might be with Him. Not even the beloved John could be there when He took the cup from His Father's hand.

"Watch with me," He said, as He left them. The request was prompted by His humanity, for who does not know the priceless value of sympathy in the supreme hours of life? But as He came three times to see how they fared, they failed Him. Their eyes were heavy with sleep; and finally an angel had to furnish the strengthening that man might have rendered, but failed. Could Peter ever forget the pathos of the Master's remonstrance: "What, could ye not watch with me one hour?" But though Peter had failed Him, notwithstanding all his protestations, Jesus sent for him.

b. *Peter misconceived of His Spirit and plan and greatly endangered Him.* All the apostles misread the situation. They had no doubt that Jesus was the Son of the Highest and the King of Israel. They were not altogether surprised at the approach of the armed band that Jesus had taught them to expect. They had even provided for such an emergency by bringing along two swords, of which Peter had one.

Though Peter trembled before the servant woman, he was not a coward. He would have fought like a lion if the Lord had permitted it. The others, when they realized the situation, asked the Master to give the signal for smiting with the sword; and Peter, not waiting for the Master's word, was already in the midst of the band hacking and hewing. He struck a mighty blow on the helmet of Malchus, which glanced aside and severed his right ear. It was well meant, but it could not be permitted. The dignity of the Savior's voluntary surrender would be impaired, and His deliberate acceptance of the cross would be beclouded.

Jesus had repeatedly insisted that no one took His life from Him, but that He laid it down of Himself. The voluntary element in His suffering would be lost sight of if He were led off after a struggle. He therefore sought to quell the rising excitement, asked permission for the freeing of one hand that He might reach as far as the wounded man, and after a brief rebuke of His allowed the soldiers to lead Him away as a lamb to the slaughter. This prompt action saved the situation that Peter's impulsive act had created. But notwithstanding all, and with the knowledge that his misconceptions were still clinging to him, Jesus mentioned Peter specifically, and sent this special summons for him to come.

c. *Peter had falsified his vows and denied Him three times with oaths—but He sent for him.* The band—their captive in the midst—turned back to the city. John first recovered from the panic-stricken flight that had carried all the apostles from their Master's side, and seems to have followed closely in the rear, while Peter followed afar off. On the opening of the great gates of Annas's palace, where the first informal trial for extracting further evidence was held, John entered with the crowd; but not discovering Peter, and sure that he was waiting outside, he went back and spoke to the maid, who operated the gate, on his friend's behalf. She recognized him as an acquaintance of the high priest, and admitted Peter, scanning his features as he passed under the oil lamp that lighted up the porch.

This porch led to a quadrangle, open to the sky; and as the night was cold, the servants kindled a fire in the big brazier, which shed its flickering rays on the faces of the motley group that had shared in the night's adventure. John had gone "with Jesus" into the council chamber, the windows of which looked out on the quadrangle; but Peter joined the group around the fire. "He stood and warmed himself." He had lost heart and hope. Still he wanted to see the end, and he thought to evade discovery by joining with the rest, as though he was one of them.

The portress, who had admitted him, leaving her post, came up to the fire, recognized Peter, and spoke to him before the entire circle with the challenge: "This man also was with the Galilean." He was taken unawares, but answered the attack—"I neither know nor understand what thou sayest."

Seizing a favorite opportunity, when probably the attention of the others was drawn in another direction, he withdrew toward the porch, and as he reached it a cock crowed in the gray dawn. While there he was recognized by another maid, who had probably heard the words of her fellow-servant at the fire. She remarked to a group of bystanders: "This man also was with Jesus the Nazarene." Again Peter denied, and this time with an oath—"I know not the man." About an hour later he was back again at the fire, perhaps with the intention, made in his own strength, of retrieving the situation. But when he opened his mouth, his inability as a Galilean to pronounce the Hebrew gutterals gave the lie to his repeated and emphatic disavowals of any attachment to Jesus. One after another denounced him; his brogue betrayed him; and the kinsman of Malchus recognized his relative's assailant. The hapless disciple began to curse and to swear, saying, "I know not this man of whom ye speak."

A second time, while he was yet speaking, a cock crowed, and Peter remembered the words that Jesus had spoken. Jesus also had heard for the second time, the same sound, and had heard Peter's strident voice where He was standing. Then, forgetting His own griefs, He turned and looked at Peter not with anger or reproach, but remembering and reminding. And yet He sent for him. Many waters cannot drown His love! We too may fail Him, deny, and crucify Him afresh. But when our heart turns back in an agony of grief and remorse, He will renew us again to repentance. "Only so look on us, when we fail Thee, blessed Lord, that we too may be recalled from our relapse, and brokenhearted may be forgiven and restored!"

15

"He Was Seen of Peter"
Luke 24:13–35; 1 Cor. 15:5

Peter fled from the hateful scene of his denial. That last look of tender, pitying love haunted him! Was this the end? Could he ever be happy again? Even if God forgave him, could he forgive himself? How could he have been entrapped in so false a deed?

Tradition says that whenever, in coming years, he heard a cock crow, he was accustomed to fall on his knees and weep; and that he was accustomed daily to awaken at cockcrow and spend in prayer the fateful hour in which he failed his Lord. Probably neither of these is a correct version of the subsequent expression of his repentance. It is more likely that his old strong, boastful spirit received its deathwound, that he became very pitiful and tender toward the fallen, and that he came to believe, as never before, in the love of the Savior, the coals of which gave so vehement a heat as to melt his heart into a fountain of tears.

1. THE SCENE OF HIS BITTER SORROW IS NOT REVEALED. Where did he go when he left the palace of Annas? Surely to the garden, that he might lie full length on the very spot of his Master's agony, and wet with his tears the ground that had been bedewed by the sweat of blood. And when the sun was up, he would make his way to the house of John, where he knew he would be hidden even from the prying eyes of the others, who were bewildered with the events that had so suddenly swept their Master from their midst, and with Him all their hopes for this world and the next. At least they had this to be thankful for, that even if they had forsaken their Lord, yet they had not denied Him.

The morning hours passed slowly. He could hear that the city was moved, but probably only snatches of information floated through the open window. Now Crucify from ten thousand throats, and then the strange word "Barabbas." John was too engrossed with all that was happening to return, and no other could have guessed that he was there.

About noon there were heavy steps in the doorway, and on going to see who was there he found John supporting, almost carrying, Mary, Jesus' mother. In her agonized face, and in John's, he learned that the worst had happened, and probably refrained from questioning them.

From his first epistle we learn that Peter was an eyewitness of the sufferings of Christ. If, as is probable, that phrase includes the sufferings of the cross, he may have stolen through the streets over which the midday gloom was beginning to gather, that he might, even from a distance and obscurely, see the outlines of the cross, which bore the One whom he loved with all the passion of a strong and penitent heart. He could not tarry, however, for John probably awaited his return to care for Mary, while he went back to stand so near the cross as to hear the last dying cry that announced a finished Redemption and the committal of the Redeemer's Spirit to the Father.

With these details and others he returned home; and in the weary waiting time of the following hours Peter confided all the tragic story of his fall. Happy are they who under such circumstances have such a friend to listen.

2. THE FACT OF THE RESURRECTION BROKE ON HIM GRADUALLY. Had the whole wonder and glory broken on the apostles suddenly, it would have overwhelmed and dazed them. It was therefore wisely ordered that it should be tempered, and made "by divers portions and in divers manners."

a. *The tomb was empty.* Early on Easter morning Mary of Magdala, breathless with haste, broke in on the sleepless anguish of John's home. "They have taken away the Lord out of the sepulchre, and we—women who visited the spot further to embalm His body—know not where they have laid him."

Instantly Peter was on his feet and hurried for the tomb, followed by John. On reaching the tomb first, because he was younger and more fleet of foot, John contented himself with looking in. But Peter, true to his impulsive nature, could brook no delay, but went immediately into the chamber from where his Master had risen an hour or two before. It had not been robbed either by friend or foe. The careful disposition of the clothes made that hypothesis impossible. They had fallen together so naturally as though the body that had laid within their folds had been withdrawn without removing them, and the head cloth was carefully folded up, as only deliberate hands would fold it. John was so impressed with what he saw that he almost guessed the truth; and Peter became thoughtful and wondering. But they needed further confirmation, for they did not know the Scripture that He must rise again from the dead; so they went away again to their own home.

b. *The Lord appeared to Mary Magdalene.* This was the next stage in the unveiling of the great wonder of the Lord's resurrection; and evidently it made a profound impression on Peter, for it is in Mark's Gospel that we are told that when Jesus arose early on the first day of the week He appeared first to Mary Magdalene, "out of whom he had cast out seven demons." That last clause probably reveals the secret of the comfort that Christ's interview with Mary brought to his distraught soul. He reasoned that if Jesus had revealed Himself to *her*, had spoken *her* name in the old tone of voice, and had commissioned *her* to go to the disciples with the message of Resurrection and Ascension, there was good reason to believe that in his own case also, though all unworthy, the Lord would resume His old intimacy and comradeship.

c. *The message of the women.* They had departed quickly from the sepulcher, and ran to bring His disciples word; but they were stopped by the appearance of their Lord who met them saying, "All hail!" They took hold of His feet and worshiped Him, and He repeated the angel's instruction, saying, "Fear not, go tell my brethren." All this delayed them. It would appear also that, whereas Mary had gone to John and Peter, the women probably made for the other eight apostles who were gathered in the Upper Room; and as the Magdalene evidently hastened from the two apostles to the eight, so the women hastened from the eight to the two, who were discussing the events of the morning.

The women broke in on them like a ray of the sun through a cloud drift in a murky sky. They had seen the Lord! He had spoken to them! He had commissioned them to bring them glad tidings of great joy! But before they met Him, the angel had instructed them to inform His brethren *and Peter* that He was risen, and was preceding them into Galilee, where they would see Him. The women had no idea of the relevancy of those words. When they had passed on to tell "the rest," did he not quietly adore the love that would not let him go, the love that never failed, until it had found and brought back the sheep that had gone astray?

3. FINALLY THE LORD APPEARED TO HIM. In his enumeration of the witnesses of our Lord's resurrection in 1 Corinthians 15, Paul records that "he was seen of Cephas"; and when Cleopas and his friend entered the Upper Room on Easter Eve they were saluted by a chorus of glad voices, saying: "The Lord is risen indeed, and hath appeared to Simon." That is all we know.

What passed in that interview is not recorded, but from our own experience we can fill in the blank page. We know that there must have been bitter tears, broken words, long breaks of silence when speech was overwhelming, assurances that the penitent did really love, whatever might be argued to the contrary from word or act. Yes, we know all that passed. We have gone through it! We too have been lifted from the dust and made to sit at the King's table, though, like Mephibosheth, we have been "lame in both our feet."

What delicate thoughtfulness there was in the Master's arrangement of this personal interview prior to the later gathering of the day, when He revealed Himself to the entire company. In their presence Peter could never have poured out his soul, or made full confession, or have kissed His feet. That first hour of radiant fellowship cast its sheen on all subsequent hours of that memorable day.

16

The Renewed Commission
John 21

It is almost certain that the final chapter of John's Gospel—which has been described as a postscript—was appended by the beloved apostle as a tribute to the memory of his friend who, according to universal tradition, had sealed his long and glorious ministry by martyrdom—the martyrdom of the cross. In noble loyalty to Peter's memory, he desired to show how, notwithstanding his denial, the Lord had Himself replaced the keys in his hand and returned his sword. The primitive church had already recognized him as one of its pillars, but the story of his actual rehabilitation had not been placed on the canvas of history.

Jesus knew that the Peter of the denial was not the real Peter, and since his future leadership depended on the concurrence of the other disciples, He skilfully contrived to bring about a revelation of Peter's innermost soul, that the effect of his denial might be neutralized, and that unquestionable proof might be given of his possession of the qualities required for the leadership of the church. The unanimity with which his leadership was agreed to proves the infinite wisdom that inspired the Lord's action when they met for the last time on the shores of the Lake of Galilee.

1. THE SCENE. In obedience to their instructions, the apostles returned to Galilee and to the lake, every headland and inlet of which was fragrant with hallowed associations. Simon Peter said, "I go a-fishing." They immediately agreed with his suggestion, and replied, "We also go with thee."

Boats and nets were at hand, and with the eager alacrity with which men will respond to the call of an old-time but long-discarded habit, seven of them pushed off from shore in one of the larger fishing boats, a smaller one being attached to the stern, and made off for the familiar fishing grounds; but when the gray morning began to break—they had caught nothing.

They failed to recognize the Figure standing on the white, sandy shore, enwrapped in the golden shimmer of the morning mist. Surely He was some early fish dealer; and the two inquiries addressed to them across the quiet water failed to correct their mistake. That fishermen, returning from a night of toil, should be asked by one standing on the shore, if they had fish to sell, or that they should be asked directions for catching a shoal were familiar incidents. But John, with the unerring instinct of love, discerned the presence of the Lord, and in a whisper passed his happy discovery to Peter. None of the others could, for the moment, have understood why Peter suddenly jumped up and wrapped around himself the outer coat that he had cast aside to expedite his labors, and plunged into the water, regardless of the morning chill. Those swift strokes, however, gave him a brief additional opportunity of lonely personal intercourse with Jesus.

We may not linger on the tender thoughtfulness that had kindled a fire, at which exhausted fishermen might warm their limbs and dry their clothes, and which had prepared the bread and fish. Nor may we dwell on the frugality of the miraculous, which urged the disciples to bring of the fish they had caught. It is enough if we learn from the entire incident that, from our Lord's resurrection and onward, the seine net of the gospel must be cast into the multitudinous waters of the human world, that the Master's presence and direction are absolutely essential to success, that He will welcome them as they near the heavenly shore and will feast with them and they with Him.

The outstanding qualification for religious leadership are three: passionate devotion to Christ, unfeigned humility, and indomitable courage. In each of these Peter had been proven deficient by the incidents of the betrayal night. But they were latent in his soul and only waited for favorable circumstances to call them forth.

a. *Passionate devotion to Christ.* Had it not been for the denial, none of the apostolic band would have questioned Peter's attitude toward the Master. But a shadow of grave doubt now overspread the sky, and as they spoke together they may have questioned the strength and steadfastness of his devotion. Our Lord realized this, and knew that before He entrusted to him the care of His sheep and lambs, He had to secure a very decisive and unquestionable expression of the love that He at least recognized as a dominant factor in His apostle's character.

So, when breakfast was over, Jesus repeated the same question three times: "Lovest thou me?" and in each case addressed him as Simon Bar-Jona, i.e., Simon, son of

John. Our Savior laid this stress on His servant's earlier name because He desired to give him a fresh opportunity of acquiring the title of "rock."

Love to Jesus is the indispensable qualification of service. Love is needed for the fathering of tired and sick lambs to the shepherd's bosom, for the weary mothers finding the mountain path steep and difficult, and for the straying sheep, possessed by an incessant tendency to break through bars, or wander browsing on forbidden pastures. The first, second, and third qualification of the true Shepherd is love. Therefore the Master asked persistently, "Dost thou love me?" And to the thrice-repeated question Peter returned the same reply, "Thou knowest that I love thee."

b. *Unfeigned humility.* Two Greek words stand for love. The one expresses the reverent and adoring love with which we should regard the holy God. The other expresses love in its more human and affectional aspect. In His two first questions, Jesus asked His apostle whether he loved with the former love. This Peter modestly disclaimed. "No," he said, "but I love you with the ardor of personal affection." Finally, our Lord descended to his level and asked if indeed He loved Him this way, eliciting the immediate response: "Assuredly, and whether as Son of God or Son of man, you know it is true."

With evident reference to Peter's boast made at the supper, that though his fellow disciples might desert the Master, yet he never would, Jesus asked him if he loved Him more than the rest. But by his silence and his grief, he confessed that he dared not claim any priority in love. He was prepared to take the lowest seat, and consider himself last and least. In this also he proved that he was worthy for the foremost place, because he was willing to take the lowest. He had become as a little child; and our Lord did not hesitate, with the hearty assent of the disciples who stood by, to take him by the hand and place him in the old foremost position that he seemed to have forfeited forever.

c. *Indomitable courage.* From the beginning our Lord saw the cross standing clearly on the horizon before Him. Amid all the excitement of His early appearance, He told Nicodemus that the Son of man must be lifted up. Do we sufficiently estimate His courage in treading resolutely a path that led ever deeper into the valley of death?

This was our Lord's experience. And it was to be Peter's also. "Thou shalt stretch forth thy hands, and another shall gird thee, and carry thee whither thou wouldest not. This spake he, signifying by what death he should glorify God." In his proud self-confidence Peter once said: "Lord with You I am ready to go to prison and to death." The Savior replied: "Thou canst not follow me *now*, but thou shalt follow me afterwards." And the time had now dawned. The disciple was not to be above his Lord. He was to follow Him to prison in Acts 12, and to death at the end of all—the death of the cross, as tradition assures us, and this prediction suggests. In his second epistle Peter refers to these words of Jesus: "Knowing that shortly I must put off my tabernacle, even as our Lord Jesus hath shewed me" (2 Peter 1:13). Clearly for him also the cross was the ultimate goal; but he never swerved from the chosen path of service because of its menace. The courage that could stand that strain was of rare and splendid quality, and approved his fitness for leadership.

By evincing his ownership of these three qualities Peter established his right to the foremost place in the glorious company of the apostles, and he nobly fulfilled the position.

17

A Witness of the Resurrection
Acts 1:1–26; 2:1–11

With his brethren Peter returned from the scene of the ascension to the city with great joy. Though he must have realized that the blessed intercourse of the last six weeks was now ended, and that his Master had definitely gone to the Father, yet the indubitable evidence of His great power and glory, the memory of those hands outstretched in benediction as He went, the assurance that they were to be endued with the power of the Comforter within the next few days, and the assurance that Jesus when He came again, as He certainly must, would be the same unchangeable Lord and Friend, were sufficient to lift them all into an ecstasy of joy and triumph, which exceeded and overflowed their sense of deprivation. It was even as He had said, their master had not left them comfortless.

Naturally they returned to *the* Upper Room, hallowed by so many precious associations. It may have been part of the house of the mother of John Mark, which afterward became the gathering place for the harried church; and probably it was filled to its utmost capacity when the entire group of apostles, disciples, holy women, and the brethren of the Lord, was assembled. Peter seemed naturally and by universal consent to become their leader; but he simply acted as chairman or moderator for the time being, because the Lord Himself, though unseen, was recognized by them all as still literally present; and it was to Him that the choice between the two candidates for the apostolate was referred. "Thou, Lord, which knowest all hearts of all men, shew whether of these two thou hast chosen." They were to be witnesses to the fact of the resurrection of their Lord. His words are very definite. "It is necessary," he said, "that of the men who have been associated with us from the beginning of our Lord's ministry in the days of John the Baptist until now, one must be chosen to become *with us* a witness to His resurrection."

1. THE SALIENT FEATURE OF PETER'S LIFE WORK. It was bearing witness to the Resurrection. The word translated witness is fraught with solemn and sacred associations. It is "martyr." We cannot utter the word lightly. It is significant of tears, and blood, and death agony, and the light reflected from the face of Jesus on the death pallor of upturned faces.

The resurrection of Jesus is not primarily to be argued for as a doctrine; it rests on attestation to a fact. It is indeed a gospel, a theology, and a philosophy. It was the fitting consummation of the work of Jesus. But it is primarily a historical fact, communicated and vouched for by a sufficient number of unimpeachable witnesses.

There is a vast difference therefore between the arguments on which Plato and others based their belief in the immortality of the soul and our belief in the resurrection of the Christ. But at the best, it was only a probability. In the resurrection of Jesus men were confronted with a fact, which could not be disputed, in that the resurrected body of Jesus was "seen many days of them which came up with him from Galilee to Jerusalem, who are his witnesses to the people" (Acts 13:31). There is a clear distinction, therefore, between the Platonic philosophy which argues for immortality, and the Christian faith in the Resurrection which, as a well-attested fact, has brought life and immortality to light.

2. PETER'S EQUIPMENT FOR HIS LIFE WORK. Before our Lord entered on His ministry He was anointed with the Holy Spirit, and from the wilderness He returned in the power of the Spirit into Galilee. May we not say that He also tarried until He (so far as His human nature required it) was endued with power from on high? That was our Savior's Pentecost. How much more must His followers stoop beneath the anointing of Pentecost.

This is what He had promised. He said: "I go to the Father, and will ask of Him, on your behalf, and He will give you another Paraclete, that He may abide with you for ever, even the Spirit of Truth."

Day after day they waited, sometimes in the Upper Room, but perhaps more often, as Luke tells us, in the temple, worshiping Christ, blessing God with great joy, and wondering how soon, and in what manner, the promised gift of power would be bestowed.

It was the first day of the week, and a notable day at that, for the priests in the special temple service would present the first loaves of the new harvest before God. It was the early morning, the embryo church probably was assembled in one of the courts or precincts of the vast temple area. They were all together in one place, when there was a sound from heaven as of the rushing of a mighty wind, and there appeared what seemed to be tongues as of flame that rested on each of them. Peter looked on John and saw the expressive symbol on his bowed head, little realizing that the same sublime event had also happened to himself. Then looking around, and seeing each similarly crowned, he concluded that an equal share in this fiery baptism had been imparted to him also. The whole company was filled, and began to speak with other tongues, as the Spirit gave them words—Peter with the rest.

Meanwhile, summoned by the extraordinary sound that evidently emanated from the temple, a vast crowd gathered. It was composed of Jews and proselytes, religious men, gathered from every part of the known world. As this torrent of excited and questioning multitudes poured into the temple area, they were accosted by the newly-anointed disciples who, with an assurance that their new experience had given, went freely among them, attesting the risen glory of Him whom their rulers had recently rejected and nailed to the cross. One of them accosted a Jew from Greece, and in the purest Attic, told him that Christ had risen. Another met a Jew who had, by residence in Rome, acquired the right of citizenship, and told the story of Jesus in language that Cicero or Horace could not have excelled. A third encountered a group which, by their dress, had evidently hailed from Arabia, and poured into their astonished ears the gospel story.

Then Peter stood up and began to speak. His sermon was little else than the citation of long passages of Scripture, accompanied by brief comments, showing their application to the present hour; but the effect was extraordinary. As this Galilean fisherman began to speak, the mob suddenly became a congregation, and the crowd became as one body, swayed and inspired by a common impulse. Presently the silence was broken by the cry, and from the entire congregation the question arose: "Men and brethren, what shall we do?"

That anointing or infilling came to Peter at least twice afterward, according to Scripture, but it probably came again and again. He was filled with the Holy Spirit on the Day of Pentecost, and a second time when he addressed the court, and was filled again on returning with John from the presence of the Sanhedrin to their own company.

Why, then, should we go on without claiming our share in this Pentecostal power? Ah, why do we fail to make use of that vast spiritual dynamic of which Pentecost was the specimen! We are not held back by God, but by ourselves. We have not, because we ask not, or because we ask amiss.

The blessing, originally confined to Jews, may become the heritage of Gentiles also who believe in Christ. They also may receive the Holy Spirit through faith. There is not a single believer who reads this page who may not claim a share in the Pentecostal gift. The Spirit may be *in* us, regenerating and renewing from within, as Jesus was born of Mary through the Spirit; but it is necessary that He should be *on* us also, as He descended and remained on Jesus in His baptism, if we are to fulfill our ministry to mankind. No learning, no polished speech, no amount of evangelical teaching short of the Holy Spirit can avail. Why not acknowledge that there is a blessing here, which is yours by right, but not yours by possession? Why not confess that it is your failure and fault not to have claimed it? Why not humbly open your heart to the entrance of that blessed Spirit who changes the cowardly into courageous confessors, and makes the weakest mighty as the angel of the Lord?

3. THE CHARACTERISTICS OF PETER'S LIFE WORK OF WITNESSING.

a. *It was persistent.* On the day of Pentecost in Acts 2; in his next great address, on the healing of the lame man in chapter 3; in his apology before the rulers, elders, priests, and scribes in 4:10; by the great power with which he gave witness to the resurrection of the Lord Jesus, in 4:33; in his second conflict with the council in 5:32; in the answer that he gave to the inquiries of Cornelius and his friends in 10:39–41—Peter was constantly and consistently a witness to the same outstanding fact that though Jesus was crucified through weakness, yet He was living through the power of God.

b. *It was steeped in Scripture quotation.* We have already noticed this in the Pentecostal sermon, where out of twenty-two verses, twelve are taken up with quotations from the prophets and psalms. We meet with the same features in the next chapter, where Peter refers twice to the predictions of the holy prophets, that it was fitting that Christ suffer, and to rise from the dead the third day. It seemed as though a very special illumination had been given him by the Holy Spirit of inspiration, that he might understand the Scriptures and perceive the relevance to Jesus of all things written in the law of Moses, the prophets, and the psalms.

This is always the case. The Spirit bears witness to the Word. Spirit of the risen Lord, open our eyes that we may see the face of Christ reflected in every Scripture, as in a mirror, now darkly, but which one day we shall see face to face!

c. *It grew in clearness of perception.* Peter begins with "Jesus of Nazareth approved of God." Then "Lord and Christ." Then "Jesus Christ of Nazareth." Then "His Son Jesus." Then the "Holy One and the Just." Then the extraordinary sublime phrase is piled as a climax and top stone on all the rest—"the Prince of Life."

Prince! He is royal, and deserves the homage of all the living. Prince of life! In the literal rendering of this great word He is the Author and Giver of life, so that he who believes in Him, though he has died, yet shall he live; while he who lives and believes in Him will never die. Prince of life! All hail!

d. *It was based on present experience.* It is remarkable that in Peter's witness to the Master's risen life he does not refer to the spectacle of the empty grave, the ordered clothes, the garden interview, the vision of His hands and side, the breakfast by the lake, or the ascension from Olivet. He says: You may judge for yourselves by *this*, "which ye now see and hear." In other words, he felt that not only was Jesus on the other side of the thin veil, which hides the unseen world, but that He was doing things. He had reached the Father's right hand, and was sending the Spirit, as He promised. He was empowering them with boldness, insight, and utterance. He was working with them, and confirming their words with signs following. He was making lame men walk, prison doors open, hard hearts to break. Peter said: "He whom ye delivered up and denied in the presence of Pilate, is alive, of this we all are witnesses, and *so is also the Holy Spirit.* Thus the testimony of those early witnesses came not only in power, but also in much assurance. He stood beside them.

Similarly a holy life will corroborate our witness to the living Christ. If contrary to our former habit we seek the things that are above; if we derive from an unseen source the power that overcomes the world; if our joy abounds in pain and sorrow, if though poor, we make many rich, being hated, we love, being refused, we entreat, being crucified, we invoke forgiveness on the agents of our shame—we prove that Jesus lives.

We are not called to live always in the far-off scenes of His agony and death. We have direct and immediate fellowship with the Prince of Life. We have the mind of Christ. We speak of things that we know, and testify of things we have seen.

If only we, who profess the name of Jesus, would wait at His doors until He gave us audience, we would go to people with His accent on our tongues, and His light on our heart. Let us not abdicate from our high privilege; then we shall go forth into the world bearing such evident traces of a life that cannot be accounted for, that those who know us best will be compelled to look from us to Him who lives forever.

18

"In the Name"
Acts 3:16

"His name through faith in his name." These two are inseparable. No great work of salvation or renewal is possible apart from the clear enunciation of preacher, teacher, or Christian worker, first of His name, and second, of faith in His name. Not the name without the faith, and not the faith apart from the name, but the name *and* faith in the name.

Under the teaching of the Holy Spirit Peter had learned this lesson well, and in his second great Pentecostal sermon he announced and bequeathed the eternal truth that the nature of the risen Lord, appropriated by a living faith, will give perfect soundness.

1. WHAT PETER SAW.

The begger at the gate, now more than forty years of age, who from his birth had never walked, was daily carried by kindly hands from the poor slum where he dwelled to that spot near the Beautiful Gate, on which he lay year after year, begging a pittance from the crowds that passed him through the gate to gain the temple plateau. He was evidently a well-known figure to the citizens who made constant visits to the sacred shrine.

In company with his friend and fellow apostle John, Peter passed up the temple steps on his way to the afternoon service, and beheld the glory of the magnificent structure in all its wealth. He saw also the familiar spectacle of this lame man in his misery. But he saw something else, which was hidden from unanointed eyes. He beheld that crippled life as God meant it to be—whole, sound, healthy, vigorous. The ideal man was there hovering as a beautiful vision above the travesty that lay on that well-worn mat.

The Lord of the temple was beside him, ready to cooperate, yearning to communicate the strength and vigor so urgently needed by this crippled existence. Here was weakness, there immortal life. Here the depression of prolonged ill-health, there the radiance of the dawn. The one problem was to bring these two together. There must be His name, but something more was necessary. Faith in His name had to be called into operation before the lame man could receive that perfect soundness, resident in the Prince of Life.

2. WHAT PETER DID. The instant response given by the lame man to Peter's use of "the name of Jesus Christ of Nazareth" suggests that it was the result of a long process of thought that had evidently been at work previously in the heart of the cripple.

Without doubt he was perfectly familiar with the person of Jesus of Nazareth. He had seen Him pass up those stairs scores of times. But He had no appearance of wealth, nothing to encourage the hope that He could give him alms. But of late strange rumors had gathered around the Nazarene. All Jerusalem knew of His arrest, trial, and consignment to the cross. The preternatural darkness that veiled His anguish and the earthquake that had synchronized with His death had been the subject of universal comment. The cripple was lying on the accustomed spot when the frenzied priests and Levites rushed out of the temple court with the tidings that the veil had been grasped and torn from top to bottom, as by unseen hands. The story of the empty tomb and of the mysterious disappearance on the Mount of Olives may also have been discussed in his hearing; and the recent marvel of the Day of Pentecost and its results had been matters within his own cognizance, for the temple itself had witnessed them. He had heard the people talking as they came away from Peter's sermon; and the baptism of 3,000 converts in the great temple reservoirs was too astounding not to have come to his ears. Thoughts of this kind had been floating for days through his mind. As yet they had not crystallized into resolve or action. They were waiting for some additional impulse.

Led by a divine prompting, the apostle realized, by a gleam of incipient faith on the cripple's face, that he had faith to salvation, and by his voice and gesture called it into expression.

One of our Lord's injunctions, when He sent the apostles forth was: Get you no gold, nor silver, nor brass in your purses, and no wallet for your journey; it was literally true as Peter phrased it: "Silver and gold have I none."

There are four classes of persons in the world:

1. The people who have neither silver nor gold nor anything else to give—these are the driftwood on the ocean.

2. The people who have silver and gold, and no moral or religious property—these are the paupers of the universe.

3. The people who have neither silver nor gold, but, they have vision, inspiration, faith, hope, and love—these are those rich to God.

4. The people who have silver and gold, and also all the things that are honorable, just, pure, lovely, and of good report.

The apostles belonged to the third of these classes. They were poor, yet making many rich, as having nothing, and yet possessing the key to the divine treasuries. Silver and gold they did not have.

Yonder a little girl is sobbing piteously on the grave of her mother! I am touched, and offer her a gold piece! She snatches it from my hand, flings it into the open grave, and continues to sob convulsively! What more can I do? That is all that I had to give, and it couldn't help! Presently a poor woman, in plain and shabby clothes, kisses the child, strokes the little head, presses her to her bosom, and comforts her with gentle crooning! See the eyes droop in sleep, and the little one is soothed and quieted! That woman had neither silver nor gold, but she possessed what was infinitely more precious, and that she gave without stint. This is what the world needs today.

In the present case Peter communicated the inspiration of his own strong faith in Jesus of Nazareth. He summoned the beggar to act on such faith as he had. Peter took him by the right hand and raised him up, as he had seen his Master raise up his wife's mother years before. Immediately the man's faith sprang into vigorous exercise. His feet and ankle bones *received* strength. The life of the risen Lord was not able to enter his anemic frame. He entered with them into the temple, from which his congenital deformity had always excluded him, according to Levetical precept, "walking, and leaping, and praising God."

3. How PETER PREACHED. When the temple service concluded and the two left the upper court, a vast concourse of people followed, and in reply to the buzz of questioning and the awestruck wonder of the crowd Peter delivered his second great address.

He turned the thoughts of his audience from John and himself to their Lord. It was not by their power or holiness that the man stood there before them whole, but by the act of Him whom they had denied in the presence of Pontius Pilate, overpowering his ardent wish to release Him. He charged them with preferring a murderer to God's Holy and Righteous One. He insisted that the evidence of Christ's resurrection consisted not simply in the witness of those who had been in His company after He had left the grave, but in the fact of the miracle wrought on the impotent man, which was evident to them all. He branched out into an eager entreaty that they would repent and turn again that their sins might be blotted out.

Peter assured them that this sin might be blotted out. The Oriental merchant keeps his accounts on little tablets of wax. On these, with the blunt point of the stylus or pencil, he makes the indented record of a debt, and when it is paid, with the blunt end of his instrument he flattens down the wax, so that all record of the debt is entirely obliterated. If we erase a debt from our account book, there is still the trace of it having been there, but on the wax there is no trace whatever. The handwriting that was against the debtor is entirely blotted out. What a vision Peter had of the completedness of the divine forgiveness! Once he had hazarded the suggestion that seven times was the limit to which forgiveness could go. Now he has entered into a more adequate conception of the love of God, which forgets as it forgives, and drops our sins when we confess into the fathomless depths of the ocean of His love. They shall never be found or remembered or mentioned again.

Notice the two sendings of the Christ. He was sent in the first Advent to bless His people, in turning them away from their iniquities; He will be sent a second time to bring on the Golden Age, to set up His kingdom, to put down all rule and authority and power, until such time as God shall be All-in-All, and the eternal timeless era of blessedness shall be inaugurated.

19

"You Builders"
Acts 4:1–37

Peter was still addressing the hushed crowd that the healing of the crippled man had gathered. Suddenly a band of officials moved quickly toward the congregation, and forcibly arrested the men. There were priests, who detected in these unordained and unrecognized laymen serious rivals. There were Sadducees, who were disbelievers in the world of Spirit, and in the doctrine of a life after death—a sect not numerous, but wealthy, powerful, and holding the chief offices of state. There was also the captain of the temple, with his band, charged with the duty of maintaining public order.

The Sadducean party was "indignant that they taught the people and preached through Jesus the Resurrection of the dead." If the story was true, Sadduceeism was ended. It is therefore probable that this arrest was instigated by Annas and Caiaphas, and the other leaders of this powerful party. Before Jerusalem was aware of what was happening, the apostles and the healed man were clapped in prison, and messengers were hastening through the city to summon the members of the Sanhedrin to meet early on the following morning.

That night must have been to the imprisoned duo one of unspeakable emotion. This was the treatment their Master had taught them to expect. It was an opportunity also to redeem the cowardly desertion of the betrayal night. Peter remembered that he had vowed to follow Jesus to prison. As to the next day's trial, they had no anxiety, now had they prepared a defense, for the words spoken three years before came back to memory: "When you are brought before rulers and kings, do not premeditate what ye shall answer, for it shall be given you in the same hour. It is not you who speak, but the Spirit of your Father who speaks in you."

The Sanhedrin was the most venerable and authoritative assembly and court in the world. The high priest presided, and around him in a semicircle sat the heads of the twenty-four priestly classes, the doctors of the law, and the fathers of ancient Jewish families. The names of some of these are given, such as the crafty Annas and the unscrupulous Caiaphas, his son-in-law. It was the same body that had handed Jesus of Nazareth to the Roman executioners, and now, in the same chamber they were preparing, by one supreme effort, to stamp out the Galilean heresy. Note their procedure! It was foolish to question the miracle—the healed man was standing there before them. It was perilous to discuss the general question of the Resurrection, because on this matter there was a distinct cleavage between the Pharisees and the Sadducees, each party being strongly represented. But the point at issue was as to the source of his healing. "In whose name and by what power." If Peter and his associates had ascribed the miracle to the mighty power of Jehovah, with the stories of Elijah's and Elisha's miracles in view, nothing more could have been said. But if it were attributed to some other name, the apostles would bring themselves within the ancient prescription of death as sorcerers. If they ascribed it to Jesus, they would risk the infliction of the death that had already been inflicted on Him. But Peter was entirely oblivious to all questions of policy, and beneath the inspiration of the divine Spirit, spoke thus: "Rulers of the people and Elders, you question us about the deed done to this cripple and ask how he was made whole—we take this opportunity of saying publicly to you and to the whole nation that it was accomplished through the name of Jesus Christ of Nazareth, whom ye crucified, but whom God raised from the dead. It is in Him that this man stands before you whole. You builders rejected Him, but none the less is He the headstone of the corner. Neither is there salvation by any other."

1. THE RIVAL BUILDERS. The reference to this rejected headstone recalls an ancient tradition woven into the structure of Psalm 118—the climax of the great national Hallel.

The position accorded to that cornerstone in the national structure was the real cause of divergence in the assembly. Two ideals confronted each other. The one group was composed of that brilliant and powerful body that comprised all that was most illustrious in the Hebrew commonwealth. The other group was represented by those simple "unlearned and ignorant" men. The former refused the Stone, and covered it with neglect. The other made it the keystone of the structure, which was beginning to arise, and has since spread through the world.

Of course, his primary reference was to the healing of the impotent man, who stood there saved and whole before their eyes. But there was more in his thought. Was it not clear that Israel was the real cripple? Beneath the rude Roman power the nation lay there bound, prostrate, and powerless. It was crippled morally and spiritually. If only the Jewish leaders had been induced to acknowledge his Master and Lord, their national influence would have revived, and they would have become what God meant them to be, the religious leaders of mankind. There was no salvation in any other.

We may apply this nationally, ecclesiastically, and individually.

a. *Nationally.* If a nation refuses to build according to the great truths that Jesus taught, exemplified, and died for, it must pass as all the great empires of the world— Assyrian, Babylonian, Persian, Grecian, and Roman—have passed. The only hope of salvation for the State is to be built foursquare with the gospel of the Son of man.

b. *Ecclesiastically.* The church that substitutes doctrinal formularies, the pomp and splendor of high ritual, or priest craft, learning, or wealth, for a vital contact with Jesus Christ, the living Savior, may enjoy a temporary success of popularity; but it is not destined to endure. The only salvation for any church is in union with Jesus Christ.

c. *Individually.* We all build from our childhood. Who of us has not built with wooden bricks in winter, and sandcastles on the beach in summer? When we are older we build businesses, stories, tragedies, poems, pictures, systems of philosophy, fortunes, or statesmanships. Too many build to the neglect of Christ. They can do without Him—so they say. But they cannot continue. For a while they flourish and grow up, but the wind passes over them and they are gone, and the place thereof knows them no more. But he who does the will of God abides forever.

2. THE IRREPRESSIBILITY OF THE CHRIST LIFE. As the Sanhedrin listened to the words, and watched the two apostles closely, they were irresistibly reminded of Jesus. They were animated by His Spirit, and spoke as He had done. They took knowledge of them

that they had been with Jesus. He was living in their hearts, and pouring through them the spirit of His own glorious existence as the Prince of Life.

When the court was cleared, with a view to private conference, they confessed to each other that they dared not permit these men to continue to preach and teach. They could not deny the miracle or disprove the Resurrection, but they had to take thought for themselves. When the apostles were recalled they were strictly charged not to speak further in the name of Jesus. Their judges would have been glad to punish them, but this would so enrage the people that it could not be entertained. So they threatened them again and let them go.

These men could do nothing else than bear witness to the things they had heard and seen. Oh, that we knew more of these irresistible impulses.

3. THE ATTESTATION OF THE HOLY SPIRIT. They returned to their own company, who had doubtless spent the intervening hours in prayer. How intensely their narrative was listened to! Then what an outburst of adoration and prayer! There was no entreaty that God would stop the persecutor or save their lives. The sole request was that they might have power to give an unfaltering testimony, and that God would stretch out His hand to heal, so that wonders and signs might be performed in the name of Jesus. If only that dear name could be magnified, extolled, and revered, they would be content to suffer to the extreme of human anguish! Let Jesus Christ be praised!

Can we wonder at heaven's response? The tremor of it shook the place, as before on the Day of Pentecost. There was a second infilling of the Holy Spirit; not now for the hundred and twenty only, but for all of them.

20

Peter's Deepening Experiences of the Holy Spirit
Acts 4:32; 5:33

One of the greatest affirmations possible to man is, "I believe in the Holy Ghost." All knowledge, power, success, and victory over the world, the flesh, and the devil depend on the recognition and use of the fellowship or partnership of the Holy Spirit. When our Lord passed through all the heavens to the right hand of power, He asked the Father and received from Him the authority to confer on each member of His mystical body the infilling and anointing by the Holy Paraclete, as He had Himself received it at His baptism.

1. PETER'S PREVIOUS EXPERIENCES. On the evening of the Resurrection Day the Lord had breathred on him and the rest as they gathered in the Upper Room. "Then said Jesus to them again, Peace be unto you: as my Father hath sent me, even so send I you. And when he had said this, He breathed on them, and saith unto them, Receive ye the Holy Ghost" (John 20:21–22). We therefore gather that their reception of the Spirit was directly intended to qualify them for their mission. It was a distinct equipment for service.

For ten days Peter waited for the promise of the Father, in obedience of the Master's command: "Tarry ye in the city of Jerusalem, until ye be endued with power from on high" (Luke 24:49).

When the Day of Pentecost was fully come he, like the rest, was filled by His Advent, and began to speak as the Spirit gave him words to speak. When he faced the Sanhedrin on the morning after the miracle on the cripple at the Beautiful Gate, he was again suddenly and gloriously filled with the Holy Spirit.

On the return of Peter and John to their own company, the place where they were assembled was shaken as by waves of holy power. They were all filled with the Holy Spirit, and spoke the word of God with boldness. "With great power gave the apostles witness of the resurrection" (Acts 4:32). Evidently this added experience of the incoming tides of God fell also to Peter's lot equally with the whole rejoicing and triumphant company.

Peter had also had repeated evidences of the convicting power of the Spirit of God. "When they heard this, they were pricked in their heart." But further experiences were to be granted before he and his fellow apostles fully explored their inheritance as leaders of the infant church. They were to be taught that the divine Spirit had to do with the collective church as well as the individual, and that He is the president of the church on earth, and the vicegerent of Christ, the supreme guide and teacher of His body, the cowitness of His resurrection, the superlative source of eternal life.

Our Lord may have revealed this great mystery during the forty days in which He instructed His friends in the things concerning the kingdom of God. But their practical realization was gradually unfolded to Peter and the rest. The experience of Peter in this matter is very illuminating. He was led step by step into the full apprehension of the Spirit's association with the church.

2. THE HOLY SPIRIT'S PRESIDENCY OF THE CHURCH. It became apparent in connection with the finances of the church. The multitude of those who believed were of one heart and soul, so that none of them claimed any of his possessions as his own. Those who were possessors of lands or houses sold them, and brought the amount that had been realized and gave it to the apostles, by whom distribution was made to everyone according to his wants. Out of this fund a certain amount would be laid aside for the rooms and meals they had in common. So much would be allotted for the maintenance of the apostles and their fellow workers. Also the destitute, sickly, and widowed would be relieved according to their requirements. This practice is not to be confused with communism, because the latter system abolishes all property by force, and imposes a compulsory division of profits. This system was clearly a temporary expedient for the special circumstances of the Jerusalem church, and the apostles made no attempt to institute it in any of the churches formed among the Gentiles.

The church differs from all other assemblies in this, that it is the body of Christ and the seat or throne of the Holy Spirit. If a handful of people, however obscure, gather in the name of Christ to consider and further the interests of His kingdom, the Holy Spirit is not only present, but He presides. He holds court as the representative and vicegerent of Christ. He sees to it that in their unanimity after united prayer, the will of Christ is reflected, and that through their united action it is done. What is bound or loosed on earth is in harmony with what is bound and loosed in heaven.

Wherever a group of people meet in the name of Jesus, and for the maintenance of the holy ordinances that He directed, and unite for mutual edification and for the purposes of His kingdom, *there* you have the divine seat and throne, and *there* you may count on the living presence of the sevenfold spirit of the eternal.

3. THE COWITNESS OF THE HOLY SPIRIT. The public sentiment of Jerusalem was strongly in favor of the church. This was largely accounted for by miraculous works of healing that gathered the crowds around the apostles, as formerly to the person of the Lord. In the early days of His popularity the people pressed to touch Him. Those scenes were repeated in the narrow streets of Jerusalem, that as Peter came by his shadow might be cast at least on some of the sick who were laid on beds and couches along his pathway. The tidings of the marvelous cures that were effected spread to the cities and towns round about and attracted immense multitudes to see and hear and be healed. The country rang with the tidings of the wondrous cures performed in the name of Jesus.

For a time the rulers stood rigidly aloof. "Of the rest," i.e., of those who were not of the ranks of the common people, "durst no man join himself to them." But finally the smoldering embers of their jealousy burst into fire, and the whole apostolic band was arrested and thrust into the public prison. On the following morning, when the Sanhedrin, reinforced by others of the elders, or senate of Israel, met to discuss the matter, the prison was empty, and news came that their prisoners were standing in the temple and teaching the people. Notwithstanding the miraculous character of their liberation, the trial was proceeded with, and Peter, as spokesman of the whole body, had another opportunity to proclaim before the ruling classes of the nation the resurrection and exaltation of his Lord. "We are his witnesses of these things; and so is the Holy Ghost, whom God hath given to them that obey him."

The Master had promised that this should be their experience. "When the Comforter is come, whom I will send unto you from the Father, even the Spirit of truth, which proceedeth from the Father, he shall testify of me: and ye also shall bear witness, because ye have been with me from the beginning" (John 15:26–27).

4. THE SUPERLATIVE SUPERIORITY OF THE HOLY SPIRIT. The evangelist Philip had been the means of a marvelous spiritual revival at Samaria, and had there encountered in Simon a crafty and ambitious man, adept in the black arts of sorcery and witchcraft. Miracles were wrought by his collusion with demon influence. As in Egypt Jannes and Jambres withstood Moses, so Simon endeavored to counterfeit the beneficent achievements of Philip, using only the name of Jesus. Immediately unclean spirits surrendered their victims with loud cries, and many that were palsied and lame were healed. But the evangelist was not content with these manifestations of spiritual powers; he preached to them the Christ, and the people gave heed with one accord and believed. "There was great joy in that city!"

Presently a demand arose for more help than Philip could give, and the apostles, who had remained in Jerusalem, notwithstanding the persecution that broke out after Stephen's death, that they might focus and guide the entire Christian movement, sent Peter and John to give on their behalf formal recognition to the infant Christian church that had arisen from the gracious work of this revival. During the solemn act that sought and received a further bestowal of the Holy Spirit, there seems to have been such a conspicuous manifestation of spiritual power as astounded the beholders and especially Simon. If only he could have a similar power it would be worth a mine of gold; so he hazarded the offer that has forever stamped his name with the infamy, and made it, as Simony, the brand of similar proposals. Turning on the wretched and misguided man, Peter sternly rebuked him. "Thy money perish with thee, because thou hast thought that the gift of God may be purchased with money. Thou hast neither part nor lot in this matter: for thy heart is not right in the sight of God" (Acts 8:20–21).

21

The Door of Faith to the Gentiles
Acts 6:1–7, 8:14–25, 9:31, 10:16

We open at this point a new chapter in the history of the unfolding of the divine purpose for our race. From the first the divine objective was to include in the one church, not Jews alone, but also Gentiles who had not received the seal and sign of the Abrahamic covenant, but who had entered directly from the Gentile world by the simple act of faith. Until the reception of Cornelius into the church, the idea had hardly dawned on the apostles or the body of disciples that the body, and fellow partakers of the promise of Christ. Gentiles, it was generally supposed, could enter the door of the Christian church only by first becoming Jews. When our Lord commissioned His apostles to go into all the world and make disciples from all the nations, they probably supposed that the rite of circumcision would precede their administration of baptism. It was only by a very gradual process that the whole truth broke on them that in Christ Jesus there is neither Jew nor Greek, circumcision nor uncircumcision, bond nor free, male nor female, but all are one in Him.

For eight years with his fellow apostles Peter had confined himself to the consolidation of the "mother church," but he was now to learn that her children would be gathered equally from a great multitude, whom none could number, of every nation, and kindred, and people, and tongue. We have therefore to consider the steps by which he was led forth into a larger concept of the divine purpose.

Peter was a strict Jew. He was inclined to view with suspicion even the Hellenist, or Greek-speaking Jews, who were scattered throughout the Roman Empire. And he knew the Gentiles, only as he had, from boyhood, for he beheld the glitter of their civilization, that transformed the Lake of Galilee into a Roman pleasure resort. He had never entered a gentile home, had never sat at a gentile table, and had never transgressed the rigid prescriptions of the Levitical dietary. He shrank from familiar intercourse with Gentile. Hence his exclamation, when invited to eat of the heterogeneous contents of the great sheet: "Not so, Lord; for I have never eaten any thing that is common or unclean" (Acts 10:14).

The divine Master is willing to take infinite pains with us, before He demands the ceding of our wills and the taking of an irrevocable step.

Let us watch the stages of the process in the present case.

1. THERE AROSE A MURMURING OF THE GRECIAN, THE HELLENIST JEWS AGAINST THE HEBREWS. The Hellenist always regarded Jerusalem and the temple with fond and reverent affection. He turned there as he prayed. There he came with his family, as often as the cost permitted, to the annual festivals. In the Holy City he desired to die, and in its precincts be buried. A large contingent of these Jews of the dispersion were present on the Day of Pentecost, and had then, as in the following years, identified themselves with the Christian community. Many of them, like the good Barnabas, had parted with their

possessions, placing the proceeds in the common stock, and their poor were in the habit of receiving their sustenance from the common purse. But their widows complained that undue partiality was shown in the daily distribution, and that home-born women fared better at the hand of the apostolic almoners than they did.

The peril of a serious rent in the seamless robe of the church became at length so imminent that Peter and his brethren were compelled to take action. After anxious consideration, they arrived at the conclusion that their highest vocation was to prayer and the ministry of the Word, and that this service of tables should be entrusted to seven men of good report, full of the Holy Spirit and wisdom. They advised the church, therefore, as the ultimate authority, that they should proceed to choose that number from among themselves.

It is remarkable that they were all Hellenist Jews, with the exception of the last, who was a Gentile proselyte. The unanimity of the church in this solemn act was so evidently due to the presence and direction of the Spirit, that Peter could say nothing to the contrary, however startling to his preconceptions such action must have appeared.

2. THEN CAME THE GREAT ARGUMENTS, APOLOGY, AND MARTYRDOM OF STEPHEN. In the familiar intercourse that ensued, Peter would have been attracted to the eloquent young Hellenist. He often listened to the burning words with which Stephen insisted that throughout their history the chosen people had resisted the divine Spirit, when He summoned them to a new advance. As he listened, Peter may have recalled the Master's words, that it would be found impossible to put the new wine in the old bottles. Already the breath of a new age fanned his cheek, as the door was being slowly opened for the admission of the gentile world.

3. THE MISSION TO SAMARIA FOLLOWED. Because of Philip's preaching vast numbers of Samaritans had been baptized in the name of Jesus. This movement needed to be regularized, and the apostles, who had dared to remain in Jerusalem, despite Saul's fiery persecution, determined to commission Peter and John to visit the scene of revival, and lead the new converts forward into the full enjoyment of the gifts of Pentecost.

Here again Peter used the keys of teaching, prayer, and the imposition of hands, with the result that the miracle of Pentecost was repeated. "They received the Holy Ghost." To the obvious astonishment of the apostles, the Holy Spirit, in answer to their prayer, descended on these believing Samaritans with absolute impartiality. Indeed, Peter was so impressed with what he saw that he could do no other than keep in the current of the divine purpose; and therefore he and John, in their leisurely return to Jerusalem, preached in the villages of Samaria through which they passed. Here again was a further unfolding of the horizon of God's purpose.

4. BUT THE PROCESS WAS STILL FURTHER ACCELERATED BY THE CONVERSION OF SAUL OF TARSUS. It was a startling rumor that reached Jerusalem, that the arch persecutor of the church had been arrested by the direct intervention of the Lord, and had become His humble follower. But as more news filtered in, and fuller details were furnished of this wonderful event, they learned that Saul had been compelled to flee from Damascus and had gone to Arabia. Some time elapsed, and finally, to Peter's surprise, Saul presented himself at his humble dwelling in Jerusalem, and remained as his guest for fifteen days.

Suddenly the younger man came to Peter with a strange glory on his features. "Brother," he said, "what do you think, as just now I was praying in the temple I seemed to lose myself, and saw the Lord, and He said to me, Get out of Jerusalem quickly because they will not receive of you testimony concerning Me. Depart: for I will send you far away to the Gentiles. You see, therefore, I have no alternative, and must be gone."

Peter must have been sorely troubled at the danger that beset his newfound friend, and took instant steps to arrange his passage out of the danger zone for Cæsarea, and ultimately to Tarsus. When he was safely away, however, those parting words must have rung in his heart—"far away to the Gentiles." He could not challenge those words. Clearly they were spoken by the Master, but they still further prepared him for the fresh demand that would soon be made on him.

5. THE PROCESS WAS COMPLETED AT JOPPA. After the departure of Paul the church throughout Judæa and Samaria had peace. Peter took advantage of this halcyon period to make an itinerary through the smaller congregations that were scattered throughout Judæa, and in course of time came to Lydda where, as the medium for the health giving word of Christ, he lifted Æneas from his eight-years' paralysis. Therefore he was summoned by an urgent message to Joppa, six-and-a-half miles distant on the rocky seacoast, to the room of death, where the beloved Dorcas lay. His prayer on her behalf prevailed with God, and when he gave her his hand she arose to become once more the gentle friend of all the saints and widows in the little town. The house in which he lodged—the house of Simon the tanner—had associations with death and its accompanying ceremonial pollution, which must have been extremely distasteful to a conscientious Jew. The Jerusalem church had become so diminished by persecution, and flight, that its concerns failed to give him the wide scope and sphere to which for eight years he had been accustomed. What was to be the next step in the fulfillment of his life work? Was some new development of the divine pattern at hand that he must realize for himself and others?

At this juncture, one noon, when the blazing sunshine poured down on the burnished mirror of the sea, and on the white houses of the little town, he went up to the housetop for prayer—prayer probably for further light. While the midday meal was prepared, he fell into a trance, and through the opened heavens he caught the vision of a redeemed world, like a great white sheet. The variety of its contents—four-footed beasts, creeping things, birds clean and unclean, startled him; and still more the declaration that God had cleansed them all, that the old Levitical restrictions were removed, and that any of them were fit for food. Rise, Peter, slay and eat.

Then, while he was much perplexed in himself as to what the vision that he had seen might mean, the knocking at the gate, the voices of men that rose in the noon silence, as they called his name, together with the assurance of the Spirit that there was no need for fear or hesitation—all indicated that the hour of destiny had struck, that a new epoch was inaugurated, and that he was to lead the church into the greatest revolution she had known since the ascension of her Lord.

22

The Breaking of the Yoke
Acts 10:17; 11:18

The gentile world was viewed as strangers and foreigners, "far off," aliens from the commonwealth of Israel, and strangers to the covenants of promise. If they desired to be received into the palace of the Great King, they had to gravel around by the tents of Abraham and the wilderness of Sinai. It was consonant with this that certain men came down from the mother church to the earliest church formed exclusively of Gentiles, saying—"Except ye be circumcised after the manner of Moses, ye cannot be saved" (Acts 15:1).

It was clearly necessary that the canceling of Levitical distinctions should be as clearly defined as their imposition; and therefore Peter's vision, the embassy from Cornelius, and the many corroborations by the Holy Spirit were concentrated in this remarkable episode. Peter and Cornelius were brought together, and so was opened the new and living way that the Lord had already consecrated through His flesh.

The unveiling of the mystery took three days.

1. CÆSAREA: 3.00 P.M. Cornelius came of one of the noblest of Roman families. He belonged to the same stock as the Scipios, Sulla, and the mother of the Gracchi. An earnest seeker after God, he had grown weary of the polytheism, idolatry, and superstitions of his age, and had sought satisfaction in the one faith that presented the conception of the unity and spirituality of God, together with a strenuous demand for purity, righteousness, and mercy. Amid widespread atheism, the ceaseless conflict of rival schools, and the foul corruption of morals, the severe ideals of the Hebrew Scriptures stood as a white sunlit peak shooting up amid the profound shadows of departing night; and large numbers of the heathen world were attracted.

When Cornelius took up his quarters in the splendid city Herod had created, some thirty miles to the north of Joppa, he was brought into yet closer contact with the religion and literature of the Old Testament. As he studied them he became increasingly impressed. He was a devout man, generous in his gifts to the poor, careful to maintain religion with all his household, and constant in prayer. His domestics and his orderly regarded him as "a just man," and he was "of good report among the Jews." He was probably a proselyte of the gate, and carefully observed the prescribed hours of daily prayer. But with all this he was not satisfied.

He knew that he was ostracized by the Jews—was it his duty to submit to their initial rite and be received into their synagogue as one of them? He had heard of Jesus of Nazareth, His holy life, His miracles, His teaching—would it be wise to enroll with His followers? He set apart one quiet day to discover by prayer and fasting what God's will might be. He had offered many previous prayers of the same kind: "Thy *prayers* and thine alms are come up for a memorial before God." But this prayer was more specific and urgent: "Cornelius, your *prayer* is heard." He had reached such a pitch of intensity that his soul was dissolved in one passionate cry for help. Suddenly an angel stood beside him. His messengers, in recounting the incident to Peter, described him as "a holy angel." Cornelius himself spoke of him as "a man in bright apparel." At first, brave soldier as he was, and accustomed to face danger, Cornelius was greatly startled by this sudden contact with the spirit world. Recovering himself, he asked: "What is it, Lord?" and was told that his prayer for light and guidance would be answered through the instrumentality of one Simon, surnamed Peter, who was lodging at a tanner's house in Joppa, along on the shore.

It is well worth our notice that God does not commission angels to evangelize the world or instruct His saints in the mysteries of the kingdom. The treasure is placed in earthen vessels. Men and women, full of human sin and frailty, are chosen as His ambassadors to their fellow citizens. The angel could have spoken almost all Peter's sermon and more, but all that he was sent to do was to tell Cornelius to send for the fisherman—apostle. He was not to call for Philip the evangelist, though he was residing in the same city, because he had not passed through the same exercises of soul or had reached the same point of vision as Peter. God always knows where to find His chosen instruments. Their addresses are registered in heaven.

2. JOPPA: 12:00 NOON. Cornelius lost no time in acting on the vision. He called for, and sent to Joppa, two household servants and a devout soldier, all of whom sympathized with his religious convictions. They were able to cover part of the distance during the remaining hours of the afternoon, and finished their journey at noon on the following day.

Peter, as we have seen, was just emerging from an ecstasy in which he beheld the vision of a redeemed world, and God had shown him that he should not call any man common or unclean. He naturally realized that if the distinction between clean and unclean animals was abolished, the abolition of the distinction between Hebrew and Gentile was necessarily implied. Salvation was as impartial as the dew or rain, which refreshes with equal love the adjacent fields of just and unjust, bond and free, Samaritan, Gentile and Jew.

Before we step out on an unknown path, let us wait for our visions to be corroborated by the knocking at the door and the clear bidding of the Spirit. Peter was encouraged and assured by the concurrence of these three. "While Peter thought on the *vision*, the *Spirit* said unto him, Behold, *three men* seek thee."

All Peter's doubts vanished. His hesitation was ended. He invited the three men into the house, shared with them the meal that had been prepared, lodged them for the night, and on the following morning started with them on the journey to Cæsarea. They must have traveled by the great high road that skirted the shore of the Mediterranean. During the afternoon, while the messengers were resting, Peter had secured the companionship of six believing Jews, under the evident impression that he was taking a step that would be closely scrutinized by the apostles and leaders at Jerusalem. The journey of these ten men occupied more than a day, and it was on the morning of the third day from Peter's vision that the party entered Cæsarea—the city of marble palaces, and seat of Roman government.

3. CÆSAREA: 3:00 P.M. Cornelius seems to have been the center of a religious circle of relatives and near friends, whom he had informed of his recent experiences, and had invited to share with him the help of which the angel had given the assurance. At the appointed hour many came together to hear the things with which the Lord had entrusted His servant on their behalf.

When it was announced that the party had arrived, Cornelius met them at the outer gate, and with instinctive reverence and courtesy prostrated himself before the man who had been commissioned by a message from the unseen. Peter instantly stooped to raise him, saying, "Stand up; I myself also am a man." It would have been wise if all his successors had imitated his manly simplicity and humility. As they passed together to the assembly room, where the expectant gathering awaited them, he spoke so pleasantly and familiarly that his host was placed entirely at his ease, and was able to detail the marvelous circumstances that had led to the present meeting. At the close of his brief address he added. "Thou hast done well that thou art come." Then, amid the awed hush, and with the consciousness that he was in the current of the divine purpose, Peter opened his mouth and spoke.

His address fell into three distinct sections. He told again the well-known story of Jesus who, though clothed in great humility, was nevertheless Lord of all. He gave his emphatic personal testimony to His resurrection from the grave—"We ate and drank with him after he rose from the dead." Finally he proclaimed the forgiveness and remission of sin through faith in His name. Not a word was uttered about circumcision. There was no suggestion that they had to pass through the synagogue to the church. The one condition of forgiveness was faith in Him, whom the Jews slew, hanging Him on a tree, but whom God raised from the dead. The offer was made to men of every nation, wherever they feared God and worked righteousness.

No burst of eloquence or charm of speech adorned this simple address. Indeed, Peter had only begun to speak when an indescribable impression swept over the audience, as the summer breeze breathes over the rustling corn. It was as though the Spirit of God was eager to get to work at once, and put Peter gently aside. The Holy Spirit fell on all who heard the word. There was no startling sound from heaven, and no moving flame, but there was the gift of tongues. And the six brethren who had accompanied Peter were amazed as they heard them speaking with tongues and magnifying God.

While Peter witnessed that scene, as he said afterward, it reminded him of Pentecost. "As I began to speak, the Holy Ghost fell on them, as on us at the beginning. Then remembered I the word of the Lord, how that he said, John indeed baptized with water; but ye shall be baptized with the Holy Ghost. Forasmuch as God gave unto them the like gift as he did unto us, who believed on the Lord Jesus Christ" (Acts 11:15–17). There were the same upturned gaze, the same enraptured look into the face of Jesus, the same desire to speak of His beauty, the same consciousness of supernatural power. The whole company, which before had been a group of separate units, was suddenly welded into a unity and became a church.

Is this scene not full of encouragement? There is doubtless a sense in which the advent of the Holy Spirit, first to the Jews on the Day of Pentecost, and second to the Gentiles in the house of Cornelius, can be no more repeated than the birth and nativity of our Lord; but there is another sense in which each gentile soul may experience the same divine infilling. Such faith always exists in union with an entire surrender of the will, and devout fellowship with God through Scripture. Why should not each reader study once more Galatians 3, and at verse 14 claim his inheritance? Are we not joint heirs with Christ? There may be no emotional response, but the computation of faith cannot cause shame. Would that every minister and teacher were so filled, that the Holy Spirit might fall as soon as we began to speak. Have we received that same gift? There are five tests that supply an infallible answer. If so:

1. The Lord Jesus will be an abiding presence in our lives.
2. The prayer life will become increasingly real.
3. The self-life will be kept on the cross.
4. There will be unmistakable but quiet power in service.
5. The spirit of grace and love will be conspicuously present in our behavior and conversation. Have we received? If not, why not?

In the case of Cornelius and his friends, the baptism by the Spirit was immediately followed by baptism in water. The inward grace was ratified by the outward act. Following the rule that Paul observed afterward, Peter did not himself baptize, probably to guard against the impression that the sacrament derived special sanctity from the person who administered it. He left it therefore to the six men from Joppa to complete the formal acceptance of these gentile disciples into the Christian church. Cæsarea today, but Rome presently!

4. THE CHALLENGE OF THE MOTHER CHURCH. The tidings of what Peter had done soon reached Jerusalem, and he lost no time in returning to give in his personal impression and reports. Not Jerusalem only, but the believers throughout Judæa had heard that the Gentiles also had received the Word of God, from which we may infer that the news had occasioned vast excitement and probably misunderstanding. The circumstances that had led the leader of the church to make so serious an innovation on recognized custom and procedure required careful consideration before they could recognize his act or welcome the new converts. The evangelist tells us that when Peter was come up to Jerusalem, "they that were of the circumcision" argued with him. From this we gather that within the church there was already forming a strong conservative party, which afterward gave much trouble and insisted with obstinate tenacity that the Gentile must submit to the Jewish rite before admission to their ranks. There was a tone of arrogant contempt in their reference to the uncircumcised men with whom Peter had sat down to eat.

Our apostles met their charges by a careful narration of the facts. He appealed from men and from himself to God. The descent of the Spirit, identical as it was with their own experience, was the divine vindication of his action. "As God gave them the like gift . . . what was I, that I could withstand God?" Surely, then neither circumcision counted anything, nor uncircumcision, but faith working by love. Nothing more could be said. "When they heard these things, they held their peace, and glorified God, saying, Then also to the Gentiles hath God granted repentance unto life."

The question, however, came up in a more acute form at the First Council of the Church, the proceedings of which are recorded in Acts 15. There again Peter told his wonderful story. God at least made no distinction between the Hebrew and the Gentile. Why burden them with the intolerable yoke of rites and ordinances? He stated therefore as his convinced belief that Gentile and Jew alike would be saved by faith only, through the grace of the Lord Jesus, and altogether apart from the presence or absence of any rite.

These were noble words, but neither they nor the decision of the council were able to settle the strife between the two parties that rent the church with their contentions. Indeed, the conservative view became so strong that, as Paul tells us in Galatians 2, Peter quailed before it, and even the amiable Barnabas was led away. It fell then to

Paul, the younger man, to take up and defend the sentiments that the elder apostle had so boldly enunciated years before. He withstood him to the face because he was to be blamed.

We may be thankful for the unswerving loyalty with which the apostle of the Gentiles contended throughout his harassed career for this principle. It is not through obedience to law that a man can be declared free from guilt, but only through faith in Jesus Christ.

23

"I Will Go With Thee to Prison"
Acts 12:1–25

Again it was the Passover. "Then were the days of unleavened bread." Fourteen years earlier Peter had been sent with John to prepare the Passover Feast for his Lord, and as the apostles were gathered around the table he had stated his willingness to go with his Master even to prison. Here he was nobly fulfilling his vow. At that Passover also he had slept, but it was the sleep of unwatchfulness, of self-confidence, of the weakness of the flesh. He failed to watch even for one hour with Christ. Here again he slept, but it was the sleep of absolute confidence in the grace of Christ, who would yet deliver him, if it were His will; but if not, would enable him to be faithful to death. Previously he had slept while Jesus prayed; now as he slept, not only did the great High Priest pray that his faith might not fail, but many were fathered together in Mary's house, and were praying for him. But he was not to die.

1. "The kings of the earth set themselves." "About that time Herod the king stretched forth his hands to vex certain of the church." He was known as Herod Agrippa, and his character bore the infamous brand of the Herod stock. By unscrupulous subservience to the caprices and crimes of Roman emperors, he had become possessed of regal power hardly inferior to that of Herod the Great. In order to ingratiate himself with the Jewish leaders he made a great show of zeal for the requirements of the Mosaic ritual. Josephus tells us that he did not allow one day to pass without its appointed sacrifice. But his further steps in the same direction were taken in the blood of Christian martyrs.

James, one of the Master's innermost circle, was the first to suffer. He had been surnamed Boanerges, and had on one occasion called fire from heaven. He proved himself able to drink of his Master's cup and be baptized with His baptism.

Agrippa saw that it pleased the Jews, and he was encouraged to strike again, but harder; and this time to arrest the leader of the hated sect, who more than once had defied the whole strength of the Sanhedrin. Peter was the strongest element in the Christian community. The precautions taken to secure him suggests that the king feared lest his arrest might lead to an attempt at rescue, and also that his advisors and supporters had a lively memory of the two previous occasions on which the prison doors had been opened for the release of this same man. A body of sixteen soldiers was set to watch and hold the prisoner. Four were on duty for three hours, and were then relieved. Two were in the cell with him, his hands fastened to one on either side. A third stood outside the bolted door, while a fourth was posted along the corridor, which led to the great iron gate. Already Herod's doom was prepared, and the angel who was to release Peter was ready to smite the tyrant oppressor in the hour of his greatest triumph. When the people were shouting in mad adulation, "It is the voice of a god, and not of a man," the angel of the Lord immediately smote him, because he did not give God the glory: and he was carried from the theater to his palace, a dying man. For five long days he lay in excruciating agony, and on the sixth of August expired, unlamented.

2. THE PRAYER OF THE CHURCH. The situation appeared desperate, so far as human judgment was concerned. If Herod succeeded in his designs against Peter, what could the rank and file look for but wholesale massacre? But there is always a weapon left to the children of God. With God all things are possible. Peter was kept in prison "until the days of unleavened bread had passed"; but prayer was made without ceasing of the church to God for him.

Day after day passed, and the seven days of the Feast had expired. On the next day Herod would bring his prisoner to a mock trial and then a cruel death. As yet there had been no answering voice from heaven. The Passover moon was waning, the next day was climbing the sky. We are informed that Peter was not missed until it was day, i.e., sunrise, about six o'clock. Clearly then his release must have taken place between three o'clock, when a fresh quarternion had come on duty, and six o'clock when they were relieved. Some time must be allowed for the watch and their ward to become drowsy and fall into a sound sleep. Therefore it may have been about five o'clock in the April dawn that the light shone into the darkness of the cell, and the angel of the Lord stood by His servant's side.

Meanwhile He was answering prayer by the great peace that He breathed into Peter's soul. He was sleeping between two soldiers, bound with two chains, and guards before the door kept the prison. Perhaps he pillowed his heart on the never-to-be-forgotten words, which the Lord had addressed to him on the shores of the lake: "*When thou shalt be old,* thou shalt stretch forth thy hands, and another shall gird thee, and carry thee whither thou wouldest not." But he was not old. His power was yet in its maturity; and death by crucifixion was not in Herod's power. So he rested in the Lord, and his mind was kept in perfect peace. Was not this a part at least of God's answer to the protracted intercessions of the church?

3. THE OPENING OF THE IRON GATE. God's angel cast off his enshrouding veil, and instantly a mild and gentle light fell on the sleeping group, awaking none of them. He had to smite Peter on his side, and call him to arise. Naturally enough he arose, hardly aware that the fetters and chains had ceased to hold him. The apostle seems to have been dazed, and needed constant reminders of what he should do in tightening his girdle, putting on his sandals, and assuming his warm outer cloak. In answer to the angel's summons to follow him, he passed through the door of the cell as though in a dream. "He wist not that it was true which was done by the angel; but thought he saw a vision." The gleaming light from his form led him past the first and second sentries, but they gave no sign of awakening. "A deep sleep from God had fallen upon them." Did he question whether that mighty iron gate would open? But when they reached this last barrier it silently opened to them of its own accord. It was swung open and closed again by strong and invincible hands. The morning breath was in Peter's face, as in company

273

with his angel guide he passed through one street; but that was all, and it was enough, for God is sparing of the miraculous. When our own judgment is adequate for our tasks, we are left to use it. When, therefore, they had passed through one street, the angel left him, "and *when he had considered the thing,* he came to the house of Mary, the mother of John, where many were gathered together and were praying." Mary was sister to Barnabas and the mother of John Mark. There had been no sleep in that home that night. Peter's coming martyrdom was on every heart; and perhaps the hope of his deliverance had faded from their thought. They were resigning themselves to what seemed to be the Lord's will, and only asking that he might be strengthened and upheld in his last hours. This may explain their incredulity when Rhoda, the servant girl, rushed into their midst with the announcement that Peter was standing at the gate. For precaution's sake she had asked who it was who sought for admittance at that unusual hour; and when she heard his voice, with which she was intimately familiar, for he was a constant visitor there, she recognized it instantly, and in her joy actually forgot to admit him, so he continued knocking.

"It is his angel," they said, "and thou art mad." But her confident affirmations, and the continued knocking, at last prevailed, and they opened the door to find that it was as the girl had said. Peter did not enter the house. As soon as he was missed by his guards, search would probably be instituted in the homes of his closest friends. There must be no presumption on his part. He must use his own wit to evade his foes. Therefore, with a few hurried explanations and directions, with loving greetings to James and the others, he departed while it was yet dark and went to another place.

24

"My Decease"
2 Peter 1:12–16

When the great issue that led to the summoning of the First Church Council, described in Acts 15, had been arrived at, there appears to have been a further agreement as to the respective areas of influence to be alotted to the leaders of the church. It was obvious that "the gospel of the uncircumcision"—to use the phrasing of Galatians 2, had been entrusted by the divine Lord to the apostle Paul. To Paul therefore was given the vast Roman world toward the West. To this arrangement a hearty agreement was given by James, the president of the church, Peter, and John. They gave the right hands of fellowship to Paul and Barnabas, that they should go unto the Gentiles, while they gave themselves to the scattered sheep of the house of Israel that lay eastward.

1. PETER'S ITINERANT LABORS. In following this arrangement we find the apostle of the Gentiles visiting Syria and the seaboard of Asia Minor, passing from there to Greece and Rome. It was in his heart to cover the whole Western world with a network of evangelization. "Round about to Illyricum he fully preached the gospel of Christ," and even contemplated a visit to Spain, the extreme limit of the empire toward the setting sun. Peter, on the other hand, if we may make inferences from hints in his epistles, corroborated by the statements of ecclesiastical tradition, concentrated his labors on the vast multitudes of Israelites who were scattered through the eastern portion of the

empire. It will be remembered that representatives of the "Diaspora," or scattered Jews, are especially mentioned in Acts 2 as forming part of the vast wondering crowd that gathered on the Day of Pentecost. Parthia, Media, Persia, Mesopotamia, Pontus and Cappadocia, Phrygia and Pamphylia, had sent their contingents; and it is more than probable that these very districts were embraced in the wide area that constituted what we may describe as Peter's diocese. Unless tradition is mistaken, the last sixteen or seventeen years of his life were occupied by a wide system of evangelistic ministry.

Forty years after his death, Pliny, whom Trajan had appointed governor of part of the region superintended by Peter, described in a state paper the wonderful predominance of Christianity. The temples dedicated to Jupiter and Mars were deserted, the usual sacrifices were unoffered, while the entire population frequented the assemblies of "the pestilent Christian heresy." He admits the purity and blamelessness of the Christian ideals and practice, their solemn oaths to abstain from sin, and their freedom from sins of violence. This testimony is confirmed by others, and as we connect their various testimonies, we get the vision of a widespread Christian community animated by passionate devotion to Christ and to the spread of His gospel. "It is incredible," writes one of the historians of the period, "with what alacrity these poor people support and defend their cause. They are firmly persuaded that one day they will enjoy eternal life; therefore they despise death with wonderful courage, and offer themselves voluntarily to punishment. They look with contempt on all earthly treasures, and hold everything in common." Such was the harvest, plentiful and rich, that resulted from the labors of Peter and his fellow workers in these prolific fields.

The contention that he worked mainly in the eastern part of the empire is further supported by the inscription of his first epistle. He addresses the elect, who are sojourners of the Dispersion in Pontus, Galatia, Cappadocia, Asia and Bithynia, and it is interesting to notice that the order of enumeration is that which an author would use who was writing in the East and not in the West. The enumeration begins with the easternmost province, proceeds westward, and ends with the most distant in the South.

This vast area, as large as the whole of France, containing 500 cities and towns, was repeatedly traversed by the apostle, but it is clear that he was something more than an itinerant evangelist. His epistles supply evidence that he remained long enough in each place to build healthy churches, appoint elders, and shepherd, according to the Lord's command, both lambs and sheep. The tone of his epistles is so affectionate and intimate, that we realize as we read that there was a very evident and tender personal relationship which knit him to them, and they to him. The fact also that the epistle is addressed, not to churches, but to the elect sojourners of the dispersion, supports the view that Peter exercised a very distinct pastoral office, which could only have originated in a prolonged residence in the main centers of population.

It must not be supposed, however, that he addressed himself only to Jews. He expressly mentions those who had not been a people, but were now the people of God; who had not obtained mercy, but had now obtained it. It had been inferred from his warnings against the luxurious plaiting of the hair, the wearing of gold, and the putting on of apparel, that the new faith had attracted some of the wealthier classes. Perhaps also his desire that, when called on, believers would be able to give an apology, or defense, of their hope, indicates that some among them were of sufficient culture to do so with efficiency. But clearly there was a vast popular movement toward Christianity that filled the devotees of the old systems of idolatry with dismay.

There are references to Peter in the First Epistle to Corinth that suggest that he had visited that important city, through which the commerce poured between Rome and Babylon, on account of its central position between the two hemispheres. "I am of Paul, and I of Apollos, and I of *Cephas*"; also, "Have we no right to lead about a sister, a wife, even as *Cephas?*" These may simply refer to the strong conservative party in the early church that ranged itself under the powerful ægis of his name, as contrasted with the more advanced and liberal school of thought led by Paul. But it is not unreasonable to accept these references in their most literal sense, and to believe that, even after the unfortunate incident at Antioch, Peter, in Corinth, and perhaps elsewhere, personally cooperated with and supported that noble gospel-pioneer, whom in his second epistle he designates as his "beloved brother" Paul.

2. HIS FINAL RESIDENCE IN BABYLON. In its closing sentence, Peter dates his first epistle from Babylon, and there is no valid reason for doubting that toward the end of his life, when the increasing infirmities of age placed a necessary restraint on his labors, he made his home in that ancient and historic city, which was densely peopled by Jews.

When Nebuchadnezzar captured Jerusalem, the first chance he got he transported to Babylon "the chief men and all the men of might, and all that were strong and apt for war"; and, a few years later, when Zedekiah had revolted after burning the house of God and breaking down the wall, the great king carried away to Babylon all who had escaped the sword. There was therefore a very large Jewish population in the province of Babylonia. The bands that followed Ezra and Nehemiah to their desolated city and denuded lands were a comparatively small percentage of the whole number that had been removed. The rich, the learned, and the highborn seem to have chosen to remain in the beautiful land of Babylon, with its mighty rivers, its luxuriant vegetation, its delicious climate.

These Babylonian Jews were extremely loyal to the great traditions of the past. They have been described as Hebrews of the Hebrews. They gave lavish contributions annually to the maintenance of the temple services, and in religious matters obeyed the mandates of the Sanhedrin. Despite the distance and the difficulties of travel they brought their children to worship in the sacred shrine. It was toward Jerusalem that they turned when they prayed.

It was there that the chief pastor of the scattered flock indited the first epistle, which was distributed through Silvanus, or Silas; and the second, which may be regarded as his final testimony to the truth of the gospel, for which he was prepared to die, even as the Lord had foretold. His mention of Silas is most interesting, for we know that he had been the close companion and associate of the apostle Paul. It is a fair inference that he had been sent by his great leader with a message of love and courage to Peter, amid the growing weakness of age; and that he brought with him a collection of all the epistles in which the apostle of the Gentiles had enshrined his profound thoughts on the excellency of the knowledge of Christ Jesus his Lord. It is evident from the closing verses of his second epistle that Peter read them all, and had found some things hard to be understood; but he loved his friend and brother with chivalrous affection, and acknowledged thankfully "the wisdom which had been given him."

It was in Babylon also that he collaborated the second Gospel with Mark, "my son." The fathers of the church, including Tertullian, Clement and Irenæus, agree that in an important sense Mark was the "interpreter" of Peter. There are many characteristics in the Gospel itself which harmonize with this tradition. A multitude of graphic touches betray the observation of an eyewitness and participator in the wondrous events of the Savior's ministry. The pillow in the boat, the green grass of the five thousand feast, the colt tied outside the house, the taking of little children *in His arms*, the mother-tongue of Talitha cumi, that the face of Peter was toward the light of the fire when he was detected, and that the resurrection message included "and Peter"—have been quoted as evidences that behind Mark's vivid pen there was the recollection of one who had been an eyewitness of the Master's majesty and beauty.

3. THE CLOSING SCENE. Much controversy has centered around the question whether the "Babylon" of Peter's epistle is a figurative name for Rome. It has not been absolutely settled, but from what we have learned in previous pages of the vast Jewish population of Babylon, there seems no reason for refusing to admit that the apostle referred to the literal city on the banks of the Euphrates. We know that his chief work was among Jews, that there was a large colony of Jews in Mesopotamia, that the five districts addressed in his epistle are all Eastern ones, and that their order suggests Babylon as the point of view from which the writer regarded them. But there remain strong grounds for the belief that the decease, or exodus, of the venerable apostle took place at Rome.

Dean Alford quotes the following sentence from one of the early fathers, Lactantius: "Execrable and noxious tyrant as he was, Nero determined to destroy the heavenly Church and to abolish righteousness; and becoming the persecutor of God's servants, he crucified Peter and slew Paul." This at least is perfectly consistent with the Lord's prediction that when Peter was old he would be carried where he did not want to go and that his hands would be outstretched in death—a remarkable expression that signified the kind of death by which he would be called to glorify God.

After reducing Rome to ashes by the conflagration that his wanton cruelty had kindled, Nero cringed before the passionate resentment of his subjects, and in his endeavor to divert it from himself, imputed the hideous crime to the Christians. In his search for victims he scoured the empire, striking first and hardest at the most illustrious and well-known Christian leaders. Among these Paul was certainly one, and Peter was almost certainly another.

What befell them in Rome is not chronicled by inspiration. Dionysius, Bishop of Corinth in the second century, states that Peter and Paul suffered martyrdom at the same time; and Jerome, in the fourth century, attests that Peter was crucified and crowned with martyrdom, his head being turned earthward and his feet in the air, because he held that he was unworthy to be crucified as his Lord was. Such was the death that he experienced at Rome. By such an exodus—for that is the Greek word—he passed out from this world to the bosom of the Redeemer, whom he had so ardently loved.

In his two Pentecostal sermons, and in both his epistles, Peter is revealed as an earnest student of prophecy. In his last epistle he stirs up our minds that we may remember the words that were spoken earlier by the holy prophets. When the full radiancy of glory broke on his spirit, and the daystar that had long shone in his heart was extinguished in the full-orbed splendor of God's presence-chamber, and as he remembered the Mount of Transfiguration, we can imagine him saying again, "Lord, it is good for me to be here." There was no need to build a small and vanishing tabernacle, for he was in the Father's house of many mansions; and there was no fear of the vision fading, or of the faces of the blessed vanishing. The long night of fishing was over, and Jesus had come down to the water's edge to welcome him. He had come forth, girded to serve him. The fire of His Love greeted his spirit. His wounds were healed with the leaves of the tree of life; his weariness was forgotten as the Lord kissed his welcome. Then dear and familiar forms began to gather around him, and none of them asked Who art thou? or What place is this? For they knew that it was the Lord, and that they were in the home that He had promised to prepare.

25

Life's Afterglow
2 Peter 1:15

In his epistles the apostle stored the thoughts that he was especially anxious should be associated with his memory, and we should linger a little longer to consider them; and they may be thus enumerated:

1. COMFORT AMID TRIAL. The Lord had especially commissioned him to strengthen his brethren, and indeed they were passing through experiences that especially called for comfort and strength. They were reproached for the name of Christ. The trials to their faith, patience, and constancy were "fiery." They were called to be partakers of the sufferings of Christ. Arraignments before arrogant and pagan judges, the lost of property, the infliction of torture, the scattering of families, cruel scourgings, prolonged imprisonment, death in the arena or by fire—these were their experiences.

In these circumstances, what could be more exhilarating than the apostle's repeated reminder of the example and constancy of the Savior, who had suffered for them, leaving them an example that they should follow in His steps? "Rejoice," he said, "inasmuch as ye are partakers of Christ's sufferings." Before his eyes the martyr's death was always present, as his Lord had told him; and he passed on to others the source of his own steadfastness and courage.

2. THE SACRIFICIAL NATURE OF THE SAVIOR'S DEATH. That was no ordinary death before which the sun veiled his face and the rocks rent in sympathy. It was the death of the Redeemer. It was a sacrifice, as of a Lamb without blemish or spot. The Son of God had borne the sins of men in His own body on the tree. He had died, the just for the unjust, to bring them to God. The blood shed on the cross was "precious" blood. Its sprinkling on the conscience brought peace, and severed the soul from its vain lifestyle received by tradition from the past.

3. THE CERTAINTY OF FUTURE GLORY. Those whom Peter addressed were reminded that they had been begotten to a living hope by the resurrection of Jesus Christ from the dead. For them an inheritance had been purchased and awaiting them, which was incorruptible, undefiled, and does not fade away. They would receive a crown of glory that could not fade away.

4. THE URGENCY FOR A HOLY LIFE. He who had called them was holy, and they had to be holy also. They were called to be a chosen generation, a royal priesthood, a holy nation, a people for Christ's own possession.

Our space does not permit a discussion of all the exhortations to holiness that are found in these epistles, nor to indicate the qualities of Christian character on which the apostle insists; but we may specify the one grace of humility on which he lays special and repeated stress. How different are these injunctions from the old proud, boastful, and imperious spirit, which in his earlier life had so often betrayed him!

5. THE NATURE OF DEATH. He thought and spoke of it as the putting off of the tent or tabernacle, which symbolized the pilgrim character of his earthly life, that he might enter the house not made with hands, his permanent dwelling place, eternal in the heavens. He said that it was a decease, or exodus. For him death was not a condition, but a passage. It was no bridge of sighs from a palace to a dungeon, but one of smiles and jubilation from a cell to the blaze of the eternal day. But all was summed up in the vision of that dear face, which he hoped to see as soon as he had crossed over. Jesus had been the daystar of his heart, and He would be the light of all his future, in the city that needs neither sun nor moon, because the Lamb is the light of it.

PAUL

1

Prenatal Grace
1 Tim. 1:14

The source of a stream must be sought, not where it arises; but in the mighty sea, drawn upward in evaporation, or in the clouds that condense against the cold slopes of the hills. So with the life of God within us. In its earlier stages we are apt to suppose it originated in our will and choice, but as we review it from the eminence of the years, we discover that we chose because we were chosen; that we loved because we were first loved. All mature piety extols the grace of God—that unmerited love, which each man thinks was magnified most abundantly in his own case. "By the grace of God, I am what I am."

Paul is very emphatic in his acknowledgments of this prenatal grace.

I. FOREKNOWN. "Known unto God," said James, "are all his works from the beginning of the world"; and if His works were foreknown, how much more His saints! Before time began it was known in heaven who would be attracted by the love of the cross to trust, love, and obey; who would be drawn to the dying and risen Son of God; who would have eternal affinity with Him in death and resurrection: and of these it is said, "Whom he did foreknow, he also did predestinate to be conformed to the image of his Son, that he might be the firstborn among many brethren" (Rom. 8:29).

As the eye of omniscient love glanced down the ages, it must have lighted with peculiar pleasure on the eager devoted soul of Paul. God foreknew and predestinated him. The divine purpose descrying his capicity for the best, selected him for it, and it for him.

2. CREATED IN CHRIST JESUS TO GOOD WORKS. He has been showing the place of works in the gospel scheme, revealing that neither our salvation, nor our faith, is a matter for boasting. "It is the gift of God; not of works," he cries, and then proceeds to the magnificent assertion, "We are his workmanship, created in Christ Jesus unto good works, which God hath before ordained that we should walk in them" (Eph. 2:10).

The Greek word translated workmanship is "poem." We are God's poem. As a great poet may adopt various kinds of rhythm and measure, such as may suit his conception, but has nevertheless a purpose in each poem that issues from his creative fancy, so God means something as He sends each life forth from the silence of eternity; and if we do not hinder Him He superintends the embodiment of that conception, making our entire life, from the cradle to the grave, a symmetrical and homogeneous poem, dominated by one thought, though carried out with an infinite variety of illustration and detail.

In a poem the expression is adapted to the conception. The poet's art demands that no touch of description or narrative, in the earlier lines, should be fruitless or redundant. To allow the canvas to be covered by figures or objects that are not conducive to the main intention of a picture is reprehensible.

So in human life. God knows the works that are prepared, that we should walk in them. And as He has created them for us, so He has created us for them, in Christ Jesus.

3. RAISED IN CHRIST'S RESURRECTION. Paul's education differed widely from that of his fellow apostles. They had grown up with Christ. It is likely that the Master was familiar with many of them before He called them. They grew gradually therefore into those mysteries of His death and resurrection. They knew Jesus the man before they recognized Christ the Messiah.

To Paul, on the other hand, the first conception of Jesus was in His risen glory. He knew perfectly, for it was common talk when he was resident in Jerusalem, that Jesus had been crucified under Pontius Pilate; but now he beheld Him risen, living, speaking, His face shining with light above the brightness of the sun. He had to think his way back from the ascension and resurrection glory to Calvary, Gethsemane, the human life, and the faraway scenes of the Lord's nativity and early years.

But more than this, Paul had a very vivid belief in the identification of all who believe with the risen Lord. He held and taught that all the members of the mystical body shared in the experiences and exploits of their Head. What happened to Him happened to them also, and to each of them. There was no single believer therefore who could not claim as his own all that had befallen Jesus, though at the time he might have been dead in trespasses and sins, or had not begun to exist.

Paul always taught that the death of the cross was a propitiating sacrifice for the sins of the whole world—a sacrifice that stands alone in its sublime and unapproachable glory. But he loved to dwell on that other and secondary aspect of the Savior's death, by virtue of which, in the divine intention, all who believe are considered one with Him in His death, resurrection, and ascension into the heavenlies.

In one memorable text he connects these two aspects of the cross. "He loved me; He gave Himself *for* me," is bound by a golden link to the words, "I have been crucified *with* Christ." He loved to consider that he had died with Christ, and to claim that he should daily receive the power of His risen life. He longed to know Jesus Christ, and the power of His resurrection being quite prepared to taste the fellowship of His sufferings and to become conformed to His death, if only he might day by day attain to the resurrection from the dead (Phil. 3).

It was a radiant vision, and one of which the apostle never wearied. When the world would cast the spell of its blandishments over you, dare to answer the challenge by the assertion that it has no further jurisdiction over you, since you have passed from its territory and control, by virtue of your union with Him who, in that He died, died to sin once, and in that He lives, lives to God.

Get up into the high mountains, believing children of God, and view the everlasting love of your Father toward you in Jesus! "O the depth of the riches both of the wisdom and knowledge of God! how unsearchable are his judgments, and his ways past finding out! For of him, and through him, and to him, are all things:to whom be the glory for ever. Amen" (Rom. 11:33, 36).

2

"When I Was a Child"
Phil. 3:1–11

Not far from the easternmost bay of the Mediterranean, in the midst of a rich and luxuriant plain, stood Tarsus, "no mean city," as one of its greatest sons tells us, but at the time of which we write a thriving emporium of trade, and a focus of intellectual and religious activity.

In the Jewish quarter of this thriving city at the beginning of this era (perhaps about A.D. 4, while Jesus was still an infant in his mother's arms at Nazareth), a child was born, who by his life and words was destined to make Tarsus famous in all for years to come, and to give a new impulse to men's religious convictions. At his circumcision he probably received a double name, that of Saul for his family, and that of Paul for the world of trade and municipal life.

The stamp of the great city left an ineffaceable impression on the growing lad, widely different from his Master's. Paul was reared amid the busy streets and crowded bazaars of Tarsus, thronged with merchants, students, and sailors from all parts of the world. Unconsciously, as he grew he was being prepared to understand human life under every aspect, and to become habituated to the thoughts and habits of the store, the camp, the arena, the temple. He became a man to whom nothing that touched human life was foreign. He loved the stir of city life, and drew his metaphors from its keen interests.

1. HE CAME OF PURE HEBREW STOCK. "A Hebrew of [sprung from] the Hebrews." On both sides his genealogy was pure. His father must have been a man of considerable position, or he would not have possessed the coveted birthright of Roman citizenship. Though living away from Palestine, he was not a Hellenist Jew; but as distinctly Hebrew as any who dwelled in the Holy City. His father was perhaps given to sternness with his children; or it might not have occured to his son, years later, to warn fathers against provoking their children to wrath, lest they should become discouraged.

The Hebrew tongue was probably the ordinary speech of that home. This may in a measure account for the apostle's intimate acquaintance with the Hebrew Scriptures, which he so often quotes. It was in Hebrew that Jesus spoke to him on the road to Damascus, and in Hebrew that he addressed the crowds from the steps of the castle. His pulse beat quickly as he remembered that he belonged to the chosen race, God's first born, whose were the adoption, and the glory, and the covenants, and the giving of the law, and the service of God, and the promises.

2. HIS EARLY EDUCATION WAS VERY RELIGIOUS. "He was a Pharisee, and the son of a Pharisee." In our day the word Pharisee is a synonym for religious pride and hypocrisy; but we must never forget that in those old Jewish days the Pharisee represented some of the noblest traditions of the Hebrew people. Amid the prevailing indifference the Pharisees stood for a strict religious life. As against the scepticism of the Sadducees, who believed in neither spirit nor unseen world, the Pharisees held to the resurrection of the dead, and the life of the world to come. Amid the lax morals of the time, which infected Jerusalem almost as much as Rome, the Pharisee was austere in his ideals, and holy in life.

Paul was also proud that at the earliest possible moment he had been initiated into the rites and privileges of his religion, being "circumcised the eighth day."

3. HE WAS BLAMELESS IN OUTWARD LIFE. As touching the righteousness that is of the law, as far as outward observances went, he was blameless. There was no precept in the moral or ceremonial law that he would consciously disregard. "Brethren," he said on one occasion, "I have lived in all good conscience before God until this day" (Acts 23:1).

The ardent soul of the young Pharisee was bent on standing in the front rank of saints. Perhaps he encountered disappointment from the first. Possibly the cry, "O wretched man that I am," began to formulate itself long before he became a Christian. Though outwardly his conduct was exemplary, his soul may have been rent by mortal strife. Often he saw and approved the better, and did the worse; often he lamented the infirmity of his motives and the infirmity of his will.

4. HIS NATURE MUST HAVE BEEN WARM-HEARTED AND FERVID FROM THE FIRST. The tears that flowed at Miletus, the heart that was nearly broken on his last journey to Jerusalem, the pathetic appeals and allusions of his epistles, his capacity for ardent and constant friendships—were not the growth of his mature years; but were present, in germ at least, from his earliest childhood. He must always have been extremely sensitive to kindness; and the contrast between his remembrance of his friends years later, and his entire reticence about his parents, and brothers or sisters, shows how bitter and final was that disowning that followed on his avowal of Christianity. There is more than appears on the surface in his remark, "For whom I have suffered the loss of all things."

The zeal, which years later led him to persecute the church, was already stirring in his heart. "I am a Jew," he once said, "born in Tarsus of Cilicia, instructed according to the strict manner of the law of our fathers, being zealous for God." Indeed, he tells us that he advanced in the Jew's religion beyond many of his own age among his country-men.

As a child he would have learned by heart Deuteronomy 6:4–9 and Psalms 113–118. It is not likely that he received the culture of the Greek philosophy. Between the ages of thirteen and sixteen he would be sent to Jerusalem to pursue his training for the office of a rabbi, to which he was evidently designated by the ambition of his father. It was easy for the boy to do this, as he had a married sister in Jerusalem with whom he could lodge during his attendance on the classes of the illustrious Gamaliel. "I was brought up in this city," he said later, "at the feet of Gamaliel."

We must not forget to record that during these boyish years he acquired a trade that served him usefully when he was hard pressed for means of livelihood.

Every Jew was taught a trade, generally that of his father. Paul's family for generations back had probably been engaged in weaving a dark coarse cloth of goat's hair. This handicraft was poorly remunerated; but in Paul's case it was highly suitable to the exigencies of a wandering life. Other trades would require a settled workshop and expensive apparatus; but this was a simple industry, capable of being pursued any-where, and needing the smallest possible apparatus and tools.

It was not a small thing to have come of noble and godly parentage, to be a child of Abraham, and heir of the promises made to his seed. *But he counted it loss.*

It was not a small thing to have built up by constant obedience and scrupulous care a fabric of blameless reputation. *But he counted it loss.*

It was not a small thing to be conscious of the throbbing of a fervent spirit that would brook no indolence or lethargy, and which transformed duty to delight. *But he counted it dross.*

a. *There was no irreverence* in his allusions to the rites of the venerable system in which he had been nurtured. For long years Judaism had been the only interpreter to him of the divine, the only nourishment of his religious instincts. In these probably lay the rudiments of all he has afterwards learned. But not withstanding the noble reverence of the apostle's soul, he could not but affirm that what he had counted gain was loss.

b. *The grounds for this verdict* are probably to be found in two directions. On the one hand, he discovered that the sacrifices of Judaism, as was obvious from their constant repetition, might bring sins to remembrance, but they could not remove them; he discovered that outward rites, however punctiliously observed, did not help to cleanse the conscience; he discovered that in Judaism there was no power to salvation, nothing to reinforce and renew the flagging energies of the soul. On the other hand, he had found something better.

Paul had seen Jesus. Before the glory of that heavenly vision all other objects of attraction had paled. He counted all things to be loss for the excellency of the knowledge of Christ Jesus his Lord. In comparison with His finished work, all his own efforts were futile. It was a relief to turn from his own righteousness, which was of the law, and to avail himself of God's method of righteousness, which was through faith in Christ. With great thankfulness he abandoned his own strivings and efforts, and counted all his former gains but dross and dung, that he might win Christ and all that Christ could be and do.

It is an awful experience, when the soul first awakens to find that he has been making a mistake in the most important of matters, and has nearly missed the deepest meaning of life.

There is only one test that can really show whether we are right or wrong: it is our attitude to Jesus Christ. If our religious life revolves around anything less than Him—though it be the doctrines of Christianity, work for Him, the rules of a holy life—it will inevitably disappoint and fail us. But if He is Alpha and Omega; if our faith, however feeble, looks up to Him; if we press on to know Him, the power of His resurrection, and the fellowship of His sufferings; if we count all things but loss for the excellency of His knowledge—we may possess ourselves in peace amid the mysteries of life, and the lofty requirements of the great white throne.

3

Separated From Birth
Gal. 1:15

God has a purpose in every life; and where the soul is perfectly yielded and acquiescent, He will certainly realize it. Blessed is he who has never thwarted the execution of the divine ideal.

One of the most interesting studies in human life is to see how all the circumstances and incidents of its initial stages have been shaped by a determining will, and made to serve a beneficent purpose. Every thread is needed for the completed pattern; every piece of equipment stands in good stead at the final test.

1. THE FUTURE APOSTLE MUST BE DEEPLY INSTRUCTED IN THE JEWISH LAW. "The law" must stand here as a convenient term, not only for the moral and Levitical code as given in the Pentateuch, but for the minute and laborious additions of the rabbis. No one could have appreciated the intolerable burden of this yoke of legalism—which even Peter said neither they nor their fathers were able to bear—unless he had been taught, as Paul was "according to the perfect manner of the law of the fathers" (Acts 22:3).

2. HE NEEDED TO BE SKILLFUL IN HIS QUOTATION AND APPLICATION OF THE HEBREW SCRIPTURES. Every question in religious and ordinary Jewish life was settled by an appeal to the Scriptures. No speaker could gain the audience, or hold the attention of a Jewish congregation for a moment, unless he could show, the more ingeniously the better, that his statements could be substantiated from the inspired Word. To the law and the testimony every assertion had to be brought. Before that venerable bar every teacher had to stand.

It was above all things necessary that Christianity should be shown to be, not the destruction but the fulfillment of the ancient law. What made Paul so "mad" against Christianity was its apparent denial and betrayal of the obvious meaning of Old Testament prophecies and types. Neither he nor any of his co-religionists were prepared to accept a humiliated, suffering, dying Messiah, unless it could be shown without controversy that such a conception was the true reading of Moses, the Prophets, and the Law. Throughout the entire course, "the sacred oracles" were the only textbook; and every day was spent in the careful and minute consideration of words, lines, and letters, together with the interpretations of the various rabbis.

Men might chafe at Paul's renderings of the ancient words, but they could not dispute his intimate acquaintance with them, and his profound erudition. He knew the whole ground perfectly. There was not a single argument with which he was not familiar, and for which he was not instantly ready with a reply. The field of Scripture had been repeatedly plowed over by that keen mind, and its harvests gathered into that retentive memory. It was this power that gave him an entrance into every synagogue, and carried conviction to so many candid Jews. How richly, for instance, it was appreciated by Bible students, like those he met at Berœa!

3. HE NEEDED TO HAVE LARGE AND LIBERAL VIEWS. Jewish intolerance and exclusivism had reared a high wall of partition between Jew and Gentile. The Jews had no dealings with the Samaritans; how much less with the Gentile dogs that crouched beneath the well-spread table of the children!

The majority of the apostles were largely influenced by this caste spirit. It was hard for them, though they had been molded by the Lord Himself, to break through the fence of early training. Had the shaping of the primitive church been left to them, though theoretically they might have acknowledged the equality of Jew and Gentile in God's sight, yet practically they would have drawn distinctions between the Jewish Christians and those other sheep that their Shepherd was bringing, but which were not of the Hebrew fold. The need of a trumpet voice was urgent, to proclaim that Jesus had abolished in His flesh the enmity, that He might create in Himself of two one new man, so making peace.

Through the ordering of divine providence this qualification also was communicated to the future apostle of the uncircumcision. By birth, as we have seen, he was a Hebrew: otherwise he could have influenced Jews, or obtained admission into their synagogues. But he had been brought up at the feet of the great rabbi who, while reverenced as "the beauty of the law," was recognized also as the most large-hearted of all the Jewish doctors. But he went so far as to permit and advocate the study of Greek literature. In his speech before the Sanhedrin, given in Acts 5, we trace the movements of a human and generous mind.

The influence of such a teacher must have been strong on the young Tarsus student, who had come to sit at his feet, and who regarded him with a boundless enthusiasm.

4. THERE WAS NEEDED AN ESPECIALLY WIDE KNOWLEDGE OF THE WORLD. The man who was to be a missionary to men had to know them. He who would be all things to all men, that by all means he might win some, had to be familiar with their methods of life and thought. A Jerusalem Jew could not possibly have adapted himself to cultured Greeks and practical Romans, to barbarians and Scythians, to bond and free; to Festus the imperial governor, and Agrippa the Hebrew king; to Onesimus the slave, and Philemon the master, as Paul did.

When his training at Jerusalem was complete he must have returned to Tarsus. In these years he probably married, or else he would not afterward have occupied a seat in the Sanhedrin; and steadily pursued his trade, or exercised his profession as a rabbi in the local synagogue, or traveled far afield on some religious mission, compassing sea and land to make proselytes.

Imagine what those seven or eight years must have meant to the young Pharisee. All the while he would be keenly observing and noting every phase of gentile heathendom. The pictures of the world of that age given in the first chapter to the Romans and the first epistle to the Corinthians, could only have been given by one who obtained his information first-hand, and by personal observation.

5. HE NEEDED ALSO TO BE EQUIPPED WITH THE PREREQUISITES OF A GREAT TRAVELER. For this there were three necessary conditions: speech, safety, sustenance. And each was forthcoming.

a. *Speech.* Greek was the common language of the world, the medium of intercourse among educated persons, as English is in India today. And Paul was even more familiar with Greek than with the sacred Hebrew. When quoting the Scriptures he habitually employed the Septuagint (i.e., the Greek) version; and he was able to speak their tongue fluently enough to hold the attention of Athenian philosophers.

b. *Safety.* All the world was Roman. Roman governors in every province; Roman usages in every city; Roman coins, customs, and officials. To be a Roman citizen gave a man a standing and position in any part of the empire. He might not be beaten without trial; or if he were, the magistrates were in jeopardy of losing their office, and even their life. He could demand trial at the bar of Cæsar; if he appealed to Cæsar, to Cæsar he must go. He would be permitted to plead for himself before the bar of Roman justice.

c. *Sustenance.* This was also granted to him. On whatever shore he was cast there were always goats, and always the demand for the coarse cloth at which he had worked from his boyhood.

In all this how evidently was the divine purpose at work, shaping all things after the counsel of its own will.

4

"Thy Martyr Stephen"
Acts 22:20

Sometimes God charges a man with a message, and launches him forth suddenly and irresistibly. Such a man was Elijah, with his "Thus saith the LORD, before whom I stand"; John the Baptist, with his "It is not lawful for thee to have thy brother's wife"; such also was Savonarola of Florence, and many others. And such was Stephen.

We know little or nothing of his antecedents. That he was a Hellenist Jew is almost certain; and that he had personally known and communicated with the Son of Man, whom he afterward recognized in His glory, is more than probable. But of father, mother, birthplace, and education, we know nothing. We have the story of one day, the record of one speech—that day his last, that speech his apology and defense for his life.

Stephen caught for a brief space the glory of the departed Lord, and reflecting it, was transformed into the same image; "and all that sat in the council, looking steadfastly on him, saw his face as it had been the face of an angel" (Acts 6:15).

Stephen's life and death must always have attracted reverent interest; but how much more so as we trace his influence on the method, thought, and character of the great apostle.

1. THE MOVEMENT OF WHICH STEPHEN WAS THE PRODUCT AND REPRESENTATIVE MAY FOR A MOMENT CLAIM OUR ATTENTION. It casts a suggestive sidelight on the career of "the young man Saul."

Three streams of thought were meeting in tumultuous eddies in Jerusalem.

There were *the Jews of the Pharisee party*, represented by Gamaliel, Saul of Tarsus, and other notable men. They were characterized by an intense religiousness that circled around their ancestry, their initial rite, their law, their temple. Were they not Abraham's children? Had not God entered into special covenant relations with them, of which circumcision was the outward sign and seal? And as for the temple, the whole of their national life was anchored to the spot where it stood. There was the only altar, priesthood, shrine, of which their religion admitted. Narrow, casuistical, bigoted, intensely fanatical; priding themselves on their national privilege as the chosen people, but resentful against the appeals of the greatest of their prophets; counting on the efficacy of their system, but careless of personal character—such was the orthodox and conservative Jewish party of the time.

Next came the *Hebrew Christian church*, led and represented by the apostles. Of founding a new religious organization they had no plans. That they should ever live to see Judaism superseded by the teaching they were giving, or Christianity existing apart from the system in which they had been nurtured, was a thought that never occurred to them. Their Master had rigorously observed the Jewish rights and feasts; and they followed in His steps, and impressed a similar course of action on their adherents. The church lingered still in the portals of the synagogue. The disciples observed the hours of prayer, were found in devout attendance at the temple's services, had their children circumcised, and would not have dreamed of being released from the regulations that bound the ordinary Jews as with iron chains. And it seems certain that, if nothing had happened of the nature of Stephen's apology and protests, the church would have become another Jewish sect, distinguished by the piety and purity of its adherents, and by their strange belief in the Messiahship of Jesus of Nazareth, who had been crucified under Pontius Pilate.

Lastly, there were *the converts from among the Hellenist Jews.* The origin of the Hellenist or Grecian Jews must be traced back to the captivity, which God overruled to promote the dissemination of Jewish conceptions throughout the world. It was but a small contingent that returned to Jerusalem with Nehemiah and Ezra; the vast majority elected to remain in the land of their adoption for purposes of trade. They slowly spread from there throughout Asia Minor to the cities of its seaboard and the highland districts of its interior, planting everywhere the synagogue, with its protest on behalf of the unity and the spirituality of God. Egypt, and especially Alexandria; Greece, with her busy commercial seaports; Rome, with her imperial cosmopolitan influence—became familiar with the peculiar countenance and customs of this wonderful people, who always contrived to secure for themselves a large share of the wealth of any country in which they had settled. But their free contact with the populace of many lands wrought a remarkable change on them.

While the Jews of Jerusalem and Judæa shrank from the defiling touch of heathenism, and built higher the wall of separation, growing continually prouder, more bitter, more narrow, the Jews that were scattered through the world became more liberal and cosmopolitan. Compelled, as they were, to relinquish the temple with its holy rites, except on rare and great occasions, when they traveled from the ends of the earth to be present at some great festival, they magnified in its place the synagogue, with its worship, its reading of the law, its words of exhortation; and they welcomed to its precincts all who cared to avail themselves of its privileges.

After some years of absence, Paul returned to settle at Jerusalem. It is possible that its Jewish leaders, having been impressed by his remarkable talents and enthusiastic devotion to Judaism, had summoned him to take part in, or lead, that opposition to Christianity, to which events were daily more irrevocably committing them. It is almost certain, also, that to facilitate his operations he was at this time nominated to a seat in the Sanhedrin, which enabled him to give his vote against the followers of Jesus (Acts 26:10).

His first impressions about the followers of "the Way," as the early disciples were termed, were wholly unfavorable. It seemed to him sheer madness to suppose that the crucified Nazarene could be the long-looked-for Messiah, or that He had risen from the dead. He therefore threw himself into the breach and took the lead in disputing with Stephen, who had just been raised to office in the developing church; and, not content with the conservative and timid attitude that the apostles had preserved for some five years, was now leading an aggressive and forward policy.

2. THE BURDEN OF STEPHEN'S TESTIMONY. It was the first attempt to read the story of God's dealings with Israel in the light of Christ; the earliest commentary on the Old Testament by the New; the fragmentary draft of the Epistle to the Hebrews. His eyes were the first that were opened to see that the old covenant was becoming old, and was

almost vanishing away, because on the point of being superseded by that better hope, through which all men might draw nigh to God.

Like most who speak God's truth for the first time, Stephen was greatly misunderstood. We gather this from the charges made against him by the false witnesses, whom the Sanhedrin bribed. They accused him of uttering blasphemous words against Moses, of speaking against the temple and the law, of declaring that Jesus of Nazareth would destroy the temple, and change customs delivered by Moses. And as we attentively follow his argument, we can see how it was that these impressions had been caused.

He spoke of the God of glory; of the great ones of the past as "our fathers"; of the angel that spoke at Sinai; and the living oracles of Scripture. And yet it is undeniable that he saw with undimmed vision that Jesus of Nazareth must change the customs that Moses delivered, and lead His church into more spiritual aspects of truth.

3. HIS MARTYRDOM. We know little of Stephen's life. It was more than probable, as we have already said, that he knew Jesus in his earthly life, for he instantly recognized Him in the heavenly vision. Surely he must have seen Him die, for the traits of His dying beauty molded his own last hours. How meekly to bear his cross; to plead for his murderers with a divine charity; to breathe his departing spirit into unseen hands; to find in death the gate of life, and amid the horror of a public execution the secret of calm and peace—all these were rays of light caught from the cross where his Master had poured out His soul to death.

This, too, powerfully affected Paul. That light on the martyr's face; that evident glimpse into the unseen Holy; those words; that patience and forgiveness; that peace which wrapped his mangled body, crushed and bleeding, as he fell asleep—he could never forget them. Not only did he mold his own great speeches on the model of that never-to-be-forgotten address; not only did those conceptions of the spiritual nature of Christ's kingdom affect his whole after teaching and ministry years later, but the very light that radiated from that strong, sweet, noble character seemed to have been absorbed by his spirit, to be radiated forth again in much patience, in afflictions, in necessities, in distresses, in strifes, in tumults, in pureness, in knowledge, in longsuffering, in kindness, in the Holy Spirit, in love unfeigned.

The blood of the martyrs is the seed of the church.

The power of the persecutor is overcome by the patience of his victims. Saul, at whose feet witnesses lay down their clothes, is catching up and assuming the mantle of the departing prophet and saint.

5

A Light From Heaven
Acts 26:13

If the importance of events can be estimated by the amount of space given in Scripture to their narration, the arrest placed by the risen Lord on the career of Saul of Tarsus must take the second place in the story of the New Testament. It is described three times, with great minuteness of detail—first by Luke, and twice by himself—and the narration occupies more space than the story of any other event, except the crucifixion of our Lord.

It was one of the deepest convictions of the apostle during his life that he had veritably and certainly seen the Lord; and was therefore as really empowered to be a witness of His resurrection as any who had lived and traveled with Him, beginning from the baptism of John until the day that He was received up. "Am I not an apostle? have I not seen Jesus Christ our Lord?" he asks (1 Cor. 9:1). And after enumerating the Lord's appearances after His resurrection, he adds, placing that scene on the road to Damascus on a level with the rest, "Last of all he was seen of me also, as of one born out of due time" (1 Cor. 15:8). Ananias said, "The Lord, even Jesus, that appeared unto thee in the way as thou camest, hath sent me" (Acts 9:17).

Six days before, Saul had left Jerusalem with a small retinue furnished as his escort by the high priest. The journey was long and lonely, giving time for reflection, of which he had known but little during the crowding events of the previous months. It was high noon. Unlike most travelers, he forbore to spend even an hour in the retirement of his tent for shelter from the downward rays of the sun, piercing like swords, while all the air was breathless with the heat. He was too weary of his own musings, too eager to be at his work.

The goal of the long journey was well in sight. Within an hour or two he would be within the gates and traversing the street called Straight, to deliver his commission to the authorities and to ascertain the best point for commencing proceedings. But suddenly a great light shone around him; and a voice, amid the blaze, unintelligible and inarticulate to his companions, though clear enough to himself, was heard, speaking in the familiar Aramaic, and calling him by name (Acts 26:14).

In the light of that moment the apostle saw many things. It was like a sudden flashlight flung over an abyss, revealing secret things that had been entirely hidden, or but dimly understood.

1. IN THE GLORY OF THAT LIGHT HE BECAME CONVINCED OF THE TRUTH OF CHRISTIANITY. There was only one thing that could convince him. He had to see this Jesus of Nazareth, whom he knew to have been crucified, living on the other side of death; he had to be able to recognize and establish His identity; he had to hear Him speak. Such evidence given to himself would be conclusive; but nothing less would avail. He saw the Lord in the way, and the Lord spoke to him." He felt instantly that life henceforward had to have a new meaning and purpose, and he had to live to establish the faith of which he had made such determined havoc.

2. IN THE GLORY OF THAT LIGHT HE BEHELD THE SUPREME REVELATION OF GOD. Nature had told something of God. The heavens had told His glory, and the firmament shown His handiwork. But *this* light was above the brightness of the sun, and made all Nature's wonders pale, as stars at dawn. There is no conceivable method of divine manifestation that can excel the light that shines from the face of Jesus. He beheld the glory of God in the face of Jesus whom he had persecuted.

Would you know God? You must study Him in Jesus. We need nothing beyond; there is nothing beyond. In heaven itself we will still behold the light of the glory of God in the face of Jesus. That light shone before the first ray of sunlight gleamed over the abyss; and it will shine when sun, moon, and stars are dark and cold.

3. IN THE REVELATION OF THAT LIGHT SAUL OF TARSUS SAW THE REAL NATURE OF THE WAR THAT HE HAD BEEN WAGING AGAINST THE RELIGION OF JESUS. The earliest name of the new sect was *the Way*. It was a pathetic and significant title; these simple souls had found a new and living way to the knowledge and worship of God, consecrated through the rent flesh of Him whom their chief priests and rulers had delivered up to be condemned to death.

The young man Saul was exceedingly mad against the pilgrims of the Way. He made life miserable for them, and the word is that which would be used of wild boars uprooting tender vines. He was so angry against them, that when the church at Jerusalem lay desolate, and its garden was torn and trampled into a desert, he pursued the same methods in distant cities, and on the present memorable occasion had received letters to bring those of the Way that were there in bonds to Jerusalem to be punished.

This work of extermination seemed to him part of his religious duty. He owed it to God to stamp out the followers of Jesus. Might not these efforts satisfy for a falling short in respect to the demands of God's law, which now and again forced itself home on his inner consciousness? But, like the Roman soldiers who crucified the Lord, he did not know what he did. "I was a blasphemer, and a persecutor, and injurious: but I obtained mercy, because I did it ignorantly in unbelief" (1 Tim. 1:13).

However, as that light fell on his path, he suddenly awoke to discover that, instead of serving God, he was in collision with Him, and was actually uprooting and ravaging that for which the Son of His love had expended tears and blood. In persecuting the sect of the Nazarenes he was persecuting the Son of God. It was a terrible and overwhelming discovery. Somehow his religion had brought him into collision with God in the persons of those who were dear to Him; instead of his fanatical zeal being pleasing to God it was grievous to Him, and was heaping up wrath against a day of wrath.

4. THAT LIGHT ALSO REVEALED THE INADEQUACY OF HIS RELIGIOUS LIFE. He had lived out all that he thought to be right. But of late he had been compelled to confess to a dull sense of uneasiness and dissatisfaction. He studiously fought against it by immersing himself more sedulously than ever in the work of persecution; yet there it was.

Two causes further instigated this uneasiness. First, he felt that his religion did not satisfy him; it seemed ineffective to curb the imperious demands of sin. Often the good he would he did not do, while the evil he hated he did. Was there nothing better?

Then it seemed as though these humble disciples of Jesus of Nazareth had something better. The meekness with which they bore their suffering; the light that shone on their dying faces; the prayers for their persecutors, which they offered with their dying breath, evidenced the possession of a secret of which he knew that he was destitute. Yet how could He be the Messiah who had come to such an end! And how absurd it was to say that He had risen, when the Roman sentries had solemnly averred that His body had been stolen by His disciples while they slept.

But all these questionings were brought to a head and confirmed when suddenly he beheld Jesus of Nazareth enthroned on the right hand of power, and shining with a light above the brightness of the sun.

5. HE NOW DISCOVERED THE SOURCE OF HIS UNEASINESS OF HEART AND CONSCIENCE. He now saw that these strivings were the prickings of the great Husbandman's goad, by which He had long been attempting to lead him to undertake that life work that had been prepared for him from the foundation of the world. From now on he was not to do

his own prompting, but God's; not to be clothed in his own righteousness, but in God's; not to oppose the Nazarene, but to take His yoke to bear His burden, to do His will.

6. THAT LIGHT ALSO REVEALED TO HIM THE COURSE OF HIS FUTURE LIFE. He was from this day on to be a minister and a witness of those things that he had seen, and of those in which Christ would still appear to him.

It was enough. He meekly asked what he must do. And in answer, he was told to take the next step, which lay just before him, and allow himself to be led unto the city.

And then there arose before him in a flash on the high road, and in fuller development during the three days' retirement in the house of Judas, the Lord's ideal of his life—that he should be sent to Jew and Gentile; that by his simple witness he would be used to open blind eyes; that men might turn from darkness to light, from the power of Satan to God. That concept molded his life, lingered always in his memory, and formed the basis of one of his noblest outbursts (Col. 1). He felt that he had been apprehended; he realized something of the purpose for which he had been apprehended; and with patient faith he resolved, so far as in him lay, to apprehend it.

How could he be other than obedient? As a token of his meek submission, he allowed himself to be led by the hand into the city, which he had expected to enter as an inquisitor; and bent low to receive instruction from one of those simple-hearted believers whom he had expected to drag captive to Jerusalem. Such are the triumphs of the grace of God, and in his case it was shown to be exceedingly abundant.

6

The Inner Revelation of Christ
Gal. 1:15–17

How different to his anticipation was Saul's entrance into Damascus! He had probably often encouraged himself during his weary six-days' journey by picturing the reception that would be accorded to him by the authorities at Damascus, on his arrival at their city as the commissioner of the high priest, charged with the extirpation of the Nazarene heresy. But instead of honor, there was consternation and surprise. No one could quite explain or understand what had taken place. Dismounted from his horse, he went afoot; instead of the haughty bearing of the Inquisitor, the helplessness of a sightless man appealed for hands to lead him; shrinking from notice and welcome, he was only too eager to reach a lonely room where he might recover from the awful effects of that collision between his mortal and sinful nature and the holy, glorious Son of God, whom he had so ruthlessly persecuted.

He seemed a stricken, dejected, broken man—but his soul was radiant with the light of the glory of God in the face of Jesus.

It is interesting to notice how much of the teaching that the apostle gives us later may be discovered in germ in the records of his conversion.

"I am Jesus, whom thou persecutest": *here* is the believer's identification with the Lord, involving all that wonderful teaching of the oneness of the Head and members.

"To make thee a minister and a witness": *here* is the origin of his constant reference to witness and testimony.

"The Gentiles, unto whom now I send thee": *on this* he rested his claim to be considered in a special way the apostle of the Gentiles, and perhaps at this time those two great revelations may have passed for a moment before the eyes of his heart; the one that the Gentiles should be fellow members, fellow heirs, and fellow partakers with the chosen nation in all the privileges and rights of the gospel; the other, to make all men see what is the fellowship of the mystery which from eternal ages has been hidden in the heart of God.

In Acts 26:17–18, we find an epitome of the first chapter of the Epistle to the Colossians. It is, in fact, the seed plot of the apostle's thoughts on the justification and sanctification of the soul. The whole of his message might be focused around these two points—remission of sins, and an inheritance among the sanctified, through faith in the living Christ.

At this formative period of his life three effective agencies were brought to bear on him: the work of God on his heart; contact with Ananias; and the education of the desert solitudes.

1. THE WORK OF GOD ON HIS HEART. Imagine the abundance of revelations made to the blinded man during those three days and nights of silence and solitude in the house of Judas. It is wonderful that he became oblivious to the needs of the body, and did neither eat nor drink.

What mysteries began to pass before him! During those wondrous hours God unveiled secrets that had been kept in silence through times eternal, but were manifested to him according to the commandment of the eternal God, that he might make them known to all nations, to obedience of faith.

But the crowning revelation of all was that on which he lays special stress. It was much to learn that Jesus of Nazareth was in very deed the Son of the Highest, but more than all was the unveiling of the indwelling Christ, living literally within him by His Spirit, so that while he was in Christ, Christ was also in him, as the branch has its place in the vine, and the vine lives through the branch.

God was pleased to make this known to Saul of Tarsus. He will be equally pleased to make it known to you. Ask for a breath of heavenly grace to part the veiling mist, and to show you the line of sunlit Alps, radiant with the morning glow!

2. CONTACT WITH ANANIAS. Holy and humble natures are sometimes permitted to help the spirit that is on the point of emerging from bondage. The offices that one can perform for another are beautifully illustrated in that simple-hearted saint, Ananias, whom the Lord at this moment called on the scene, and to whom He entrusted the keys of the kingdom, that he might unlock Saul's way into perfect peace.

We know very little of Ananias, except that he was a devout man according to the law and was well reported of by the Jews, but evidently he was on intimate terms with his Master. A very slender taper, if it has caught the fire, may communicate its glow to the powerful wicks of a lighthouse tower.

a. *He gave him a brother's welcome.* Though he was fully acquainted with the object of Saul's visit to the city, he accosted him with the sweet and generous term, "brother." *Brother* Saul. What a thrill that address sent through the heart of the new convert! The human love was the sign of the divine. Ah! Love of God, what must you not be, though I have persecuted you so sorely, if the love of man be so strong and tender!

b. *He communicated priceless blessings.* First, under the laying on of his hands, sight came clear to eyes that had beheld nothing since they had been smitten by the glory of "that light." And the touch of this devout man, accompanied as it must have been with the upward glance of prayer and faith, was also the signal for the reception of the anointing grace of the Holy Spirit, infilling, anointing, and equipping for blessed service.

c. *He baptized him.* What a baptism that must have been! What a tidal wave of emotion must have swept over him, as he realized that he was being united with Jesus by the likeness of his death! That baptism was his final and irreversible break with his past life, the Pharisaic party, and his persecution of the adherents of "the Way." From that point on he was avowedly one with the followers of the Nazarene. The cross and grave of Jesus must now stand between him and all that had been—all his friends, ambitions and opinions—while he must turn his face toward labor and travail, hunger and thirst, perils and persecutions, together with the daily deliverance to death for Jesus' sake.

It does not appear that Ananias was aware of all that baptism meant to his new brother Saul. To him it was an act of obedience, a symbol of the washing away of sins. How little do we know, what is passing in the thoughts of those next to us in life's strange school! But Ananias's honest help must have been very comforting to the new disciple. All he knew was that the Lord had said, "I will shew him how great things he must *suffer* for my name's sake."

3. THE EDUCATION OF THE DESERT SOLITUDES. "Immediately I conferred not with flesh and blood: neither went I up to Jerusalem to them which were apostles before me; but I went into Arabia." It is not quite clear whether he began to preach before going; probably not. He wanted to be alone, to reflect on all that he had seen. For this he had to have uninterrupted leisure, and he hungered for the isolation and solitude of the wilderness. Men like Ananias might reassure him; the apostles of the Lord might communicate much of His teachings and wondrous ministry.

Arabia probably stands for the Sinaitic peninsula, with its sparse population, its marked physical features, its associations with Moses, and the Exodus, and Elijah.

Probably the most important work of those years was to review the entire course of Old Testament truth from the new standpoint of vision suggested by the sufferings and death of the Messiah. There was no doubt that He had been crucified in weakness, and now lived in the power of God. But how was this consistent with the anticipations of the prophets and seers of the Old Testament, who had been understood by generations of rabbis to predict an all-victorious prince? How eagerly he turned to all the well-known messianic passages! What ecstasy must have thrilled him as he discovered that they were all consistent with Christ's suffering to death as the way to enter His glory! And how greatly he must have wondered that he and all his people had been so blind to the obvious meaning of the inspired Word (2 Cor. 3).

We can well understand how, on his return to Damascus, he would immediately proclaim that Jesus was the Son of God; and that he should especially confound the Jews who dwelled there, proving that this is the Messiah.

It is almost certain also that he was led at this time to understand the relation of the law to the older covenant into which God had entered with Abraham. Now he was led to see that he and all his people had made too little of the promise made to Abraham, which was conditioned, not on works; but on faith. The law, which came four hundred and thirty years after the giving of the covenant, could not disannul it, so as to make the promise of none effect (Gal. 3:17). He graduated backward from Moses to Abraham.

In the light of this revelation he could better understand his own call to minister to the Gentiles, for this was one of the special provisions of the Abrahamic covenant: "In thee and in thy seed shall all the nations of the earth be blessed."

But deeper than all was God's work within his soul. No longer confident in himself, he was now more than content to be the slave of Jesus Christ, going where he was sent, doing as he was bidden, and serving as the instrument of His will. We all need to go to Arabia to learn lessons like these.

7

The Emergence of the Life Purpose
Acts 22:17–21

At the beginning of his Christian career, the apostle felt strongly drawn to minister to his own people. He was a Hebrew, and the son of Hebrews. What was the meaning of his having been cradled and nourished in the heart of Judaism, except that he might better understand and win Jews? Did not his training in the strictest sect of their religion, and at the feet of Gamaliel, give him a special claim on those who held "that jewel of the law" in special reverence and honor?

But he was destined to discover that his new-found Master had other purposes for his life, and that he had been especially prepared and called to preach *among the Gentiles* the unsearchable riches of Christ, and make *all men* see the fellowship of the mystery which from all generations had been hid in God.

1. PAUL'S CHERISHED HOPE.

a. *During his sojourn in the Sinaitic penninsula* we may well believe that his soul turned toward his people with ardent desire. Was he not an Israelite, of the seed of Abraham, of the tribe of Benjamin; and could he be indifferent to the needs of his brothers and sisters according to the flesh? That the law given from Sinai had been fulfilled and reedited in the holy life of Jesus of Nazareth; that the sacrifices, offered on those sands, had pointed to the death of the cross; and that the fire which burned in the bush had also shone on his face—to teach all this, and much more, and to lead his people from the desert wastes of Pharisaism to the heavenly places of which Canaan was the type, was the hope and longing of his heart. What work could be more congenial to his tastes and attitudes than this?

b. *On his return to Damascus* he at once began his crusade in the synagogues. "Straightway," we are told, "he preached Christ in the synagogues, that he is the Son of God. But all that heard him were amazed. . . . But Saul increased the more in strength, and confounded the Jews which dwelt at Damascus, proving that this is very Christ" (Acts 9:20, 22). How encouraged he was by these early successes!

But the vision was soon overcast. So violent was the hatred with which he was regarded by his fellow countrymen, that he was in imminent danger of his life. The gates were watched day and night, that he might be killed if he endeavored to escape. And finally he was lowered under cover of the night by a basket over the city wall.

c. *Still, however, his purpose was unchanged.* He went up to Jerusalem with the intention of seeing Peter. But in this he would probably have failed had it not been for the intervention of Barnabas who, according to an old tradition, had been his fellow student, educated with himself at the feet of Gamaliel. Through his good offices he was brought into contact with Peter and James. A blessed time followed. He was with them, and was especially engaged in holy and loving fellowship with Peter, the acknowledged leader of the church.

It is surely an innocent use of the imagination to think of these two conversing of the great past. On one occasion their theme would be the Lord's early ministry in Galilee, so closely associated with Peter's opening manhood; on another, the discourses and scenes of the last hours before His crucifixion; on another, the precious death and burial, the glorious Resurrection and Ascension, and the appearances of the forty days. "Tell me all you can remember of the Master," would be the frequent inquiry of the new disciples of him who had been so specially privileged as a witness of that mystery of love.

But Saul had other business in those happy days. He again sought the synagogues. "He spake and disputed against the Grecian Jews." How well he could understand the passion with which his statements were received; but how skillfully would he drive home the goad, which had at last compelled his own surrender! But here also his efforts were met by rebuffs: "They went about to slay him."

Yet in spite of coldness and aversion, he clung tenaciously to his cherished purpose. He had great sorrow and unceasing pain in his heart; he could have wished himself anathema from Christ for his kinsmen according to the flesh.

In a similar manner we have all cherished our life purposes. Only very slowly have we yielded and accepted the inevitable. Then suddenly we have awakened to discover that while we were desiring to do one thing, God was leading us to do another.

2. THE CLOSING DOOR. It began to close at Damascus; it closed still further when persecution arose at Jerusalem: but the final act was as Saul was praying in the temple.

As he knelt in prayer in some quiet spot, he saw Him, whom his soul loved and sought. And the risen Lord gave clear and unmistakable directions, "I saw him saying unto me, Make haste, and get thee quickly out of Jerusalem: for they will not receive thy testimony concerning me" (Acts 22:18).

Saul, as we have seen, did not willingly accept this as the ultimatum, and still argued that Jerusalem would afford the most suitable sphere for his ministry. But all debate was at last summarily closed by the words, "Depart: for I will send thee far hence unto the Gentiles."

Ah, Saul! you have argued, and strived, and tried to carry your way. The Lord loves you too well to yield to you. Some day you will come to see that He was doing better for you than you knew, and was sending you into yet a wider and more productive sphere of service.

3. THE OPENED DOOR. So the disciples brought the hunted preacher down to Cæsarea, and sent him forth to Tarsus; and not improbably he resumed his tent making there, content to await the Lord's will and bidding. But the years passed slowly. Possibly four or five were spent in comparative obscurity and neglect. That he worked for Christ in the immediate vicinity of his home is almost certain, as we shall see; but the word of the Lord awaited fulfillment.

At last one day he heard a voice saying in the doorway, "Does Saul live here?" And in another moment the familiar face of his old college friend was peering in on him, with a glad smile of recognition. Then the story was told of the marvelous outbreak of God's work in Antioch, and Barnabas pleaded with him to return to help him gather in the whitening harvest of the first great gentile city that the gospel had moved. "And he brought him unto Antioch. And it came to pass, that a whole year they assembled themselves with the church, and taught much people."

8

"Always Led in Triumph"
2 Cor. 2:14–16

While Saul was waiting in Tarsus, where he remained some four or five years, he appears to have concentrated his energies in the direction suggested by two references in Acts 15. In the 23rd verse, the apostles and elders address their circular letter expressly to the brethren who were of the Gentiles in Antioch, Syria, and Cilicia. And in the 41st verse we learn that Paul, with Silas as his fellowtraveler, went through Syria and Cicilia, confirming the churches. Evidently there were infant churches scattered throughout Saul's native province; and the conclusion is almost irresistible that they were born into existence beneath the fervid appeals and devoted labors of the new disciple.

His work, however, was chiefly concerned with the synagogues which, since the Dispersion, had been established in most of the large cities of the empire. As with the earliest churches in Judæa, the main constituents of these would be converted Jews and proselytes. It is doubtful if the apostle would have felt himself justified in receiving the Gentiles, as such, into the church. He was feeling his way in that direction, and was being prepared for the full acceptance of the commission with which he had been entrusted on the way to Damascus, and when worshiping in the temple.

It has been supposed that some of his deep experiences of privation and peril must have taken place during these years. We all remember that marvelous enumeration— labors more abundant, stripes above measure, deaths oft, five times the forty stripes save one; thrice beaten with rods, thrice shipwrecked, a night and day in the deep; in perils, labor, travail, watchings, hunger and thrist, cold and nakedness (2 Cor. 11). There is positively no room in his life, as narrated by the chronicler of the Acts of the Apostles, for many of these.

It is therefore more than probable that from the very hour that he began to follow the Savior he became identified with His sorrowful progress through the world.

This conception was closely associated in the apostle's mind with his unprecedented experiences, as will appear to any thoughtful student of the Second Epistle to the Corinthians. Mark especially the second chapter and fourteenth verse: "Thanks be unto God, which always causeth us to triumph in Christ, and maketh manifest the savior of his knowledge by us in every place. For we are unto God a sweet savour of Christ, in them that are saved, and in them that perish."

The metaphor was gathered from the scene of a Roman triumph, one of the most notable events in the old world, when some great general, a Cæsar or Marius, returning from distant scenes of triumph, ascended the Capitoline Hill amid the plaudits of the assembled citizens and the fragrance of sweet odors. Before his chariot were paraded captive kings and princes; after it came long lines of prisoners laden with the spoils of war.

To the vivid imagination of the apostle it seemed as though the pageantry of the scene, which so often stirred Rome to its heart, was a fitting emblem of the progress of Christ through the world.

Is not this an apt picture of every age? Each great crisis in the past has helped to advance the glorious reign of Christ. Was the fall of Babylon a crisis? It gave mankind a universal speech—the language spoken by Alexander and his soldiers—the delicate, subtle Greek in which the New Testament was written. Was the fall of Rome a crisis? It opened the way to the rise of the northern nations, which have ever been the home of liberty and the gospel. We may look without dismay on events that cast a shadow on our hearts. They also shall serve the cause of the gospel. In ways we cannot tell, they shall prepare for the triumph of our King.

The apostle's personal position in his Master's procession was clearly apprehended and perpetually accentuated. He never wearied of describing himself as *the slave of Jesus Christ.* "Paul a slave of Jesus Christ, called to be an apostle, separated unto the gospel of God." From that hour in which he had been smitten to the ground on the road to Damascus, he had been content to be led from city to city, from continent to continent, in the triumphal progress of his Lord, a trophy of His mighty power to bring the most stubborn under His yoke. "Thanks be unto God," he cries, "which always causeth us to triumph."

Those whom Jesus leads in triumph share His triumph. They may be a spectacle to angels or to men. Sometimes in the stocks; often accounted the offscouring of all things; yet, in the spiritual realm, they are made to triumph always. If you are conquered by Jesus, you shall always be made to triumph!

The influence of Christ on the character of those who follow Him is also clearly delineated. The metaphor is changed, and the apostle considers himself no longer a slave, but a freed servant, a citizen, a friend. God makes manifest through him in every place the sweet savor of the knowledge of Jesus. Wherever he went, men knew Jesus better.

What an ideal this is for us all, so to live that though we are unable to speak much or occupy a commanding position, yet from our lives a holy savor may be spread abroad, which will not be ours, but Christ's!

Yet once again the thought changes. The apostle imagines himself to be no longer the hand that swings the incense bowl, but the incense itself. He says, "We are unto God a sweet savour of Christ." How marvelously scent awakens memory! In a moment it will waft us back through long years.

When therefore we are told that we may be to God a sweet savor of Christ, it must be meant that we may so live as to recall to the mind of God what Jesus was in His mortal career. It is as though, as God watches us from day to day, He would see Jesus in us. What a test for daily living! Is my life fragrant of Jesus? Do I remind the Father of the blessed Lord?

It was in such a mood that Saul of Tarsus spent the years of preparation that preceded the great opportunity of his life. It was in the cultivation of such virtues that he awaited the coming of Barnabas.

9

The Apostle of the Gentiles
Rom. 11:13

It is probable that during his years of quiet work in Cilicia and Syria, Saul of Tarsus was being led with increasing clearness to apprehend God's purpose in his life—that he should be the apostle of the Gentiles. The vision in the temple had culminated in the worlds, "Depart: for I will send thee far hence unto the Gentiles" (Acts 22:21). Until now Judaism had been the only door into Christianity; from now on the door of faith was to stand wide open to Gentiles also, without circumcision. Some suggestion of this is furnished by his own lips. But still the true direction of his life was hardly discovered until circumstances transpired that will now demand our notice.

1. SUMMONED TO ANTIOCH. Halfway through Luke's narrative the center of interest shifts from the mother church at Jerusalem to one that had been founded shortly before the time we are describing, in the gay, frivolous, busy, beautiful city of Antioch. It was an emporium of trade, a meeting place for the Old World and the New. It is forever famous in Christian annals because a number of unordained and unnamed disciples, fleeing from Jerusalem in the face of Saul's persecution, dared to preach the gospel to Greeks, and to gather the converts into a church, in entire disregard of the initial rite of Judaism. There, also, the disciples of "the Way" were first called Christians. From Antioch went the first missionary expedition for the evangelization of the world. In postapostolic days it was famous as the see of the great bishop, saint, and martyr, Ignatius.

It was left to a handful of fugitive, Hellenistic Jews, men of Cyprus and Cyrene, to break through the barriers of the centuries, and to begin preaching the Lord Jesus to the Greeks at Antioch. Instantly the divine Spirit honored their word, gave testimony to the word of God's grace, and a great number believed and turned to the Lord (Acts 11:19–21).

As soon as tidings of these novel proceedings reached Jerusalem, the church sent Barnabas, who was himself a Cypriot, to make inquiries and report. His verdict was definite and reassuring. He had no hesitation in affirming that it was a definite work of God's grace; and he carried on the work that had been inaugurated with such success that "much people was added unto the Lord."

His success, however, only added to the perplexity and difficulty of the situation, and he found himself face to face with a great problem. The Gentiles were pressing into the church, and taking their places on an equality with Jews at the Lord's Supper and love feasts, an action that the more conservative Jews greatly resented. The single-hearted man was hardly able to cope with the problem. But he remembered that at his conversion his old friend and fellow student had been especially commissioned to preach to the Gentiles; and he departed to Tarsus to seek Saul, and brought him to Antioch. "And it came to pass, that a whole year they assembled themselves together with the church, and taught much people" (Acts 11:26).

But this year's experience at Antioch was of the utmost consequence to Saul. He learned from Barnabas the conclusion to which the church at Jerusalem had come, on hearing Peter's recital of God's dealings with Cornelius and his household (11:18). God made no distinctions; why should he? All the while Paul's horizon was broadening, his confidence increasing, his concept of God's purposes deepening, and he was formulating the gospel that he afterward preached among them (Gal. 2:2).

We need not linger over his brief visit to Jerusalem at the end of his year's ministry at Antioch, to carry alms from the gentile Christians to their suffering Jewish brethren. On this occasion he does not seem to have met the apostles, who probably had withdrawn from Jerusalem to avoid the murderous hate of Herod (Acts 12); and the gift of the church at Antioch was therefore left with the elders of the mother church.

2. SET APART BY THE HOLY SPIRIT. It was a momentous hour in the history of the church when, on the return of Barnabas and Paul from Jerusalem, they met, with three others, for a season of fasting and prayer. What was the immediate reason for this special session we cannot say; but it is significant that the three prophets and two teachers represented between them five different countries. Were they yearning after their own people, and wistful to offer them the gospel, as they now saw they might offer it, apart from the trammels and restraints of Judaism? We cannot tell. That, however, was the birth of modern missions. The Holy Ghost, Christ's Vicar, the Director and Administrator of the church, bade the little group set apart two out of their number to a mission that He would unfold to them, as they dared to step out in obedience to His command.

In Cyprus, to which they were first attracted, because Barnabas was connected with it through his birth and estate, though they proclaimed the word of God from one end to the other in the synagogues of the Jews, they had no fruit until the Roman governor called them before him, and sought to hear their message, which after hearing he believed.

After landing on the mainland Paul, contrary to the judgment of John Mark, struck up from the seacoast to the far-reaching tablelands of the interior, four thousand feet above sea level, with the evident intention of establishing churches on the great trade route that ran through Asia Minor from Tarsus to Ephesus. What might not be the result for East and West, if this great mutual bridge were to become a highway for the feet of the Son of God! But there the same experience awaited him.

The Jews in Antioch and Pisidia refused, while the Gentiles welcomed them. Indeed he was compelled to turn publicly from his own countrymen, and hold up the gospel as light and salvation to those whom the prophet described as at the uttermost end of the earth. Then it was that the word of the Lord spread throughout all the region.

At Iconium, where they fled before a persecution that made it unsafe to remain in Antioch, they again found the malice of the Jews so persistent that they were driven into the gentile cities and district of Lycaonia, where there were probably no synagogues at all. There, too, they preached the gospel, and made many disciples.

Everywhere it was the Jewish element that was obstructive and implacable; while the Gentiles, when left to themselves, received them and their message with open arms. His love was not abated. How could it be? Were they not his brethren, his kinsmen according to the flesh? But he had to follow the divine plan.

Probably Paul's greatest experience of this journey was his first visit to the warm-hearted Galatians, whose country is probably referred to in the vague allusion of Acts 14:24. In any case, his insistence in his epistle that he had preached to them the gospel as he had received it direct and undiluted from Christ, compels us to locate his first acquaintance with them at this time, and before that memorable visit to Jerusalem, to which we shall refer presently, and in which he consulted the apostles concerning the gospel he proclaimed (Acts 15; Gal. 2). It is probable that he was detained among them by a painful attack of his habitual malady, aggravated by climatic changes, or malaria. "Ye know," he says, "how through infirmity of the flesh I preached the gospel unto you at the first. And my temptation which was in my flesh ye despised not, nor rejected" (Gal. 4:13–14). So far from rejecting him on this account, his sorrows and afflictions only touched them more and bound them to him. "I bear you record," he says, "that, if it had been possible, ye would have plucked out your own eyes and given them to me" (v. 15).

His success among this affectionate people was remarkable, and still further deepened the impression that he had to bend his strength to the salvation of the Gentiles, whose cause had been laid on his heart at the hour of his conversion.

3. HIS APOSTOLATE RECOGNIZED BY THE APOSTLES. We do not propose to add anything to the discussion in which so much has been urged on either side, as to the time when the visit to Jerusalem, referred to in Galatians 2, took place. We fall back on the more generally received view that Galatians 2 refers to the visit mentioned in Acts 15, when he was sent as a deputation from Antioch to Jerusalem to obtain the view of the apostles on the admission of Gentiles into the church.

Paul sought the opinion of those in repute among the apostles on his teaching, lest by any means he should be running, or had run, in vain. In the course of several interviews it became increasingly evident to James, Peter, and John, that their former persecutor had received a divine commission to the Gentiles. They realized that he had been entrusted with the gospel of the uncircumcision. The responsible leaders of the mother church could not help perceiving the grace that was given to him; and finally they gave to him the right hand of fellowship, that he should go to the Gentiles, while they went to the circumcision.

This was the further and final confirmation of the purpose that had been forming in his heart. He never failed to begin his work in any place by an honest endeavor to save some of his own flesh; but he always realized that his supreme stewardship was to those who were called uncircumcision by that which was called circumcision in the flesh made by hands.

Surely, then, it is befitting that the church that bears his name should stand in the heart of the greatest Gentile city of the age, and bear the emblem of the death of Christ above its smoke and turmoil.

10

"Fourteen Years Ago"
2 Cor. 12:2–5

If we count back fourteen years from the writing of this epistle, we will find ourselves amid the events narrated in the thirteenth and fourteenth chapters of the Book of the Acts, especially at that momentous hour in the history of Christianity when five men, representing five different countries, met together to fast and pray about the state of the world and their duty in respect to it. The evangelist tells us of the separation and sending forth of the two missionaries; and of the hardships, difficulties, and sufferings through which they fulfilled their high calling. We may be thankful therefore that we can supplement the narrative of Luke by the words of the apostle, as he recalls what happened to him fourteen years before he wrote.

1. THE DESCRIPTION THE APOSTLE GIVES OF HIMSELF. "A man in Christ." There are three qualities in a truly manly character:resolution, fortitude and courage.

a. *Resolution*—that a man will take up one high ambition and aim, prosecuting it through good and evil report, through sun and storm. How evidently this characterized the apostle, who pursued his purpose of ministering to the Gentiles from Antioch to Iconium, and from there to Lystra and Derbe. The hatred of the Jews did not dissuade; the fickleness of the crowds did not daunt; the hailstone storm of stones at Lystra did not turn him aside. It was his persistent ambition to preach the gospel where Christ had not been named.

b. *Fortitude*—that a man should be able to sustain sorrow and heartrending anguish. There is no one without his hours of heartrending grief, when it seems as though the heart strings must break and the lifeblood be shed. Paul manifested this when he bore with uncomplaining nobility the cowardice of Mark and the relentless hatred of his fellow countrymen. Also, after his stoning at Lystra, aroused from what had seemed to be his death-swoon, he struggled back to the city from which he had been dragged to all appearance a corpse, and having saluted the brethren, and especially the young Timothy, started on the following morning to continue his loved work in the neighboring cities of Lycaonia.

c. *Courage*—Paul never lacked courage. He never flinched from facing an amphitheater full of raging fanatics, or braving consuls and procurators, or from withstanding an apostle who deserved to be blamed. And his heroic courage was conspicuously manifested in this very journey, that instead of taking an easier and more direct route home by way of his native city and the Cilician Gates, he dared to retrace his steps to each of the cities in which he had preached, confirming the souls of the disciples, exhorting them to continue in the faith. At great personal risk he stayed long enough in each place to appoint elders in the infant communities, and to pray with fasting, commending them to God, on whom they believed.

When we become Christians we do not forfeit these characteristics. No, but they become purified of ingredients that might vitiate and corrupt them. Apart from Christ, resolution may become obstinacy, fortitude stoicism, and courage fatalism. As soon as a person is in Christ, however, all danger of exaggeration is done away, and the native strong character is invigorated from the Lion of the Tribe of Judah, and sweetened by the meekness and gentleness of the Lamb who was slain.

2. TO SUCH, BRIDAL MOMENTS COME. These are days of the bridal of heaven and earth—high days—hours of vision and ecstasy—when the tide runs high and fast, and the cup of life brims to overflow. "I knew such an one caught up even to the third heaven, to Paradise, and heard unspeakable words, which it is not lawful for a man to utter. On behalf of such a man will I glory."

At first we might suppose that the apostle was really describing the experience of someone else. He appears to distinguish between that blessed man, whose experience he was describing, and himself. "Of myself I will not glory, but in mine infirmities." But as his story proceeds, it becomes clear that he is describing some radiant experiences through which he passed during that first missionary tour.

Such experiences may come in hours of great pain. The conjecture has been hazarded that this rapture into Paradise took place during the apostle's stoning at Lystra. But be this as it may, he could find no words to tell what he saw and heard. Paradise would indeed be a place if words could describe it. The third heaven would not be worthy of its Maker if its glories did not transcend our furthest imaginings.

But these hours are as evanescent as they are unspeakable. Why? *Lest* we should be exalted above measure, and become proud. If the apostle feared this, much more should we.

Through God's wise providence such radiant hours do not linger, because our strength is not fed from them. We will not get much energy out of whipped cream, however pleasant it may taste to the palate; and if we only rely on the raptures of Paradise for our sources of spiritual power, we will also be short of spiritual strength.

Do not regret the passage of the blessed, rapturous hours, light of step and fleet of pace. Do not think that you have fallen from grace when their flush and glow are over. Whether they fall to you often or not, or even if they never visit you, you are still in Christ, still joined to the Lord, still accepted in the Beloved. Be content, then, to turn as Jesus did from the rapture of Paradise, presented on the Transfiguration Mount, to take the way of the cross.

3. THE DISCIPLINE OF PAIN. We need not spend time discussing the nature of Paul's thorn in the flesh. Paul calls it "a stake," as though he were impaled. In infinite wisdom God permitted the messenger of Satan to buffet His servant; and all through that first missionary journey he had to face a long succession of buffetings. There were perils of robbers, of waters, of mountain passes, and of violent crowds; but in addition to all, there was the lacerating thorn.

He probably suffered from weak eyes, or some distressing form of ophthalmia. We infer this from the eagerness of his Galatian converts to give him their eyes, from his dependence on an amanuensis, and from the clumsy letters with which he wrote the postscripts to his epistles (Gal. 6:11). And if this were the case, the pain would be greatly aggravated as he faced the sharp blasts that swept the mountain plateau on which the Pisidian Antioch was situated.

Was it during this journey that he asked the Lord on three separate occasions for deliverance, and received the assurance that though the thorns were left, more than sufficient grace would be given? If so, like a peal of bells, at Antioch, Iconium, Derbe, and Lystra, he must have heard the music of those tender words: My grace is sufficient, *sufficient,* SUFFICIENT for you!

And how greatly does our appreciation of the apostle rise when we remember that he was incessantly in pain. Instead of sitting down in despair, however, and pleading physical infirmity as his excuse for doing nothing, he bravely claimed the grace that waited within call.

11

The Conflict of Paul's Life
Acts 15; Gal. 2

In the separation of Abraham from country, kindred, and father's house, the story of his people was foreshadowed. Their dress, rites, customs, and religious habits were carefully and expressly determined to accentuate their separation that, being withdrawn from the influence of surrounding nations, they might be fitted to receive, keep, and transmit the knowledge of God. In no other way could they have borne the precious deposit entrusted to them down the centuries.

The laws of separation were so rigid that Peter did not hesitate to remind Cornelius and his friends of the risk he ran in crossing the threshold of a Gentile's house. And when Peter came up to Jerusalem, even his fellow believers, who were of the circumcision, found grievous fault with him: "They contended with him, saying, Thou wentest in to men uncircumcised, and didst eat with them" (Acts 11:3). The law of commandments, contained in ordinances, some of them ordained through Moses, and many added later by successive generations of doctors and rabbis, stood like a middle wall of partition between Jew and Gentile.

The rigor of these observances was heavy enough in Jerusalem. But in foreign cities it became customary to relax the stringency of the bonds of Judaism, though always maintaining circumcision, the intermarriage of Jew with Jew, and that particular method of preparing animal flesh for food that is still in vogue among Jews. We are not surprised, therefore, that Antioch became the scene of that forward movement, led by Barnabas and Paul, which consisted in openly welcoming Gentile converts into the Christian community, without insisting on their previous conformity to the venerable rite of circumcision.

This marked a great advance. Up to this time, especially in Judæa, the Christians were regarded by the people as a Jewish sect; and as long as they were prepared to attend the temple services, conform to the regulations, and maintain the institutions of Judaism, their belief in Jesus as the long-promised Messiah was regarded as a peculiarity that might be condoned and winked at. It was permissible that they should meet in the love feast, as long as they did not forsake the temple; they might pray to Jesus as God if they acted in all other respects as devout Jews. But if this rule had been universally maintained, Christianity would have speedily been lost to view. After a few brief years it would have been indistinguishable.

All this, however, was prevented by the policy to which Barnabas and Paul had been led. In the Epistle to the Galatians (2:4, 12) we have a pleasant glimpse of the liberty that the converts in Antioch had in Christ Jesus. Circumcised and uncircumcised joined in the common exercises of Christian fellowship. They ate together without question; and even Peter, when on a visit to Antioch, was so charmed with the godly simplicity and beauty of their communion, that he joined freely with them, and partook of their love feasts and common meals.

The conservative party in the Jerusalem church, however, on hearing these tidings, was ill at ease. As the first step, they sent down false brethren, who were privately brought in, and came to spy out the liberty that the church at Antioch practiced. Then, when they were assured of the facts, certain men came down from Judæa, and taught the brethren, saying, "Except ye be circumcised after the manner of Moses, ye cannot be saved."

It was an important crisis, and led to the breaking out of a controversy that embittered many succeeding years in the apostle's life; but it led to some of his noblest epistles, and to his exposition of the principles of the gospel with unrivalled clearness and beauty.

1. GREAT QUESTIONS WERE AT STAKE. This, for instance: Was Christianity to be a sect of Judaism? And this: Were the Levitical institutions of rites and ceremonies, of feasts and fasts, as important as the great moral code of Sinai and Deuteronomy, or might they be regarded as temporary and fugitive, to be laid aside when that purpose was fulfilled? But this most of all: What were the conditions on which people could be saved?

Salvation is not obtained by obedience to a rite, by the observance of a code of rules, or even by obedience to a creed, pronounced orthodox. The only condition of salvation is faith, which believes in Him who justifies the ungodly, and receives into the heart the very nature of Jesus to become the power of the new life. How infinitely unimportant, then, compared with faith, is any outward rite. It may have its place, as the outward sign and seal of the covenant, but it has no efficacy apart from the spiritual act.

Let us never forget then that circumcision avails nothing, nor uncircumcision; but faith that works by love, a new creature, and the keeping of the commandments of God.

2. THE ARGUMENTS ON EITHER SIDE. "There was much contention."

Did not Jesus fulfill the law of Moses? Was He not circumcised? And did He not rigorously observe the temple fasts and feasts, and even pay his share in the temple tax?

Certainly, said Barnabas and Paul; but you must remember that when He died He said, "It is finished"; and the veil of the temple was rent from the top to the bottom, to show that Judaism had finished its God-given mission. From that moment He became not a Savior of Jews only, but the world's Redeemer.

But surely the law given by Moses is permanent? Did not Jesus of Nazareth assert that not one jot or tittle should pass away until all was fulfilled?

Precisely. But surely we must distinguish between the outward and inward, the ritual and ethical, the form and the substance? It is impossible to believe that the sublime ceremonial of Leviticus, which was imposed for a special purpose, can be of the same binding force and moment as the ten words of the law that are borne witness to by the conscience of all men.

But if you do away with the restrictions of the law, will you not loosen all moral restraint, and lead to a general relaxation of all bonds in the family and the states?

There is no fear of this, the stalwart defenders of the simplicities of the faith answer from the other side. Souls that are united to Jesus Christ by faith are cleansed by receiving from Him tides of spiritual life and health; so that they become more than ever pure, and holy, and divine. The law of the spirit of life in Christ Jesus makes us free from the law of sin and death.

3. THE APPEAL TO JERUSALEM. The disputing and questioning, however, showed no signs of abating, and it was finally decided that Paul and Barnabas, and certain others with them, should go up to Jerusalem to consult the apostles and elders about this question.

They traveled slowly through Phœnicia and Samaria, declaring the conversion of the Gentiles in each of the little Christian communities on their route, until they reached Jerusalem where, in a great missionary convocation, especially convened, they told all things that God had done with them. But their statements were interrupted by the uprising of certain Pharisees that believed, and the heated interjection of the reiterated statement, "It is needful to circumcise them, and to keep the law of Moses."

Again a special meeting was summoned: in which there was much questioning. Then Peter arose, and said, "This matter was settled in my judgment by God Himself, when in the house of Cornelius the Holy Spirit descended on uncircumcised Gentiles, as on us at the beginning; and as He made no distinction, why should we?"

Next, Barnabas and Paul repeated their wondrous story, and showed how greatly the Gentiles had been blessed, and were being blessed, altogether apart from circumcision.

Lastly, James summed up the whole debate by enumerating some three or four minor points on which he thought it well to insist, for the right ordering of the young communities; but he did not mention circumcision among them, nor insist on obedience to the Mosaic and Levitical institutions. To his sage counsel the apostles and elders agreed.

This unanimity between the leading apostles and the two evangelists, who were the cause of the whole controversy, was probably largely due to the private interview that Paul had sought with them, and which most commentators allocate to this period (Gal. 2:2). He tells us that he went up by revelation as though, in addition to the request of the church, there was strong spiritual pressure exerted on him; and when he reached Jerusalem he laid before those who were of repute the gospel he was preaching among the Gentiles, lest he was running in vain. But to his great satisfaction they did not comment adversely on his statements, nor insist on Titus, a young Greek, being circumcised; and they even went so far as to recognize that the gospel of the uncircumcision had been entrusted to him, giving him and Barnabas the right hand of fellowship, that they should go to the Gentiles, as themselves to the circumcision. The power of the risen Jesus was so mightily in His servants, that there was no speaking against their vocation.

The Pharisee party was defeated, and a decree signed in the sense of James' address; but from that moment a relentless war broke out, which followed the apostle for the next ten years of his life, and cost him many bitter tears. Every church he planted was visited by the emissaries of his virulent opponents, who asserted that Paul was no apostle because he had only seen Christ in vision, and had never companied with Him during the days of his flesh. They attacked his personal character, misrepresented his reluctance to take the gifts of his converts, dwelt with cruel animosity on his personal defects, and in many cases succeeded in alienating the love and loyalty of his converts.

This cruel persecution is constantly alluded to in the Epistles to the Galatians and Corinthians, and cut Paul to the quick. However, he never considered himself defeated. By prayers and tears, by arguments and persuasions, by threatenings and expostulations, the heroic lion-heart fought the good fight to the end.

12

A Lesson of Guidance
Acts 16

After a brief respite, Paul proposed to Barnabas that they should return to visit the believers in every city in which they had proclaimed the word of the Lord, and see how they fared. This was the beginning of his second missionary journey, which was to have far-reaching results.

Barnabas suggested that they should take Mark with them as before, a proposition that his companion positively refused to entertain. Mark had deserted them on the threshold of their previous expedition, and there was grave fear that he might do so again. Barnabas was as strong on the other side. Perhaps he felt that he had some rights in the matter, as the senior in age, because of the tie of blood between himself and his sister's son. At last the contention reached such an acute stage that the church became aware of it, and took Paul's side, for the narrative of the Acts tells us that when Paul chose Silas, and went forth, "being recommended by the brethren unto the grace of God."

Paul and Silas traversed Syria and Cilicia, confirming the infant churches, which probably owed their existence to Paul's earliest efforts. So through the Cicilian Gates to Tarsus, his native city. But there was no welcome for him there. Probably the old home was either broken up or forever closed to him; and the two companions in travel threaded the narrow passage in the mountains behind Tarsus. After some days' toilsome journey associated with the former journey.

What a welcome Paul would receive! How much to tell and hear! There was, however, a special burden on the apostle's heart. On the occasion of his previous visit his attention had been arrested by a young man who had been strongly attracted to him. He asked for Timothy, and was glad to learn that he had not been faithless to the teachings and training of the godly women who had watched over his opening character, and who had instructed him in the Holy Scriptures.

All the reports about Timothy were favorable. He was well reported of by the believers that were at Lystra and Iconium. The more Paul knew of him the more he was attracted to him, and finally proposed that Timothy should accompany him on his travels as his own son in the faith. He administered the rite of circumcision, not because he deemed it obligatory, but as a matter of convenience, that there might be no obstacle to the admission of his young assistant to Jewish synagogues.

A simple ordination service was then held, in which Timothy was solemnly set apart for his great work. The elders gathered around and laid their hands on his bowed head, and prayed. In answer to their believing intercession, he received the gift of sacred speech; and Paul, in later years, reminded him to stir up the gift that was in him through the laying on of his own hands and of those of the presbytery.

Leaving Lystra, Paul and his companions, visited the churches in the highland region of Phrygia and Galatia, everywhere distributing the letter of James. They next purposed to go into the populous and influential cities of Asia Minor, such as Colossæ, Laodicæ, and Ephesus. Yet it was not to be: "They were forbidden of the Holy Ghost to preach the word in Asia." Years later Paul would do some of the greatest work of his life in that very region; but just now the door was closed against him by the Holy Spirit. Paul and Barnabas were needed more urgently elsewhere.

The travelers therefore took a northern route, with the intention of entering the important province of Bithynia, lying along the shores of the Black Sea; but when they came to a point in the great Roman road, opposite Mysia, and were attempting to go out of Asia Minor into Bithynia, the spirit of Jesus would not let them go.

Checked when they attempted to go to the West, they were now stopped as they sought to go northeast; and there was nothing for it but to keep straight on, until they came out at the terminus of the road, on the seacoast, at the famous harbor of Troas, the ancient Troy. There they met with Luke, whose presence is from that point on denoted by the significant personal pronoun *we;* and from there the man of Macedonia invited the little missionary band across the straits to set up the banner of Christ on the hitherto untouched continent of Europe. It is interesting to study the method of the Spirit's guidance as it was extended toward these early heralds of the cross. It consisted largely in prohibitions, when they attempted to take another course than the right one. When they would turn to the left, to Asia, He stopped them; and when they sought to turn to the right, to Bithynia, again He stopped them. He shut all the doors along their route, and bolted them, so that they had no alternative but to go straight forward. In the absence of any prohibition, they were left to understand that they were treading the prepared path for which they had been created in Christ Jesus.

Whenever you are doubtful as to your course, submit your judgment absolutely to the Spirit of God, and ask Him to shut against you every door but the right one. In the meanwhile, continue along the path which you have been already treading.

13

"Ye Philippians"
Phil. 4:15

To many of the world's greatest benefactors, home life has been denied. Theirs has been a solitary and lonely lot. This was largely the case with Paul, a self-contained, strong, heroic soul. Few have been dowered with a more tender, warmer disposition. But it was his appointed lot to have no settled dwelling place—no spot he could call Home.

> Yes, without cheer of sister or of daughter;
> Yes, without stay of father or of son;
> Lone on the land and homeless on the water,
> Pass I in patience till the work be done.

Yet the apostle had marvelous powers of attracting men and women to himself. We have seen how he threw the mantle of his magnetic influence over Silas and Timothy; and the Galatians were ready to give him their eyes. But he was now to win a group of friends who would never cease to love him while life lasted; and Philippi was to become to him the one bright sunny spot in all the earth, more than Tarsus which had disowned him, more than Jerusalem which would cast him out, and next to the "far better" of Paradise.

1. LUKE. The beloved physician seems to have met him first at Troas. It is conjectured that Luke, himself a native of Philippi, had followed in the wake of commerce to

pursue his profession as a physician to his countrymen. Paul's temporary sojourn in the crowded ghetto may have induced a return of the acute disease from which he had suffered in Galatia, or he may have been laid low by malarial fever, for which the nearest available physician was summoned, and this was Luke. The servant of God won his medical attendant for the Savior. In the enthusiasm of an ardent attachment the new disciple elected to become his fellow traveler, so as to be able at all times to minister to the suffering and frail tenement of his friend's dauntless and vehement spirit.

He is immediately taken into the closest confidence; forms one of the little group to whom one morning Paul tells of the vision of the man of Macedonia; helps to formulate the conclusion, in which Silas and Timothy and he agreed, that the apostle's path lay across the blue waters of the Ægean, dancing and sparkling in the morning light; goes forth to seek a passage in one of the many ships that lay at the wharves; and records with much love of the sea and knowledge of the land the successive stages of their voyage and journey to Philippi.

How dear he became to the apostle, and how tenaciously he clung to his charge, is clear from two expressions penned, the one from the hired house of the first Roman imprisonment, the other from the chill prison cell of the second. "Luke, the beloved physician"; "only Luke is with me" (Col. 4:14; 2 Tim. 4:11).

2. Lydia. She was probably a widow, a woman of considerable business capacity, with energy enough to leave her native city of Thyatira, and cross the sea to establish herself in Philippi as agent for the sale of the purple-dyed garments for which her native town was famous. She was above all else an eager seeker after God. The Jewish community at Philippi, being too small and poor to have a synagogue of its own, was obliged to meet by the riverside in an enclosure or garden screened from public observation. But there she stayed as the Sabbath came around, with members of her household, listening to the Jewish Scriptures, and seeking after God, if perchance she might find Him.

On one memorable Sabbath, when only women were present, four strangers, Jews, appeared in the little circle, "sat down, and spake unto the women which resorted thither." This was the first gospel sermon in Europe. And it is somewhat remarkable that it was addressed to a handful of women in the open air.

The result of that morning service was Lydia's conversion; whether she received the apostle's message of the crucified and living Lord at once or gradually, is not clear, but the result was that she, with her entire household, came to believe in Jesus, whom Paul preached, and she felt as sure about her own conversion as she was eager for Paul to come and abide in her house: "If ye have judged me to be faithful to the Lord, come into my house, and abide there." It was a blessed change, which led to far-reaching consequences in her own life, and in Paul's.

How much this warm-hearted and resolute woman did in days to come, it is impossible to gather from the record of the past. We know of four separate occasions in which the Philippian church sent supplies to their beloved founder and teacher (2 Cor. 11:9; Phil. 4:10, 18). And this was probably due to Lydia's foresight and generosity. No other church performed so large a ministry, because no other church could perform it. As Paul intimates, they were for the most part in deep poverty. And it is probable that the Philippians would have been as paralyzed as the rest had it not been for Lydia and her household, who thrived on the proceeds of their trade. It had even been surmised that Paul owed much of the comfort of succeeding days, when he spent two years in the palace of Cæsarea waiting for his trial, and two more years in his hired house at Rome, to the same source; and it may have been some inkling of the well-to-do friend who held Paul dear, that induced Felix to keep him in bonds.

3. MINOR CHARACTERS are cast on the canvas, drawn from life, and filling up the picture. The hysterical girl, demon-possessed, who marked and followed the evangelists. The syndicate of owners who fattened on the proceeds of her divination, as she showed miners where to find the gold, girls the day to wed, merchants the period to speculate; and who were correspondingly chagrined when Paul's challenge to the spirit released his wretched victim and ended their hopes of further gain. The Roman magistrates, who strangely forgot the high traditions of their office, were swept off their feet by the urgency of the rabble and, without going through even the formality of a trial, tore the clothes off the backs of the accused with their own hands, and laid "many stripes upon them," uncondemned, being Romans. There was also Silas, who well justified Paul's choice of him, for he showed himself well able to bear shame and suffering for Jesus. But from these our thought turns to the third principal actor in this scene, the story of whose conversion has shed the light of unspeakable comfort into myriads of broken hearts.

4. THE JAILOR. A rough, coarse man probably! What else could be expected from one who had spent his early days in the Roman army, and his later ones amid the hardening and brutalizing experiences of a provincial Roman prison? Barbarous usage would certainly be meted out by his hands to the two Jews, about whom he had received the significant hint that he was to keep them safely. The inner prison was a dark underground hole beneath his house (Acts 16:34); into this he thrust them. They would probably lie extended on the bare damp ground, their bleeding backs in contact with the soil, and their legs stretched to such an extent by the stocks as to almost dislocate their hips.

By midnight the two prisoners became so happy that they could no longer contain themselves, and began to sing, chanting the grand old Hebrew Psalms, and in the intervals praying. It was an unwanted sound to the prisoners who stood or lay around in the pitch dark, their chains bolted to the walls—not one of them thought of sleep; "the prisoners," we are told, "were listening."

An earthquake broke in on the singing, the doors flew open, and the chains fell off. The jailor, being roused from sleep, came into the prison yard and found the doors open. As Paul and Silas caught sight of him, to their horror they saw him draw his sword and prepare to kill himself rather than face an ignominious death for his infidelity to his charge. With a loud voice Paul stopped him and reassured him; then the call for the light, the springing into the cell, the trembling limbs, the courtesy that led them out, the inquiry for salvation, the answer of peace, the motely midnight audience that gathered around the two servants of God, the loving tendance of their wounds, the baptism, the hastily-prepared food, the glad rejoicing of the transformed believer and of all his beliving house. One event crowding on the heels of another.

He doubtless became one of the members of the Philippian church, a community of singular purity and loveliness, to whom the apostle wrote his tenderest words without a syllable of rebuke. He could only thank God on every remembrance of them, and in every supplication for them made request with joy.

14

From Philippi to Athens
Acts 17; 18

Leaving Luke at Philippi, Paul and his companions travelled through Amphipolis and Apollonia to Thessalonica, a name that lives forever in the inscriptions of his two earliest epistles. It may be that Paul was especially attracted to this city because of the synagogue and a weekly Jewish service there, in which he could prosecute his favorite work of opening and alleging from the Hebrew Scriptures that the Messiah had to suffer, and that He had appeared in the person of Jesus of Nazareth. He did this for three Sabbath days, maintaining himself and his friends by the work of his own hands, and lodging with one Jason, who afterward became a devoted disciple and follower (Rom. 16:21).

At the end of that period the strong feeling raised among the Jews made it unwise to continue in the synagogue: he therefore moved his conferences to some neutral ground. How long he remained there we cannot tell, but it must have been long enough to give time for the formation of a healthy and vigorous church. There was something about these Macedonian converts that was immensely attractive to him.

More than in other cases, his teaching led them to anticipate the Advent of the Lord. The pressure of the anguish that lay heavily on them all may have made them peculiarly susceptible to those radiant visions of the Lord's return that filled the apostle's thought. They even outran his teaching, and fell into the error of supposing that that day had already come—an error that the apostle by a second epistle hastened to correct. He recalls, with lively satisfaction, that the Gospel came to them in power and the Holy Ghost.

This blessed ministry must have taken some months, and the strain on the apostle was evidently greatly lessened by the gifts that came from Philippi, relieving him from the necessity of manual toil (Phil. 4:16).

At last, however, Thessalonica was closed to them. Paul and Silas were compelled to flee by night before the anger of the populace, incited by the Jews.

Fifty miles of night journey brought them to Berea; and there for a brief space they had respite, as the Jews were less bigoted and more willing to search the Scriptures, to discover for themselves the reasonableness or otherwise of Paul's views. But his heart yearned for the beloved brethren whom he had left to stem the strong tide of hatred that his teaching had evoked; and more than once he would have returned had it not been for the fear of implicating Jason and others, who appear to have been bound over to prevent him from setting his foot again in Thessalonica. This was in his mind when he said Satan hindered him (1 Thess. 2:18).

The project of Paul's return to Thessalonica was, however, rendered impossible by the rising of another storm, caused by Jewish emissaries from that city, who pursued his steps with relentless hate. There was at last no help for it but to leave Silas and Timothy in Berea, to see what could be done further to keep the pathway to the rear open, and to hurry down to the harbor to take the first boat that was sailing. This happened to be for Athens.

Athens. The messengers hastened back to Berea, bearing the charge that Silas and

Timothy should come to him with all speed. While he waited for them and hoped they would assure him that he might return to the infant communities he had founded, he passed through the streets of Athens, surveying the monuments of their religion. On every side were the achievements of human genius. Temples that a Phidias had designed; statues that a Praxiteles had made.

It is not clear that the heart of the apostle was stirred with classic memories or artistic appreciation. To him the city was simply full of idols. He was greatly moved; and, not content with reasoning in the synagogue with the Jews and proselytes, he went forth every day into the market place to reason with whoever he met, urging all to turn from these vanities to worship the only God. No ordinary Jew could have entered so thoroughly into the spirit of the place as the great apostle did, or have excited sufficient interest among its philosophers to justify their calling a special assembly of the council of the Areopagus to hear a full statement of the new teaching he brought to their ears.

It was the greatest audience Paul had ever addressed. Before him philosophers, pedants, lecturers, and students, accustomed to discussing the loftiest themes within the horizon of human thought, and to making distinctions to which the delicate refinement of the Greek language lent itself with marvelous subtlety.

The address Paul gave on that occasion is quite unique. For its grace, intellectual sequence, grandeur of conception and range, stately march of eloquent words, it stands alone among the addresses recorded for us by the evangelist. It reveals the opulence of the apostle's intellect and power of ready sympathy, which enabled him to adapt himself so easily to all sorts and conditions of men. We can only notice the contrasts between himself and his audience. They taught a dreary kind of Pantheism, as though God were no longer distinct from the matter of the world; he said that He was a Person, a Father to be sought after. Some held the immortality of the soul, as Socrates had proclaimed it on that very spot, but they had no idea of the resurrection of the body; he, however, unhesitatingly affirmed that spirit would mate again with body, not only that there would be a literal resurrection, but that there had been one, and that a day was coming in which God would judge the world by the Man who died in mortal weakness, but whom He had raised from the dead.

At this mention of the Resurrection, many in his audience began to mock. The Greek found the perfect fruition and glory of life in the present. So Paul departed from among them with comparatively small results. Dionysius, a member of the august tribunal before which he had stood; a woman, Damaris, who was probably the result of his more general work in the city; and a few others, stayed with him, and believed. The Gospel attracted the simple-minded merchants and artisans of Macedonia more readily than the educated *literati* of Athens.

So far as we know the apostle never visited Athens again. He went sadly on his way to Corinth, his heart filled with a tumult of thoughts, anxiety for the infant churches behind him, yearning to see Timothy and Luke, questioning what reception he might receive amid the cultured and eloquent Corinthians; but more than ever determined not to know anything among them except Jesus Christ and Him crucified, while steadfastly refraining from all attempts at wisdom or grace of speech, lest the cross of Christ should be made void.

15

"In Weakness and Fear"
1 Cor. 2:3

Five hours' sail across the Saronic Bay brought the apostle to Cenchrea, the port of Corinth to the east; for this great and busy city commanded two waterways. Through her western port, Lechum, she was in communication with the Adriatic; and through her eastern port, Cenchrea, with the Ægean. Vast crowds were attracted to her precincts for the purposes of trade. This commanding position thus gave her an unusual importance in the eye of the apostle, ever eager to seize on any advantage that he could use for the gospel of his Lord. To establish a strong Christian church there would be to cast seeds of Christian teaching on waters that would bear them east and west.

But the apostle entered the proud and beautiful city "in weakness, and in fear, and in much trembling." He could not forget the frigid contempt that he had encountered at Athens, and which was harder to bear than violent opposition. He was profoundly conscious of being deficient in those gifts of learning and eloquence on which the Corinthians set such store. He knew that his speech and his preaching could never be in persuasive words of human wisdom.

There were many other difficulties to be encountered, which made his ministry in Corinth the more difficult, and his consequent success the more conspicuous.

1. THE NECESSITY FOR CONTINUAL MANUAL TOIL. In his first Epistle to Corinth, Paul lays great emphasis on this. Always maintaining the right of those who preached the Gospel to live by the Gospel, he did not use it. No chance should be given to the merchants and traders that thronged the city from all parts to allege that he was actuated by mercenary motives. He therefore resumed his trade of tent-making, and was thankful to come across two Christian Jews who had been flung on this shore by the decree of the emperor, which expelled all Jews from Rome. Suetonius, the historian, tells us that this decree was due to tumults caused by one Chrestus, evidently referring to violent disputes in the Jewish community concerning the claims of Jesus to be the long-expected Messiah. With them, therefore, he lived and worked, for they were of the same craft; and a friendship sprang up between him and Aquila, with his wife Priscilla.

2. THE VIRULENT HATRED OF THE JEWS. According to his usual practice, Paul went every Sabbath to the synagogue and reasoned, persuading the Jews and Greek proselytes that the conception of the Hebrew Scriptures was precisely that of a suffering and crucified Messiah. This went on for some weeks; but the measure of his labors was somewhat curtailed by the heavy drain of his daily toil. It was not until Timothy and Silas arrived, the one from Thessalonica, and the other from Berœa, bringing cheering news of the steadfastness of his converts, their hands full of generous benefactions, that he was able to give himself with more leisure and intensity to the cherished object of his life.

The influential men of the Jewish community opposed, blasphemed, and drove him from the synagogue. Their attitude was more than usually virulent. Their hatred culminated when the apostle gladly accepted the offer of a God-fearing proselyte, Titus Justus, whose house was close to the synagogue, to hold meetings there. This new move was attended with instant and remarkable success. Among those who migrated with the apostle from the synagogue was Crispus, its chief ruler, who believed in the Lord with all his house. As the new meeting house became more crowded, and the movement increased in numbers and influence, the Jews became more and more exasperated, and at last rose in a body, seized Paul, and dragged him before the Roman governor, who happened to be Gallio, brother to Seneca, the famous philosopher, and Nero's tutor. He was a man of unusual culture and refinement, sweetness, and lovableness. He represented the broad and liberal views of educated Romans, and when he discovered that the charge against Paul involved only words, and names, and Jewish law, he would have nothing more to do with Paul's accusors or their accusations, but had his attendants drive them from the judgment seat.

The Greeks were only too glad that contempt should be heaped on the hated Jews, and took the opportunity of seizing Sosthenes, the new chief ruler of the synagogue—who had succeeded to the post vacated by Crispus—and beating him in the very presence of the Proconsul. He regarded their horseplay, however, with perfect indifference. What did it matter if a Jew got a few stripes more or less?

But the incident must have greatly aggravated the hatred of the Jews against the apostle and his converts; the more so when, as it would appear, Sosthenes himself became a convert, and so intimately associated with the apostle as to be coupled later with himself in the inscription of the first Epistle to the Corinthians—"Sosthenes our brother."

3. THE CHARACTER OF HIS CONVERTS. How often to His tried and persecuted servants does the Master come as He came to the apostle! They may be conscious of weakness and much fear, may speak His word in trembling, may be derided as a spectacle and laughing stock, may be encompassed with toil and pain and persecution; but He stands beside in a vision, and says: "Be not afraid, but speak, and hold not thy peace: for I am with thee, and no man shall set on thee to hurt thee" (Acts 18:9–10).

With this encouragement in his heart, Paul labored for a year and six months in this sinful city, with marvelous success. It is true that not many of the wise, or mighty, or noble of this world, were among the chosen ones. There might be a Crispus and Gaius, a Stephanas and his household, but these were exceptions to the general rule. Perhaps women predominated in the young community, as the apostle devotes so much space in his epistle to regulating their behavior. We know, at least of Phœbe, the deaconess of the church at Cenchrea, who bore his epistle to Rome; and of Chloe, whose household slaves were the medium of intelligence when Paul was at Ephesus.

The majority of his converts, however, were of the lowest caste, and of those who had been deeply stained with the vices that made Corinth notorious. But under the preaching of the cross, in the power of the Holy Ghost, a marvelous change had passed over them—they had become washed, sanctified, and justified, in the name of the Lord Jesus, and in the Spirit of our God. Delivered from the power of darkness, they had become children of the light and of the day: heirs of God, and joint heirs with the Son of His love.

But it is evident that the apostle was far from satisfied. He complained that he could not speak to them as to spiritual; but as to carnal, as to babes in Christ; that he was obliged to feed them with milk, and not with meat. Even before he left there was probably manifestations of party spirit, of the mistaking license for liberty, of greed in the love feasts, and heresy in the doctrine of the Resurrection.

At last, however, he resolved to leave Corinth. Many reasons prompted this step, and among them the desire to proceed to Jerusalem to ascertain the feeling of the mother church. Still further to conciliate the conservative element there, he had bound himself in the vow of a Nazirite, and was anxious to perform the concluding ceremonial within the temple. He was obliged to have his head shorn at Cenchrea, because the month had expired; but he carried the hair with him to be burned on the great altar within the temple court. Aquila and Priscilla probably thought that Ephesus would be a better market for their wares than Corinth, so they sailed with him. But though he left the city, it produced an ineffaceable effect on his methods of thought and expression. It was there that he came under the influence of those imperial conceptions that were embodied in Rome, the undisputed mistress of the world. There he wrote his first two epistles, those to the Thessalonians. And thus the first memorable missionary tour in Greece came to an end, and for the fourth time since his conversion the apostles approached the city that was doubly dear to him—memories of his Lord being now entwined with the sacred associations of David, Solomon, Hezekiah, and Ezra.

16

More Than a Conqueror
Rom. 8:36–37

It was toward the close of Paul's third missionary journey. About three years before, he had left the Syrian Antioch for the third time, after a stay of some duration (Acts 18:23). His eager spirit could not rest amid the comparative comfort and ease of the vigorous church life that was establishing itself there, but yearned with tender solicitude for his converts throughout the region of Galatia and Phrygia. He therefore again passed the Cilician Gates, traversed the bleak tablelands of the upper or highland country, establishing all the disciples, and working toward the Roman province of Asia. This lay to the southwest, on the seaboard. He had been previously forbidden to enter it (16:6); but his steps were now as clearly led to it as they had formerly been restrained. Thus does our sovereign Lord withhold His servants from the immediate fulfillment of their dreams, that they may return to them again when the time was ripe.

It was to redeem a pledge he had solemnly made that the apostle at last came down to Ephesus. He had spent one Sabbath day there previously, on his way from Corinth to Jerusalem. On that occasion his ministry had so deeply interested the Jews, that they had urged him to stay for a longer period; but this being impossible, on account of the necessity of hastening to Jerusalem to fulfill his vow, he said, "I will return again to you, if the Lord will." It was in fulfillment of that promise that the apostle now visited the metropolis of Asia the Less.

A good deal had happened in the interval. Apollos, the eloquent Alexandrian, had visited the city, had met there Paul's friends, Aquila and Priscilla, who were awaiting their fellow worker's return. By them he had been led into a clear appreciation of the truth, in consequence of which his ministry had become more fruitful, both in helping those who had believed, and powerfully confuting the Jews.

But Apollos had now left for Corinth, and Paul arrived to take up and extend the work so auspiciously begun. He probably but dimly realized as he entered Ephesus how long he would remain, or the far-reaching results of his residence.

As a matter of fact it was a conflict from first to last. "I have fought with beasts at Ephesus," was his comment after it was all over.

1. THE BATTLEFIELD. There were several difficulties to be encountered. In the first place there was the pressure of the strange, eager mass of human beings, whose interests, aims, and methods of thought were so foreign to his own. But, besides, there was the vast system of organized idolatry that centered in the temple of Diana. Her image was said to have fallen from Jupiter (possibly a meteorite), and it was enshrined in a temple, counted to be one of the wonders of the world. The magnificence of uncalculated wealth, the masterpieces of human art, the fame of splendid ceremonials, the lavish gifts of emperors and kings, the attendance and service of thousands of priests and priestesses, combined to give it an unrivalled eminence of influence and prestige. Sooner might some humble Protestant missionary working in a back street of Rome expect to dim the magnificence of St. Peter's or diminish the attendance of its vast congregations, as Paul hope that his residence in Ephesus could have any effect whatever on the worship of Diana.

In connection with the temple, a great trade in amulets and charms thrived. Each individual in the vast crowds that came up to worship at the shrine was eager to carry back some memento of his visit. What the trade in strong drink is among ourselves, that was the business in these miniature shrines manufactured by Demetrius and his fellow craftsmen. How impossible it seemed that one man, in three years, employing only moral and spiritual weapons, could make any difference to this ancient and extensive craft!

But still further, Ephesus was deeply infected with the black arts of the exorcist, the magician, and the professor of cabalistic mysteries. Even the converts to Christianity found it hard to divest themselves of their former association with these practices, and treasured their books greatly. It is no child's play to turn a nation of savages from their confidence in witchcraft and medicine men to sane views of life and divine providence.

But perhaps Paul's most inveterate foe was the Jewish synagogue, entrenched in ancient prejudices and persistent disbelief. They were hardened and disobedient, speaking evil of "the Way."

Such were the giant obstacles that confronted the humble tentmaker as he settled down to his trade in company with Aquila and Priscilla. But greater was He who was for him than all who there were against him.

2. LET US VERIFY THIS ASSERTION. Let us turn to the Acts of the Apostles, and ask if Paul was indeed more than conqueror. The answer is unmistakable. After three months' conflict with the Jews in their synagogue, the apostle was driven to the course he was wont to adopt under similar circumstances—he moved his disciples to the schoolhouse of one Tyrannus, and taught there daily, as soon as noon was past, and a break was given alike to the schoolmaster and the artisan. In consequence of this ministry, "all they which dwelt in Asia heard the word of the Lord Jesus, both Jews and Greeks"—a very strong statement, when we bear in mind the population of that crowded province.

The trade in amulets and charms fell off so seriously that the craftsmen realized that unless they did something about it their gains would be at an end. The magicians and exorcists were utterly baffled and confounded by the much greater miracles that were wrought through Paul; so much so that the handkerchiefs he used to wipe the sweat from his brow and the aprons he wore at his trade, were made the medium of healing virtue as they were carried from his person to the sick and demon-possessed. So mighty was the impression that Christ had secrets superior to the best contained in their ancient books, that many of them who had believed came confessing and declaring their deeds. And many of those who practiced magical arts brought their books together in one of the open squares and burned them in the sight of all. So mightily grew the word of the Lord, and prevailed.

The exorcist Jews also were silenced. The name of Jesus, spoken even by those who did not believe in Him, had a power over evil spirits such as no other name exerted; and it had been blasphemously used by strolling Jews, who had taken on themselves to call that sweet and holy name over some who were possessed. But in one notable instance the demon himself had remonstrated, crying, "Jesus I know, and Paul I know; but who are ye?" (Acts 19:15) and he had leaped on them, and mastered them, so that they fled from the house naked and wounded.

3. LET US CONSIDER THE TALISMAN OF VICTORY. If we turn from his outward life to study the diary of this wonderful man who seemed to be alone in his conflicts and victories, we find a pathetic record of his sorrows and trials. We wonder how such a man, under such drawbacks and in face of such opposing forces, could be more than a conqueror.

The only matter about which the apostle, therefore, felt any anxiety was whether anything could occur to cut him off from the living, loving Lord. "Can anything separate me from the love of Christ?"—that was the only question worth consideration. He is like a man proving every link of the chain on which he is going to swing out over the abyss. Carefully and fervently he has tested all, and is satisfied that none of them can cut him off from the love of God; and since that is so, he is sure that nothing can ever intercept those supplies of the life and strength of God that will avail to make him more than a conqueror.

Oh, blessed love that comes down to us from the heart of Jesus, the essence of the eternal love of God. It is not our love that holds God, but God's that holds us. He will go on loving us forever, so that whatever our difficulties, we will be kept steadfast, unmovable, always abounding in the work of the Lord, and ever more conquerors through Him who loved us.

17

Gathering Clouds
Acts 20:22

After the great uproar excited by Demetrius was over, Paul sent for his disciples and exhorted them; commending them to the grace of God, and then sadly bade farewell. This done, he departed into Macedonia by way of Troas.

At Troas, which he now visited for a second time, the apostle expected to meet

Titus, who had probably been the bearer of the first Epistle to Corinth—a letter elicited by the sad story of the dissensions and disorders of the church there, which had been brought to Ephesus by members of the household of Chloe. He had dealt with the whole situation in very stringent terms, and was intensely anxious to learn the result of his words. Often since writing he had questioned whether he might not have imperilled his entire influence for good over his converts, and driven them into defiance and despair. The delay of Titus confirmed his worst fears; and though a great door of ministry was opened at Troas, he could find no relief for his perturbed and eager spirit, but taking leave of them went forth into Macedonia (2 Cor. 2:13).

In all probability Paul headed at once for his beloved Philippi; but even there, since there was still no tidings of Titus, his flesh had no relief. He was afflicted on every side; without were fightings, and within were fears.

At last, God comforted him by the coming of the overdue traveler. He was glad, not only to have his friend at his side, but to learn that the effect of his first letter had brought results, and had led to an outbreak of godly repentance and affectionate yearning to himself. It was after conference with Titus on the whole state of affairs at Corinth that he wrote his second epistle.

1. HIS MULTIPLIED SORROWS. Throughout the epistle Paul speaks of the great anguish through which he was passing; and while he casts off the many unkind and slanderous allegations made against him, he does so with pathetic references to his sufferings.

In one of the most extraordinary enumerations of antitheses in any language, he mentions, among other sources of anguish, his spells of sleeplessness, his repeated fastings, the blows, imprisonments, tumults, toils, and pressure of his daily life. But there must have been other and deeper reasons—perhaps that he was being so persistently maligned, and his teachings so flagrantly misrepresented; or because the love of many was waxing cold; or that the infant churches, on which he had expended so many prayers and tears, were proving themselves unworthy.

But the Father of mercies and God of all comfort drew near and comforted him, and in spite of all, this deeply suffering soul never abated for a moment its devoted labors for the cause of God. His letters abound with references to the offering that he was raising for the poverty-stricken saints at Jerusalem from all the churches he had established. Being ambitious to preach the gospel where Christ had not been already named, and unwilling to build on another man's foundation, he fully preached the gospel even to Illyricum, on the Adriatic.

2. HIS FRIENDS. Some men have a marvelous power in attaching men to themselves. They possess a kind of spiritual magnetism for others. Paul had this power in a pre-eminent degree. He was loved as few have been loved, and he loved in return. It must have therefore been a peculiar pleasure to him, as at last he came to Corinth, to find himself the center of a large gathering of devoted friends.

There was Timothy, his "beloved child", his "true child in faith"; Tychicus, "the beloved brother and faithful fellow servant in the Lord," who was with him in his last imprisonment; Titus, his "partner and fellow worker," his "true child after the common faith"; Luke, "the beloved physician," who accompanied him to Rome, and was with him to the last; Trophimus, the Ephesian, who would have been with him to death had not sickness detained him at Miletus; Aristarchus and Secundus, the former of whom probably contrived to become his fellow prisoner that he might minister to his illustrious friend; Sopater, his kinsman, well known to the Roman church; Gaius, a trophy of that first missionary tour that had taken him to Derbe; and the other Gaius, at this time his host; and Jason, who had sheltered him at Thessalonica at the risk of his life. And these were only a sheaf of the great harvest of his friends. Writing at this time from Corinth, he greets twenty-six persons by name in the closing verses of the Epistle to the Romans.

At last it became necessary for the party to break up. Paul was eager to get to Jerusalem for the Passover, and a passage had been taken for him in one of the pilgrim vessels that started each spring from every port on the Ægean for Palestine. Before his embarkation, however, a plot was discovered on the part of the Jews to assassinate him, and he was compelled to alter his route, going with an escort of friends through Macedonia, and getting on a sailing vessel from Troas. He took advantage of this change in his plans to say another farewell to the endeared circle at Philippi, always nearest his heart; and then he hastened to rejoin the little band that awaited him at Troas, sworn to care for him and the treasure that he had been at such pains to collect.

3. SAD FOREBODINGS. That journey from Troas, down the ragged shores of Asia Minor, sailing by day and anchoring by night, must in some senses have been sadder to the little band of devoted followers than to Paul.

He had no doubt as to its destination. He went bound in the spirit to Jerusalem, sure that there, as in every other city, bonds and afflictions awaited him. Of this the Holy Spirit gave unequivocal testimony. He prolonged his speech at Troas until midnight, and sent for the elders of the Ephesian church to meet him at Miletus, because he knew that all those among whom he had gone about preaching the kingdom should see his face no more. He said farewell to the little groups, who waved their goodbys across the waters to his receding ship, as though it were his last. What the Spirit said through the disciples at Tyre only corroborated what He had said to the heart of Paul (Acts 20:23). What Agabus foretold in striking symbolism, had been prognosticated already by that inward prophet whose voice cannot be bribed. It excited no surprise when he found himself the center of a frenzied mob, hurrying him down the temple steps to the lowest court, where they meant to take his life without sacrilege to the holy shrine.

To those who loved him, the successive and unanimous prognostications of coming disaster were like the falling of the earth sods on a coffin containing the earthly remains of one's dearest friend. Luke gives us a pathetic picture of the scene in the house of Philip, their host at Cæsarea. Agabus came there from Jerusalem, and unbinding Paul's girdle bound himself with it, announcing that in like manner the Jews would bind its owner. "And," says Luke, "when we heard these things, both we, and they of that place besought him not to go up to Jerusalem" (Acts 21:12). They wept; enough, Paul said, to break his heart.

But he was marvelously sustained. It seemed as though he were going rather to a wedding than a funeral. He was ready not to be bound only, but also to die at Jerusalem for the name of the Lord Jesus.

18

The Furtherance of the Gospel
Phil. 1:12–13

Space forbids us to tell in detail the story of his transportation from the lower platform of the temple at Jerusalem to the hired house at Rome; but we may at least consider its successive stages.

1. THERE WAS THE AWFUL RIOT IN THE TEMPLE COURT. The Jews of Asia, perhaps led by Alexander the coppersmith, laid hold of Paul, under the impression that he had introduced Trophimus, whom they knew as an Ephesian, into the court reserved for Jews. They dragged him down the steps, furiously beating him, and with the intent of murdering him when they reached the bottom. With the greatest difficulty he was rescued by Lysias and his legionnaires, who rushed down from the adjoining Castle of Antonia, surrounded him with their shields, and carried him back on their shoulders from the frenzy of the mob. It was not simply the result of natural coolness and self-command, but because he was at rest in Christ, and desired to magnify his Master, that he was able to hold a brief conversation with his deliverer in the midst of the tumult. He obtained permission to address the people in their national tongue, weaving the story of the risen Jesus so ingeniously into his personal narrative, that they could do nothing but listen.

There was a manly strength in his quiet remonstrance with those who were set to examine him by scourging, and avowal of Roman citizenship, which must have filled them with profound respect. Here was no common criminal!

In a vision the Lord urged him to be of good cheer, and assured him that the witness that he had given from the steps of the castle and in the halls of the Sanhedrin should be repeated in Rome herself, at the very heart of the empire, where all the Gentiles could hear.

There must have been something very noble and heroic in his bearing; or his nephew, who was evidently secretly involved with his foes, and must have passed as a bigoted Jew, would never have run the risk of being torn limb from limb for divulging the secret plot of the Zealots, who had bound themselves by a solemn vow neither to eat nor drink until they had forever silenced the tongue that gave them more cause to fear than all the legions of Felix's escort.

2. HIS JUDICIAL TRIALS. He was presently hurried by a strong body of soldiers in a forced march, by night, to Antipatris, thirty-five miles away, and twenty-five miles further, on the following day, to Cæsarea, to undergo trial before Felix, the Roman governor of Judæa. But as on repeated occasions he stood before Felix, he seemed less eager for himself, and bent on snatching every opportunity of so public a position to explain the nature of "the Way," and to reason with the judge concerning the faith in Christ Jesus. Indeed, on one occasion he spoke so powerfully in the presence of Felix and the woman with whom he was living in adultery, that Felix trembled as the prisoner compelled him to review a life of shameless infamy beneath the searchlight of an awakened conscience.

When Festus came in the room of Felix, who had been recalled in disgrace, the apostle, within a few days, so impressed the newcomer with his faith in Jesus, that the

Governor was able to state the case with wonderful accuracy to King Agrippa, who, with his sister Bernice, came to pay their respects to the new representative of the emperor.

Perhaps Paul's greatest opportunity, and one of which he availed himself to the full, was that in which he was able to preach the gospel to an assembly that comprised all the fashion, wealth, and distinction of the land. Festus was there in state, and the Herods, brother and sister, seated on golden chairs; the officers of the garrison, and the principal men of the city. How great a contrast between the splendid pomp of that occasion and the poor chained prisoner at the bar! How enthusiastically he preached Christ that day under the guise of making his defense! The story of the suffering and risen Lord; the fulfillment of the predictions of Moses and the prophets; such topics were recited with all the passionate earnestness of which he was capable, until the Roman thought him mad, and the Jew princeling needed all his courtly wit to turn aside the barbed dart of the prisoner's appeal.

In one of the guard rooms of the old palace of the Cæsars, Paul was kept a prisoner for two whole years, but he was permitted to see and receive help from his friends. His appreciation of the truth as it is in Jesus was greatly deepened. Contrast the Epistles to the Thessalonians, Corinthians, Romans, and Galatians, with those to the Ephesians, Philippians, and Colossians, and the difference is easily discernible. We find less polemics and defense of his motives and actions, and more of the believer's vital union with his Lord. Ah! those years spent within view of the dividing sea, restrained by the old castle walls, and the chain that he shook before Festus and his guests, were turned to good account, if only they enabled him to give the church his priceless prison epistles.

At last this term of imprisonment came to an end. The ecclesiastical authorities had never ceased to urge that he should be handed over to their jurisdiction, a claim that in God's providence the Roman governors steadfastly refused. They knew, and Paul knew, that to such a trial there would be only one end. But finally, when Festus showed signs of yielding, Paul claimed his right as a Roman citizen to have his case tried by the emperor himself.

That appeal had to be carried out. He had appealed to Cæsar, and to Cæsar he must go. As soon as possible he was placed under the care of a centurion for conveyance to the imperial city.

At every stage of the voyage Paul seems to have bent all his endeavors to use his opportunities, as far as possible, for the glory of his Lord.

They set sail, first in an ordinary sailing vessel, then from Myra, in an Alexandrian ship, one of the great fleet perpetually engaged in sending provisions to Rome. Contrary to Paul's advice, the captain attempted to cross the open bay from the Fair Havens to Phœnice, each on the southern side of Crete. But, when halfway across, the wind changed, and a sudden squall came down from the mountains and carried the big ship out to sea. In the brief respite from sailing under the lee of the little island of Cauda, they hauled in the boat that had been tearing through the water behind them, and got ropes around the straining vessel to strengthen her. This done, there was nothing for it but to drift through the open sea. Three days later, all hands (even the prisoners) were called in to lighten the ship, by casting out cargo and other movable objects; and after many days of storm, in which neither sun nor moon appeared, all hope that they would be saved gradually faded away.

It was then that Paul stood up, calm, assured, with the message of God, to cheer and encourage their fainting hearts. He received an assurance that he would yet stand before Cæsar. Here was an opportunity of preaching faith in God, and belief in the power of prayer.

Always using common sense, he detected the attempt of the sailors, when the vessel struck, to get away in the boat; but with something above common sense, with a sense of the eternal and divine, he took bread, and as though he were presiding at the Lord's table in Corinth or Philippi, he gave thanks to God in the presence of all, and broke it, and began to eat.

When they reached the shore of Malta on that drear November morning, it seemed as though nothing more could be done to further the gospel. But as the viper fell off Paul's hand, and the father of the chief man in the island was healed of dysentery through his prayer, and all else who had diseases throughout the island were cured by his touch, much was done to magnify the Lord.

They were now approaching home. Paul had often thought of this moment, and longed for it. Some three years before, writing to the church at Rome, he said, "I long to see you, that I may impart some spiritual gift." But he had never anticipated coming like this—one of a knot of prisoners in charge of Roman legionnaires. But almost certainly through his bonds he was able to effect much more good than if he had been free. Had he been free, the opportunity would never have befallen him of speaking to the Praetorian Guard and Cæsar's household. It is thus that God answers our prayers in ways and methods we do not expect.

God fulfilled Paul's desire to see Rome in this way probably for two reasons. First, for safety's sake, and second, for the wider audience that awaited him. And these two reasons may necessitate our being conducted to our Rome in chains.

Do not fret at the limitations and disabilities of your life. They are required to present your opportunity. Storm and shipwreck, centurion and sea captain, soldier and fetter, Cæsarea and Rome—all are part of the plan, all work together for good, all are achieving God's ideal, and making you what, in your best hours, you have asked to become.

19

"More Abundantly Than They All"
1 Cor. 15:10

Even in these days of easy and universal communication the apostle's record as a traveler would have been a remarkable one; but how much more remarkable it appears when we recall the bandits that infested the mountain passes of Asia Minor; the impetuous torrents that crossed the track; the vast distances that had to be traversed on foot; the hardships of the wayside inns; the suspicion and dislike of which Jews must have always been the object.

But what a record he has left! In his first missionary journey he establishes churches as Christian garrisons along the central highway of Asia Minor, and attracts the enthusiastic Gauls with the tenderest affection. In his second, he proclaims the gospel to Europe, and founds churches in some of the most famous and influential cities— Philippi, Thessalonica, Berea, Athens, Corinth, flame out as successive beacon lights in the darkness. In the third, like a Colossus, he strides the Ægean, planting one foot in Asia Minor and the other in Greece, where he preaches even to Illyricum. In the fourth, after pleading his cause before at least three different tribunals, he traverses the Mediterranean, saves the crew and passengers of the storm-driven ship by his prayers and heroism, compels the respect and affection of an island of barbarians, and reaches Rome in the guise of a prisoner, but really as a conqueror, to unfurl the banner of his Master in the palace of the Cæsars. After his release he again sets forth on journeys that carried him, perhaps to Spain, but certainly to familiar scenes in Asia Minor and Greece. So he fulfills his course until Rome and martyrdom again come in sight.

We may well inquire into the secret of this marvelous work, to which, after that of our Lord, the position of Christianity in the world at this moment is to be ascribed. And if we do, we will discover it not in his intellectual talent and eloquent speech, for these were more than neutralized by his physical weakness, his "thorn," and his "contemptible" utterance (2 Cor. 11:6); but in sources of power that are within the reach of us all.

1. WE NOTICE THE APOSTLE'S VIVID REMEMBRANCE OF THE MERCY THAT HAD BEEN SHOWN HIM. It was as though he never could forget how deeply he had sinned, and how strenuously he had resisted that very grace he now proclaimed. How could he ever despair of men, since such a one as he had found mercy? Like a silver refrain, it came back on him in all times of anguish, distress, and virulent opposition, "I obtained mercy, therefore I dare not, must not faint."

2. WE MUST ALSO MENTION THE GREAT AND SIMPLE PURPOSE FOR WHICH THE APOSTLE LIVED. He bent his strength to save men, and for this he was prepared to make any sacrifice. He was equally careful to the last to institute and organize little Christian communities, which were absolutely necessary to conserve and develop the life that had been implanted. Would that this also were our single aim! It would greatly simplify our lives.

To each of us is committed a stewardship. With Paul, each of us can say, "I have a stewardship entrusted to me" (1 Cor. 9:17). Now surely it is required in stewards, not that they should realize all the dreams that suggest themselves to their imagination, but that they be found faithful to Him who appointed them.

3. HIS PLAN OF LIVING ALSO GREATLY MINISTERED TO HIS SUCCESS. In point of fact, he had no plan at all. For him the way had been prepared in the counsels of God before the worlds were made, and he had only to discover its track.

This made the apostle so cautious in referring to his future. Whatever would betide, he had to keep in the current of the will of God. And there was no interval between his apprehension of the divine purpose and his endeavor to strike his tent and follow wherever it might lead (Acts 16:6–7). "What did you mean for me, O God, in my creation, redemption, and the ordering of my life? Teach me to do your will, for you are my God. Your Spirit is good: lead me into the land of uprightness." Such should be the prayer of each Christian worker.

a. *But, perhaps, the secret of Paul's success lay most of all in his faculty of extracting power from his weaknesses.* He had eminent gifts of character, of energy, of power to command and lead and organize, of thought and speech; but had it not been for the presence of his infirmity, he might never have become the great apostle of the Gentiles, or accomplished such splendid work.

Judging from the words of his detractors, which he seems to endorse, his bodily presence was weak, and his speech contemptible (2 Cor. 10:10), the former phrase referring to his thorn in the flesh, of which we have spoken; and the latter to a lack of those graces of oratory that the Greeks had come to expect in their public teachers. It was very humbling to the flesh; but it drained away the last remains of human pride, and left him a vessel meet for the Master's use, because he was so utterly dependent on the Master's hand to direct and empower.

In early life he was one of Gamaliel's most promising pupils, strong, self-reliant, vehement, clear in thought, incisive in speech, swift in action. Among the men of his age few could outmatch Saul of Tarsus, who earlier than was customary became a member of the Jewish Sanhedrin. Would you recognize him in the weakness, the fear, and the much trembling of this broken man? But had Paul been strong, he might have been—we borrow the expression—an Apollos, a Chrysostom, an Augustine, a Luther, but never Paul. Because he was weak he was strong; because he bore chains he was the great emancipator from chains; because he was poor he succeeded in making so many rich.

b. *Another element in the success of the apostle's work must be found in his self-abnegation.* This, too, is a path in which we may follow the steps of this great servant of Jesus. All Christian workers, zealous for the coming of God's kingdom, must at once forego indulgences and practices that are not in themselves unlawful, that the ministry may not be blamed, nor souls hindered. The more widespread our influence over souls, the more absolute the necessity of considering the effect on others of methods and actions in which we are left with large liberty of self-determination and choice.

c. *Let us not forget the eloquence of his tears.* "Remember," he said to the elders of the Ephesian Church, "that by the space of three years I ceased not to warn every one night and day with tears" (Acts 20:31). Each word is significant! Not content with appealing to them by day, he had to invade his nights; when worn by emotion, labor, and teaching, his tired body might surely claim repose. He did not cease this ministry for three long years; but pursued it without relaxation, without interruption, without pause, but with the tears of a soul lover.

Why is it that this fount of tears seems denied us? We have tears for all things except the infinite loss of those who have rejected the Gospel. For this no single drop trickles down our faces. In losing the power of tears we have lost one great power of causing them. It is by broken hearts that hearts are broken; by wet eyes that eyes are made to brim over with the waters of repentant sorrow.

d. *Last, let us not forget the apostle's individual interest in his converts.* "Warning *every one of you* night and day with tears," is one evidence of this; and for another we turn instinctively to Colossians 1:28: "Whom we preach, warning *every man*, and teaching *every man* in all wisdom; that we may present *every man* perfect in Christ Jesus." All the fruit he gathered for God was hand picked. He was more fond of the hand net than the seine. Like his Master, he would go far out of his way if he might cast the demon out of one possessed spirit, or persuade an Agrippa to become a Christian. One soul, for whom Christ died, was in his sight of unspeakable worth.

4. UNDERLYING ALL THESE, THERE WAS THE FUNDAMENTAL CONCEPTION THAT IT WAS NOT HE, BUT THE GRACE OF GOD THAT WAS WITH HIM, AND THE POWER OF GOD THAT WORKED THROUGH

HIM. This is, after all, the first and last lesson for the Christian worker. Be clean, pure of heart, and simple in motive. See to it that there is no friction between your will and Christ's. Be adjusted, in gear, well set and jointed. Subdue your own activities as much as your own natural lethargy. Stand still until God impels you. Wait until He works in you to will and to do of His good pleasure. Nothing will make you so intense and ceaseless in your activity as this.

Be it ours so to live, testify, and minister, that we may be workmen not needing to be ashamed, good stewards of God's great grace, coworkers with God, ambassadors through whom God Himself may beseech men to be reconciled.

20

"In a Strait, Betwixt Two"
Phil. 1:23

Paul, on his arrival in Rome, was treated with great leniency. He was permitted to rent a house or apartment in the near neighborhood of the great Prætorian barracks, and live by himself, the only sign of his captivity being the chain that fastened his wrist to a Roman legionary, the soldiers relieving each other every four or six hours.

There were many advantages in this arrangement. It kept him from the hatred of his people, and gave him a marvelous opportunity to cast the seeds of the gospel into the head of the rivers of population that poured from the metropolis throughout the known world. At the same time, it must have been very irksome. Always to be in the presence of another, and that other filled with gentile antipathy to Jewish habits and pagan irresponsiveness to Christian fervor; to be able to make no movement without the clanking of his chain, and the consent of his custodian; to have to conduct his conferences, utter his prayers, and indite his epistles, beneath those stolid eyes, or amid brutal and blasphemous interruptions—all this must have been excessively trying to a sensitive temperament like the apostle's. But this also he could do through Christ who strengthened him. And it also helped to further the cause he loved. Many of these brawny veterans became humble, earnest disciples. With a glow of holy joy, he informs the Philippians that his bonds in Christ have become known through the whole Prætorian Guard; and we know that this was the begining of a movement destined within three centuries to spread throughout the entire army, and compel Constantine to adopt Christianity as the religion of the State.

Three days after his arrival in Rome, Paul summoned to his temporary lodging the leaders of the Jewish synagogues, of which there are said to have been seven, for the 60,000 Jews who were the objects of the dislike and ridicule of the imperial city. At the first interview they cautiously occupied neutral ground, and expressed the wish to hear and judge for themselves concerning the sect that was only known to them as the butt of universal excration. At the second interview, after listening to Paul's explanations and appeals for an entire day, there was the usual division of opinion. "Some believed the things which were spoken, and some believed not." His testimony having thus been first offered, according to his invariable practice, to his own people, there was now no further obstacle to his addressing a wider audience. The message of salvation was sent to the Gentiles, and these would certainly hear (Acts 28:28). We are therefore not surprised to be told that for the next two years "He received all that came in unto him, preaching the kingdom of God, and teaching those things which concern the Lord Jesus Christ, with all confidence, no man forbidding him."

It might be said of the apostle, as of his Lord, that they came to him from every quarter. Timothy, his son in the faith; Mark, now "profitable"; Luke, with his quick physician's eye and delicate sympathy; Aristarchus, who shared his imprisonment, that he might have an opportunity of ministering to his needs; Tychicus, from Ephesus, "the beloved brother and faithful minister in the Lord"; Epaphras, from Colossæ, a "beloved fellow servant, and faithful minister of Christ," on the behalf of the church there; Epaphroditus, from Philippi, who brought the liberal contributions of the beloved circle, that for so many years had never ceased to remember their friend and teacher; Demas, who had not yet allowed the present to turn him aside from the eternal and unseen—these, and others, are mentioned in the postscripts of his epistles as being with him. Members of the Roman church would always be welcomed, and must have poured into his humble lodging in a perpetual stream; Epænetus and Mary, Andronicus and Junia, Tryphena and Tryphosa, Persis the beloved, and Apelles the approved, must often have resorted to that apartment that was irradiated with the perpetual presence of the Lord. They had come to meet him on his first arrival as far as the Appii Forum and the Three Taverns, and would not be likely to neglect him, now that he was settled among them.

Then what interest would be aroused by the episodes of those two years! The illness of Epaphroditus, who was sick to death; the discovery and conversion of Onesimus, the runaway slave; the writing and dispatching of the epistles, which bear such evident traces of the prison cell.

It is almost certain that Paul was acquitted at his first trial, and liberated, and permitted for two or three years at least to engage again in his beloved work. He was evidently expecting this when, writing to the Philippians, he said: "I trust in the Lord, that I also myself, too shall come shortly" (2:24). In his letter to Philemon also, he goes so far as to ask that a lodging be prepared for him, as he hopes in answer to their prayers. Universal tradition affirms an interspace of liberty between his two imprisonments; and without this hypothesis, it is almost impossible to explain many of the incidental allusions of the Epistles to Timothy and Titus, which cannot refer, so far as we can see, to the period that falls within the compass of the Acts.

Once more a free man, Paul would certainly fulfill his intention of visiting Philemon and the church of Colossæ. From there he would make his way to the church at Ephesus. Leaving Timothy behind him with the injunction to command some that they should preach no other gospel than that which they had heard from his lips (1 Tim. 1:3), he traveled onward to Macedonia and Philippi. What a greeting must have been given him there! Lydia and Clement, Euodias and Syntyche, Epaphroditus and the jailor, together with many other fellow workers whose names are in the Book of Life, must have gathered around to minister to that frail, worn body, to be inspired by the heroic soul.

From Philippi he must have passed to other churches in Greece, and among the rest to Corinth. Finally he set sail with Titus for Crete, where he left him to set in order the things that were wanting, and to appoint elders in every city (Titus 1:5). On his return to the mainland he wrote an epistle to Titus, from the closing messages in which we gather that he was about to winter at Nicopolis surrounded by several friends, such as Artemas, Zenas, Tychicus, and Apollos, who were inspired with his own spirit, and were gladly assisting him in strengthening the organization and purifying the teaching in these young churches.

This blessed liberty, however, was cut short. One of the most terrible events in the history of the ancient world—the burning of Rome—took place in the year A.D. 64; and to divert from himself the suspicion that indicated him as its author, Nero accused the Christians of being the incendiaries. As soon as the fierce flames of the first general persecution broke out, those who were resident in the metropolis, and who must have been well known and dear to the apostle, were seized and subjected to horrible tortures, while a strict search was made throughout the empire for their leaders, the Jews abetting the inquisitors. It was not likely that so eminent a Christian as the apostle would escape.

He was staying for a time at Troas, in the house of Carpus, where he had arrived from Nicopolis. His arrest was so sudden that he had not had time to gather up his precious books and parchments, which may have included copies of his epistles, a Hebrew Bible, and some early copies of the sayings of our Lord; or to wrap around him the cloak that had been his companion in many a wintry storm. From there he was hurried to Rome.

A little group of friends accompanied him, with faithful tenacity, in this little sad journey: Demas and Crescens, Titus and Tychicus, Luke and Erastus. But Erastus stayed at Corinth, through which the little band may have passed; and Trophimus fell ill at Miletus and had to be left there, as the Roman guard would brook no delay. So, for the second time, Paul reached Rome.

But the circumstances of his second imprisonment differed widely from those of the first. Then he had his own hired house; now he was left in close confinement, and tradition points to the Mamertine prison as the scene of his last weeks or months. Then he was easily accessible; now Onesiphorus had to seek him out very diligently, and it took some courage not to be ashamed of his chain. Then he was the center of a large circle of friends and sympathizers; now the winnowing fan of trouble had greatly thinned their ranks, while others had been dispatched on distant missions. "Only Luke is with me," is the rather sad expression of the elderly man's loneliness. But now, as he was reviewing his career, he could say humbly and truthfully, "I have fought the good fight, I have finished my course, I have kept the faith; henceforth there is laid up for me a crown of righteousness."

What were the following processes of Paul's trial? How long was he kept in suspense? Did Timothy arrive in time to see him, and to be with him at the last supreme moment? What was the exact method of his martyrdom? To these questions there is no certain reply. Tradition points to a spot, about three miles from Rome, on the Ostian road where, at the stroke of the headsman's ax, he was beheaded, and his spirit leaving its frail tenement, entered the house not made with hands, eternal in the heavens. If Christ arose to receive Stephen, may He not also have stood up to welcome Paul? Again he beheld the face that had looked down on him from the opened heavens at his conversion, and heard the voice that had called him by his name. His long-cherished wish of being "with Christ" was gratified, and he found it "far better" than he had ever thought.

As he had kept Christ's deposit, so Christ had kept his. And as he gave in the account of his stewardship, who can doubt that the Lord greeted him with, "Well done, good and faithful servant, enter thou into the joy of thy Lord." What a festal welcome he must have received from thousands whom he had helped turn from darkness to light, from the power of Satan to God, and who were now to become his crown of rejoicing in the presence of the Lord! These from the highlands of Galatia, and those from the seaboard of Asia Minor. These from Judaistic prejudice, and those from the depths of gentile depravity and sin. These from the degraded slave populations, and those from the ranks of the high-born and educated.

21

"How Large Letters"
Gal. 6:11

It has been supposed, with much show of reason, that at the close of the Epistle to the Galatians the apostle took the pen from the hand of his amanuensis and wrote somewhat more than his usual brief autograph. Generally he contented himself with such words as those with which the Epistle to the Colossians close, "The salutation by the hand of me, Paul. Remember my bonds. Grace be with you." But in the case of the Galatians, among whom his authority had been greatly impugned, it seemed incumbent to give rather more emphasis and importance to his words by a prolonged personal closing paragraph. He practically begs them excuse the clumsy shape and appearance of his handwriting, on account of his defective sight; to which he may also be alluding when he touchingly describes himself as branded with the marks of Jesus (Gal. 6:17).

How largely his letters bulk in the make-up of the New Testament! They make a fourth part of the whole. And their importance must be measured not by length but by weight. Consider the precious treasures you are handling. The sublime chapter on love (1 Cor. 13); the matchless argument on justification (Rom. 4:5); the glorious exposition of the work of the Holy Spirit (Rom. 8); the triumphant resurrection hope (1 Cor. 15); the tender unveiling of the love between Jesus and His own (Eph. 5)—what priceless treasures these are which the church owes first to the Holy Ghost, and next to the apostle Paul, acting as His organ and instrument. How many of the most precious and helpful passages in Scripture bear the mark of the tender, eager, fervent, and devout spirit of the apostle of the Gentiles.

The epistles marvelously reflect his personality. It has been said of one of the great painters that he was accustomed to mix his colors with blood drawn from a secret wound; and of Paul it may be said that he dipped his pen in the blood of his heart.

It is not too much to say that, humanly speaking, the gospel of Christ would never have taken such fast hold on the strong, practical, vigorous nations of the West, had it not been for these epistles. They are characterized by a virility, a logical order, a style of argument, a definiteness of statement and phraseology, which are closely akin to our Western civilization. It is for this reason that Paul has been the contemporary of Western civilization through all the centuries. It was he who taught Augustine and inspired Luther. His thoughts and conceptions have been worked into the texture of the foremost minds of the Christian centuries. The seeds he scattered have borne fruit in the harvests of modern education, jurisprudence, liberty, and civilization.

"Ah!" it has been eloquently said, "what does the world owe to this apostle; what has it owed to him; what will it owe: of pious pastors, zealous missionaries, eminent Christians, useful books, benevolent endowments, examples of faith, charity, purity, holiness? The whole human race will confess that there is no one to whom it proclaims with so much harmony, gratitude and love, as the name of the apostle Paul."

We have thirteen letters bearing the inscription and signature of Paul. The evidence of their genuineness and authenticity is generally admitted; even the extreme school of destructive criticism has been compelled to admit that the Epistles to the Corinthians, Galatians, and Romans are undoubtedly his. They were written at different periods between the years A.D. 52 and 68; and under very different circumstances. Each is largely tinctured with the complexion of the worlds without and within, but all are full of that devotion to the risen Lord that led him to subscribe himself so often as his devoted bond servant. "Paul, the bond servant of Jesus Christ."

Let us place these epistles in order of their composition, and see how they mark the successive stages of progress in the apostle's conceptions of Christ. All his life was a going from strength to strength. And as he climbed the craggy steeps of obedience and faith, of growing likeness to Jesus, of self-sacrifice and experience of the cross, his horizon of knowledge widened to tread the lengths and heights and depths of the knowledge of the love of Christ, which still passed his knowledge. We have only to compare the first epistle to the Thessalonians with that of the Ephesians, to perceive at once how greatly this noble nature had filled out and ripened under the culture of the divine husbandman.

The best and most natural division of the epistles that I have met with is the following:

The Eschatological Group: 1 and 2 Thessalonians.

The Anti-Judaic Group: 1 and 2 Corinthians, Galatians, Romans.

The Christological, or Antignostic Group: Philippians, Colossians, Philemon, Ephesians.

The Pastoral Group: 1 Timothy, Titus, and 2 Timothy. Let us consider them in this order.

1 and 2 THESSALONIANS. The first of these was probably written toward the close of the year 52, and certainly from Corinth. Timothy had been left in Macedonia. After doing all he could to comfort and help the infant churches, he came with Silas to Paul, and the three held solemn and prayerful conferences on the best way of directing and assisting the disciples with the great storm of opposition through which they were passing. It was impossible for any of them to go to their relief, and so this first epistle was sent. And the second from the same city, a few months later, when the apostle heard that the first had been interpreted to mean that the Lord's coming was near enough to justify the expectation of the speedy dissolution of existing society.

In each of these epistles, the apostle dwells more largely than in any of the others on the Second Advent. Its light was illuminating his whole being with its glow. "The Lord himself shall descend from heaven with a shout, with the voice of the archangel, and with the trump of God: and the dead in Christ shall rise first: then we which are alive and remain shall be caught up."

The motive for Christian living is less in the sense of the indwelling Christ and more in the expectation of the coming Christ: there is less of the cross, and more of the glory; less of the invisible headship over all things in heaven and earth, which comes out so prominently in later epistles, and more of the *parousia,* the personal presence of Jesus.

1 CORINTHIANS. Toward the end of Paul's three years' residence in Ephesus, news came, partly through Apollos and partly through members of the house of Chloe, of the very unfavorable condition of affairs at Corinth. Shortly after this a letter arrived from the church itself, brought to Ephesus by Stephanas, Fortunatus, and Achaicus, asking advice on a number of practical difficulties. It was a terrible revelation of quarrels, disputings, inconsistencies, and grosser evils, and was enough to daunt any man. How could he hope to remedy such a state of things without going in person? And if he went, how would he be received? At that time he was pressed with the terrible conflict that was being waged at Ephesus, and he had to stay at his post. There was nothing else to do but to write as the Holy Spirit might direct; and the result is the marvelous epistle, which more than any other has supplied practical direction to the church in the following centuries, showing her how to apply the principles of the gospel to the most complicated moral and social problems. It was carried to Corinth by Titus. In this epistle there is still the pulse throb of the Second Advent; but there is, in addition, the sublime conception of the Second Adam.

2 CORINTHIANS. When the riot broke out in Ephesus, the apostle was eagerly looking for the coming of Titus with tidings of the reception of his epistle. On his expulsion from the city he went to Troas, making sure that he would meet him there; but failing to do so, he became feverishly anxious, and hastened on to Macedonia to seek him. He was afflicted on every side: "without were fightings, within were fears," until he was finally comforted by the coming of Titus, who brought good news as he told of their longing, their mourning, their zeal for him. Thereupon he wrote his second epistle, and sent it to the church by the hands of Titus and another.

This is the most personal of all his epistles. He lays bare his heart; he permits us to see its yearning tenderness, its sensitiveness to love or hate, its eager devotion to the best interests of his converts. The deep spiritual aspects of the Christian life, which are so characteristic of the later epistles, are especially unfolded.

GALATIANS. Paul followed Titus to Corinth and remained there a happy three months. But the joy of fellowship with the large and happy band of friends that gathered around him there must have been greatly blurred by tidings of the fickleness of the Galatians, who were moving "from him that had called them into the grace of Christ unto another gospel." Proselytisers had gone among his converts professing to represent the church at Jerusalem, and in the name of promitive Christianity had disparaged Paul's apostleship, questioned his authority, and insisted on the necessity of Gentiles being circumcised and submitting to the Levitical law.

It was a critical hour. If these views had prevailed, Christianity would have dwindled into a Jewish sect. Gentile Christianity was in the balance; the hope of the world at stake. Profoundly stirred in spirit, the apostle's righteous indignation flames in almost every sentence, and with glowing passion he meets the arguments of those who were seducing the Galatians from the simplicity and freedom of Christ.

Under the glow of his indignation there is not only clear and strong thinking, but there is indication of yet further areas of Christian knowledge that were being unfolded to Paul. He is led to realize that not Moses but Abraham, not Sinai but the tents of the patriarch, were the true origin of the Jewish people. Abraham was called when yet in uncircumcision; he believed, and was justified by faith thirty years before he received the distinctive Jewish rite. From that moment Paul sprang up to an altogether new position, from which he was able successfully to meet the assaults of the Judaizer, and vindicate all believing Gentiles as children of believing Abraham, and heirs of the covenant of promise.

ROMANS. As his stay at Corinth drew to a close, the apostle's mind was attracted to the church in the world's metropolis, which he hoped very soon to visit; and by way of preparation for his coming he prepared a succinct and connected view of the truths that had been revealed to his profoundest thought by the divine Spirit. Thus originated the greatest of his epistles, that to the Romans.

In this, as in the former, there is not only a clear appreciation and presentation of the great doctrine of justification by faith, but an ever-enlarging view of our identification with Christ, and of His indwelling. He says we were *reconciled* to God by the *death* of His Son, but we are *saved* by His *life*. His words glow with rapture as he speaks of being joined to Him who was raised from the dead, and of our freedom from the old bondage in which we were held. He had yielded his members as weapons in his mighty warfare against sin; had been crucified with Christ, and now no longer lived, but Christ lived in him. His life was one of faith in the Son of God, who loved him and gave Himself for him.

PHILIPPIANS. There is nothing polemical in this epistle. The former epistles have met and silenced his detractors and enemies. The peace of God that passes all understanding keeps his mind and heart, and out of that tranquil heart pours forth a tide of deep and tender love to his beloved friends at Philippi.

The hope of being alive at the coming of the Lord is still his heart's guiding star. He saw, however, that the will of God was best, and learned from his Master the secret of self-sacrificing humility. Epaphroditus had brought gifts of love from Philippi, and by his hands this letter of love and gratitude was returned.

COLOSSIANS. Among those who visited Paul in his hired house, toward the end of his detention in Rome, was Epaphras of Colossæ, who also represented Laodicea and Hierapolis—cities of Asia Minor in the valley of the Lycus. He told the apostle of a strange new heresy that was developing with alarming rapidity in the churches that had been planted in those distant cities.

The falsely called Christian philosophy of the time was endeavoring to fill the gulf between sinful man and the holy God by a ladder of mythical existences, through which man's prayers might ascend to God and His blessing descend on man.

The necessity of dealing with this absurd concept of the imagination was used by the Spirit of God to unveil a wider, deeper view of the fullness that there is in Jesus; and a disclosure was made to the apostle of the full meaning of the Lord's ascension to the right hand of power. He saw that all principalities and powers, all creature existences, all beings in heaven and earth, and under the earth, were beneath his feet. He was Lord and King, ruling all, filling all, maintaining all.

At the same time, his conviction of his union with the risen Lord was ever more definite, and his appreciation of His indwelling more full of hope and glory. Tychicus bore this letter to the Ephesians.

PHILEMON. Onesimus, the runaway slave, fugitive from his master Philemon, driven by want to the apostle's house or discovered in some low haunt of crime by his companions in their errands of mercy, had been begotten to a new life, and was now not a slave only, but a brother beloved. Paul sent him back to his master, who was a friend of his, and with whom he seems to have had a business account (vv. 18–19). This epistle, which is a perfect model of Christian courtesy, was given him as an introduction to his owner.

The chief point to notice here is the perfect patience and certainty with which the apostle awaits the ultimate triumph of divine love. He must have felt that in the sight of God, Onesimus had a perfect right to freedom; but it would have been highly improper for him to interfere between master and man. Let Philemon be taught to look at Onesimus as one with him in the Gospel, and it would not be long before he would himself propose his emancipation. But until he did, Paul would not precipitate matters, and Onesimus had to return to serve. The principle of action in this single instance doubtless became the ultimate law for the solution of many other difficult problems, that were left to the gradual conquest of the spirit of love.

EPHESIANS. This epistle reiterates the great conceptions of the empire of the Lord Jesus, and of His ability to fill the whole gulf between God and man, which the former epistle had foreshadowed. The doctrine of identification with Christ, in His death, resurrection, and ascension, is set forth with remarkable vividness and power. The conception of the church as the body and bride of Christ is elaborated with peculiar beauty of detail. But the commanding peculiarity of this epistle is its allusion to the home life of husband and wife, parent and child, master and slave. But in these later epistles he holds marriage up as the model of the love that subsists between the heavenly Bridegroom and His own: as Christ loved the church and gave Himself for it.

1 TIMOTHY and TITUS. After his release, Paul visited the scenes of his former ministry round the shores of the Ægean; and it was during his journeys at this time that he wrote these epistles to direct the young evangelists in the right ordering of the churches under their care. They are of extreme interest because they deal with so many domestic and practical details. He is never weary of showing that the great principles of the gospel are meant to elevate the more common incidents and duties of life.

2 TIMOTHY. It was a mellow and softened old age. Lonely as far as dear companions were concerned; full of privations, without cloak, or books, or friend; shivering in the prison; waiting to be offered, weigh anchor, and drop down the stream. He wanted once more to see his beloved son in the faith, and wrote to speed his steps. It is very pathetic, very beautiful, very human. But the ray of an indomitable courage and faith is flung across the heaving waters: he has kept his Lord's deposit, and knows that the deposit that he had made years before had been no less safely kept. And so the pen is taken in hand for the last time. A few tender messages are added as a postscript. And with large

letters he appends the closing sentences, "The Lord Jesus Christ be with thy spirit. Grace be with you."

Who but God can number the myraids of souls that have come in contact with his words, and have themselves become epistles, ministered by him, "written not with ink, but with the Spirit of the living God."